THE FIRST CRUSADE

THE FIRST CRUSADE

THE ACCOUNTS OF EYE-WITNESSES
AND PARTICIPANTS

BY
AUGUST C. KREY
ASSOCIATE PROFESSOR OF HISTORY IN THE
UNIVERSITY OF MINNESOTA

Martino Publishing
Mansfield Centre, CT
2006

Martino Publishing
P.O. Box 373,
Mansfield Centre, CT 06250 USA

www.martinopublishing.com

ISBN 1-57898-561-7

© 2006 Martino Publishing

All rights reserved. No new contribution to this publication may be reproduced, stored in a retrieval system, or transmitted, in any form or by any means, electronic, mechanical, photocopying, recording, or otherwise, without the prior permission of the Publisher.

Library of Congress Cataloging-in-Publication Data

The First Crusade the accounts of eye-witnesses and participants / [edited] by August C. Krey.
   p. cm.
  Includes bibliographical references.
  Originally published: Princeton: Princeton University Press, 1921.
  ISBN 1-57898-561-7 (cloth: alk. paper)
  1. Crusades--First, 1096-1099, I. Krey, August C. (August Charles), 1887-1961.

D161.1.F56 2005
956'.014--dc22   2005051061

Printed in the United States of America On 100% Acid-Free Paper

THE FIRST CRUSADE

THE ACCOUNTS OF EYE-WITNESSES
AND PARTICIPANTS

BY
AUGUST C. KREY
ASSOCIATE PROFESSOR OF HISTORY IN THE
UNIVERSITY OF MINNESOTA

PRINCETON UNIVERSITY PRESS
PRINCETON
LONDON: HUMPHREY MILFORD
OXFORD UNIVERSITY PRESS

1921

Copyright, 1921, by
PRINCETON UNIVERSITY PRESS

Published 1921
Printed in the United States of America

To
DANA CARLETON MUNRO
DODGE PROFESSOR OF MEDIAEVAL HISTORY
IN PRINCETON UNIVERSITY

PREFACE

When Henry Adams sought to triangulate the progress of modern civilization he fixed his historical transit at Mont St. Michel and Chartres in the days of the First Crusade and sighted from them across the centuries. No earlier place in the Middle Ages would have afforded a foundation of equal breadth in its description of society. The spiritual character of the Crusade lent a halo to even the most commonplace details connected with it and thus gave to them a literary immortality hitherto confined rather narrowly to matters of ecclesiastical interest. The widespread enthusiasm for the movement and participation in it assured its commemoration not only in monuments of stone but in a variety of writings as well. The authors of these accounts were neither sophisticated nor highly trained in their art. The picture of society which they drew, though relatively complete, has stood forth with all the simple and stark realism of a charcoal sketch, full of feeling, action, and scenery, but lacking in finish. The polish and finish have come with the later centuries. For those, however, who would understand that society even in its more finished form, a knowledge of the preliminary sketch is still essential.

In these lack-o-Latin days students seeking to accomplish this find their path too much beset with linguistic obstacles. It is to ameliorate these difficulties that the present volume has been compiled. The plan of this work will be found reminiscent of *Archer's Crusade of Richard I* and the *Parallel Source Problems of Mediaeval History*. The author gratefully acknowledges indebtedness to both. For assistance in the preparation of these

PREFACE

translations he is under great obligation to several of his former students. Special acknowledgment is due to Sister Frances Rita Ryan, M.A. (Sisters of St. Joseph) for her contributions of the passages from Fulcher and to Mrs. Willoughby M. Babcock, M.A. for a like service in the case of Ekkehard. Both have also assisted in reading the proof sheets. In the preparation of the introduction and notes the works of numerous scholars in the field have been placed under contribution. A few of these are mentioned, but it would be quite impossible to enumerate them all. The author must content himself with the expression of his gratitude to Professor D. C. Munro, through whose seminar he, like so many others, was first introduced to the study of this period. Finally, I wish to acknowledge my indebtedness to my wife, without whose help at all stages this work would not have been completed.

A. C. K.

Minneapolis, Minn.
May 31, 1921.

TABLE OF CONTENTS

	PAGE
Introduction	1
Prologue	22
Chapter I. The Summons	24

    1. Conditions in Europe at the beginning of the Crusade——2. Urban's plea for a Crusade——3. The immediate response——4. Urban's instructions to assembling Crusaders.

Chapter II. The March to Constantinople.................. 44

    1. The Departure——2. The March of the Peasants——3. The Main Body.

Chapter III. Alexius and the Crusaders.................... 69

    1. Alexius and the Peasants. Fate of the Peasants' Crusade——2. The Emperor's treatment of Hugh——3. Godfrey at Constantinople——4. Alexius and the minor leaders——5. Bohemund and the Emperor——6. Raymond and the Emperor——7. Robert of Normandy and Stephen at the Emperor's Court——8. Siege and capture of Nicaea——9. Alexius at the surrender of Nicaea——10. The views of Alexius on his relations with the Crusaders.

Chapter IV. From Nicaea to Antioch...................... 112

    1. Battle of Dorylaeum——2. Hardships of the march through Asia Minor——3. Baldwin and Tancred depart from the main army——4. The march through Armenia——5. Beginning of the siege of Antioch——6. Summary of the march to Antioch and the beginning of the siege——7. The foraging expedition of Bohemund and Robert of Flanders——8. Sufferings in camp before Antioch——9. Call for reinforcements——10. The erection of a fortress. Fights with the Turks——11. Capture of Antioch——12. Summary of the siege of Antioch.

Chapter V. Kerbogha and the Finding of the Lance.......... 163

    1. Kerbogha lays siege to the Crusaders in Antioch——2. Dire straits of the Crusaders——3. Revelation of the Lance——4. Defeat of Kerbogha——5. Summary of events.

TABLE OF CONTENTS

PAGE

Chapter VI. Dissension among the leaders................. 194

    1. Disorganization of the army——2. Disputes between Raymond and Bohemund——3. Raymond finally starts for Jerusalem. Archas——4. Continued quarrels among the leaders. The trial of the Lance——5. Another view of the revelation and trial of the Lance.

Chapter VII. Capture of Jerusalem...................... 242

    1. March to Jerusalem——2. The Siege——3. Final assault and capture——4. Arrangements for holding Jerusalem——5. Battle of Ascalon——6. Bohemund and Baldwin fulfil their vow ——7. Official Summary of the Crusade.

Epilogue 280

Notes 282

INTRODUCTION

It is now more than eight hundred years since Christian Europe was first aroused to arms in an effort to wrest the Holy Land from the hands of the Infidel, and yet the interest in those expeditions still persists. Scarcely a generation has passed without demanding a fuller and fresher account of the Crusades for its own perusal. Sober historians have sought earnestly to answer the call, but, voluminous as their work has been, the fanciful poet and novelist have succeeded in keeping a pace in advance. It would require many pages to list only the titles of the books and articles which the last generation alone has produced. Apparently the subject will not cease to appeal to the interest of the world so long as the history of Syria remains a treasured memory. And the story of the first and most successful Christian effort to retake possession of the Holy Land will continue to be read with feeling by the descendants, blood and spiritual, of those first Crusaders. It seems, therefore, not out of place to make available for the English reader the story of that expedition as related by the men who witnessed it and participated in it.

I. General Importance of the Chronicles

Modern writers have viewed the Crusades with varying opinion. Scholarly enthusiasts have seen in them "the first great effort of mediaeval life to go beyond the pursuit of selfish and isolated ambitions; . . . the trial feat of the young world essaying to use, to the glory of God and the benefit of many, the arms of its new knighthood."[1] Others, like Gibbon, more cynical in their attitude, have seen in them only the mournful spectacle of hundreds of thousands of human beings led on to inevitable slaughter by a spirit of ignorant fanaticism.[2] However varied the opinion on the wisdom and the expediency of the undertaking, there is less room for difference in regard to the importance of the movement as a phase in the development of European civilization. The highly localized life of the eleventh century, in which the immediate horizon so often served to limit men's vision of knowledge, was shaken from end to end. Not all who started on this expedition to the Holy Land ever reached the other end of Europe, to be sure, but even these saw for the first time strange cities and men and returned home, if not with glory, certainly with more experience than they had had before.

As for the thousands who finally succeeded in overcoming the almost superhuman obstacles involved in the conquest of the holy places, what wonders did they not have to relate! Individuals and occasional bands of pilgrims had journeyed over the same route before the Crusaders, but they were relatively so few that their experiences were absorbed within their own limited localities and left few traces. The First Crusade, however, enlisted people of all classes, of both sexes, and every age, drawing them from practically all parts of Christian Europe. As the first bands proceeded through district after district, others caught the spirit and started after them. And thus the narrow highways were choked with a constant stream of Crusaders, some hurrying eastward, others returning home. Nor did the movement cease with the capture of Jerusalem. Ten years later there were Crusaders still going East in answer to Urban's call for the First Crusade, while the actual possession of the Holy City by the Crusaders afforded the necessary impetus for a steady stream of pilgrims between West and East. With the pilgrim and the Crusader went also the merchant, courier, minstrel, and adventurer. Thus wayfaring, with all its attendant good and evil, became a habit over all of Europe. What this exchange of ideas and wares meant transcends statistics and must be looked for in the accelerated progress of Europe which followed, in the so-called Renaissance of the Twelfth Century.

Quite apart from the Crusade itself, the eye-witness accounts of the expedition have a peculiar value for the student of history as the first fairly full description of European society since the fall of the Roman Empire in the West. It is difficult to find in the period between the fifth and twelfth centuries any writings which describe contemporary life and society. Einhard's *Life of Charlemagne* is the striking exception. Just as the meagre *Germania* of Tacitus has been remorselessly tortured into a confession of Germanic civilization, frequently made to serve all centuries from the prehistoric to the eighth, and even beyond, so Einhard, with but little help, has been pressed into equally heroic service for the eighth and ninth centuries. The next two centuries, for lack of a Tacitus or an Einhard, have been constrained to linger under the infamy of the name "Dark Ages." This darkness, however, is effectively dispelled at the end of the eleventh century, largely through these chronicles of the First Crusades, while the steadily swelling volume of writings thereafter obviates the danger for succeeding ages. The religious character of the Crusades drew the sympathetic attention of clerical writers, the only writers of the time. All that the leaders did on this journey "of the Lord," whether petty or great, trivial or important, was thought worthy of commemoration for the benefit of posterity. Under the circumstances, the varied composition of the crusading host was particularly fortunate. Practically the only classes of Europe not personally represented on the Crusade were Emperor and King, Pope and Archbishop. In other words, that portion of society which alone was deemed worthy of attention in the ordinary brief annals and chronicles of the time was absent, and those who detailed the story of the expedition lavished their enthusiasm upon ordinary nobles, knights, and foot soldiers, even the poor being accorded a generous measure of notice. These accounts, accordingly, present a picture of society in which the relationship of all classes, ecclesiastical and lay, masculine and feminine, is portrayed in its intimate aspects. Although ordinary affairs are at times slighted, the extraordinary recur so frequently and with such variety as to make the inference of the ordinary fairly easy. The descriptions are so full and touch so many activities of society that they illumine not only the civilization of the time, but also cast considerable light on the preceding and following periods. As a result, it has been a common practice for master historians to initiate their apprentices into the study of European history through the accounts of the First Crusade.

The literary value of these writings is rather indirect than otherwise. They have afforded apparently inexhaustible material for literature, but as literary productions themselves have been only lightly appraised. Nevertheless, they are fair specimens of the writings of that time, and, as such, they deserve some consideration in a comprehensive history of literature. Some of them, such as the letters of Stephen of Blois and Anselm of Ribemont, have a charm which entitles them to much higher consideration. Here and there in the chronicles the authors soar to fairly great heights. It would be difficult to find anywhere a more graphic description of deep despair than is presented by the anonymous author of the *Gesta* in his account of the reception by Alexius and his army of the fate of the Crusaders at Antioch. In like manner, the fanciful account of the interview of Kerbogha and his mother before Antioch may be ranked with many a better known piece of imagery. In general, however, the literary merit of the following accounts consists chiefly in their vivid realism, which the very crudeness of expression only serves to accentuate. The hopes and fears, mournful sorrows and exultant joys, the profound despair and terror of the army, as it marched through one trial after another, are described with the awful earnestness and sincerity of men who have actually shared these experiences. It is this quality which causes the chronicles themselves to be read with interest long after their material has been adorned with finer language by more skilful writers.

II. THE DISTRIBUTION OF NEWS

But the absence of a polished literary finish was not wholly due to a lack of skill on the part of the writers. It was partly due, also, to the fact that these writings were intended for the information of the contemporary world. They were the newspapers of the time and in this they mark a distinct advance in the art of disseminating current information. Hitherto, writing had been almost exclusively confined to the Latin language and, hence, to churchmen. The few exceptions in vernacular tongues before the twelfth century have been deservedly treasured as rare monuments of philology. In the Latin writings only such matters as were of interest to the clergy were accorded much consideration. Theological writings, Scripture, the writings of the Church Fathers, books of Church service, textbooks for the schools, and treatises on kindred subjects constituted the chief themes for writers. Laws of kingdoms and meagre entries in monastic annals composed the major portion of secular information committed to writing. Occasionally the career of some ruler was chronicled in panegyric fashion, usually because of some past or expected favor to the Church. Even the histories of nations—e.g., *The History of the Franks* by Gregory of Tours, or *The Ecclesiastical History of England* by the Venerable Bede— were ecclesiastical histories, in which the purely secular played but an incidental part.

The written description of contemporary events for contemporary men was left to letters. But in the narrow life of the time people were rarely so far removed from their friends that they found it necessary to resort to such means for exchanging information. The churchmen, whose organization radiated from Rome, and whose training had made them more familiar with the art of writing, alone employed letters to any great extent. Here again, however, ecclesiastical and scholastic matters received the preponderant share of attention, though often current bits of general interest were included. These latter items might be transmitted to Church gatherings and, doubtless, were frequently so treated. But for the most part the news of the day was passed orally from neighbor to neighbor, or wider areas were momentarily linked together by the tales of some warfaring minstrel or other traveller. As the monasteries and castles were most famous for their hospitality, so these were the best informed centers of the time.

The Crusade, however, created abnormal conditions. Most of

the people who went on the expedition did so with the expectation of returning home after the fulfillment of their purpose. As a result, the social interests of the local communities were suddenly expanded even to Palestine itself. Since, moreover, there were few regions of western Europe which did not furnish some of their people for the cause, many different lines of interest focused themselves upon the army and were constantly crossing one another. Secular Europe was no longer limited by a local horizon; it was ever eager for news, and more news, from the East. Neighborhood gossip could serve only as a local distributing agency in this work. Wayfarers were eagerly accosted for news and probably supplied the localities with much real information. But where the interest was great and so constant, the temptation to expand small items to magnificent proportions was too great to be resisted, and many a glib-tongued impostor exchanged the fabrication of his fertile imagination for full fare and comfortable lodging. Some of these wild tales found their way into writing and were transmitted to a credulous posterity with all the authority which the written page could lend. Authentic information—and even the common world was soon forced to discriminate between kinds—had to be obtained through more assured channels. The service of couriers, long known to the official world, was expanded to meet the need.

III. Letters

In the earlier stages of the march it was a relatively easy matter to detach squires or foot-soldiers and send them back with messages and news. This continued even to the time when the army left Nicaea; thereafter this method became impracticable, if not quite impossible. Chance meetings with ships from the West then offered almost the only opportunity to exchange greetings, and, as the accounts show, these opportunities occurred but rarely. Letters alone could be used under such circumstances. It was, therefore, fortunate that the expedition represented a union of ecclesiastical and secular interests, for the churchmen, priests, or clerics lent themselves willingly to the task of drawing up letters—in Latin, of course. The churchmen in the West, upon receiving these letters, copied them and rapidly passed on the information to the waiting world. Such letters, even when addressed to individuals, were regarded as common property, unless they were carefully sealed, and their contents were widely diffused, usually at Church gatherings of some sort. How eagerly the congregations everywhere must have looked forward to such meetings for news from relatives, friends, and acquaintances, gone so long and so far away!

These letters,[3] of which fourteen are here translated and distributed at their appropriate places in the narrative, constitute the most important sources of our knowledge of the events which they describe. The authors are all men of prominence and responsibility. Two of the letters are from popes. One is from the Emperor Alexius. Five are from the leaders of the Crusade and may be regarded as official reports of progress, while the remaining four, though also the works of leaders, are of a more personal nature. The two letters of Stephen of Blois to his wife, Adele, are among the literary gems of the period. In addition to the responsible character of their writers, the letters have the further merit of greater proximity both of time and place to the events which they narrate. The emotions of the moment grip the writers irresistibly, beyond the power of epistolary formality to efface and thus lend a vividness which the later chronicles sometimes lack. Our chief regret is that there are not more of them.

IV. Chronicles

The interest of the world in the events of the First Crusade could not be satisfied by letters alone. Numerous motives combined to keep this interest inflamed. Patriotic pride in the achievements of countrymen, natural enjoyment of the marvelous and adventurous, the continued need of both men and money to insure the permanence of the conquest, and, no less, the pardonable pride of the Crusaders themselves in preserving the memory of their deeds—all these influences tended to the telling and the retelling of the story. Book-making in itself offered little inducement, for the absence of publishing houses and the lack of copyright laws denied prospective authors hope either of fame or wealth. Publishing, if the multiplication of copies by the laborious process of hand-writing may be so called, was done chiefly in the scriptoria of monasteries or episcopal schools. But parchment was expensive, and only the clerics could write. Ordinarily the military exploits of contemporary men seemed too ephemeral to justify description. However, the Crusade was a different matter in that its exploits, though largely military and material, nevertheless had a deep religious significance. Urban's remark at Clermont, that the recovery of the Holy Land would be a deed comparable to those of the Maccabees, was not forgotten. The thought that he was really adding a chapter to Sacred History served to carry more than one writer over depressing periods of discouragement to the successful completion of his history of the expedition. These varied motives, both sacred and profane, combined to inspire the composition of the following detailed accounts of the First Crusade.[4]

The first complete account of the Crusade which has come down to us is commonly known as the *Gesta*. Its author has attained some measure of distinction as the Anonymous. What is known to him, therefore, rests solely upon the inferences to be drawn from his work. He accompanied the Italian Norman prince, Bohemund, from the siege of Amalfi to the capture of Antioch. From there he went to Jerusalem with the general band under Raymond's leadership, whether with Raymond himself or, which is more likely, with Tancred or Robert of Normandy, who were associated with Raymond, is not clear. His book was written before the close of 1101, for Ekkehard saw and used a copy of it at Jerusalem in that year. So much may be stated fairly positively; the rest is only inferential, for in his book personal references are singularly few. There is no preface or dedication, no parting remark to the reader. However, certain expressions, certain modifications of the Latin which he employs, betray a high degree of familiarity with the verbal habits of southern Italy, while his constant laudation of Bohemund, even though he abandoned him after the capture of Antioch, tends to confirm the belief that his home was in that region. He may have been a Norman; if so, he left Normandy long before the First Crusade. His somewhat secular point of view in regard to events, occasional impersonal remarks upon the clergy, or participation in battle, have led modern critics to the belief that he was a knight, though his lack of intimacy with the leaders would indicate that he was a lesser knight. The style of his work and the general lack of literary allusions do not bespeak a very high degree of education. His use of language is that of an amateur, and his vocabulary is decidedly limited. Unable adequately to describe the achievements of the various crusaders, he strains the superlative degree of his adjectives so constantly that occasionally he finds it necessary to lapse into the simple positive as a means of actual distinction. The Bible is practically the only work which he quotes. His real piety is sustained both in his book and in his own career, as is indicated by the fact that he chose to go on to Jerusalem, instead of remaining with his leader at Antioch. What he lacks elsewhere is greatly outweighed by his judgment in evaluating the relative importance of events, his restraint in preventing intimate details from obscuring the perspective of his story, his unusual fairness and impartiality toward the rival Christian leaders, as well as toward his Turkish foes, and a certain native instinct for the dramatic apparent throughout the book. Guibert, Balderic, and Robert the Monk all criticized his style, but unwittingly paid him the lavish compliment of incorporating nearly the whole of his work in their "literary" accounts of the expedition. The great historical value of the work rests not only in the fact that it was written by an eye-witness and participant, but also upon the fact that it was probably composed from time to time on the journey and finished immediately after the battle of Ascalon in September 1099, the last event which it mentions. It is the first full account of the Crusade still extant, and almost every other history of the First Crusade is based either directly or indirectly upon it. Six MS copies of it still remain, and all of the material has been preserved in one form or another in the later accounts of the Crusade.

The second chronicle listed, on the other hand, does not at all efface its author, for the preface sets forth the authorship and the purpose in full:

"To my Lord Bishop of Viviers and to all the orthodox, from Pontius of *Balazun* and Raymond, Canon of Puy; greeting, and a share in our labor.

"We have concluded that we ought to make clear to you and to all who dwell across the Alps the great deeds which God in the usual manner of His love performed, and did not cease constantly to perform, through us; especially so, since the unwarlike and the fearful left us and strove to substitute falsehood for the truth. But let him who shall see their apostacy shun their words and companionship! For the army of God, even if it bore the punishment of the Lord Himself for its sins, out of His compassion also stood forth victor over all paganism. But since some went through Slavonia, others through Hungary, others through Longobardy, and yet others by sea, it would be tedious for us to write about each. Therefore we have omitted the story of others and have taken it as our task to write about the Count, the Bishop of Puy, and their army."

Pontius of *Balazun,* a knight in the Provençal army, was killed at Archas, and Raymond was thus left to complete the task alone. Raymond had been elevated to the priesthood while on the Crusade and had become the chaplain of Count Raymond of Toulouse, who was the wealthiest leader on the expedition. The expense of compiling the book was, therefore, a trivial matter. His intimacy with Count Raymond and with Bishop Adhemar gave him access to much information not available to such writers as the Anonymous. Critics have been exceedingly harsh in their condemnation of both the form and the content of the book. They condemn it as crude, bigoted, intensely partisan, and a mass of confused and credulous mysticism. Partisan it undoubtedly is, for Raymond was writing to correct a probable impression conveyed by the returning Crusaders both as to the bravery of the Provençal host and the validity of the Holy Lance, especially the latter. He himself had been among the first to accept the visions of Peter Bartholomew, had participated in the digging for the Lance, and even the apparently adverse judgment of the Ordeal was not sufficient to shake his faith in it. A large part of his work, therefore, is a brief in defense of the Lance, in support of which he adduces vision after vision and numerous witnesses. The rest of his book is devoted to the part played by Count Raymond, Bishop Adhemar, and the Provençal host in the Crusade. All this is true, but it cannot be said in justice that he is totally blind to the faults of either leader or people. To the historian the book is second in importance only to the *Gesta*, for it was the work of an eye-witness, written possibly no earlier than 1102, though undoubtedly on the basis of notes taken during the journey. It must be regarded as an independent account, even though, as Hagenmeyer conjectures, its author may have used details from the *Gesta* to correct his own account. For what may be termed the sociological aspects of the Crusade, Raymond's history is the most valuable of all the accounts. Six MS copies of the work are extant.

The third account of the Crusade as a whole was written by Fulcher of Chartres, whose career can be traced more fully than that of any other eye-witness chronicler of the Crusade. Born probably at Chartres in 1059, he was trained for the service of the Church, and when the Council of Clermont was held in 1095 he was a priest either at Chartres or at Orleans. The enthusiasm which swept over the land claimed him, as it did so many of his countrymen, so that when the army of Stephen of Blois moved from Chartres, late in 1096, Fulcher was one of the band. He was with Stephen's army until October, 1097, when he became the chaplain of Baldwin, Godfrey's brother. From this time until Baldwin's death in 1118 he remained in that capacity, closely associated with the energetic leader. As a result, he was present neither at the siege of Antioch nor at that of Jerusalem, being then at Edessa, which place he did not leave until late in 1099, when he made a pilgrimage to Jerusalem with Baldwin and Bohemund. When Baldwin was summoned to take the reins of government upon the death of Godfrey, Fulcher accompanied him to Jerusalem, where he remained until the time of his own death in 1127 or 1128.

His *Historia Hierosolymitana*, of which only the portion relating events actually witnessed by Fulcher on the First Crusade is here translated, was written upon the urgent solicitation of his friends. It first appeared in 1105, and the welcome then accorded it encouraged him to go on with it. The latter part of his work takes the form of an annalistic account of the Latin Kingdom of Jerusalem, for the early history of which it is undoubtedly the most important single source of information. He seems to have revised the earlier portions of his history at least twice, and the final version ends somewhat abruptly with the mention of a plague of rats in the year 1127. Fulcher apparently had a more extensive literary training than either of the two preceding writers. His fondness for quotation has been charged against him as an affectation by modern critics, but, as a fault, it mars only the latter portion of his work, written when he was quite old. On the whole, his book is free from either partisanship or bias. He seems to have been interested chiefly in describing the events as they occurred, with possibly an additional desire to attract soldiers from the West to the support of the needy Latin state in Syria. He displays a strong interest in nature and describes strange plants, animals, and natural phenomena in a naïve manner. His interest in the intrigues of the lords, both lay and ecclesiastical, is very slight, but the general welfare of the people he views with all the kindly concern of a simple French curé. As a whole, the book is exceedingly valuable and very soon was widely read and copied. It was second only to the *Gesta* as a mine for exploitation by later writers on the Crusade. More than fifteen MS copies of the original are still extant.

Of the writings which contribute eye-witness testimony to but a portion of the history of the Crusade, the *Alexiad*, by Anna Comnena, is one of the most important. The writer was the daughter of Alexius, and, though she was barely fourteen years of age when the Crusaders came to Constantinople, it may be assumed that the presence of so many rude strangers in the imperial city made a most vivid impression on her mind. Both Anna and her husband, Nicephorus Briennius, had been highly educated, and when the palace intrigue in which they were both concerned proved unsuccessful and she was shut up in a convent by her brother's order, she undertook to complete the history which her husband had begun. Forty years after the first Crusaders had passed through Antioch she began her task. In the meantime there had been various bands of Crusaders from the West. Bohemund had taken Antioch in defiance of the Emperor and had even made war upon him. The relations of Alexius with Count Raymond of Toulouse had undergone changes, and many other events relating to the Latins and the Crusades had occurred. Thus, with so much to confuse her memory, her chronology is uncertain, her statement of fact often inaccurate, and her style highly rhetorical and affected. Never very certain of the identity of the Latin leaders, as she herself confesses, she calls them all counts and confuses one group with another in hopeless fashion. Nevertheless, her work is exceedingly valuable as a presentation of the Byzantine attitude toward the Latins, and her conception of her father's feeling toward the Westerners can probably be relied upon as correct. A MS copy of the account, corrected by Anna herself, is preserved at Florence. Other fragments also remain.

It is necessary to include in the list of eye-witness accounts of the First Crusade the work by Peter Tudebode, a priest of Civray.[5] This work, once regarded as the original of the *Gesta*, has been dethroned from that position by recent criticism. It is almost a verbatim copy of the latter, with portions added from the account of Raymond of Agilles, together with a very few personal remarks and observations. He speaks of the death of his brother in Antioch and his own share in the funeral services. His account differs from that of the *Gesta* primarily in the change of adjectives qualifying Raymond of Toulouse and Bohemund, for Tudebode was a follower of Count Raymond. However, this policy is not consistently maintained. At best, the work may be regarded as an eye-witness corroboration of the *Gesta*. It was written after both the account by the Anonymous and by Raymond had been composed, and sometime before 1111, after which date it was quoted by other writers. Four MS copies are preserved.

Ekkehard of Aura, who is still regarded as one of the greatest of the German historians of the Middle Ages, was a monk at Corvey when the First Crusade was preached. He accompanied a later band of crusaders in 1101 as far as Constantinople by land, and by sea from there to Joppa. At Jerusalem he saw a copy of the *Gesta*, which he made a basis for his own history. This work he wrote for the Abbot of Corvey in 1112, after he himself had become Abbot of Aura. The language and the style of this book reveal a greater familiarity with classical authors than is shown by any of the preceding accounts of the Crusade. Its value rests chiefly upon his eye-witness account of the Crusade of 1101, and his brief items about the Peasants' Crusade, of which no direct chronicle has come down to us. Only the latter material has been included in the following translation. Six MS copies of the work are extant.

Raoul de Caen, a Norman knight too young to accompany the

Crusaders of 1096, enlisted in the army which Bohemund assembled in 1107. He reached Syria and entered the service of Tancred, then prince of Antioch, whom he served until the latter's death. In his early years he had received instruction in letters from Arnulf, who became Patriarch of Jerusalem after 1112. He was an accomplished knight and seems to have enjoyed the friendship of Tancred. During the first five years of this relationship he learned much about the First Crusade, especially Tancred's view of events. He also visited Jerusalem and there conversed with his former teacher, Arnulf, now the Patriarch, to whom he dedicated his work, the *Gesta Tancredi*. Though an important source of information, this work is not, strictly speaking, an eye-witness account. It is a panegyric of the Norman princes of Antioch and is very hostile to the Emperor Alexius and to Count Raymond. It deals with the history of the First Crusade and of Tancred up to 1105, and its chief value lies in the reflection of the Norman point of view. It also contains some information not afforded by other writers. The Latin is polished and adorned with numerous passages and quotations from classical authors. Raoul writes chiefly in prose, but he sometimes attempts to soar to poetic form in describing unusually great achievements. On the whole, Patriarch Arnulf had reason to be proud of his former pupil's achievement. The book was written sometime between Tancred's death in 1112 and that of Arnulf in 1118. A single MS copy is preserved at the Royal Library of Brussels. His account of the Holy Lance, in which he takes an opposite view from Raymond, is here translated in full. Other material from the work is included in the notes.

The value of the account by Albert of Aix has been much disputed. Little is known of the author, who is said to have been a canon of the church of Aix-la-Chapelle about the middle of the twelfth century. By his own confession he never visited the Holy Land himself. Nevertheless, he wrote a history of the First Crusade and the Latin Kingdom of Jerusalem down to the year 1120, of which twelve MS copies exist. The date of this writing has, therefore, been placed somewhere between 1120 and the middle of the century. He obtained his information, he says, from the oral and written testimony of participants. Much of the material is palpably legendary; more of it, however, seems entirely probable and stands the test of comparison with well established accounts. The work contains so much not treated by other writers and, therefore, incapable of corroboration that its value must stand or fall with the reader's attitude toward the author. It has been conjectured that much of the material was taken from a Lorraine chronicle now lost, an explanation plausible enough, though thus far not substantiated. At any rate, his items of information cannot be ignored, and they may be of full value. Until further evidence is discovered, the question cannot be settled positively.[6] Only excerpts on the Peasants' Crusade and Godfrey's march to Constantinople are here translated from Albert.

The other three works included in this translation because their authors were present at the Council of Clermont may be grouped together as literary histories. None of the writers accompanied the expedition, but each wrote a history of the whole Crusade, thus illustrating the deep interest of the people of Europe in the subject. All three were churchmen of high position, and each sought to rewrite the crude account of the *Gesta* in more literary form. They succeeded in varying degree, but their names are remembered, while that of the original author has been irretrievably lost. Robert the Monk is generally identified as the monk chosen Abbot of Saint-Remi of Rheims in 1094, and later forced to retire to the priory of Senuc. His work was written at the request of Bernard, Abbot of Marmoutier, sometime before 1107. It adds little to the *Gesta*, but was very popular in the twelfth century. More than eighty MS copies of it are still extant. Balderic, Abbot of Bourgeuil, and Archbishop of Dol after 1107, added little more than Robert to the *Gesta* account. His work was written after 1107 and was also quite popular. Seven MS copies remain. The best of these three accounts is that of Guibert, who was Abbot of Nogent from 1104 to 1121. He composed his book between 1108 and 1112 and dedicated it to Lisiard, Bishop of Soissons. Guibert was one of the leading scholars of his time, well versed in classical lore, which he used to adorn his accounts of the Crusade. He was also fairly well informed about matters in northern France. His additions to the *Gesta* contain many valuable items about the crusading leaders from that region. Four MS copies of his work are preserved.

V. Terminology.

In the translation of these accounts a conscious effort has been made to reproduce as nearly as possible the style and manner of expression of the original. Though the writers all used the same language, they employed different words and idioms to describe the same occurrences, even the ordinary incidents of life. Under the circumstances, it was felt that too much would be lost if the expressions were all translated in the standard idiom of today. The person of the twentieth century who is interested in the manners and customs of that time will find enough pleasure and profit in this treatment, it is hoped, to repay him for whatever confusion the variety of expressions may create. A brief explanation of some of the more distinctive habits in the terminology of the period may be of use.

1. *Names of persons and places.*

The names of the same persons and the same places are spelled in many different ways not only by the different writers, but often, too, by the same writer. While this is more true of Eastern persons and places, it is, also, quite generally true with regard to the West, a revelation of how much of the world was strange to the people of eleventh century Europe. It must be remembered, however, that dictionaries, gazetteers, and similar works of reference, which greet the twentieth century person at every turn, were virtually unknown, while newspapers and other periodicals, which serve to standardize so much of life today, did not then exist. Almost the only common descriptions of the world known at that time were those contained in either the classical writings or in those of the Church fathers. It is not strange, therefore, to find the names of old Roman provinces and cities applied to places by some of the more highly educated writers, such as Ekkehard, Raoul, or Guibert. Less trained writers—and most of our writers fall within this category—had to trust chiefly to their powers of hearing and their ability to reproduce in writing what they heard. They had to follow their own rules of phonetic spelling and, considering the difficulties under which they labored, their results deserve genuine admiration. In order to avoid undue confusion, a uniform spelling has been adopted for the names of places which have been identified. In most cases the mediaeval name has been employed, but where the modern equivalent is much better known that form has been chosen.

The identification of the places mentioned by the writers presents considerable difficulty at times. It would be asking almost too much to expect the chroniclers to recall vividly and correctly both the name and exact location of all the strange places which they mention five or more years after they had passed through them. Important towns and places in which they spent some time, or with which they were able to associate some dramatic event, are usually located quite accurately; other lesser places cannot always be positively identified. All places mentioned whose location can be identified appear on the accompanying maps. The others, whose location is uncertain, have been italicized.

Names of persons, such as Robert, Godfrey, Baldwin, and

Stephen were common enough, and little variation occurs. But Adhemar, papal leader of the expedition, seems to have had a baffling name, probably due to its similarity to a variety of names. As a result, his name appears as Haymarus, Aimarus, Ademarus, or Adhemarus, or not at all. Guibert, in describing the Pope's appointment of a vicar for the Crusade, confesses that he does not know his name, an interesting comment on the isolation of the time. His use of the name later may be an indication that he was using his original too closely, for the author of the *Gesta*, too, was ignorant of the name until later in the expedition. For the purposes of this translation, however, the names of the Western leaders are standardized. This is not the case with Oriental names, the unusual character of which occasioned the chroniclers a great deal of trouble. The name of the Turkish ruler of Antioch may be cited as a typical instance. The common spelling of his name today is Yagi-Sian or Iagi-Sian. It appears in the accounts, however, wth the Latin ending as Aoxian-us, Cassian-us, Caspian-us, and even Gracianus. Fulcher, who coined the first of these, succeeded remarkably well on the whole. In the case of less prominent men who are mentioned only once or twice, the variations have caused considerable confusion, leading even to the belief that they were different persons—e.g., Godfrey of Lastours, who appears as Gulferrus de Daturre, Golprius *de turribus*, and Gosfridus de Dasturs. This example seems to indicate the beginning of the use of surnames, but it is probably fortunate for the reader that the movement had not yet developed far. The efforts of the Crusaders to distinguish between the numerous Raymonds, Roberts, Stephens, Baldwins, and Godfreys, are of interest as early factors in the movement which led to the growth of heraldry and the multiplication of names.

2. *Expressions of time.*

The reader will doubtless be impressed by the absence in the chronicles of precise and minute statements of time, which are such a marked feature of modern industrial life. The year seems to have been of little account as a basis for reckoning time, for the author of the *Gesta* mentions it only once during the whole narrative which extends over a period of four years, and Raymond of Agilles scarcely more often. The more learned Fulcher uses it, to be sure, but rather as an ornament than because he feels the need of such a measure of time. The great festival days of the Church constituted the chief standards of time, and here, thanks to the influence of the Church, we find a fairly uniform practice among the writers. The necessity of determining the variable date of Easter compelled the Church to keep a calendar, while the custom of regulating the ordinary affairs of life with reference to the chief festival days of the Church had long since become an established habit of Christian Europe. The old Roman Calendar, too, continued to exert some influence despite the efforts of the Church to supplant it with a Christian scheme. As a result, the days of the month are reckoned both by Kalends, Nones, and Ides, and by the numerical count of days from the incoming or outgoing month. Days of the week bear the old Roman names and the canonical enumeration from the Lord's Day, as well. Time of day is expressed usually by means of the canonical hours, Matins, Prime, Terce, Sext, None, Vespers, and Compline, though such expressions as cock-crow, earliest dawn, and sunrise also occur. Time of day, and day of year are sometimes noted by the psalms and prayers customary at those times. Local variations in reckoning the beginning of the year and seasons, or in expressing dates by festivals of loyal saints, a practice quite common in the West, appear rather infrequently in these accounts.[7]

3. *Numbers.*

The figures used by mediaeval writers in stating numbers of people have baffled modern investigators. In order to discover the actual numbers involved, it has become almost a rule to divide the figures of the chroniclers by ten. Perhaps it would be fairer to regard almost all numbers over one thousand as figures of speech, intended only to convey the impression of a very large number. Roman numerals alone were in use, and neither the average writer nor the average reader of the period had very much training in arithmetic. It was certainly a difficult task to describe, if not a more difficult task to decipher, a very uneven number of six figures in Roman numerals. Quite aside from the mere mechanical difficulty of the task, few, if any persons, had had experience in dealing with large numbers. Neither commercial, ecclesiastical, nor military establishments dealt accurately in very large amounts or numbers at this time. As a result, when these chroniclers found themselves in the midst of the vast host which composed the crusading army they were struck with amazement. Nothing in their previous experience afforded them a satisfactory basis for estimating the size of the army. The numbers implied in their frequent resort to the term "countless" and "innumerable," or "as the sands of the sea," and "as the leaves of autumn," are probably almost as accurate as the numerals which they employ. The actual number of persons who took part in the First Crusade cannot be fixed with any certainty. Army rosters were not yet in use. It is, furthermore, extremely doubtful whether even among the better organized bands, such as those of Raymond and Godfrey, the leaders themselves knew exactly how many persons were in their following. The more adventurous knights were constantly digressing in smaller or larger companies from the main line of march; the more timid were dropping behind or deserting; and new enthusiasts were joining the march at almost every halting place. Thus the total number in the army fluctuated from day to day. Fulcher's statement that if all who had signed themselves with the cross had been present at Nicaea, there would have been six million, instead of six hundred thousand, armed men is probably more accurate in its proportions than in its actual figures. A modern estimate of the number in the army as it left Nicaea, ingeniously computed from the length of time required to cross a certain bridge in Asia Minor, is 105,000 persons.[8] The combined army was then at its maximum size. It dwindled rapidly thereafter, and the figures offered by the chroniclers themselves became more and more accurate, so that when Fulcher reports the number of Crusaders left to garrison Jerusalem as a few hundred, his statement may be accepted without great question.

If they had so much difficulty in describing their own numbers, little surprise need be felt at their estimate of the enemy's forces. After chronicling battles against the Turks and Saracens for almost thirty years, Fulcher reaches the following conclusion: "As to the number of dead or wounded in this or any other battle, it is not possible to determine the truth, for such great numbers cannot be computed by anyone, except approximately. Often when different writers deceive, the reason for their deception is to be attributed to adulation; for they try to enhance the glory of the victors and to extol the valor of their own land for people present and to come. From this it is very clear why they so foolishly and falsely exaggerate the number of dead among the enemy, and minimize, or remain entirely silent, about their own loss." This critical attitude, however, was not taken by the earlier writers, not even by Fulcher himself in the period with which this translation deals.

4. *Money and prices.*

Europe was still dealing largely on a basis of natural economy when the First Crusade started on its way. Money was regarded rather as a luxury than as a matter of general need, and even ordinary state obligations were discharged in kind rather than coin. Indeed, there was no standard coin in the West, and coinage was a right exercised by all the great feudal vassals. There were expressions of value common to all Europe—e.g., the *liber*, or pound, which equalled 20 *solidi*, or shillings, which equalled 240 *denarii*, or pennies; and a *marc* which equalled two-thirds of a liber, or 160 *denarii*. But when these terms were applied to coins in actual circulation, their meaning varied with the character of the coin involved. The coin in most general use was the *denarius*, or penny. This was usually of silver, but might be made of an alloy, or sometimes of copper alone. A large and a small *denarius* were known, the latter often called an *obol*. The intrinsic value of the coin varied somewhat according to the particular mint at which it was coined, weight constituting, on the whole, the safest method of determining value. Raymond mentions seven different *denarii* from a limited region of the West as current in the army. Variation was caused by debasement through coin-clipping and kindred practices, which, however, appear to have been less common at this time than later. In view of such facts, generalizations about monetary matters are exceedingly hazardous. However, it is usually safe to assume when Western coins are mentioned that *denarii* are meant. *Solidi, liberi*, and *marci* are moneys of account, convenient in expressing large sums of *denarii*. The ordinary silver *denarius* weighed from 20 to 24 gr. as compared with the American dime which weighs 38.5 gr. In the East the Crusaders met with gold coins, the *besant* and *perperus* of Constantinople, and the gold *besant* of the Saracens. The *besant* of Constantinople weighed about 65 gr. as compared with the American gold coinage, which weighs about 25 gr. per dollar. The *perperus*, called also *purpuratus, yperperus, yperperon*, and *perpre*, is less well known. Its value, as stated by the author of the *Gesta*, was equal to 15 *solidi*, or 180 *denarii*. The gold *besant* of the Saracens, a Latin term for the Arabian *dinar*, was about equal in weight and intrinsic value to the *besant* of Constantinople. In seeking the modern equivalents of these coins, it is necessary to bear in mind the relative value of gold and silver in the middle ages. Another coin encountered in the East was the *tartaron*, which appears to have been a cheap copper coin of somewhat varying value.

From an economic point of view the First Crusade must be regarded as one of the most important factors in transforming the basis of European exchange from the natural to the monetary. The change was by no means complete with the end of the Crusades, but a long step had been taken toward that goal when the first of these expeditions was launched. Money was necessary to defray the ordinary living expenses on the march, and the Crusaders resorted to almost every conceivable device to obtain it. They tortured Jews, melted plate, mortgaged their possessions, and sold their goods for ridiculously small sums. Money, ordinarily scarce, rose in value until, as Albert recounts, one peasant sold seven sheep for a single *denarius*. Normally, a *denarius* was the equivalent of a workman's dinner, but the Crusade created abnormal conditions. Unfortunately, this abnormal state of affairs accompanied the Crusaders along their whole line of march, for just as their arrangements for departure caused the exchange value of money to soar, so the arrival of so many people at one town or another caused the limited food supply to take on incredible prices. Occasionally, in time of famine, food rose to almost impossible heights, so that the peasant who exchanged his seven sheep for one *denarius* in the Rhine country might have exchanged his *denarius*, in turn, for a single nut at Antioch during its siege by Kerbogha. The student of economics will be able to find many such equations in the following pages. The Crusaders had unwittingly become steady victims of the law of supply and demand, but for lack of such knowledge they blamed their misfortunes upon the cupidity of the Armenians and Greeks. Thus, however, they learned to esteem the possession of money, and in Saracen territory they lost few opportunities to secure it either as tribute, extortion, or plain robbery. Sometimes they even burned the dead bodies of their foes to obtain the coins which they believed these people had swallowed or secreted about their bodies. Actual money and its value was one of the most important contributions of the returning Crusaders to Western life, so much so that the *besant* of Constantinople and the Saracen *besant* became well known coins in Europe.

5. *Military arrangements.*

A definite organization of the army as a whole did not exist. The Pope's representative, Adhemar, who met all of his charges at Nicaea for the first time, was social and ecclesiastical head of the expedition until his death at Antioch, August 1, 1098. For military purposes, the Crusaders chose Stephen of Blois as their leader on the march across Asia Minor, and, after his withdrawal, Bohemund acted in that capacity for a time. Little real authority, however, was accorded these leaders, except for the brief period of Kerbogha's siege, when Bohemund was entrusted with full powers. Ordinarily, matters of policy were decided at a council of all the leaders, both lay and ecclesiastical. For all practical purposes, each band was almost a separate army in itself, and even within each band matters were usually decided by a common council. Leaders of the separate bands frequently had to resort to all the arts of persuasion at their command in order to keep their many-minded and impulsive vassals in leash. Eloquence, entreaty, offers of pay, and even threats were used time and time again. The feudal oath of allegiance of vassal to over-lord was the only basis of obedience, but the conditions under which the campaign was conducted were so different from those of the West as to render the ordinary feudal obligations quite inadequate. As a result, adventurous knights frequently went off on raiding expeditions without regard for the wishes of their lords, and companies of knights for these forays were formed from many different bands. Disorganization was further increased by the presence of great numbers of non-combatants. Persons of both sexes and all ages had attached themselves to the army from various motives—serfs to perform menial tasks; peasants with their families seeking improvement, material, social, or spiritual; women, wives of Crusaders, or mere adventurers; pious pilgrims of all ages; and clergy, both regular and secular. At Nicaea this multitude probably largely outnumbered the fighting men, and, as a rule, they were a great hindrance to the army.

The fighting men were of two classes—the mounted and armored knight, and the more or less armored foot-soldiers. At first the mounted knights were probably all of noble birth, but, as the exigencies of the campaign multiplied, this condition was changed. At times noble knights were compelled to ride on oxen or other beasts, or to proceed on foot, and, again, ignoble foot-soldiers found mounts and suits of armor. In the course of time, many of the latter proved themselves worthy of knighthood, so that by the time the army reached Jerusalem a great number of the so-called knights were not of noble birth.

The knight, protected by his breastplate and his suit of chain-mail, and equipped with shield, lance, and two-edged sword, was the mainstay of the army. His squires, also mounted, usually accompanied the knight in battle. The foot-soldiers, whose chief weapons were the cross-bow and javelin, were used both to break up the line of the enemy in the opening charge and to dispose of the dismounted enemy after the main charge of the knights. Non-combatants were of some service in refreshing the fighters with drinks, caring for the wounded, and helping to collect the spoils. The clergy played an important part by administering the sacrament before battle and offering up prayers during the course of the fighting. Such was the practice against an enemy in the open field. The tactics of the Turks, however, caused some modifications. This foe, usually mounted on swift horses and armed with dangerous small bows, insisted upon encircling the Crusaders without coming to close quarters. Their arrows, which they shot quickly and in profusion, were calculated to shatter the ranks of the Crusaders and usually did great damage to the less heavily armored foot-soldiers. If this device failed to open up the ranks, they scattered in feigned flight, hoping thus to draw the Crusaders after them in disorganized pursuit, when it was an easy matter to turn and cut them down. The Emperor Alexius gave the Crusaders some very valuable advice on these matters. Actual experience proved an even more effective teacher, so that the Crusaders regularly placed a strong line at their rear and on the flanks, as well as in front, and did not pursue the enemy until they were actually in rout.

To the Westerners siege warfare was less well known than open fighting. In most of Western Europe there was little of the heavy masonry of Roman days, such as had never gone out of use in the East. The Italians had had relatively more experience than the people north of the Alps, but both had much to learn. The military engineers of Constantinople gave the Crusaders some important lessons in siege-craft at Nicaea. The development of more powerful hurling engines for both stones and arrows became a necessity. These were of two kinds: the *ballistae*, used to shoot large arrows or bolts with great force, and the *Petraria*, which hurled large stones. The motive power was provided by the torsion of twisted ropes or the sudden release of a heavy counter-poise, and great ingenuity was exercised to increase their force. During the whole expedition, however, they were not developed sufficiently to make any considerable impression upon the walls. They were chiefly effective in clearing the walls of defenders, which facilitated other siege operations. Battering rams of various kinds were also used, and, as a protection for the manipulators, mantlets made of wattled stakes were constructed. Undermining the walls was an operation also resorted to, but the most effective devices in overcoming strongly fortified towns were the great movable towers and the blockade. The first was used successfully both at Marra and Jerusalem, the latter at Nicaea and Antioch. These are fully described in the text (see pages 256, 205, 105). Scaling ladders of wood were of subsidiary value, but played a part at Marra and Jerusalem and especially at Caesarea. In all these operations there was a great demand for skilful engineers, as well as for unskilled labor. It is significant that Greek engineers were employed at Nicaea and Antioch, Italian at Antioch and Jerusalem. The Westerners had much to learn, it is true, but that they were quick to do so is shown not only by their success at Jerusalem, but also by the stronger castles and fortifications which appeared in Western Europe during the twelfth century.

THE FIRST CRUSADE

PROLOGUE

(*Fulcher.*) It is a joy to the living and even profitable to the dead when the deeds of brave men, and especially of those fighting for God, are read from writings, or, committed to memory, are recited with prudence in the midst of the faithful. For upon hearing the pious purposes of those who have gone before them—how, rejecting the honor of the world, leaving their parents, wives, and goods of whatsoever kind, they clung to God and followed Him according to the counsel of the Gospel—those who live in the world are themselves animated by His inspiration and aroused to love Him most ardently. It is even beneficial to those who are dead in the Lord, since the faithful, hearing their good and pious deeds, therefore bless their souls and in charity offer alms and prayers for them, whether these dead were known to them or not.

Moved, therefore, by the requests of former comrades, I have related in careful and orderly fashion the illustrious deeds of the Franks in honor of the Saviour, when at the command of God they made an armed pilgrimage to Jerusalem. In homely style, but, nevertheless, truly, I have recounted what I deemed worthy to be committed to memory, and I have told it as well as I can and just as I saw it myself. Although I do not dare to put this work of the Franks that I have mentioned on an equality with the distinguished achievements of the people of Israel, or of the Maccabees[1], or of many other peoples whom God has honored by such frequent and such wonderful miracles, still I consider it not far inferior to those works, since in connection with it miracles worked by God were often witnessed. These I have taken care to report in writing.

In what way, indeed, do these Franks differ from the Israelites and the Maccabees? In those lands, by my very side, I have seen them dismembered, crucified, flayed, shot with arrows, butchered, or killed by other kinds of martyrdom for the love of Christ; or I have heard of it when I was far away. And yet they could be overcome neither by threats nor blandishments! Nay, even if the slayer's sword had come, many of us would not have refused to perish for the love of Christ. Oh, how many thousands of martyrs died a happy death on this expedition! Who is so hard of heart that he can hear these deeds without being moved by deepest piety to break forth in His praise? Who will not wonder how we, a few people in the midst of the lands of our enemies, were able not only to resist, but to live? Who has ever heard such things? On one side of us were Egypt and Ethiopia; on another Arabia, Chaldea, Syria, Parthia, Mesopotamia, Assyria, and Media; on another Persia and Scythia.[2] A great sea separated us from Christendom and shut us up in the hands of our destroyers, as if God allowed it. But His arm mercifully defended us. "Blessed indeed is the nation whose God is the Lord."[3]

The history which follows shall explain how this work was begun, and how all the people of the West, once aroused to undertake so great an expedition, more than willingly applied their hearts and hands to it.

CHAPTER I

THE SUMMONS

(After Fulcher's preface, which seems admirably suited to this account, the chapter deals with the call for Crusaders from the West. The condition of Europe on the eve of the Crusade is too large a subject to be treated adequately here, but Fulcher's brief summary contains a very suggestive survey of the situation and is interestingly supplemented by Ekkehard's contrast of conditions in East and West Frankland. Most of the causes of the movement may be inferred from Urban's speech at Clermont.

The Council of Clermont was held in November 1095 and lasted for ten days, from the eighteenth to the twenty-eighth of the month, the famous address of Urban being delivered on the day before the close of the Council. The four writers who were presumably present wrote their versions of the speech several years after it occurred, that of Fulcher being perhaps the earliest. Each may have preserved notes taken at the time, but it is extremely interesting to observe that each stresses that phase of the speech which especially appealed to him. Robert the Monk seems to have responded as a patriotic Frenchman, Balderic as a member of the Church hierarchy, Guibert as a mystic, Fulcher, here, as always, as the simple curé—all as churchmen.[4] Enough has been added by the writers to indicate that most of Urban's audience, which consisted principally of the clergy, became unofficial preachers of the Crusade when they returned to their own districts. This is indicated also by Urban's letter to the Crusaders in Flanders, written less than a month after the Council, which was half plea and half instruction to men already aroused. Urban himself spoke at other places in France before returning to Italy to stir up the people there, but he did not go to Germany for the reasons mentioned by both Fulcher and Ekkehard. The appeal there, though indirect, was powerful, as the second chapter proves. The call to the Crusade was sounded and resounded by Urban, even to the time of his death, and by hundreds of others both during his life-time and long thereafter.)

1. *Conditions in Europe at the beginning of the Crusades.*

(*Fulcher.*) In the year of our Lord 1095, in the reign of the so-called Emperor[5] Henry in Germany and of King Philip in France, throughout Europe evils of all kinds waxed strong because of vacillating faith. Pope Urban II[6] then ruled in the city of Rome. He was a man admirable in life and habits, who always strove wisely and energetically to raise the status of Holy Church higher and higher. . . .

But the devil, who always desires man's destruction and goes about like a raging lion seeking whom he may devour, stirred up to the confusion of the people a certain rival to Urban, Wibert[7] by name. Incited by the stimulus of pride and supported by the shamelessness of the aforesaid Emperor of the Bavarians, Wibert attempted to usurp the papal office while Urban's predecessor, Gregory, that is Hildebrand, was the legitimate Pope; and he thus caused Gregory himself to be cast out of St. Peter's. So the better people refused to recognize him because he acted thus perversely. After the death of Hildebrand, Urban, lawfully elected, was consecrated by the cardinal bishops, and the greater and holier part of the people submitted in obedience to him. Wibert, however, urged on by the support of the aforesaid Emperor and by the instigation of the Roman citizens, for some time kept Urban a stranger to the Church of St. Peter; but Urban, although he was banished from the Church, went about through the country, reconciling to God the people who had gone somewhat astray. Wibert, however, puffed up by the primacy of the Church, showed himself indulgent to sinners, and exercising the office of pope, although unjustly, amongst his adherents, he denounced as ridiculous the acts of Urban. But in the year in which the Franks first passed through Rome on their way to Jerusalem, Urban obtained the complete papal power everywhere, with the help of a certain most noble matron, Matilda[8] by name, who then had great influence in the Roman state. Wibert was then in Germany. So there were two Popes; and many did not know which to obey, or from which counsel should be taken, or who should remedy the ills of Christianity. Some favored the one; some the other. But it was clear to the intelligence of men that Urban was the better, for he is rightly considered better who controls his passions, just as if they were enemies. Wibert was Archbishop of the city of Ravenna. He was very rich and revelled in honor and wealth. It was a wonder that such riches did not satisfy him. Ought he to be considered by all an exemplar of right living who, himself a lover of pomp, boldly assumes to usurp the sceptre of Almighty God? Truly, this office must not be seized by force, but accepted with fear and humility.

What wonder that the whole world was a prey to disturbance and confusion? For when the Roman Church, which is the source of correction for all Christianity, is troubled by any disorder, the sorrow is communicated from the nerves of the head to the members subject to it, and these suffer sympathetically. This Church, indeed, our mother, as it were, at whose bosom we were nourished, by whose doctrine we were instructed and strengthened, by whose counsel we were admonished, was by this proud Wibert greatly afflicted.

For when the head is thus struck, the members at once are sick. If the head be sick, the other members suffer. Since the head was thus sick, pain was engendered in the enfeebled members; for in all parts of Europe peace, goodness, faith, were boldly trampled under foot, within the church and without, by the high, as well as by the low. It was necessary both that an end be put to these evils, and that, in accordance with the plan suggested by Pope Urban, they turn against the pagans the strength formerly used in prosecuting battles among themselves. . . .

He saw, moreover, the faith of Christendom greatly degraded by all, by the clergy as well as by the laity, and peace totally disregarded; for the princes of the land were incessantly engaged in armed strife, now these, now those quarrelling among themselves. He saw the goods of the land stolen from the owners; and many, who were unjustly taken captive and most barbarously cast into foul prisons, he saw ransomed for excessive sums, or tormented there by the three evils, starvation, thirst, and cold, or allowed to perish by unseen death. He also saw holy places violated, monasteries and villas destroyed by fire, and not a little human suffering, both the divine and the human being held in derision.

When he heard, too, that interior parts of Romania were held oppressed by the Turks, and that Christians were subjected to destructive and savage attacks, he was moved by compassionate pity; and, prompted by the love of God, he crossed the Alps and came into Gaul. He there called a council at Clermont in Auvergne, which council had been fittingly proclaimed by envoys in all directions. It is estimated that there were three hundred and ten bishops and abbots who bore the crozier. When they were assembled on the day appointed for the council, Urban, in an eloquent address full of sweetness, made known the object of the meeting. With the plaintive voice of the afflicted Church he bewailed in a long discourse the great disturbances which, as has been mentioned above, agitated the world where faith had been undermined. Then, as a supplicant, he exhorted all to resume the fullness of their faith, and in good earnest to try diligently to withstand the deceits of the devil, and to raise to its pristine honor the status of Holy Church, now most unmercifully crippled by the wicked.

"Dearest brethren," he said, "I, Urban, invested by the permission of God with the papal tiara, and spiritual ruler over the whole world, have come here in this great crisis to you, servants of God, as a messenger of divine admonition. I wish those whom I have believed good and faithful dispensers of the ministry of God to be found free from shameful dissimulation. For if there be in you any disposition or crookedness contrary to God's law, because you have lost the moderation of reason and justice, I shall earnestly endeavor to correct it at once, with divine assistance. For the Lord has made you stewards over His family, that you provide it with pleasant-tasting meat in season. You will be blessed, indeed, if the Lord shall find you faithful in stewardship. You are also called shepherds; see that you do not the work of hirelings. Be true shepherds and have your crooks always in your hands. Sleep not, but defend everywhere the flock committed to your care. For if through your carelessness or neglect the wolf carries off a sheep, doubtless you will not only lose the reward prepared for you by our Lord, but, after having first been tortured by the strokes of the lictor, you will also be savagely hurled into the abode of the damned. In the words of the gospel, 'Ye are the salt of the earth'?[9] But, it is asked, 'If ye fail, wherewith shall it be salted?' Oh, what a salting! Indeed, you must strive by the salt of your wisdom to correct this foolish people, over-eager for the pleasures of the world, lest the Lord find them insipid and rank, corrupted by crimes at the time when He wishes to speak to them. For if because of your slothful performance of duty He shall discover any worms in them, that is to say any sins, He will in contempt order them to be cast forthwith into the abyss of uncleanness; and because you will be unable to make good to Him such a loss, He will surely banish you, condemned by His judgment, from the presence of His love. But one that salteth ought to be prudent, foresighted, learned, peaceful, watchful, respectable, pious, just, fair-minded, pure. For how can the unlearned make others learned, the immodest make others modest, the unclean make others clean? How can he make peace who hates it? If anyone has soiled hands, how can he cleanse the spots from one contaminated? For it is written, 'If the blind lead the blind, both shall fall into the pit.'[10] Accordingly, first correct yourselves, so that without reproach you can then correct those under your care. If, indeed, you wish to be the friends of God, do generously what you see is pleasing to Him.

"See to it that the affairs of Holy Church, especially, are maintained in their rights, and that simoniacal heresy in no way takes root among you. Take care lest purchasers and venders alike, struck by the lash of the Lord, be disgracefully driven through narrow ways into utter confusion. Keep the Church in all its orders entirely free from the secular power; have given to God faithfully one-tenth of the fruits of the earth, neither selling them, nor withholding them. Whoever lays violent hands on a bishop, let him be considered excommunicated. Whoever shall have seized monks, or priests, or nuns, and their servants, or pilgrims, or traders, and shall have despoiled them, let him be accursed. Let thieves and burners of houses and their accomplices be excommunicated from the church and accursed. Therefore, we must consider especially, as Gregory says, how great will be his punishment who steals from another, if he incurs the damnation of hell who does not distribute alms from his own possessions. For so it happened to the rich man in the Gospel, who was punished not for stealing anything from another, but because, having received wealth, he used it badly.[11]

"By these evils, therefore, as I have said, dearest brethren, you have seen the world disordered for a long time, and to such a degree that in some places in your provinces, as has been reported to us (perhaps due to your weakness in administering justice), one scarcely dares to travel for fear of being kidnapped by thieves at night or highwayman by day, by force or by craft, at home or out of doors. Wherefore, it is well to enforce anew the Truce,[12] commonly so-called, which was long ago established by our holy fathers, and which I most earnestly entreat each one of you to have observed in his diocese. But if any one, led on by pride or ambition, infringes this injunction voluntarily, let him be anathema in virtue of the authority of God and by the sanction of the decrees of this council."

When these and many other things were well disposed of, all those present, priests and people alike, gave thanks to God and welcomed the advice of the Lord Pope Urban, assuring him, with a promise of fidelity, that these decrees of his would be well kept.

2. *Urban's plea for a Crusade.* (November 27, 1095.)

(*Gesta.*) When now that time was at hand which the Lord Jesus daily points out to His faithful, especially in the Gospel, saying, "If any man would come after me, let him deny himself and take up his cross and follow me,"[13] a mighty agitation was carried on throughout all the region of Gaul. (Its tenor was) that if anyone desired to follow the Lord zealously, with a pure heart and mind, and wished faithfully to bear the cross after Him, he would no longer hesitate to take up the way to the Holy Sepulchre.

And so Urban, Pope of the Roman see, with his archbishops, bishops, abbots, and priests, set out as quickly as possible beyond the mountains and began to deliver sermons and to preach eloquently, saying: "Whoever wishes to save his soul should not hesitate humbly to take up the way of the Lord, and if he lacks sufficient money, divine mercy will give him enough." Then the apostolic lord continued, "Brethren, we ought to endure much suffering for the name of Christ—misery, poverty, nakedness, persecution, want, illness, hunger, thirst, and other (ills) of this kind, just as the Lord saith to His disciples: 'Ye must suffer much in My name,'[14] and 'Be not ashamed to confess Me before the faces of men; verily I will give you mouth and wisdom,'[15] and finally, 'Great is your reward in Heaven.'"[16] And when this speech had already begun to be noised abroad, little by little, through all the regions and countries of Gaul, the Franks, upon hearing such reports, forthwith caused crosses to be sewed on their right shoulders, saying that they followed with one accord the footsteps of Christ, by which they had been redeemed from the hand of hell.

(*Fulcher.*) But the Pope added at once that another trouble, not less, but still more grievous than that already spoken of, and even the very worst, was besetting Christianity from another part of the world. He said: "Since, O sons of God, you have promised the Lord to maintain peace more earnestly than heretofore in your midst, and faithfully to sustain the rights of Holy Church, there still remains for you, who are newly aroused by this divine correction, a very necessary work, in which you can show the strength of your good will by a certain further duty, God's concern and your own. For you must hasten to carry aid to your brethren dwelling in the East, who need your help, which they often have asked. For the Turks, a Persian people, have attacked them, as many of you already know, and have advanced as far into the Roman territory as that part of the Mediterranean which is called the Arm of St. George; and, by seizing more and more of the lands of the Christians, they have already often conquered them in battle, have killed and captured many, have destroyed the churches, and have devastated the kingdom of God. If you allow them to continue much longer, they will subjugate God's faithful yet more widely.

"Wherefore, I exhort with earnest prayer—not I, but God—that, as heralds of Christ, you urge men by frequent exhortation, men of all ranks, knights as well as foot-soldiers, rich as well as poor, to hasten to exterminate this vile race from the lands of your brethren, and to aid the Christians in time. I speak to those present; I proclaim it to the absent; moreover, Christ commands it. And if those who set out thither should lose their lives on the way by land, or in crossing the sea, or in fighting the pagans, their sins shall be remitted. This I grant to all who go, through the power vested in me by God. Oh, what a disgrace, if a race so despised, base, and the instrument of demons, should so overcome a people endowed with faith in the all-powerful God, and resplendent with the name of Christ! Oh, what reproaches will be charged against you by the Lord Himself if you have not helped those who are counted, like yourselves, of the Christian faith! Let those who have been accustomed to make private war against the faithful carry on to a successful issue a war against infidels, which ought to have been begun ere now. Let these who for a long time have been robbers now become soldiers of Christ. Let those who once fought against brothers and relatives now fight against barbarians, as they ought. Let those who have been hirelings at low wages now labor for an eternal reward. Let those who have been wearing themselves out to the detriment of body and soul now labor for a double glory. On the one hand will be the sad and poor, on the other the joyous and wealthy; here the enemies of the Lord; there His friends. Let no obstacle stand in the way of those who are going, but, after their affairs are settled and expense money is collected, when the winter has ended and spring has come, let them zealously undertake the journey under the guidance of the Lord."

(*Robert the Monk.*) . . . "Oh, race of Franks, race from across the mountains, race chosen and beloved by God—as shines forth in very many of your works—set apart from all nations by the situation of your country, as well as by your Catholic faith and the honor of the Holy Church! To you our discourse is addressed, and for you our exhortation is intended. We wish you to know what a grievous cause has led us to your country, what peril, threatening you and all the faithful, has brought us.

"From the confines of Jerusalem and the city of Constantinople a horrible tale has gone forth and very frequently has been brought to our ears; namely, that a race from the kingdom of the Persians, an accursed race, a race utterly alienated from God, a generation, forsooth, which has neither directed its heart nor entrusted its spirit to God, has invaded the lands of those Christians and has depopulated them by the sword, pillage, and fire; it has led away a part of the captives into its own country, and a part it has destroyed by cruel tortures; it has either entirely destroyed the churches of God or appropriated them for the rites of its own religion. They destroy the altars, after having defiled them with their uncleanness. They circumcise the Christians, and the blood of the circumcision they either spread upon the altars or pour into the vases of the baptismal font. When they wish to torture people by a base death, they perforate their navels, and, dragging forth the end of the intestines, bind it to a stake; then with flogging they lead the victim around until his viscera have gushed forth, and he falls prostrate upon the ground. Others they bind to a post and pierce with arrows. Others they compel to extend their necks, and then, attacking them with naked swords, they attempt to cut through the neck with a single blow. What shall I say of the abominable rape of the women? To speak of it is worse than to be silent. The kingdom of the Greeks is now dismembered by them and deprived of territory so vast in extent that it can not be traversed in a march of two months. On whom, therefore, is the task of avenging these wrongs and of recovering this territory incumbent, if not upon you? You, upon whom above other nations God has conferred remarkable glory in arms, great courage, bodily energy, and the strength to humble the hairy scalp of those who resist you.

"Let the deeds of your ancestors move you and incite your minds to manly achievements; likewise, the glory and greatness of King Charles the Great, and his son Louis, and of your other kings, who have destroyed the kingdoms of the pagans, and have extended in these lands the territory of the Holy Church. Let the Holy Sepulchre of the Lord, our Saviour, which is possessed by unclean nations, especially move you, and likewise the holy places, which are now treated with ignominy and irreverently polluted with filthiness. Oh, most valiant soldiers and descendants of invincible ancestors, be not degenerate, but recall the valor of your forefathers!

"However, if you are hindered by love of children, parents, and wives, remember what the Lord says in the Gospel, 'He that loveth father, or mother more than me, is not worthy of me.'[17] 'Every one that hath forsaken houses, or brethren, or sisters, or father, or mother, or wife, or children, or lands for my name's sake shall receive an hundred-fold and shall inherit everlasting life.'[18] Let none of your possessions detain you, no solicitude for your family affairs, since this land which you inhabit, shut in on all sides by the sea and surrounded by mountain peaks, is too narrow for your large population; nor does it abound in wealth; and it furnishes scarcely food enough for its cultivators. Hence it is that you murder and devour one another, that you wage war, and that frequently you perish by mutual wounds. Let therefore hatred depart from among you, let your quarrels end, let wars cease, and let all dissensions and controversies slumber. Enter upon the road to the Holy Sepulchre; wrest that land from the wicked race, and subject it to yourselves. That land which, as the Scripture says, 'floweth with milk and honey'[19] was given by God into the possession of the children of Israel.

"Jerusalem is the navel of the world; the land is fruitful above others, like another paradise of delights. This the Redeemer of the human race has made illustrious by His advent, has beautified by His presence, has consecrated by suffering, has redeemed by death, has glorified by burial. This royal city, therefore, situated at the center of the world, is now held captive by His enemies, and is in subjection to those who do not know God, to the worship of the heathen. Therefore, she seeks and desires to be liberated and does not cease to implore you to come to her aid. From you, especially, she asks succor, because, as we have already said, God has conferred upon you, above all nations, great glory in arms. Accordingly, undertake this journey for the remission of your sins, with the assurance of the imperishable glory of the kingdom of heaven."

When Pope Urban had said these and very many similar things in his urbane discourse, he so influenced to one purpose the desires of all who were present that they cried out, "God wills it! God wills it!" When the venerable Roman pontiff heard that, with eyes uplifted to heaven he gave thanks to God and, with his hand commanding silence, said:

"Most beloved brethren, to-day is manifest in you what the Lord says in the Gospel, 'Where two or three are gathered together in My name there am I in the midst of them.'[20] Unless the Lord God had been present in your minds, all of you would not have uttered the same cry. For, although the cry issued from numerous mouths, yet the origin of the cry was one. Therefore I say to you that God, who implanted this in your breasts, has drawn it forth from you. Let this then be your battle-cry in combat, because this word is given to you by God. When an armed attack is made upon the enemy, let this one cry be raised by all the soldiers of God: 'God wills it! God wills it!'

"And we do not command or advise that the old, or the feeble, or those unfit for bearing arms, undertake this journey; nor ought women to set out at all without their husbands, or brothers, or legal guardians. For such are more of a hindrance than aid, more of a burden than an advantage. Let the rich aid the needy; and, according to their means, let them take with them experienced soldiers. The priests and clerks of any order are not to go without the consent of their bishops; for this journey would profit them nothing if they went without such permission. Also, it is not fitting that laymen should enter upon the pilgrimage without the blessing of their priests.

"Whoever, therefore, shall determine upon this holy pilgrimage and shall make his vow to God to that effect and shall offer himself to Him as a living sacrifice, holy, acceptable unto God, shall wear the sign of the cross of the Lord on his forehead, or on his breast. When, having truly fulfilled his vow, he wishes to return, let him place the cross on his back between his shoulders. Such, indeed, by two-fold action will fulfil the precept of the Lord, as He commands in the Gospel, 'He that doth not take his cross and follow after me, is not worthy of me.' "[21] . . .

(*Balderic of Dol.*) . . . "We have heard, most beloved brethren, and you have heard what we cannot recount without deep sorrow—how, with great hurt and dire sufferings our Christian brothers, members in Christ, are scourged, oppressed, and injured in Jerusalem, in Antioch, and the other cities of the East. Your own blood-brothers, your companions, your associates (for you are sons of the same Christ and the same Church) are either subjected in their inherited homes to other masters, or are driven from them, or they come as beggars among us; or, which is far worse, they are flogged and exiled as slaves for sale in their own land. Christian blood, redeemed by the blood of Christ, has been shed, and Christian flesh, akin to the flesh of Christ, has been subjected to unspeakable degradation and servitude. Everywhere in those cities there is sorrow, everywhere misery, everywhere groaning (I say it with a sigh). The churches in which divine mysteries were celebrated in olden times are now, to our sorrow, used as stables for the animals of these people! Holy men do not possess those cities; nay, base and bastard Turks hold sway over our brothers. The blessed Peter first presided as Bishop at Antioch; behold, in his own church the Gentiles have established their superstitions, and the Christian religion, which they ought rather to cherish, they have basely shut out from the hall dedicated to God! The estates given for the support of the saints and the patrimony of nobles set aside for the sustenance of the poor are subject to pagan tyranny, while cruel masters abuse for their own purposes the returns from these lands. The priesthood of God has been ground down into the dust. The sanctuary of God (unspeakable shame!) is everywhere profaned. Whatever Christians still remain in hiding there are sought out with unheard of tortures.

"Of holy Jerusalem, brethren, we dare not speak, for we are exceedingly afraid and ashamed to speak of it. This very city, in which, as you all know, Christ Himself suffered for us, because our sins demanded it, has been reduced to the pollution of paganism and, I say it to our disgrace, withdrawn from the service of God. Such is the heap of reproach upon us who have so much deserved it! Who now serves the church of the Blessed Mary in the valley of Josaphat, in which church she herself was buried in body? But why do we pass over the Temple of Solomon, nay of the Lord, in which the barbarous nations placed their idols contrary to law, human and divine? Of the Lord's Sepulchre we have refrained from speaking, since some of you with your own eyes have seen to what abominations it has been given over. The Turks violently took from it the offerings which you brought there for alms in such vast amounts, and, in addition, they scoffed much and often at your religion. And yet in that place (I say only what you already know) rested the Lord; there He died for us; there He was buried. How precious would be the longed-for, incomparable place of the Lord's burial, even if God failed there to perform the yearly miracle![22] For in the days of His Passion all the lights in the Sepulchre and round about in the church, which have been extinguished, are re-lighted by divine command. Whose heart is so stony, brethren, that it is not touched by so great a miracle? Believe me, that man is bestial and senseless whose heart such divinely manifest grace does not move to faith! And yet the Gentiles see this in common with the Christians and are not turned from their ways! They are, indeed, afraid, but they are not converted to the faith; nor is it to be wondered at, for a blindness of mind rules over them. With what afflictions they wronged you who have returned and are now present, you yourselves know too well, you who there sacrificed your substance and your blood for God.

"This, beloved brethren, we shall say, that we may have you as witness of our words. More suffering of our brethren and devastation of churches remains than we can speak of one by one, for we are oppressed by tears and groans, sighs and sobs. We weep and wail, brethren, alas, like the Psalmist, in our inmost heart! We are wretched and unhappy, and in us is that prophecy fulfilled: 'God, the nations are come into thine inheritance; thy holy temple have they defiled; they have laid Jerusalem in heaps; the dead bodies of thy servants have been given to be food for the birds of the heaven, the flesh of thy saints unto the beasts of the earth. Their blood have they shed like water round about Jerusalem, and there was none to bury them.'[23] Woe unto us, brethren! We who have already become a reproach to our neighbors, a scoffing, and derision to them round about us, let us at least with tears condole and have compassion upon our brothers! We who are become the scorn of all peoples, and worse than all, let us bewail the most monstrous devastation of the Holy Land! This land we have deservedly called holy in which there is not even a foot-step that the body or spirit of the Saviour did not render glorious and blessed; which embraced the holy presence of the mother of God, and the meetings of the apostles, and drank up the blood of the martyrs shed there. How blessed are the stones which crowned you, Stephen, the first martyr! How happy, O, John the Baptist, the waters of the Jordan which served you in baptizing the Saviour! The children of Israel, who were led out of Egypt, and who prefigured you in the crossing of the Red Sea, have taken that land by their arms, with Jesus as leader; they have driven out the Jebusites[24] and other inhabitants and have themselves inhabited earthly Jerusalem, the image of celestial Jerusalem.

"What are we saying? Listen and learn! You, girt about with the badge of knighthood, are arrogant with great pride; you rage against your brothers and cut each other in pieces. This is not the (true) soldiery of Christ which rends asunder the sheep-fold of the Redeemer. The Holy Church has reserved a soldiery for herself to help her people, but you debase her wickedly to her hurt. Let us confess the truth, whose heralds we ought to be; truly, you are not holding to the way which leads to life. You, the oppressors of children, plunderers of widows; you, guilty of homicide, of sacrilege, robbers of another's rights; you who await the pay of thieves for the shedding of Christian blood—as vultures smell fetid corpses, so do you sense battles from afar and rush to them eagerly. Verily, this is the worst way, for it is utterly removed from God! If, forsooth, you wish to be mindful of your souls, either lay down the girdle of such knighthood, or advance boldly, as knights of Christ, and rush as quickly as you can to the defence of the Eastern Church. For she it is from whom the joys of your whole salvation have come forth, who poured into your mouths the milk of divine wisdom, who set before you the holy teachings of the Gospels. We say this, brethren, that you may restrain your murderous hands from the destruction of your brothers, and in behalf of your relatives in the faith oppose yourselves to the Gentiles. Under Jesus Christ, our Leader, may you struggle for your Jerusalem, in Christian battle-line, most invincible line, even more successfully than did the sons of Jacob of old—struggle, that you may assail and drive out the Turks, more execrable than the Jebusites, who are in this land, and may you deem it a beautiful thing to die for Christ in that city in which He died for us. But if it befall you to die this side of it, be sure that to have died on the way is of equal value, if Christ shall find you in His army. God pays with the same shilling, whether at the first or eleventh hour. You should shudder, brethren, you should shudder at raising a violent hand against Christians; it is less wicked to brandish your sword against Saracens. It is the only warfare that is righteous, for it is charity to risk your life for your brothers. That you may not be troubled about the concerns of to-morrow, know that those who fear God want nothing, nor those who cherish Him in truth. The possessions of the enemy, too, will be yours, since you will make spoil of their treasures and return victorious to your own; or empurpled with your own blood, you will have gained everlasting glory. For such a Commander you ought to fight, for One who lacks neither might nor wealth with which to reward you. Short is the way, little the labor, which, nevertheless, will repay you with the crown that fadeth not away. Accordingly, we speak with the authority of the prophet: 'Gird thy sword upon thy thigh, O mighty one.'[25] Gird yourselves, everyone of you, I say, and be valiant sons; for it is better for you to die in battle than to behold the sorrows of your race and of your holy places. Let neither property nor the alluring charms of your wives entice you from going; nor let the trials that are to be borne so deter you that you remain here."

And turning to the bishops, he said, "You, brothers and fellow bishops; you, fellow priests and sharers with us in Christ, make this same announcement through the churches committed to you, and with your whole soul vigorously preach the journey to Jerusalem. When they have confessed the disgrace of their sins, do you, secure in Christ, grant them speedy pardon. Moreover, you who are to go shall have us praying for you; we shall have you fighting for God's people. It is our duty to pray, yours to fight against the Amalekites.[26] With Moses, we shall extend unwearied hands in prayer to Heaven, while you go forth and brandish the sword, like dauntless warriors, against Amalek."

As those present were thus clearly informed by these and other words of this kind from the apostolic lord, the eyes of some were bathed in tears; some trembled, and yet others discussed the matter. However, in the presence of all at that same council, and as we looked on, the Bishop of Puy,[27] a man of great renown and of highest ability, went to the Pope with joyful countenance and on bended knee sought and entreated blessing and permission to go. Over and above this, he won from the Pope the command that all should obey him, and that he should hold sway over all the army in behalf of the Pope, since all knew him to be a prelate of unusual energy and industry. . . .

(*Guibert of Nogent.*) . . . "If among the churches scattered about over the whole world some, because of persons or location, deserve reverence above others (for persons, I say, since greater privileges are accorded to apostolic sees; for places, indeed, since the same dignity which is accorded to persons is also shown to regal cities, such as Constantinople), we owe most to that church from which we received the grace of redemption and the source of all Christianity. If what the Lord says—namely, 'Salvation is from the Jews—,'[28] accords with the truth, and it is true that the Lord has left us Sabaoth as seed, that we may not become like Sodom and Gomorrah, and our seed is Christ, in whom is the salvation and benediction of all peoples, then, indeed, the very land and city in which He dwelt and suffered is, by witness of the Scriptures, holy. If this land is spoken of in the sacred writings of the prophets as the inheritance and the holy temple of God before ever the Lord walked about in it, or was revealed, what sanctity, what reverence has it not acquired since God in His majesty was there clothed in the flesh, nourished, grew up, and in bodily form there walked about, or was carried about; and, to compress in fitting brevity all that might be told in a long series of words, since there the blood of the Son of God, more holy than heaven and earth, was poured forth, and His body, its quivering members dead, rested in the tomb. What veneration do we think it deserves? If, when the Lord had but just been crucified and the city was still held by the Jews, it was called holy by the evangelist when he says, 'Many bodies of the saints that had fallen asleep were raised; and coming forth out of the tombs after His resurrection, they entered into the holy city and appeared unto many,'[29] and by the prophet Isaiah when he says, 'It shall be His glorious sepulchre,'[30] then, surely, with this sanctity placed upon it by God the Sanctifier Himself, no evil that may befall it can destroy it, and in the same way glory is indivisibly fixed to His Sepulchre. Most beloved brethren, if you reverence the source of that holiness and glory, if you cherish these shrines which are the marks of His foot-prints on earth, if you seek (the way), God leading you, God fighting in your behalf, you should strive with your utmost efforts to cleanse the Holy City and the glory of the Sepulchre, now polluted by the concourse of the Gentiles, as much as is in their power.

"If in olden times the Maccabees attained to the highest praise of piety because they fought for the ceremonies and the Temple, it is also justly granted you, Christian soldiers, to defend the liberty of your country by armed endeavor. If you, likewise, consider that the abode of the holy apostles and any other saints should be striven for with such effort, why do you refuse to rescue the Cross, the Blood, the Tomb? Why do you refuse to visit them, to spend the price of your lives in rescuing them? You have thus far waged unjust wars, at one time and another; you have brandished mad weapons to your mutual destruction, for no other reason than covetousness and pride, as a result of which you have deserved eternal death and sure damnation. We now hold out to you wars which contain the glorious reward of martyrdom, which will retain that title of praise now and forever.

"Let us suppose, for the moment, that Christ was not dead and buried, and had never lived any length of time in Jerusalem. Surely, if all this were lacking, this fact alone ought still to arouse you to go to the aid of the land and city—the fact that 'Out of Zion shall go forth the law and the word of Jehovah from Jerusalem!'[31] If all that there is of Christian preaching has flowed from the fountain of Jerusalem, its streams, whithersoever spread out over the whole world, encircle the hearts of the Catholic multitude, that they may consider wisely what they owe such a well-watered fountain. If rivers return to the place whence they have issued only to flow forth again, according to the saying of Solomon,[32] it ought to seem glorious to you to be able to apply a new cleansing to this place, whence it is certain that you received the cleansing of baptism and the witness of your faith.

"And you ought, furthermore, to consider with the utmost deliberation, if by your labors, God working through you, it should occur that the Mother of churches should flourish anew to the worship of Christianity, whether, perchance, He may not wish other regions of the East to be restored to the faith against the approaching time of the Antichrist.[33] For it is clear that Antichrist is to do battle not with the Jews, not with the Gentiles; but, according to the etymology of his name, He will attack Christians. And if Antichrist finds there no Christians (just as at present when scarcely any dwell there), no one will be there to oppose him, or whom he may rightly overcome. According to Daniel and Jerome, the interpreter of Daniel, he is to fix his tents on the Mount of Olives; and it is certain, for the apostle teaches it, that he will sit at Jerusalem in the Temple of the Lord, as though he were God. And according to the same prophet, he will first kill three kings of Egypt, Africa, and Ethiopia, without doubt for their Christian faith. This, indeed, could not at all be done unless Christianity was established where now is paganism. If, therefore, you are zealous in the practice of holy battles, in order that, just as you have received the seed of knowledge of God from Jerusalem, you may in the same way restore the borrowed grace, so that through you the Catholic name may be advanced to oppose the perfidy of the Antichrist and the Antichristians—then, who can not conjecture that God, who has exceeded the hope of all, will consume, in the abundance of your courage and through you as the spark, such a thicket of paganism as to include within His law Egypt, Africa, and Ethiopia, which have withdrawn from the communion of our belief? And the man of sin, the son of perdition, will find some to oppose him. Behold, the Gospel cries out, 'Jerusalem shall be trodden down by the Gentiles until the times of the Gentiles be fulfilled.'[34] 'Times of the Gentiles' can be understood in two ways: Either that they have ruled over the Christians at their pleasure, and have gladly frequented the sloughs of all baseness for the satisfaction of their lusts, and in all this have had no obstacle (for they who have everything according to their wish are said to have their time; there is that saying: 'My time is not yet come, but your time is always ready,'[35] whence the lustful are wont to say 'you are having your time'). Or, again, 'the times of the Gentiles' are the fulness of time for those Gentiles who shall have entered secretly before Israel shall be saved. These times, most beloved brothers, will now, forsooth, be fulfilled, provided the might of the pagans be repulsed through you, with the co-operation of God. With the end of the world already near, even though the Gentiles fail to be converted to the Lord (since according to the apostle there must be a withdrawal from the faith), it is first necessary, according to the prophecy, that the Christian sway be renewed in those regions, either through you, or others, whom it shall please God to send before the coming of Antichrist, so that the head of all evil, who is to occupy there the throne of the kingdom, shall find some support of the faith to fight against him.

"Consider, therefore, that the Almighty has provided you, perhaps, for this purpose, that through you He may restore Jerusalem from such debasement. Ponder, I beg you, how full of joy and delight our hearts will be when we shall see the Holy City restored with your little help, and the prophet's, nay divine, words fulfilled in our times. Let your memory be moved by what the Lord Himself says to the Church: 'I will bring thy seed from the East and gather thee from the West.'[36] God has already brought our seed from the East, since in a double way that region of the East has given the first beginnings of the Church to us. But from the West He will also gather it, provided He repairs the wrongs of Jerusalem through those who have begun the witness of the final faith, that is the people of the West. With God's assistance, we think this can be done through you.

"If neither the words of the Scriptures arouse you, nor our admonitions penetrate your minds, at least let the great suffering of those who desired to go to the holy places stir you up. Think of those who made the pilgrimage across the sea! Even if they were more wealthy, consider what taxes, what violence they underwent, since they were forced to make payments and tributes almost every mile, to purchase release at every gate of the city, at the entrance of the churches and temples, at every side-journey from place to place: also, if any accusation whatsoever were made against them, they were compelled to purchase their release; but if they refused to pay money, the prefects of the Gentiles, according to their custom, urged them fiercely with blows. What shall we say of those who took up the journey without anything more than trust in their barren poverty, since they seemed to have nothing except their bodies to lose? They not only demanded money of them, which is not an unendurable punishment, but also examined the callouses of their heels, cutting them open and folding the skin back, lest, perchance, they had sewed something there. Their unspeakable cruelty was carried on even to the point of giving them scammony to drink until they vomited, or even burst their bowels, because they thought the wretches had swallowed gold or silver; or, horrible to say, they cut their bowels open with a sword and, spreading out the folds of the intestines, with frightful mutilation disclosed whatever nature held there in secret. Remember, I pray, the thousands who have perished vile deaths, and strive for the holy places from which the beginnings of your faith have come. Before you engage in His battles, believe without question that Christ will be your standard-bearer and inseparable fore-runner."

The most excellent man concluded his oration and by the power of the blessed Peter absolved all who vowed to go and confirmed those acts with apostolic blessing. He instituted a sign well suited to so honorable a profession by making the figure of the Cross, the stigma of the Lord's Passion, the emblem of the soldiery, or rather, of what was to be the soldiery of God. This, made of any kind of cloth, he ordered to be sewed upon the shirts, cloaks, and *byrra* of those who were about to go. He commanded that if anyone, after receiving this emblem, or after taking openly this vow, should shrink from his good intent through base change of heart, or any affection for his parents, he should be regarded an outlaw forever, unless he repented and again undertook whatever of his pledge he had omitted. Furthermore, the Pope condemned with a fearful anathema all those who dared to molest the wives, children, and possessions of these who were going on this journey for God. . . .

3. *The immediate response.*

(*Fulcher.*) After this speech, those present were very enthusiastic in the cause, and many, thinking that nothing could be more laudable than such an undertaking, at once offered to go and diligently exhort the absent. Among these was the Bishop of Puy, Adhemar by name, who later acting as the Pope's vicegerent prudently and wisely led the whole army of God and vigorously inspired them to accomplish the undertaking. So, when those things which have been mentioned were determined upon in the council and unanimously approved of, and after the papal blessing was given, they withdrew to their homes to make known to those who were not present at the council what had been done. When these tidings were proclaimed throughout the provinces, they agreed under oath that the peace which was called the Truce should be kept mutually by all. Finally, then, many persons of every class vowed, after confession, that they were going with a pure intent whither they were ordered to go.

Oh, how fitting and how pleasing to us all to see those crosses, beautiful, whether of silk, or of woven gold, or of any kind of cloth, which these pilgrims, by order of Pope Urban, sewed on the shoulders of their mantles, or cassocks, or tunics, once they had made the vow to go. It was indeed proper that soldiers of God who prepared to fight for His honor should be signed and fortified by this fitting emblem of victory; and, since they thus marked themselves with this symbol under the acknowledgment of faith, finally they very truly obtained the Cross of which they carried the symbol. They adopted the sign that they might follow the reality of the sign.

It is evident that a good intention brings about the achievement of a good work, and that good work earns the soul's salvation. For if it is good to intend well, it is still better to accomplish a good work which has been planned. Therefore the best thing one can do is to provide for the salvation of his soul by a worthy action. Let each one then plan good deeds, which by still more worthy action he will fulfil, so that he shall at length receive the never ending reward which he has earned. So Urban, a man prudent and revered, conceived a work by which later the whole universe prospered. For he restored peace and re-established the rights of the church in their pristine condition. And with a lively determination he also made an effort to drive out the pagans from the Christian lands. Therefore, since he endeavored in every way to glorify everything which was God's, almost all voluntarily submitted themselves to his paternal direction.

(*Ekkehard.*) The West Franks[37] could easily be induced to leave their lands, since for several years Gaul had suffered, now from civil war, now from famine, and again from excessive mortality; and, finally, that disease which had its origin in the vicinity of the church of St. Gertrude of Nivelle[38] alarmed them to such an extent that they feared for their lives. This was the nature of the disease. The patient, attacked in any part of the body by invisible fire, suffered unspeakable torment for a long time, and without remedy, until either he lost his life from the agony, or he lost both the torture and the afflicted limb at the same time. There are to this day living witnesses of this disease, maimed either in hands or feet by the scourge.

Of the other nations, some peoples or individuals acknowledged that they had been called to the land of promise not only by the proclamation of the Pope, but also by certain prophets who had lately arisen among them, or by signs and revelations from heaven; others confessed that they had been constrained to take the vows by reason of embarrassed circumstances. Indeed, the majority set out encumbered with their wives and children and all their household effects.

But for the East Franks, the Saxons, the Thuringians, the Bavarians, and the *Alemanni*[39] this trumpet call sounded only faintly, particularly because of the schism between the empire and the papacy, from the time of Pope Alexander[40] even until today. This, alas, has strengthened our hatred and enmity against the Romans, as it has theirs towards us! And so it came to pass that almost all the Teutonic race, at first ignorant of the reason for this setting out, laughed to scorn the many legions of knights passing through their land, the many companies of foot soldiers, and the crowds of country people, women, and little ones. They regarded them as crazed with unspeakable folly, inasmuch as they were striving after uncertainties in place of certainties and were leaving for naught the land of their birth, to seek with certain danger the uncertain land of promise; and, while giving up their own possessions, they were yearning after those of strangers. But although our people are more perverse than other races, yet in consideration of the promise of divine pity, the enthusiasm of the Teutons was at last turned to this same proclamation, for they were taught, forsooth, what the thing really meant by the crowds passing through their lands.

4. *Urban's instructions to the assembling Crusaders.*

Urban, bishop, servant of the servants of God, to all the faithful, both princes and subjects, waiting in Flanders; greeting, apostolic grace, and blessing.

Your brotherhood, we believe, has long since learned from many accounts that a barbaric fury has deplorably afflicted and laid waste the churches of God in the regions of the Orient. More than this, blasphemous to say, it has even grasped in intolerable servitude its churches and the Holy City of Christ, glorified by His passion and resurrection. Grieving with pious concern at this calamity, we visited the regions of Gaul and devoted ourselves largely to urging the princes of the land and their subjects to free the churches of the East. We solemnly enjoined upon them at the council of Auvergne[41] (the accomplishment of) such an undertaking, as a preparation for the remission of all their sins. And we have constituted our most beloved son, Adhemar, Bishop of Puy, leader of this expedition and undertaking in our stead, so that those who, perchance, may wish to undertake this journey should comply with his commands, as if they were our own, and submit fully to his loosings or bindings, as far as shall seem to belong to such an office. If, moreover, there are any of your people whom God has inspired to this vow, let them know that he (Adhemar) will set out with the aid of God on the day of the Assumption of the Blessed Mary,[42] and that they can then attach themselves to his following.

(Written toward the end of December, 1095.)

CHAPTER II

The March to Constantinople

(Despite Urban's efforts to keep the expedition within the bounds of a common plan and to maintain some degree of organization, the enthusiasm which he aroused was too great to be restrained. Without waiting for the appointed day, various bands, commonly known as the Peasants' Crusade, started from the Rhine country, eager to be the first to gain the great rewards. Neither the character nor the conduct of the groups seems to have been such as to inspire any writer with a desire to recount their deeds. As a result, our information about them comes wholly from the none too sympathetic chronicles of the later writers. The versions given by the Anonymous, who met some of the survivors at Constantinople, by Ekkehard, and by Albert, both of whom lived in the country through which these bands passed, have been selected as the most accurate and complete. The persecutions of the Jews, so common along the march of the Peasants, was by no means, however, confined to them, being almost as widespread as the enthusiasm for the Crusade itself.[1] Though the final fate of the first of these companies is described in the third chapter, they had all started before the main body, and their conduct had left a deep impression upon the peoples through whose lands they journeyed. The difficulties of the main army in these same regions were probably due in no small measure to the excesses which the Peasants had committed. The main armies must be followed up to Constantinople, as the leaders followed four different routes. The march of Godfrey and Baldwin is described by Albert, that of Bohemund by the Anonymous, who accompanied him, that of Raymond by his chaplain, Raymond of Aguilers, and that of Robert of Normandy and Stephen of Blois by Fulcher, who was with them. Hugh the Great and Robert of Flanders had no chroniclers in their following, or, at any rate, no detailed account of their journey to Constantinople has been preserved. Due to the diverse routes chosen by the leaders, this portion of the history of the First Crusade is least well substantiated, for each of the writers could render accurate account of only his own army. References to other bands are often inaccurate and confusing, and even in the story of a single route geographical allusions are frequently uncertain or incorrect. This can be easily explained by the fact that the Crusaders were moving fairly rapidly through strange country, without the stimulus of actual warfare to fix place names in their minds. Fortunately, the well worn Roman roads through the Balkan and Danube country can still be traced, while the recognizable places mentioned by the chroniclers afford ample testimony that the Crusaders followed them in the main.)

1. *The Departure.*

(*Fulcher.*) Now then, I must turn to the history of those who went to Jerusalem and make clear to all who do not know what happened to these pilgrims on the way, how, little by little, by the grace of God, their undertaking and their labor gloriously succeeded. I, Fulcher of Chartres, went with the other pilgrims, and for the benefit of posterity I have carefully and diligently stored all this in my memory, just as I witnessed it.

In the year 1096, and in the month of March following the council, which, as has been said, Pope Urban held during November in Auvergne, some who were more prompt in their preparation than others began to set out on the holy journey. Others followed in April, or May, in June, or in July, or even in August, or September, or October, as they were able to secure the means to defray their expenses. That year peace and good crops of grain and grapes flourished everywhere, by the disposition of God, lest those who chose to follow Him with their crosses, in accordance with His precept, should fail on the way for want of food. . . .

What further shall I say? The islands of the sea and all the regions of the earth were shaken under foot, so that it would seem that the prophecy of David was fulfilled, who said in the psalm, "All the nations thou hast made shall come and worship before thee, O Lord"[2]; and that, also, which those who came later justly said, "We will worship in the place where His feet have stood." Of this journey, moreover, we have read much more in the Prophets, which it would be tedious to repeat. Oh what grief, what sighs, what weeping! What lamentations among friends, when the husband left his wife so dear to him, and his children, and all his possessions, his father, his mother, his brothers, or his relatives! But in spite of such tears which those who remained shed for departing friends in their very presence, the crusaders were still in no wise weakened by this; and for love of God they left all that they possessed, firmly convinced that they would receive that hundred-fold which the Lord has promised to those who love Him. Then husband advised wife of the time of his return, assuring her that if he lived, by God's grace, he would return to her. He commended her to the Lord, he kissed her tenderly, and, weeping, he promised to return. But she, fearing that she would never see him more, was unable to stand and fell senseless to the ground and wept for her love, whom, though living, she had lost as though already dead. He, like one who had no pity—though he had—and as if moved neither by the tears of his wife nor the grief of any friends—and still in his heart he was moved—set out, keeping his purpose firm. Sadness was the lot of those who remained, those who left were glad. What then can we add further? "This is the Lord's doings and it is marvelous in our eyes."[3]

(*Ekkehard.*) Moreover, the sign which was described before as seen in the sun, and many portents which appeared in the air, as well as on the earth, stimulated many, who had been backward before, to undertakings of this kind. Some of these portents I have deemed it desirable to insert here, but to tell all would certainly take too long. For we, too, about the Nones of October, saw a comet in the southern sky, its radiance extending out obliquely, like a sword; and two years later, on the sixth day before the Kalends of March, 1099, we saw another star in the east changing its position by leaps at long intervals. There were also blood-red clouds rising in the east, as well as in the west, and darting up into the zenith to meet each other; and, again, about midnight, fiery splendors rushed up in the north; and frequently we even saw torches of fire flying through the air, as we proved by many witnesses. About three o'clock one day some years before this, Sigger, a certain priest of exemplary life, saw two knights rushing at each other in the air, and after they had fought for a long time, the one who bore a large cross, with which he seemed to strike the other, emerged as victor. At the same time, the priest, G—, who now belongs to the monastic profession with us, having paid the sheep which is owed to Christ in place of the first born of the ass, was walking one day at the noon hour in a wood, with two companions, when he saw a sword of wondrous length (which came, he knew not whence) carried up on high by a whirlwind. Until the great height hid it from his eyes, he not only saw the metal, but heard the crashing of the weapon. Some men who were keeping watch in a horse pasture also reported that they saw the semblance of a city in the air, and that they saw divers companies, both on horseback and on foot, hastening to it from different directions. Some even showed the sign of the cross stamped by divine power upon their foreheads, or clothes, or upon some part of the body; and by this sign they believed that they had been predestined for the same army of the Lord. Again, others, pricked by a sudden change of heart, or taught by visions of the night, resolved to sell their lands and goods, and to sew upon their clothes the sign of the cross. To all these people, who flocked to the churches in incredible numbers, the priests, in a new rite, distributed swords along with a blessing and pilgrims' staves and bags. Why should I mention the fact that in those days a certain woman continued pregnant for two years and, at last, brought forth a boy who could speak from birth? Likewise, a child was born with a double set of limbs, and another with two heads; some lambs, also, with two heads. Again, foals were born which possessed at birth the larger teeth which we commonly call horse-teeth, and which nature does not provide until the colt is three years old.

While by these and like signs all creation was being summoned into the army of the Lord, that enemy of men, the evil one himself (ever on the watch, even while others are sleeping) did not delay to sow his own tares, to rouse false prophets, and, under the guise of religion, to mingle with the army of the Lord false brethren and shameless women. And so, through the hypocrisy and falsehoods of some and the gross immorality of others, the army of Christ was polluted to such an extent that, according to the prophecy of the good shepherd, even the elect were led astray. At this time, the legend about Charles the Great was invented,[4] that he had been raised from the dead for this expedition, and about some one else who was living again; and also that foolish story of the goose that acted as its mistress's guide, and many tales of that kind. Yet, since each one may be known by his fruits, even as wolves are recognized under sheep's clothing, those same deceivers, especially these who are still alive, may be questioned as to what port they sailed from, according to their vows, and how they crossed the sea without ships, or in what battles and places they worsted so many pagans with their small forces, what fortresses of the enemy they took there, and, finally, at what part of the wall at Jerusalem they had their camp, and so forth. And those who have nothing to answer as to the alms which they have hypocritically taken from the faithful, or as to the many bands which they have misled and murdered for plunder, and, above all, as to their own apostasy, may be compelled to do penance.

(*Guibert of Nogent*): Now then, while the princes who felt the need of large funds and the support of numerous followers were making preparations carefully and slowly, the common people, who were poor in substance but abundant in numbers, attached themselves to a certain Peter the Hermit[5] who appeared as a master while we were as yet still considering the project.

He was from the city of Amiens, if I am not mistaken, and we learned that he had lived as a hermit in the garb of a monk somewhere in Northern Gaul, I know not where. We beheld him leaving there, with what intent I do not know, and going about through cities and towns under the pretext of preaching. He was surrounded by such great throngs, received such enormous gifts, and was lauded with such fame for holiness that I do not remember anyone to have been held in like honor.

He was very generous to the poor from the wealth that had been given him. He reclaimed prostitutes and provided them with husbands, not without dowry from him; and everywhere with an amazing authority, he restored peace and concord in place of strife. Whatever he did or said was regarded as little short of divine, to such an extent that hairs were snatched from his mule as relics. This we ascribe not so much to the popular love for truth as for novelty.

He wore a plain woolen shirt with a hood and over this a cloak without sleeves, both extending to his ankles, and his feet were bare. He lived on wine and fish: he hardly ever, or never, ate bread. . . .

2. *The March of the Peasants.*

A. Peter the Hermit and Walter the Penniless. (March-August, 1096.)

(*Albert.*) There was a priest, Peter by name, formerly a hermit. He was born in the city of Amiens, which is in the western part of the kingdom of the Franks, and he was appointed preacher in Berri in the aforesaid kingdom. In every admonition and sermon, with all the persuasion of which he was capable, he urged setting out on the journey as soon as possible. In response to his constant admonition and call, bishops, abbots, clerics, and monks set out; next, most noble laymen, and princes of the different kingdoms; then, all the common people, the chaste as well as the sinful, adulterers, homicides, thieves, perjurers, and robbers; indeed, every class of the Christian profession, nay, also, women and those influenced by the spirit of penance—all joyfully entered upon this expedition. . . .

In the year of the Incarnation of the Lord, 1096, in the fourth Indiction, in the thirteenth year of the reign of Henry IV, third august Emperor of the Romans, and in the forty-third year of the Empire, in the reign of Pope Urban II, formerly Odoard, on the eighth day of March, Walter, surnamed the Penniless, a well-known soldier, set out, as a result of the preaching of Peter the Hermit, with a great company of Frankish foot-soldiers and only about eight knights. On the beginning of the journey to Jerusalem he entered into the kingdom of Hungary. When his intention, and the reason for his taking this journey became known to Lord Coloman,[6] most Christian king of Hungary, he was kindly received and was given peaceful transit across the entire realm, with permission to trade. And so without giving offence, and without being attacked, he set out even to Belgrade, a Bulgarian city, passing over to *Malevilla*, where the realm of the king of Hungary ends. Thence he peacefully crossed the Morava river.

But sixteen of Walter's company remained in *Malevilla*, that they might purchase arms. Of this Walter was ignorant, for he had crossed long before. Then some of the Hungarians of perverse minds, seeing the absence of Walter and his army, laid hands upon those sixteen and robbed them of arms, garments, gold and silver and so let them depart, naked and empty-handed. Then these distressed pilgrims, deprived of arms and other things, hastened on their way to Belgrade, which has been mentioned before, where Walter with all his band had pitched tents for camp. They reported to him the misfortune which had befallen them, but Walter heard this with equanimity, because it would take too long to return for vengeance.

On the very night when those comrades, naked and empty-handed, were received, Walter sought to buy the necessaries of life from a chief of the Bulgarians and the magistrate of the city; but these men, thinking it a pretense, and regarding them as spies, forbade the sale of any thing to them. Wherefore, Walter and his companions, greatly angered, began forcibly to seize and lead away the herds of cattle and sheep, which were wandering here and there through the fields in search of pasture. As a result, a serious strife arose between the Bulgarians and the pilgrims who were driving away the flocks, and they came to blows. However, while the strength of the Bulgarians was growing even to one hundred and forty, some of the pilgrim army, cut off from the multitude of their companions, arrived in flight at a chapel. But the Bulgarians, their army growing in number, while the band of Walter was weakening and his entire company scattered, besieged the chapel and burned sixty who were within; on most of the others, who escaped from the enemy and the chapel in defense of their lives, the Bulgarians inflicted grave wounds.

After this calamity and the loss of his people, and after he had passed eight days as a fugitive in the forests of Bulgaria, Walter, leaving his men scattered everywhere, withdrew to Nish, a very wealthy city in the midst of the Bulgarian realm. There he found the duke and prince of the land and reported to him the injury and damage which had been done him. From the duke he obtained justice for all; nay, more, in reconciliation the duke bestowed upon him arms and money, and the same lord of the land gave him peaceful conduct through the cities of Bulgaria, Sofia, Philippopolis, and Adrianople, and also license to trade.

He went down with all his band, even to the imperial city, Constantinople, which is the capital of the entire Greek empire. And when he arrived there, with all possible earnestness and most humble petition he implored from the Lord Emperor himself permission to delay peacefully in his kingdom, with license to buy the necessaries of life, until he should have as his companion Peter the Hermit, upon whose admonition and persuasion he had begun this journey. And he also begged that, when the troops were united, they might cross in ships over the arm of the sea called the Strait of St. George, and thus they would be able to resist more safely the squadrons of the Turks and the Gentiles. The outcome was that the requests made of the Lord Emperor, Alexius by name, were granted.

Not long after these events, Peter and his large army, innumerable as the sands of the sea—an army which he had brought together from the various realms of the nations of the Franks, Swabians, Bavarians, and Lotharingians—were making their way to Jerusalem. Descending on that march into the kingdom of Hungary, he and his army pitched their tents before the gate of Oedenburg. . . .

Peter heard this report and, because the Hungarians and Bulgarians were fellow Christians, absolutely refused to believe so great crime of them, until his men, coming to *Malevilla,* saw hanging from the walls the arms and spoils of the sixteen companions of Walter who had stayed behind a short time before, and whom the Hungarians had treacherously presumed to rob. But when Peter recognized the injury to his brethren, at the sight of their arms and spoils, he urged his companions to avenge their wrongs.

These sounded the trumpet loudly, and with upraised banners they rushed to the walls and attacked the enemy with a hail of arrows. In such quick succession and in such incredible numbers did they hurl them in the face of those standing on the walls that the Hungarians, in no wise able to resist the force of the besieging Franks, left the walls, hoping that within the city they might be able to withstand the strength of the Gauls. Godfrey, surnamed Burel—a native of the city Etampes, master and standard-bearer of two hundred foot-soldiers, himself a foot-soldier, and a man of great strength—seeing the flight of the Hungarians away from the walls, then quickly crossed over the walls by means of a ladder he chanced to find there. Reinald of Broyes, a distinguished knight, clad in helmet and coat of mail, ascended just after Godfrey; soon all the knights, as well as the foot-soldiers, hastened to enter the city. The Hungarians, seeing their own imminent peril, gathered seven thousand strong for defense; and, having passed out through another gate which looked toward the east, they stationed themselves on the summit of a lofty crag, beyond which flowed the Danube, where they were invincibly fortified. A very large part of these were unable to escape quickly through the narrow passage, and they fell before the gate. Some who hoped to find refuge on the top of the mountain were cut down by the pursuing pilgrims; still others, thrown headlong from the summit of the mountain, were buried in the waves of the Danube, but many escaped by boat. About four thousand Hungarians fell there, but only a hundred pilgrims, not counting the wounded, were killed at that same place.

This victory won, Peter remained with all his followers in the same citadel five days, for he found there an abundance of grain, flocks of sheep, herds of cattle, a plentiful supply of wine, and an infinite number of horses. . . .

When Peter learned of the wrath of the King and his very formidable gathering of troops, he deserted *Malevilla* with all his followers and planned to cross the Morava with all spoils and flocks and herds of horses. But on the whole bank he found very few boats, only one hundred and fifty, in which the great multitude must pass quickly over and escape, lest the King should overtake them with a great force. Hence many who were unable to cross in boats tried to cross on rafts made by fastening poles together with twigs. But driven hither and thither in these rafts without rudders, and at times separated from their companions, many perished, pierced with arrows from the bows of the Patzinaks, who inhabited Bulgaria. As Peter saw the drowning and destruction which was befalling his men, he commanded the Bavarians, the Alemanni, and the other Teutons, by their promise of obedience to come to the aid of their Frankish brethren. They were carried to that place by seven rafts; then they sank seven small boats of the Patzinaks with their occupants, but took only seven men captive. They led these seven captives into the presence of Peter and killed them by his order.

When he had thus avenged his men, Peter crossed the Morava river and entered the large and spacious forests of the Bulgarians with supplies of food, with every necessary, and with the spoils from Belgrade. And after a delay of eight days in those vast woods and pastures, he and his followers approached Nish, a city very strongly fortified with walls. After crossing the river before the city by a stone bridge, they occupied the field, pleasing in its verdure and extent, and pitched their tents on the banks of the river. . . . .

Peter, obedient to the mandate of the Emperor, advanced from the city of Sofia and withdrew with all his people to the city Philippopolis. When he had related the entire story of his misfortune in the hearing of all the Greek citizens, he received, in the name of Jesus and in fear of God, very many gifts for him. Next, the third day after, he withdrew to Adrianopole, cheerful and joyful in the abundance of all necessaries. There he tarried in camp outside the walls of the city only two days, and then withdrew after sunrise on the third day. A second message of the Emperor was urging him to hasten his march to Constantinople, for, on account of the reports about him, the Emperor was burning with desire to see this same Peter. When they had come to Constantinople, the army of Peter was ordered to encamp at a distance from the city, and license to trade was fully granted. . . .

B. Folcmar and Gottschalk. (May-July, 1096.)

(*Albert.*) Not long after the passage of Peter, a certain priest, Gottschalk by name, a Teuton in race, an inhabitant of the Rhine country, inflamed by the preaching of Peter with a love and a desire for that same journey to Jerusalem, by his own preachings likewise stirred the hearts of very many peoples of diverse nations to go on that journey. He assembled from the various regions of Lorraine, eastern France, Bavaria, and Alemannia, more than fifteen thousand persons of military station, as well as ordinary foot-soldiers, who, having collected an inexpressible amount of money, together with other necessaries, are said to have continued on their way peacefully, even to the kingdom of Hungary.

When they arrived at the gate of *Wieselburg* and its fortress, they were honorably received by the favor of King Coloman. They were likewise granted permission to buy the necessaries of life, and peace was commanded on both sides by an order of the King, lest any outbreak should arise from so large an army. But as they delayed there for several days, they began to roam about, and the Bavarians and Swabians, spirited peoples, together with other thoughtless persons, drank beyond measure and violated the peace which had been commanded. Little by little they took away from the Hungarians wine, grain, and all other necessaries; finally, they devastated the fields, killing sheep and cattle, and also destroying those who resisted, or who wished to drive them out. Like a rough people, rude in manners, undisciplined and haughty, they committed very many other crimes, all of which we cannot relate. As some who were present say, they transfixed a certain Hungarian youth in the market place with a stake through his body. Complaints of this matter and of other wrongs were brought to the ears of the King and their own leaders. . . .

When Gottschalk and the other sensible men heard this, they trusted with pure faith in these words, and also because the Hungarians were of the Christian profession, they counselled the entire

assembly to give their arms in satisfaction to the King, according to this command. Thus everything would return to peace and concord.
. . . .

And yet, when all their arms had been placed under lock and key, the Hungarians proved false regarding all the faith and clemency which they had promised that the King would show to the people; nay, rather they fell upon them with cruel slaughter, cut down the defenceless and unarmed and inflicted upon them frightful slaughter, to such an extent (as those affirm for a truth who were present and barely escaped) that the entire plain of Belgrade was filled by the bodies of the slain and was covered with their blood. Few escaped from that martyrdom.

(*Ekkehard.*) Now, as has been said, a band followed Folcmar through Bohemia. At the city of Neitra, in Pannonia, an uprising took place, in which a part were killed, and a part were taken prisoners, while the very few survivors are wont to testify that the sign of the cross, appearing in the heavens above them, delivered them from imminent death.

Then Gottschalk, not a true, but a false servant of God, entered Hungary with his followers, and that not without injury to East Noricum. Next, under an astonishing glamour of false piety, he fortified a certain town situated on a height and placed a garrison there and began, with the rest of his company, to ravage Pannonia round about. This town, forsooth, was captured by the natives without delay, and great numbers of the band having been killed or taken prisoners, the rest were dispersed, and he himself, a hireling, not the shepherd of the flock, was driven away from there in disgrace.

C. Emico. (May-August, 1096.)

(*Ekkehard.*) Just at that time, there appeared a certain soldier, Emico, Count of the lands around the Rhine, a man long of very ill repute on account of his tyrannical mode of life. Called by divine revelation, like another Saul, as he maintained, to the practice of religion of this kind, he usurped to himself the command of almost twelve thousand cross bearers. As they were led through the cities of the Rhine and the Main and also the Danube, they either utterly destroyed the execrable race of the Jews wherever they found them (being even in this matter zealously devoted to the Christian religion) or forced them into the bosom of the Church. When their forces, already increased by a great number of men and women, reached the boundary of Pannonia, they were prevented by well fortified garrisons from entering that kingdom, which is surrounded partly by swamps and partly by woods. For rumor had reached and forewarned the ears of King Coloman; a rumor that, to the minds of the Teutons, there was no difference between killing pagans and Hungarians. And so, for six weeks they besieged the fortress *Wieselburg* and suffered many hardships there; yet, during this very time, they were in the throes of a most foolish civil quarrel over which one of them should be King of Pannonia. Moreover, while engaged in the final assault, although the walls had already been broken through, and the citizens were fleeing, and the army of the besieged were setting fire to their own town, yet, through the wonderful providence of Almighty God, the army of pilgrims, though victorious, fled. And they left behind them all their equipment, for no one carried away any reward except his wretched life.

And thus the men of our race, zealous, doubtless, for God, though not according to the knowledge of God, began to persecute other Christians while yet upon the expedition which Christ had provided for freeing Christians. They were kept from fraternal bloodshed only by divine mercy; and the Hungarians, also, were freed. This is the reason why some of the more guileless brethren, ignorant of the matter, and too hasty in their judgment, were scandalized and concluded that the whole expedition was vain and foolish. . . .

(*Albert.*) At the beginning of summer in the same year in which Peter and Gottschalk, after collecting an army, had set out, there assembled in like fashion a large and innumerable host of Christians from diverse kingdoms and lands; namely, from the realms of France, England, Flanders, and Lorraine. . . . I know not whether by a judgment of the Lord, or by some error of mind, they rose in a spirit of cruelty against the Jewish people scattered throughout these cities and slaughtered them without mercy, especially in the Kingdom of Lorraine, asserting it to be the beginning of their expedition and their duty against the enemies of the Christian faith. This slaughter of Jews was done first by citizens of Cologne. These suddenly fell upon a small band of Jews and severely wounded and killed many; they destroyed the houses and synagogues of the Jews and divided among themselves a very large amount of money. When the Jews saw this cruelty, about two hundred in the silence of the night began flight by boat to Neuss. The pilgrims and crusaders discovered them, and after taking away all their possessions, inflicted on them similar slaughter, leaving not even one alive.

Not long after this, they started upon their journey, as they had vowed, and arrived in a great multitude at the city of Mainz. There Count Emico, a nobleman, a very mighty man in this region, was awaiting, with a large band of Teutons, the arrival of the pilgrims who were coming thither from diverse lands by the King's highway.

The Jews of this city, knowing of the slaughter of their brethren, and that they themselves could not escape the hands of so many, fled in hope of safety to Bishop Rothard. They put an infinite treasure in his guard and trust, having much faith in his protection, because he was Bishop of the city. Then that excellent Bishop of the city cautiously set aside the incredible amount of money received from them. He placed the Jews in the very spacious hall of his own house, away from the sight of Count Emico and his followers, that they might remain safe and sound in a very secure and strong place.

But Emico and the rest of his band held a council and, after sunrise, attacked the Jews in the hall with arrows and lances. Breaking the bolts and doors, they killed the Jews, about seven hundred in number, who in vain resisted the force and attack of so many thousands. They killed the women, also, and with their swords pierced tender children of whatever age and sex. The Jews, seeing that their Christian enemies were attacking them and their children, and that they were sparing no age, likewise fell upon one another, brother, children, wives, and sisters, and thus they perished at each other's hands. Horrible to say, mothers cut the throats of nursing children with knives and stabbed others, preferring them to perish thus by their own hands rather than to be killed by the weapons of the uncircumcised.

From this cruel slaughter of the Jews a few escaped; and a few because of fear, rather than because of love of the Christian faith, were baptized. With very great spoils taken from these people, Count Emico, Clarebold, Thomas, and all that intolerable company of men and women then continued on their way to Jerusalem, directing their course towards the Kingdom of Hungary, where passage along the royal highway was usually not denied the pilgrims. But on arriving at *Wieselburg,* the fortress of the King, which the rivers Danube and Leytha protect with marshes, the bridge and gate of the fortress were found closed by command of the King of Hungary, for great fear had entered all the Hungarians because of the slaughter which had happened to their brethren. . . .

But while almost everything had turned out favorably for the Christians, and while they had penetrated the walls with great openings, by some chance or misfortune, I know not what, such great fear entered the whole army that they turned in flight, just as sheep are scattered and alarmed when wolves rush upon them. And seeking a refuge here and there, they forgot their companions. . . . .

Emico and some of his followers continued in their flight along the way by which they had come. Thomas, Clarebold, and several of their men escaped in flight toward Carinthia and Italy. So the hand of the Lord is believed to have been against the pilgrims, who had sinned by excessive impurity and fornication, and who had slaughtered the exiled Jews through greed of money, rather than for the sake of God's justice, although the Jews were opposed to Christ. The Lord is a just judge and orders no one unwillingly, or under compulsion, to come under the yoke of the Catholic faith.

There was another detestable crime in this assemblage of wayfaring people, who were foolish and insanely fickle. That the crime was hateful to the Lord and incredible to the faithful is not to be doubted. They asserted that a certain goose was inspired by the Holy Spirit, and that a she-goat was not less filled by the same Spirit. These they made their guides on this holy journey to Jerusalem; these they worshipped excessively; and most of the people following them, like beasts, believed with their whole minds that this was the true course. May the hearts of the faithful be free from the thought that the Lord Jesus wished the Sepulchre of His most sacred body to be visited by brutish and insensate animals, or that He wished these to become the guides of Christian souls, which by the price of His own blood He deigned to redeem from the filth of idols! . . .

3. *The Main Body.*

A. Composition.

(*Fulcher.*) It is fitting to keep in mind the names of the leaders of the Crusades. Hugh the Great,[7] brother of the King of France, was the first hero to cross the sea. He landed with his force at Durazzo, a city in Bulgaria; but imprudently venturing forth with too small an army, he was there captured by the inhabitants and taken to the Emperor of Constantinople, where he was kept for a long time, not altogether free. After him, Bohemund of Apulia,[8] son of Robert Guiscard of Norman extraction, journeyed with his army over the same route; next, Godfrey, Duke of Lorraine,[9] passed with a great force through Hungary. Raymond,[10] Count of Provence, with Goths and Gascons, and also with Adhemar, Bishop of Puy, crossed through Dalmatia. Peter the Hermit, gathering to himself a crowd of foot-soldiers, but few knights, first passed through Hungary; afterwards the satrap of this horde was Walter the Penniless, who, together with many of his good soldiers, was killed by the Turks between the cities of Nicomedia and Nicaea. Then in the month of October, Robert, Count of Normandy,[11] and son of William, King of England, started out, after having gathered a large army of Normans, Angles[12] and Bretons. With him went Stephen, Count of Blois,[13] his brother-in-law, and Robert, Count of Flanders,[14] together with many other nobles. Therefore, since such a multitude came from all Western countries, little by little, and day by day, the army increased to such a very great number that, when finally convened, it formed an infinite host from many regions and of many tongues. However, they did not unite into a single army until we arrived at Nicaea.

(*Gesta.*) Soon they departed from their homes in Gaul, and then formed three groups. One party of Franks, namely, Peter, the Hermit, Duke Godfrey, Baldwin, his brother,[15] and Baldwin, Count of the Mount,[16] entered the region of Hungary. These most powerful knights, and many others whom I do not know, went by the way which Charles the Great, wonder-working king of France, long ago had made, even to Constantinople. . . .

The second party—to wit, Raymond, Count of St. Gilles, and the Bishop of Puy—entered the region of Slavonia. The third division, however, went by the ancient road to Rome. In this division were Bohemund, Richard of Principati, Robert, Count of Flanders, Robert the Norman, Hugh the Great, Everard of Puiset, Achard of Montmerle, Ysoard of Mousson, and many others. Next, they went to the port of Brindisi, or Bari, or Otranto. Then Hugh the Great, and William, son of Marchisus, took to the sea at the port of Bari and, crossing the strait, came to Durazzo. But the governor of this place, his heart touched with evil design, took these most renowned men captive immediately upon hearing that they had landed there and ordered them to be conducted carefully to the Emperor at Constantinople, where they should pledge loyalty to him.

B. Godfrey's march to Constantinople. (August 15 (?)-December 23, 1096.)

(*Albert.*) After the departure of Peter the Hermit and the most dire destruction of his army; after the killing of the distinguished soldier Walter the Penniless, and the grievous disaster to his army; shortly after the cruel slaughter of the priest, Gottschalk, and of his army; after the misfortune of Hartmann, Count of Alemannia, of Emico, and all the other brave men and leaders from the land of Gaul (to wit, Drogo of Nesle and Clarebold of Vendeuil); and after the cruel destruction of the army of Clarebold at the gate of

Wieselburg in the Kingdom of Hungary—after all these things, the very noble Godfrey, Duke of Lorraine, and his brother Baldwin, Werner of Grez, a kinsman of the Duke, and Baldwin of Burg, likewise a kinsman, Reinard, Count of Toul, and Peter his brother, Dodo of *Conz*, Henry of Ascha, and his brother, Godfrey, set out,[17] in the same year, in the middle of the month of August. While making a journey in direct march to Jerusalem, they halted in their course near *Tollenburg* in the realm of Austria, where the Leytha terminates the kingdom of Gaul [18] and separates it from the Austrian realm. They remained there three weeks in the month of September, to hear and to understand why sedition had arisen; why the army had perished a few days before; why those whom they met returning in despair had been turned from their purpose of going to Jerusalem with their chiefs and leaders.

Finally, after hearing very many evil rumors, they discussed what should first be done to investigate the cruel attack which the Hungarians had made against their fellow Christians; and with what circumspection and deliberation the investigation should be made. After having considered the matter at length, it seemed to all a practical plan to send from those celebrated leaders only Godfrey of Ascha to investigate so wicked and criminal a slaughter. (They decided thus) because he was known to Coloman, King of Hungary, having been sent some time before as ambassador of Duke Godfrey to this same king. They sent with him twelve others chosen from the retinue of the Duke—Baldwin, *Stabelo*, it is said, and others whose names are unknown. . . .

The King struck a treaty with Duke Godfrey, and all the chiefs of his kingdom were bound by oath not to do harm to the pilgrims who were to pass that way. When, therefore, these agreements had been confirmed on both sides, the King, upon the advice of his men, demanded as hostages, Baldwin, the brother of the Duke, his wife and family. This the Duke agreed to fulfil without dispute. After eight days, the embassy was dismissed, and the Duke ordered the army to hasten to the fortress Oedenburg, and to pitch their tents on the banks of the river near the marshes. . . . Finally, Baldwin, having put aside all doubt, consented to become a hostage and to be taken into exile for the safety of his brethren.

And thus, when so distinguished a leader had become a hostage, and when the King had returned with him to Pannonia, the entire army, by order and permission of the King, was led over the bridge across the marsh, and camp was pitched near the river Leytha. Then, after camp was pitched, and after all were settled at rest, Duke Godfrey appointed heralds to announce to each house and tent that, under sentence of death, they should neither touch nor take by force anything in the Kingdom of Hungary, and should stir up no quarrel, but that everything should be exchanged for a just price. Similarly, the King commanded that it be proclaimed throughout his realm that the army was to obtain every abundance of necessary things, bread, wine, corn, oil, beasts of the field, and flying creatures of the sky; and he commanded, under penalty of life, that the Hungarians should not burden and enrage the army by unjust selling, but, rather, should make all buying easy for them.

And so, day by day, in quiet and in peace, with full measure and just sale, the Duke and his people crossed the Kingdom of Hungary and arrived at the river Drave. A heap of wood was gathered and a large raft was made, on which they crossed the river. Without delay the King, coming from the left with a very powerful band of horsemen, together with Baldwin and all the other hostages, arrived at that place which is called *Francavilla*.[19] There they remained three days, purchasing the necessaries of life of which the army was in need. Then they all went to *Malevilla* and spent five days near the Save.

There it became known to the Duke and to the other leaders of the army that an intolerable force of the Emperor of Constantinople was present to prohibit the passage of the pilgrims through the Kingdom of Bulgaria. The Duke, therefore, and all the leaders entered upon a plan to send a part of the army across the river to drive back the hostile soldiers of the Emperor, while the people were crossing the river. Not more than three boats were found there. In these a thousand knights in armour were carried across to take possession of the shore. All the rest of the multitude gained the other bank of the river by means of rafts made of wood and bound together by twigs.

Scarcely had the people and their chiefs crossed the stream, when, behold, the King appeared with all his retinue, and Baldwin, the brother of the Duke, his wife, and all the hostages. There he restored the hostages to the Duke. Next, after very affectionately favoring the Duke and his brother with many gifts and the kiss of peace, he returned to the land of his own kingdom. But the Duke and all his army, having settled on the opposite bank, passed the night in the hospitality of the village Belgrade in Bulgaria—a city which the army of Peter the Hermit had plundered and burned not long before. But when morning came, the Duke and his army arose and advanced into the immense and indescribable forests in the Kingdom of Bulgaria.

There legates of the Emperor met them, bearing a message in

these words: "Alexius, Emperor of Constantinople, of the Kingdom of the Greeks, to Duke Godfrey and his fellow princes; sincere affection. I ask, most Christian Duke, that you do not suffer your people to plunder or to lay waste my lands and kingdom which you have entered, but that you secure the privilege of buying. By our order you will find everything in abundance for buying and selling." Upon hearing this message, the Duke promised to obey in all things the mandate of the Emperor. Thereupon, it was proclaimed to all that thereafter they should touch nothing with undue violence, except food for their horses. And so, peacefully crossing over at the request of the Emperor, they arrived at his fortress, Nish, where a wonderful abundance of food-stuff, grain, barley, wine, and oil, and very much game were brought to the Duke as the gift of the Emperor. To the others was granted the privilege of buying and selling. There, indeed, for four days they were refreshed with every abundance and pleasure. After those days, the Duke with all his army departed to Sofia, where he was supplied by the Emperor with gifts no less rich. Leaving there after some days, he went down to Philippopolis, a famous city; there during eight days he likewise received as gifts from the Emperor every abundance of necessary things.

There a message was brought to him that the Emperor held in chains and prison Hugh the Great, brother of the King of France, Drogo, and Clarebold. When he had heard this, the Duke sent an embassy to the Emperor, demanding that the Emperor should restore to liberty those princes of his land whom he was holding captive; otherwise, he himself could not keep faith and friendship with the Emperor. When Baldwin, Count of Hainault, and Henry of Ascha found out that an embassy was to be sent to the Emperor, they anticipated the journey to Constantinople by going out at daybreak, without the knowledge of the Duke, in order that by preceding the legates they might receive greater gifts from the Emperor. The Duke, hearing this, took it ill; but, concealing his wrath, he set out to Adrianople. After crossing a river by swimming his horses, he pitched his tents and passed the night there. On the next day, a bridge which crosses a river in the middle of the city was forbidden to him and his followers by the inhabitants. Then arising and hastening to *Salabria*, they pitched their tents in pleasant meadows. There the messengers of the Duke, who had returned from the Emperor, reported that he had not given up the captive princes. Thereupon the Duke and all his company burned with wrath; and they refused any longer to keep faith and treaty of peace with him. Immediately, by a command of the Duke, all that land was given over in plunder to the alien pilgrims and knights, who, delaying there for eight days, laid waste the whole region.

But the Emperor, upon learning that the country had been laid waste, sent to the Duke Rudolph *Peeldelan* and Rotger, son of Dagobert, very eloquent men, who were of the region and kinship of the Franks. He asked that the army should cease from plundering and devastating his realm; and he said that without delay he would give back the captives whom the Duke demanded. Then the Duke was pleased with the message of the Emperor; and, after entering upon a plan with the other leaders, he moved his camp and forbade plunder.

C. March of the West Franks into Southern Italy. (Late September-November, 1096.)

(*Fulcher.*) Then we West Franks traversed Gaul, and, travelling through Italy, came to Lucca, a far-famed city. Near there we met Pope Urban. Robert the Norman, and Stephen, Count of Blois, talked with him, and others who wished likewise. Having received his blessing, we joyfully advanced to Rome. And when we had entered the church of St. Peter, we found before the altar the supporters of Wibert, that pseudo-pope, who, sword in hand, wickedly seized the offerings placed on the altar. Others, too, ran about on the roof of St. Peter's itself and threw stones down where we were prostrate, praying. For when they saw any one faithful to Urban, they straightway wished to kill him. In one tower of the church were adherents of Pope Urban, who were guarding it well in faithfulness to him and, as far as they could, were resisting his adversaries. We grieved much to see such an outrage committed in that place; but we could do nothing except to desire that it be avenged by God. Many who had come thus far with us waited no longer, but at once, with disgraceful cowardice, returned to their homes.

We, however, travelling through the center of Campagnia, reached Bari, a rich seaport town. There we addressed our supplications to God in the church of St. Nicholas. Then coming to port, we decided to cross at once. But because we lacked seamen, and because fortune might play us false, and because, furthermore, it was winter time, which exposed us to dangers, Robert, Count of Normandy, was obliged to withdraw into Calabria; and there he spent the whole winter season. Robert, Count of Flanders, however, with his followers crossed over. Then many of the Crusaders, abandoned by their leaders, and fearing future want, sold their weapons there and, taking up again their pilgrim's staves, ignominiously returned to their homes. This desertion debased them before God and man, and it redounded to their shame.

D. Bohemund's march to Constantinople. (October 26, 1096-April 10, 1097.)

(*Gesta.*) But Bohemund, powerful in battle, who was engaged in the siege of Amalfi on the sea of Salerno, heard that a countless host of Christians from among the Franks had come to go to the Sepulchre of the Lord, and that they were prepared for battle against the pagan horde. He then began to inquire closely what fighting arms these people bore, and what sign of Christ they carried on the way, or what battle-cry they shouted. The following replies were made to him in order: "They bear arms suitable for battle; on the right shoulder, or between both shoulders, they wear the cross of Christ; the cry, 'God wills it! God wills it! God wills it!' they shout in truth with one voice." Moved straighway by the Holy Spirit, he ordered the most precious cloak which he had with him cut to pieces, and straightway he had the whole of it made into crosses. Thereupon, most of the knights engaged in that siege rushed eagerly to him, so that Count Roger remained almost alone.

Returning again to his own land, Lord Bohemund diligently prepared himself to undertake in true earnest the journey to the Holy Sepulchre. At length, he crossed the sea with his army. With him were Tancred, son of Marchisus,[20] Richard of Principati, and Rainulf, his brother, Robert of Anse, Herman of Cannae, Robert of *Surd*a Valley,[21] Robert, son of *Tostanus,* Hunfred, son of Raoul, Richard, son of Count Rainulf, the Count of *Roscignolo*,[22] with his brothers, Boellus of Chartres, Albered of Cagnano, and Hunfred of Mt. Scaglioso. All of these crossed the sea to do service for Bohemund and landed in the region of Bulgaria, where they found a very great abundance of grain, wine, and bodily nourishment. Thence descending into the valley of *Andronopoli*,[23] they waited for his forces, until all had likewise crossed the sea. Then the wise Bohemund ordered a council with his people, comforting and admonishing all (with these words): "Seignors, take heed all of you, for we are pilgrims of God. We ought, therefore, to be better and more humble than before. Do not plunder this land, since it belongs to Christians, and let no one, at the cost of blessing, take more than he needs to eat."

Departing thence, we journeyed hrough great plenty from villa to villa, city to city, fortress to fortress, until we reached Castoria. There we solemnly celebrated the nativity of the Lord. We remained there for several days and sought a market, but the people were unwilling to accord it to us, because they feared us greatly, thinking that we came not as pilgrims, but to devastate their land and to kill them. Wherefore we took their cattle, horses, asses, and everything that we found. Leaving Castoria, we entered Pelagonia, in which there was a certain fortified town of heretics. This we attacked from all sides and it soon yielded to our sway. Thereupon, we set it on fire and burned the camp with its inhabitants, that is, the congregation of heretics. Later, we reached the river Vardar. And then Lord Bohemund went across with his people, but not with all, for the Count of *Roscignolo* with his brothers remained behind.

Thereupon, an army of the Emperor came and attacked the Count with his brothers and all who were with them. Tancred, hearing of this, went back and, hurling himself into the river, reached the others by swimming; and two thousand went into the river following Tancred. At length, they came upon the Turcopoles[24] and Patzinaks struggling with our men. They (Tancred and his men) charged the enemy suddenly and bravely and overcame them gloriously. Several of them they seized and led them, bound, into the presence of Bohemund, who spoke to them as follows: "Wherefore, miserable men, do you kill Christ's people and mine? I have no quarrel with your Emperor." They replied, "We cannot do otherwise; we have been placed in the service of the Emperor, and whatever he commands we must fulfill." Bohemund allowed them to depart unpunished. This battle was fought in the fourth day of the week, which is the beginning of the fast. Through all, blessed is the Lord! Amen.

The unhappy Emperor sent one of his own men, whom he greatly loved, and whom they call *Corpalatius*,[25] together with our envoys, to conduct us in security through his land until we should come to Constantinople. And as we paused before their cities, he ordered the inhabitants to offer us a market, just as those also did of whom we have spoken. Indeed, they feared the most brave host of Lord Bohemund so greatly that they permitted none of us to enter the walls of the city. Our men wanted to attack and seize a certain fortified town because it was full of all kinds of goods. But the renowned man, Bohemund, refused to consent, not only in justice to the land, but also because of his pledge to the Emperor. Therefore, he was greatly angered on this account with Tancred and all the rest. This happened toward evening. When morning came, the inhabitants of the town came out, and, in procession, bearing crosses in their hands, they came into the presence of Bohemund. Delighted, he received them; and with gladness he permitted them to depart. Next we came to a certain town, which is called Serrhae, where we fixed our tents and had a market sufficient for that time. There the learned Bohemund made a very cordial agreement with two *Corpalatii;* and out of regard for their friendship, as well as in justice to the land, he ordered all the stolen animals which our men had to be returned. The *Corpalatius* promised him that he would despatch messengers to return the animals to their owners in order. Then we proceeded from castle to castle and from villa to villa to the city of Rusa. The people of the Greeks came out, bringing us the greatest market, and went joyfully to meet Lord Bohemund. There we pitched our tents in the fourth day of the week before the feast of the Lord.

There, also, the learned Bohemund left all his host and went on ahead to speak with the Emperor at Constantinople. He gave commands to his vassals, saying, "Approach the city gradually. I, however, will go on in advance." And he took with him a few knights. Tancred remained at the head of the army of Christ, and, seeing the pilgrims buying food, he said to himself that he would go off the road and lead his people where they would live happily. At length he entered a certain valley, filled with goods of all kinds that are suitable nourishment for the body, and in it we most devoutly celebrated Easter.

E. The march of Raymond of Toulouse and Bishop Adhemar of Puy. (October (?) 1096-April 21, 1097.)

(*Raymond.*) While advancing into the land of Slavonia they suffered many losses on the way, especially because it was then winter. For Slavonia was such a desert and so pathless and mountainous that we saw in it neither wild animals, nor birds for three weeks. The inhabitants of the region were so boorish and rude that they were unwilling to trade with us, or to furnish us guidance, but instead fled from their villages and their castles. Indeed, they even butchered like cattle, or, as if they had done much harm, the feeble aged and the weak poor, who, because of their weakness, followed our army at a distance. Nor was it easy amidst steep mountains and thick woods for our armed knights to pursue the unarmed brigands who were acquainted with the country. But they suffered them constantly, unable either to fight or to keep from fighting. Let us not pass over a certain illustrious act of the Count. When the Count with some of his knights had been hedged about for some little time by the Slavonians, he made a charge upon them and captured as many as six of them. And when, on this account, the Slavonians pressed upon him the more violently, and the Count was compelled to follow the army, he ordered the eyes of some of them (the prisoners) to be torn out, the feet of others cut off, and the nose and hands of still others to be slashed, so that while the pursuers were thus moved at the sight and preoccupied with their sorrow, the Count could safely escape with his companions. And thus, by the grace of God he was delivered from the straits of death and this difficult situation.

Indeed, what courage and wisdom the Count displayed in this region is not easy to relate! For we were in Slavonia for almost forty days, during which time we encountered clouds so dense that we could feel them and push them before us with a slight movement. Amidst all this, the Count was fighting constantly at the rear and ever defending his people. He was never the first, but always the last, to encamp, and though the others went to rest at midday, or at evening, the Count often did so at midnight, or at cockcrow. At length, through the compassion of God, the labor of the Count, and the advice of the Bishop, the army so crossed (Slavonia) that we lost no one there from hunger, and no one in open battle. On that account, I bear witness, God wanted his army to cross Slavonia, in order that the boorish men who did not know God, upon recognizing the valor and patience of His knights, might either lose something of their wildness or be brought without excuse to God's judgment. And then, after many labors, we came to the king of the Slavonians at Scutari. The Count swore friendship with him and gave him a large tribute, so that the army might buy or seek necessaries in security. But this was a (vain) expectation, for we did penance enough for the peace we had sought when thereafter the Slavonians, raging in their usual manner, killed our men and took from the unarmed what they could. We sought not vengeance, but a place of refuge. So much about Slavonia.

We came to Durazzo. We believed we were in our own country, thinking that the Emperor and his satellites were our brothers and helpmates. They, indeed, raging in the manner of lions, attacked a peaceful people who thought of nothing less than arms. They butchered them in secret places; they stole what they could by night, in the woods, and in villages remote from the camp. Although they raged thus, their leader promised peace. But during the intervals of peace, they killed Pontius Reinald and mortally wounded his brother, Peter, and these were most noble princes. However, when an opportunity was presented to us for revenge, we chose to continue the journey, not to avenge our wrongs. On the way, we had letters from the Emperor about peace, brotherhood, and, as I may also say, about alliance; this, however, was a snare in words. For in front and behind, to right and to left, Turks and Cumans, Uzi, *Tanaces*,[26] Patzinaks, and Bulgarians were lying in ambush for us.

On a certain day, moreover, when we were in the valley of Pelagonia, the Bishop of Puy, who, in order to find a comfortable resting place, had withdrawn a little distance from the camp, was captured by the Patzinaks. They knocked him down from his mule, robbed him, and beat him severely on the head. But since so great a pontiff was still necessary to the people of God, through God's mercy he was saved to life. For one of the Patzinaks, in order to obtain gold from him, protected him from the others. Meanwhile, the noise was heard in the camp; and so, between the delay of the enemy and the attack of his friends, he was rescued.

When we had come amidst treachery of this fashion to a certain fortress called *Bucinat*,[27] the Count learned that the Patzinaks intended to attack our army in the passes of a certain mountain. Staying in hiding with some of his knights, he came upon the Patzinaks, and, after killing several of them, he turned the rest to flight. Meanwhile, pacifying letters from the Emperor reached us, (and yet) by his evil design the enemy surrounded us on all sides. When we came to Thessalonica, the Bishop was ill and remained in the city with a few men.

After this, we came to a certain city, Rusa by name, where, since its citizens were plainly disposed to do us evil, our usual patience was somewhat disturbed. So, taking up arms, we destroyed the outer walls, seized great plunder, and forced the city to surrender; then, having taken our standards into the city and shouted "Toulouse!" which was the battle cry of the Count, we departed.

We came to another city, called Rodosto. When knights in the pay of the Emperor there sought to carry out his vengeance upon us, many of them were killed and a quantity of plunder taken. There, also, the envoys whom we had sent ahead to the Emperor came to us and, having received money from him, promised that everything boded well for us with the Emperor. What more? The message (brought) by our envoys and those of the Emperor was that the Count, leaving his army behind, should hasten unarmed and with a few men to the Emperor. For they said that Bohemund, the Duke of Lorraine, the Count of Flanders, and other princes made this prayer: that the Count should hasten to agree with the Emperor about the march to Jerusalem; that the Emperor, having taken the cross, should also become leader in the army of God. In addition to this, they reported that the Emperor had said that he would make all arrangements with the Count, both about themselves and whatever else should be necessary for the journey. They announced, furthermore, that a battle was imminent, and that without the support of so great a man it would probably be unfavorable; that the Count should therefore go ahead with a few men, so that when his army should arrive, everything would have been arranged with the Emperor, and there would be no delay for anyone. At length, the Count was persuaded to go ahead of his army, in this instance, alone, leaving his guard behind him in the camp. And thus he went unarmed to Constantinople.

F. Robert of Normandy and Stephen of Blois on the way to Constantinople. (April 5-May 14, 1097.)

(*Fulcher.*) Then in the month of March, 1097, as soon as spring had returned, the Norman Count and Count Stephen of Blois with his followers (for he likewise was awaiting an opportune time), returned again to the coast. When the fleet was ready on the Nones of April, which happened that year to be the feast of Easter, they embarked at the port of Brindisi. Oh how incomprehensible and unsearchable are the judgments of God![28] For among all these ships we saw one which was suddenly split through the middle from no apparent cause. Then about four hundred of both sexes were drowned, concerning whom joyous praises at once went up to God. For when those standing around had collected as many as possible of the dead bodies, they found on the shoulders of some signs of the cross. For since they had worn the cross on their clothes while living, it was the will of God that that same victorious sign of faith should remain on the skin of those prematurely cut off by death while in His service. So it was very fitting for such a miracle to prove to those who witnessed it that the dead had already received everlasting peace by the mercy of God; thus, in very truth, that was evidently fulfilled which is written, "But the just man, even if he die too soon, shall nevertheless be at rest."[29] Of the rest of our companions already struggling with death, few survived. Their horses and their mules were swallowed up by the waves, and much money also was lost. At the sight of this disaster we were much afraid, so much so that many weak hearted, who had not yet embarked, returned to their homes, giving up the journey, and saying that never again would they trust themselves to the treacherous sea.

As for us, however, we trusted implicitly in Almighty God and launched out upon the sea, with flags flying aloft, and many trumpets sounding, and a gentle breeze blowing. For three days the wind failed us, and we were detained in the midst of the billows. On the fourth day, we reached land, about ten miles from the city of Durazzo. Our fleet, however, anchored at two ports. Then joyfully we again resumed the dry land and advanced beyond the above mentioned city. So we passed by the regions of Bulgaria, over steep mountains and desert places. Then we all came to the rapid river, called by the natives the River of the Demon,[30] and appropriately so. For in this river we saw many people, who hoped to wade across step by step, perish suddenly, engulfed by the strong force of the torrent; and none of those looking on were able to save them. Wherefore, moved by compassion, we shed many tears, and had not knights with their mighty battle steeds brought aid to the foot-soldiers, many of them would there have lost their lives in the same manner. Then we pitched our tents near the bank and there we spent one night. Great mountains, uninhabited, were about us on all sides. Hardly had the morning dawned, when the war trumpets sounded, and, resuming our way, we descended the mountain called Bagora. Afterwards passing by the mountain and the towns Ochrida, Bitolia, Wodena, and *Stella*,[31] we came to the river called Vardar. And what could not usually be done except by boat, we did by the help of God; we waded across. The day following we camped before the city of Thessalonica, a city rich in goods of all kinds. After a four days delay here, we travelled through Macedonia, through the valley of the Strymon, and through Crisopolis and Christopolis, *Praetoria*,[32] Messinopolis, Maera, Traianopolis, Neapolis, Panedor, Rodosto, and Heraclea, Silivri, and Natura; and we arrived at Constantinople. Pitching our tents before this city, we rested fourteen days.

CHAPTER III

Alexius and the Crusaders

(The conduct of Alexius and the people of his empire toward the Crusaders, as they passed through the land on their way to Constantinople, seemed incomprehensible to the Latins at the time and has been more or less baffling to all later writers. There is some doubt as to whether or not Alexius had sent a definite appeal for help to the West at this time. Chalandon, whose study of the reign of Alexius represents probably the most authoritative modern investigation of the subject, maintains the thesis that Alexius did not call for help, and that the empire in 1096 was less in need of aid than at any time since 1071.[1] Certainly, the Emperor's conduct appears more intelligible if the Crusaders can be regarded as his uninvited guests. Their not infrequent acts of violence may even have led him to suspect their motives, which suspicion the presence of Bohemund and his Normans from southern Italy—old foes of the Eastern Empire—only served to strengthen. Possibly there were other causes, also, to arouse the Emperor. Köhler has suggested that Urban, in arousing the expedition, cherished the hope of gaining the submission of the Greek Church, either as a reward for this help, or by intimidation and force, if necessary.[2] But whether or not there was any just cause for the Emperor's suspicions, the statements of his daughter, together with his own unquestionable zeal to hasten each band away from Constantinople and across the Bosporus before the next band arrived, indicates very clearly that he did distrust the Latins. And yet, as one reads the Latin accounts, it is difficult to find in them evidence of guile toward Alexius or a covert design upon the possession of his empire. The constant combination of friendly messages from the Emperor and rough treatment from his soldiers aroused a good deal of distrust on the part of the Crusaders, but at first they seemed to give the Emperor the benefit of the doubt.

For almost every event narrated in this chapter there is testimony from at least two independent writers. The fate of the Peasants' Crusade, though not described by an eye-witness, is quite fully treated by both Anna and Albert, as well as by the Anonymous, and Fulcher's mention of the heap of bones near Nicomedia serves as a graphic confirmation of their statements. Anna's account of Hugh's experiences is confirmed only by the brief mention of his plight by Fulcher and Albert. The rather brief statement of the Anonymous about Godfrey's dealings with Alexius is too condensed to settle the disparities between the accounts of Anna and Albert, and the reader must draw his own inferences. The identity of the Raoul mentioned by Anna is somewhat uncertain. He could not have been Robert of Flanders, who was with the other leaders both at Constantinople and Nicaea. The shipment of troops to Syria by water did occur in the Crusade of 1101, which Anna may very easily have confused with earlier events. Her account of Bohemund and of Raymond, also, is colored by her knowledge of later events, but the versions given by the Anonymous, Raymond, and the others serve to establish the actual occurrences fairly well. For the arrival and treatment of Robert of Normandy and Stephen of Blois at Constantinople Fulcher's statements and those in Stephen's letter furnish ample evidence. The siege and capture of Nicaea is the most fully attested event in the history of the First Crusade. Certain minor incidents in the siege, however, are related by only one or two of the writers who were in the immediate vicinity, and the connection of the various chroniclers with one band or the other must be borne in mind. Throughout the whole chapter the contrast of western and eastern civilization, as evidenced by the frequent naïve expressions of wonder and amazement, on the one hand, and blasé contempt and horror, on the other, forms an interesting background to the progress of events,)

1. *Alexius and the Peasants' Crusade. Fate of the Peasants' Crusade.* (August 1-October 4, 1096.)

(*Anna.*) . . . Moreover, Alexius was not yet, or very slightly, rested from his labors when he heard rumors of the arrival of innumerable Frankish armies. He feared the incursions of these people, for he had already experienced the savage fury of their attack, their fickleness of mind, and their readiness to approach anything with violence. . . .

And finally, he kept ever in mind this information, which was often repeated and most true—that they were known to be always immoderately covetous of anything they strove after and to break very easily, for any reason whatsoever, treaties which they had made. Accordingly, he did not indulge in any rest, but made ready his forces in every way, so that when occcasion should demand he would be ready for battle. For it was a matter greater and more terrible than famine which was then reported. Forsooth, the whole West, and as much of the land of barbarian peoples as lies beyond the Adriatic Sea up to the Pillars of Hercules—all this, changing its seat, was bursting forth into Asia in a solid mass, with all its belongings, taking its march through the intervening portion of Europe.

A certain Gaul, Peter by name, surnamed Kuku-Peter,[3] had set out from his home to adore the Holy Sepulchre. After suffering many dangers and wrongs from the Turks and Saracens, who were devastating all Asia, he returned to his own country most sorrowfully. He could not bear to see himself thus cut off from his proposed pilgrimage and intended to undertake the expedition a second time. . . .

After Peter had promoted the expedition, he, with 80,000 foot-soldiers and 100,000 knights, was the first of all to cross the Lombard strait. Then passing through the territory of Hungary, he arrived at the queenly city. For, as anyone may conjecture from the outcome, the race of the Gauls is not only very passionate and impetuous in other ways, but, also, when urged on by an impulse, cannot thereafter be checked. Our Emperor, aware of what Peter had suffered from the Turks before, urged him to await the arrival of the other counts.

(*Gesta.*) But the above-mentioned Peter was the first to reach Constantinople, on the Kalends of August, and with him was a very large host of Alemanni. There he found assembled Lombards, and Longobards, and many others. The Emperor had ordered such a market as was in the city to be given to these people. And he said to them, "Do not cross the Strait until the chief host of the Christians has come, for you are not so strong that you can do battle with the Turks." The Christians conducted themselves badly, inasmuch as they tore down and burned buildings of the city and carried off the lead with which the churches were constructed and sold it to the Greeks. The Emperor was enraged thereat and ordered them to cross the Strait. After they had crossed, they did not cease doing all manner of evil, burning and plundering houses and churches. At length they reached Nicomedia, where the Lombards and Longobards and Alemanni separated from the Franks because the Franks were constantly swelled with arrogance.

The Lombards and Longobards chose a leader over themselves whose name was Reinald. The Alemanni did likewise. They entered Romania[4] and proceeded for four days beyond the city of Nicaea. They found a certain fortress, *Xerogord*[5] by name, which was empty of people, and they seized it. In it they found an ample supply of grain, wine, and meat, and an abundance of all goods. The Turks, accordingly, hearing that the Christians were in the fortress, came to besiege it. Before the gate of the fortress was a cistern, and at the foot of the fortress was a fountain of running water, near which Reinald went out to trap the Turks. But the Turks, who came on the day of the Dedication of St. Michael,[6] found Reinald and those who were with him and killed many of them. Those who remained alive fled to the fortress, which the Turks straightway besieged, thus depriving them of water. Our people were in such distress from thirst that they bled their horses and asses and drank the blood; others let their girdles and handkerchiefs down into the cistern and squeezed out the water from them into their mouths; some urinated into one another's hollowed hands and drank; and others dug up the moist ground and lay down on their backs and spread the earth over their breasts to relieve the excessive dryness of thirst. The bishops and priests, indeed, continued to comfort our people, and to admonish them not to yield, saying, "Be everywhere strong in the faith of Christ, and do not fear those who persecute you, just as the Lord saith, 'Be not afraid of them that kill the body, but are not able to kill the soul.'"[7] This distress lasted for eight days. Then the lord of the Alemanni made an agreement with the Turks to surrender his companions to them; and, feigning to go out to fight, he fled to them, and many with him. Those, however, who were unwilling to deny the Lord received the sentence of death; some, whom they took alive, they divided among themselves, like sheep; some they placed as a target and shot with arrows; others they sold and gave away, like animals. Some they took captive to their own home, some to Chorosan, some to Antioch, others to Aleppo, or wherever they themselves lived. These were the first to receive a happy martyrdom in the name of the Lord Jesus.

Next, the Turks, hearing that Peter the Hermit and Walter the Penniless were in Civitote, which is located above the city of Nicaea, went there with great joy to kill them and those who were with them. And when they had come, they encountered Walter with his men, (all of) whom the Turks soon killed. But Peter the Hermit had gone to Constantinople a short while before because he was unable to restrain that varied host, which was not willing to listen either to him or to his words. The Turks, indeed, rushed upon these people and killed many of them. Some they found sleeping, some lying down, others naked—all of whom they killed. With these people they found a certain priest celebrating mass, whom they straightway martyred upon the altar. Those who could escape fled to Civitote; others hurled themselves headlong into the sea, while some hid in the forests and mountains. But the Turks, pursuing them to the fortress, collected wood to burn them with the fort. The Christians who were in the fort, therefore, set fire to the wood that had been collected, and the fire, turning in the direction of the Turks, cremated some of them; but from the fire the Lord delivered our people at that time. Nevertheless, the Turks took them alive and divided them, just as they had done the others, and scattered them through all these regions, some to Chorosan, and others to Persia. This all happened in the month of October. The Emperor, upon hearing that the Turks had so scattered our people, was exceedingly glad and sent for them (the Turks) and had them cross the Strait. After they were across, he purchased all their arms. . . .

(*Albert.*) The Emperor was moved by compassion on hearing this humble narrative and ordered two hundred gold besants to be given to Peter; of that money which was called tartaron he disbursed one measure for his army. After that, Peter retired from the conference and from the palace of the Emperor. Although under the kind protection of the Emperor, he rested only five days in the fields and lands near Constantinople, where Walter the Penniless had likewise pitched his tents. Becoming companions from that very day, thereafter their troops, arms, and all necessary provisions were joined together. Next, after five days, they moved their tents and, with the aid of the Emperor, passed by boat over the Strait of St. George. Entering the confines of Cappadocia, they advanced through mountainous country into Nicomedia and there passed the night. After this, they pitched camp at the port called Civitote. There merchants were constantly bringing ships laden with supplies of wine, corn, oil, and barley, and with abundance of cheese, selling all to the pilgrims with just measure.

While they were rejoicing in this abundance of necessities and were resting their tired bodies, there came messengers from the most Christian Emperor. Because of the danger of ambushes and attacks from the Turks, they forbade Peter and his whole army from marching towards the mountainous region of the city of Nicaea, until a greater number of Christians should be added to their number. Peter heard the message, and he with all the Christian people assented to the counsel of the Emperor. They tarried there for the course of two months, feasting in peace and joy, and sleeping secure from all hostile attacks.

And so two months later, having become wanton and unrestrained because of ease and an inestimable abundance of food, heeding not the voice of Peter, but against his will, they entered into the region of the city of Nicaea and the realms of Soliman.[8] They took as plunder cattle, sheep, goats, the herds of the Greek servants of the Turks, and carried them off to their fellows. Peter, seeing this, was sorrowful in heart, knowing that they did it not with impunity. Whereupon he often admonished them not to seize any more booty contrary to the counsel of the Emperor, but in vain did he speak to a foolish and rebellious people. . . .

But the Teutons, seeing that affairs turned out so well for the Romans and the Franks, and that they returned unhindered so many times with their booty, were inflamed with an inordinate desire for plunder. About three thousand foot-soldiers were collected and about two hundred knights. . . .

And thus, after all the stronghold had been captured and its inhabitants driven out, they rejoiced in the abundance of food found there. And exulting in that victory, they in turn gave counsel that, by remaining in that fortress, they could easily obtain, through their own valor, the lands and principality of Soliman; that they would gather from all sides booty and food, and thus could easily weaken Soliman, until the promised army of the great leaders should approach. Soliman, the leader and chief of the army of the Turks, having heard of the arrival of the Christians, and of their plunder and booty, assembled from all Romania and the territory of Chorosan fifteen thousand of his Turks, most agile archers, very skilful in the use of bows of horn and bone. . . . Next, it is said, that after sunrise on the third day, Soliman with his followers arrived from Nicaea at the fortress which the Teutons had invaded. . . .

Therefore, the Turks, unable to drive out the Alemanni with this assault and shower of arrows, gathered all kinds of wood at the very gate of the fortress. They set fire to it and burned the gate and very many buildings which were within the citadel. As the heat of the flames became greater, some were burned to death; others, hoping for safety, leaped from the walls. But the Turks who were outside the walls cut down with swords those who were fleeing and took captive about two hundred who were pleasing in appearance and youthful in body; all the others they destroyed with sword and arrow. . . .

In the meantime, the truth was discovered and tumult arose among the people. The foot-soldiers came in a body to Reinald of Broyes, Walter the Penniless, to Walter of Breteuil, also, and to Folker of Orleans, who were leaders of Peter's army, to urge them to rise in a body in vindication of their brethren and against the audacity of the Turks. But they positively refused to go without the presence and the counsel of Peter. Then Godfrey Burel, master of the foot-soldiers, upon hearing their response, asserted that the timid by no means avail so much in war as the bold; and in sharp words he frequently reproached those men who prevented their other companions from pursuing the Turks to avenge their brethren. On the other hand, the leaders of the legion, unable to endure his insults and reproaches any longer, or those of their own followers, were deeply moved by wrath and indignation and promised that they would go against the strength and wiles of the Turks, even if it should happen that they died in battle.

Nor was there delay; at dawn on the fourth day, all the knights and foot-soldiers throughout the entire camp were ordered to arm themselves, to sound the trumpets, and to assemble for battle. Only the unarmed, the countless sick, and the women remained in camp.

THE FIRST CRUSADE

But all the armed men, to the number of 25,000 foot-soldiers and 500 knights in armor, pressed on their way together toward Nicaea, in order to avenge their brethren by provoking Soliman and the rest of the Turks to engage in battle. And so, divided and arrayed in six battle lines, with standards uplifted in each, they advanced on the right and on the left.

Boasting and shouting with vehement tumult and great clamor, they had scarcely advanced through the aforesaid forest and mountain region three miles from the port of Civitote, their halting place, (Peter being absent and unaware of all this), when lo! Soliman, with all his intolerable following, entered that same forest from the opposite side. He was coming down from the city of Nicaea to fall suddenly upon the Gauls in camp, intending at the point of the sword to wipe out and destroy them, unaware and unprepared. Upon hearing the approach and the violent outcry of the Christians, he marvelled greatly what this tumult meant, for all that the Christians had decided was unknown to him. Finding out straightway that they were pilgrims, Soliman addressed his men as follows: "Behold the Franks, against whom we were marching, are at hand. Let us withdraw from the forest and the mountains into the open plain, where we may freely engage in battle with them, and they can find no refuge." Accordingly, this was done without delay, at Soliman's command, and in deep silence they withdrew from the forest and the mountains.

But the Franks, unaware of Soliman's approach, advanced from the forest and the mountains with shouting and loud clamor. There they first beheld the battle lines of Soliman in the midst of the field, awaiting them for battle. When they had seen the Turks, they began to encourage one another in the name of the Lord. . . .

There Walter the Penniless fell, pierced by seven arrows which had penetrated his coat of mail. Reinald of Broyes and Folker of Chartres, men of the greatest renown in their own lands, fell in like martyrdom, destroyed by the enemy, though not without great slaughter of the Turks. But Walter of Breteuil, son of Waleramnus, and Godfrey Burel, master of the foot-soldiers, having slipped away in flight through briars and thickets, turned back along the narrow path where the entire band, withdrawn from battle, had gathered together. When the flight and desertion of these men became known, all turned in flight, hastening their course towards Civitote along the same route by which they had come, but with little defense against the enemy.

And so the Turks, rejoicing in the pleasing success of victory, were destroying the wretched band of pilgrims, whom they followed for a distance of three miles, killing them even at the camp of Peter. And going within the tents, they destroyed with the sword whomever they found, the weak and the feeble, clerics, monks, old women, nursing children, persons of every age. But they led away young girls whose face and form was pleasing in their eyes, and beardless youths of comely countenance. They carried off to Nicaea money, garments, mules, horses, and all valuable things, as well as the tents themselves.

But above the shore of the sea, near the aforesaid Civitote, was an ancient, deserted fortress. Towards that fortress three thousand pilgrims rushed in flight. They entered the ruined fortress in hope of defense. But finding no gates or other obstacles, and anxious and deprived of aid, they piled up their shields for a gate, along with a huge pile of rocks; and with lances, wooden bows, and slingstones, they bravely defended themselves from the enemy. But the Turks, seeing that they were having but little success in killing those inside, surrounded the fortress, which was without a roof, on all sides. They aimed their arrows high, so that, as they fell from the air in a shower, they would strike the bodies of the enclosed Christians, destroying the poor wretches; and that all the others, at the sight of this, might be compelled to surrender. In this way very many are said to have been wounded and killed there; but the rest, fearing yet more cruel treatment from the impious enemy, could not be compelled to come out either by force or by arms. . . .

The Emperor was moved with pity when he had heard from Peter about the siege and the fall of his men. So he summoned the Turcopoles and all the nations of his kingdom, and commanded them to go in all haste across the Strait to the aid of the fugitive and besieged Christians, and to drive the assaulting Turks from the siege. But the Turks, having learned of the Emperor's edict, moved from the fortress at midnight with their Christian captives and very great spoils, and so the pilgrim soldiers who had been shut up and besieged by the impious (Turks) were freed. . . .

(*Anna.*) But relying on the multitude of those who followed him, Peter did not heed the warning and, after crossing the strait, pitched camp at a little town called *Helenopolis*.

But since there were also Normans in his army, estimated at about ten thousand men, these, separating themselves from the rest of the body, devastated the region lying around the city of Nicaea, rioting most cruelly in every way. For they tore some of the children apart, limb from limb and, piercing others through with wooden stakes, roasted them in fire; likewise, upon those advanced in years they inflicted every kind of torture. When those in the city saw this being done, they opened the gates and went out against them. As a result, a fierce battle took place, in which, since the Normans fought ferociously, the citizens were hurled back into the fortress. The Normans, after gathering up all the plunder, again returned to *Helenopolis*. There a quarrel arose between themselves and the other pilgrims who had not gone off with them, a thing which usually happens in an affair of this kind, envy inflaming the wrath of those left behind, and a riotous fight followed the quarrel. The fierce Normans again separated (from the others) and captured *Xerogord* on their way at the first attack.

When this was learned, the Sultan sent Elchanes against them with a suitable number of troops. When he reached them, he recaptured *Xerogord*, killed some of the Normans with the sword, and carried off the rest as captives, planning at the same time, also, an attack upon those who had remained with Kuku-Peter. And he set ambushes at opportune places into which, when they left for Nicaea, they would unexpectedly fall and be killed. But knowing also of the avarice of the Gauls, he had summoned two men of bold spirit and ordered them to go to the camp of Kuku-Peter to announce that the Normans had captured Nicaea and were now sacking it to the utmost. This report, brought to the camp of Peter, excited all violently; for when the mention of plunder and riches was heard, they straightway set out in tumult on the road which leads to Nicaea, forgetful of their military training and of observing discipline in going out to battle. For the Latins are not only most fond of riches, as we said above, but when they give themselves to raiding any region for plunder, are also no longer obedient to reason, or any other check. Accordingly, since they were neither keeping order nor forming into lines, they fell into the ambush of the Turks around *Draco* and were wretchedly cut to pieces. Indeed, so great a multitude of Gauls and Normans were cut down by the Ishmaelite sword that when the dead bodies of the killed, which were lying all about in the place, were brought together, they made a very great mound, or hill, or look-out place, lofty as a mountain, and occupying a space very conspicuous for its width and depth. So high did that mound of bones tower, that some barbarians of the same race as the killed later used the bones of the slain instead of stones in constructing a wall, thus making that fortress a sort of sepulchre for them. It stands to this day, an enclosure of walls built with mixed rocks and bones.

And thus, after all had been wiped out in the slaughter, Peter returned with only a few to *Helenopolis*. The Turks, in their desire to get him into their power, again beset him with an ambush. But when the Emperor heard of the whole affair and learned how great was the slaughter of men, he held it very wrong that Peter should also be taken. Immediately, therefore, he summoned Catacalon Constantine Euphorbenus,[9] of whom mention has often been made in this history, and sent him with suitable forces on war-vessels across the sea as a succour to Peter. When the Turks saw him approach, they fled. . . .

2. *The Emperor's treatment of Hugh.* (October, 1096-January, 1097.)

(*Anna.*) As we said above, there were among the Latins such men as Bohemund and his fellow counsellors, who, eager to obtain the Roman Empire for themselves, had been looking with avarice upon it for a long time. Seeing an opening for their plans in the expedition which was promoted by Peter, they stirred up this huge movement; and, in order to deceive the more simple, they feigned a crusade against the Turks to regain the Holy Sepulchre and sold all their possessions. Moreover, a certain Hugh, brother of the King of France, who conducted himself with the spirit of a *navatus* on account of his wealth and power, and the nobility of his birth, decided to leave his fatherland, as if to set out for the Holy Sepulchre. Upon reaching this decision, he looked forward to a most glorious meeting and announced in letters full of swollen insolence to the Emperor:

"Know, O King, that I am King of Kings, and superior to all who are under the sky. You are now permitted to greet me, on my arrival, and to receive me with magnificence, as befits my nobility."

At this time the Governor[10] of Durazzo was John, son of Isaac, the *Sebastocrator*,[11] of whom we have spoken above. Nicolaus Maurocatacalon, in command of the fleet, had arranged his ships at stations around the port of Durazzo, so that he could make excursions and watch the seas, lest, perchance, pirate ships might secretly approach. To each of these men, therefore, the Emperor, after hearing this letter (from Hugh), immediately sent a message, bidding the Governor of Durazzo watch closely by land and sea for the arrival of this man, upon whose coming a messenger was to be sent quickly to the Emperor. Hugh, however, was to be received magnificently. He further ordered the commander of the fleet to be constantly alert and on the watch with every faculty awake, not with his usual negligence.

Meanwhile Hugh reached the seacoast of Longobardy; there he

sent envoys to the Governor of Durazzo, twenty-four in number, each decorated with gold and red breastplates. Along with them went Count Carpenter and that Helia who had fled from the Emperor at Thessalonica. These men addressed the following message to the Governor:

"Be it known to you, O Governor, that our lord, Hugh, will soon be here, bringing with him from Rome the golden banner of St. Peter; moreover, know that he is the highest leader of all the armies of France. Prepare yourself, therefore, to receive him and the army obeying him according to the dignity of his power; and gird yourself about to meet him."

While they were thus commanding the Governor, Hugh, as it is said, came from Rome into Longobardy; and leaving Bari toward Illyricum, he was caught by a most awful storm and lost the greater number of his ships, together with their oarsmen and passengers. The little boat in which he saved himself was cast up by the waves, as though they spewed it forth, on the seacoast which lies half way between Durazzo and another place called *Palus*. It, too, was half cut to pieces. Two men, who were on the watch for his arrival, met him after he had been saved and pressed him with these words: "The Governor is awaiting your arrival, desiring very much to enjoy your coming." Thereupon, Hugh immediately asked for a horse, and one of those men, dismounting from his horse, very dutifully gave it over to him. As a result, the Governor, after seeing that Hugh was safe, was the first to greet him and asked whither, and whence, and what dangers and evils had befallen him in sailing. And when he had been set upon his feet and refreshed with kind words, the Governor then put before him a well-prepared feast. After dinner he loosed him, but did not yet permit him to walk about freely, for all these things had been quickly announced to the Emperor, and the Governor was waiting to find out his commands from him.

When the Emperor was informed, he quickly sent Butumites to Epidamnus, which we have often called Durazzo, with orders to bring Hugh back with him and not to return by the direct road, but, by turning aside, to bring him to Constantinople through Philippopolis; for he was afraid of the forces and throngs of Gauls who followed. The Emperor treated him honorably with all kindness and gave him, in addition, considerable sums of money. He immediately urged the man to attach himself to him (the Emperor), and to bind himself by the customary oaths of the Latins. . . .

3. *Godfrey at Constantinople.* (December, 1096-May, 1097.)

(*Gesta.*) Duke Godfrey was the first of all the seignors to come to Constantinople with a great army. He arrived two days before the Nativity of Our Lord and camped outside the city, until the iniquitous Emperor ordered him to be lodged in a suburb of the city. And when the Duke had been so lodged, he used to send his squires, under pledge, day by day to fetch hay and other necessities for the horses. When now they planned to go wherever they wished, on the strength of their pledge, the evil Emperor placed a watch upon them and commanded his Turcopoles and Patzinaks to attack and kill them. Thereupon, when Baldwin, brother of the Duke, heard of this, he placed himself in ambush and then found them killing his people. He attacked them in great anger and, God helping, overcame them. Capturing sixty of them, he killed some and presented the rest to the Duke, his brother. When the Emperor had heard of this, he was exceedingly angry. Then the Duke, seeing that the Emperor was enraged, went with his men out of the suburb and encamped outside the city. Moreover, toward evening the Emperor ordered his forces to attack the Duke and the people of Christ. The unconquered Duke and the knights of Christ pursued these, killed seven of them, and drove the rest even to the gates of the city. The Duke, returning to his tents, remained there for five days, until he had entered into an agreement with the Emperor. The Emperor told him to cross the Strait of St. George, and promised to have every kind of market there, just as at Constantinople, and to distribute alms to the poor, upon which they could live.

(*Albert.*) With his entire band of pilgrims Godfrey withdrew to the city of Constantinople itself. There, after pitching their tents, they lodged, a strong and powerful band, protected by armor and all warlike equipment. And, behold, at the meeting Hugh, Drogo, William Carpenter, and Clarebold, set free by the Emperor, were present, rejoicing because of the arrival of the Duke and of his multitudes, and meeting the embrace of the Duke and of the others with many a kiss. And, likewise, the above mentioned messenger of the Emperor met the Duke, asking him to come to the palace of the Emperor with some of the chiefs of his army, that he might hear the word of the King. The rest of his multitude should remain outside the walls of the city. Scarcely had the Duke received the message when, behold, some strangers from the land of the Franks appeared by stealth in his camp. The strangers cautioned the Duke very strongly to beware of the wiles and alluring appearance of the Emperor, and by no means to go to the Em-

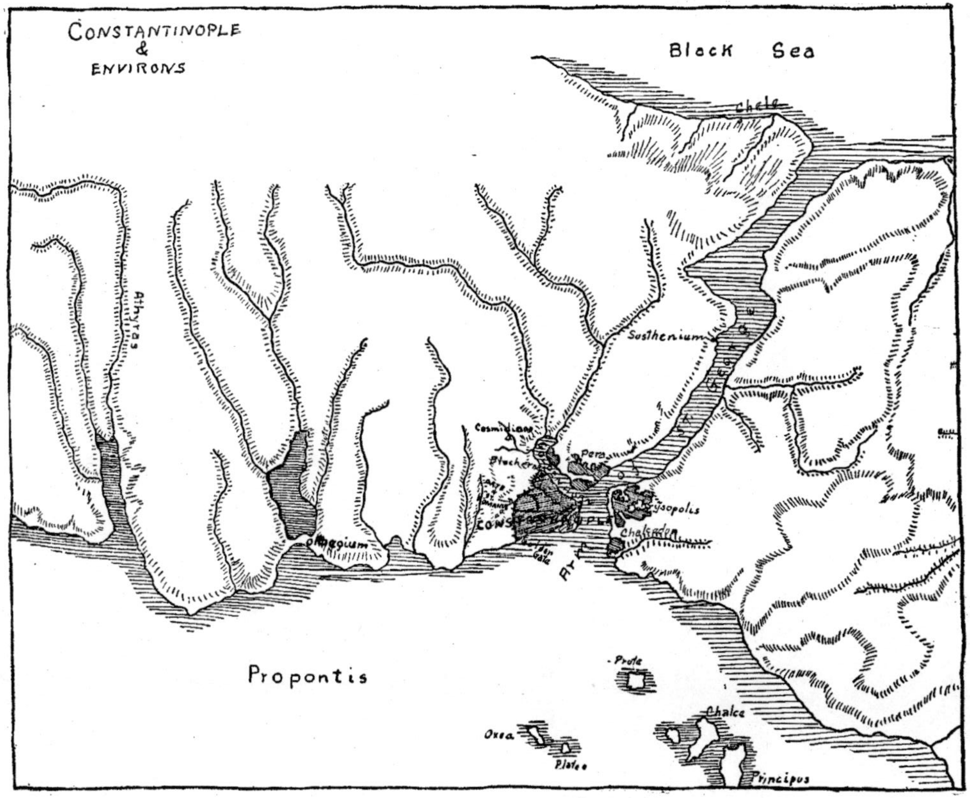

CONSTANTINOPLE & ENVIRONS
Black Sea
Chele
Athyras
Sosthenium
Cosmidion
Pera
Chrysopolis
Chalcedon
Rhegium
Propontis
Prote
Chalce
Oxea
Plateo
Principus

peror because of some flattering promise, but to sit outside the walls and listen carefully to all which the Emperor should propose to him. Thereupon, the Duke, so warned by the strangers, and taught by the deception of the Greeks, did not go to the Emperor.

For this reason, the Emperor, moved by a violent indignation towards the Duke and all his army, refused them the privilege of buying and selling. But when Baldwin, brother of the Duke, learned of the wrath of the Emperor and saw the need of the people and their very great lack of necessaries, he pleaded with the Duke and the leaders to plunder again the region and lands of the Greeks, and to collect spoils and food, until the Emperor, compelled by this damage, should again grant the privilege of buying and selling. Therefore, when the Emperor saw devastation and misfortune befalling the lands of his kingdom, he once more gave to all the privilege of buying and selling.

It was the time of the Nativity of the Lord. At that festal time, and in those days of peace and joy, it seemed to all praiseworthy, good, and acceptable before God that peace should be restored on both sides between the household of the Emperor and the Duke and all the mighty ones of the army. And so, when peace had been made, they withheld their hands from all plunder and hurt. Accordingly, during those four holy days they rested in all quiet and happiness before the walls of the city Constantinople.

Four days after, the legation of the Emperor went to the Duke asking, for the sake of the Emperor and his entreaties, that he would move his camp, and with his army lodge in the houses situated on the shore of the Strait, so that their tents might not become wet and worn from wintry cold and snow, which was threatening in that rainy season. Finally, the Duke and all the other leaders yielded to the will of the Emperor, and, after moving their tents, they, with all the Christian army, lodged in the castles and turreted buildings which were along the shore for a distance of thirty miles. From that day on successively they found and bought every abundance of food and necessities by order of the Emperor.

Shortly after, an embassy of the Emperor again appeared before the Duke, urging him to go and learn what the Emperor had to say. This the Duke absolutely refused to do, having been warned by the strangers of the craftiness of the Emperor. But he sent to him as messengers the distinguished men Conon, Count of Montaigu, Baldwin of Burg, and Godfrey of Ascha, who were to make excuses for him, speaking in this manner: "Duke Godfrey to the Emperor; trust and obedience. Willingly and eagerly would I come before you to look upon the wealth and glory of your household, were it not that many evil rumors, which have come to my ears regarding you, have terrified me. However, I know not whether these reports have been invented and spread about from envy or malice towards you." The Emperor, hearing this, warmly protested his innocence of all these charges, saying that never should the Duke or any of his followers fear any artifice on his part, but that he would serve and honor the Duke as his son, and the Duke's associates as his friends. Then the messengers of the Duke, on their return, reported favorably on all the good and faithful promises which they had heard from the Emperor's lips. But the Duke, still placing little faith in the honeyed promises of the Emperor, again refused him a conference. And so, between these messages back and forth, fifteen days rolled away.

Therefore the Emperor, recognizing the firmness of the Duke and that he could not be lured before him, again took offense and withdrew the privilege of buying barley, and fish, and then bread, so that the Duke, thus coerced, could not refuse to enter the presence of the Emperor. The Emperor, unsuccessful in changing the Duke's mind, one day had five hundred Turcopoles armed with bows and quivers taken in ships across the strait. Early in the morning, they shot the soldiers of the Duke with arrows; some they killed, others they wounded, keeping them all from the shore, so that they could not there buy the usual food.

This cruel report was carried immediately to the chair of the Duke. He thereupon ordered the trumpets to be sounded and all the people to arm themselves and return to the city of Constantinople itself, and there to replace their tents. After the trumpets had been sounded at this command of the Duke, all rushed to arms. They laid waste the buildings and towers in which they had been lodged, setting fire to some, pulling others to pieces, thus causing irreparable damage to Constantinople.

Finally, when the report of this great fire and destruction had reached the palace, the Duke became excessively alarmed, fearing that when the flaming buildings and the noise of a moving army had been noticed, the knights and archers of the Emperor would suddenly seize the bridge over which they had come from the city of Constantinople to the palatial residences. Therefore, without delay he sent Baldwin, his brother, with five hundred armored knights to seize the bridge, lest any force of the Emperor, anticipating him, should destroy it, and thus deny the pilgrims passage back and forth.

Baldwin had scarcely taken a stand on the middle of the bridge, when, behold, from right and left, Turcopoles (the soldiers of the

Emperor brought over on the ships) rushed upon them from all sides with arrows and fiercely attacked them. Baldwin, unable to resist from the bridge, hastened to escape their arrows by going across the bridge. Along the dry shore he swiftly betook himself to the other side of the bridge, (hoping) to hold it and keep watch upon the walls of the lord and master of the city while the entire army passed over that bridge, and the Duke with his men kept guard from the rear. In the meantime, from the gates opposite *St. Argenteus* an infinite band of Turcopoles and soldiers of every kind, equipped with bows and arms of every description, ran forward to attack Baldwin and the whole band of Christian people. But in the appointed place Baldwin, immovable and unconquered, withstood their every attack from early morning even to vespers, until the people were taken across the bridge and lodged in the camps placed before the walls of the city. Baldwin, with his five hundred knights, advanced fiercely upon these same Turcopoles who had come out from the gates and were attacking the people. Both sides having engaged in heavy battle, very many fell on this side and that, and very many horses of the Franks perished by arrows. But Baldwin, conquering at last, forced these harried and fleeing soldiers of the Emperor to go inside the gates. Then the Turcopoles and soldiers of the Emperor, indignant that they had been beaten and put to flight in war, rushed forth again from the gates in larger numbers to harass and attack the army.

Then the Duke arrived and, since it was night, brought an end to the fight, advising his brother to return to camp with all his forces, and to keep his men from fighting during the night. Likewise, the Emperor himself, fearing that the tempest of war would become more and more violent, and that his soldiers would fail and perish in the darkness of evening, commanded peace to be made, rejoicing that the Duke had been willing to withdraw his army from battle.

But after sunrise the next day, the people, surging forth at the command of the Duke, wandered about plundering the lands and kingdom of the Emperor for six days, so that, to say the least, the pride of the Emperor and his men seemed to be humbled. When this became known, the Emperor began to grieve and lament because his lands and kingdom were being thus devastated. Taking counsel immediately, he sent a message to the Duke to the effect that he should prohibit plunder and fire, and that he himself would give satisfaction in every respect to the Duke. The message ran as follows: "Let enmity between you and us cease. Let the Duke, upon receiving hostages as a pledge from me, advance without any doubt that he will come and return unharmed, assured of all the honor and glory which we are able to give him and his people." The Duke graciously agreed, provided hostages were given to whom he could trust his life and safety; then without doubt he would come to the Emperor, freely to speak by word of mouth.

Hardly had the legates of the Emperor departed after this response of the Duke, when, behold, certain other legates, coming to the same Duke from Bohemund, greeted him, speaking thus: "Bohemund, the most wealthy prince of Sicily and Calabria, asks that you by no means enter into peace with the Emperor; but that you withdraw to Adrianople and Philippopolis, cities of the Bulgarians, and pass the winter there. You may be certain that this same Bohemund will come to your aid with all his troops early in the month of March, to attack the Emperor and to invade his kingdom." After he had heard the message of Bohemund, the Duke put off answering it until the next day. Then, upon the counsel of his followers, he replied that neither for gain nor for the destruction of Christians had he left his country and kindred, but, rather, in the name of Christ to pursue the way to Jerusalem. He wished to accomplish this and to fight the designs of the Emperor, provided he could regain and keep his favor and good will. The messengers of Bohemund, upon learning the reply and intention of the Duke, were graciously commended by him and returned to the country of Apulia, reporting all as they had heard it from the lips of the Duke.

Learning of this new embassy and suggestion from Bohemund, the Emperor yet more earnestly urged the Duke and his friends to enter upon an agreement with him; he would give his most beloved son, John, as hostage, on condition that they would make peace, would pass through the country quietly, and would meet him in conference face to face. Furthermore, he would favor Godfrey and his followers with the privilege of buying all necessaries. When the Duke learned that these promises of the Emperor had been made in the form of a decree, he moved his camp from the wall of the city by the advice of his council and again withdrew across the bridge to take lodging in the fortified dwellings on the strait. He admonished all his people to remain at peace, and to purchase whatever was necessary without disturbance.

On the following day, he commanded Conon, Count of Montaigu, and Baldwin of Burg, most noble men and skilled in speaking, to come before him. He then confidently directed them to receive as hostage the Emperor's son, which was done. When, therefore, the Emperor's son had been brought and placed in faithful custody under the power of the Duke and his men, the Duke was carried at once by boat through the Strait to Constantinople. Accompanied by the distinguished men, Werner of Grez, Peter of Dampierre, and the other leaders, he boldly advanced to the Court of the Emperor and stood before him, that he might hear his word and reply to him by word of mouth. Baldwin, however, by no means entered then into the palace of the Emperor, but remained on the shore with the multitude.

Upon seeing the magnificence of the Duke and all his men, honorably clad, as they were, in splendid and rich apparel of purple and gold, bordered with ermine white as snow, with martin, and other kinds of fur, such as the princes of Gaul, especially, wear, the Emperor heartily admired their pomp and splendor. He first graciously received the Duke, then all his chiefs and companions, whom he honored with the kiss of peace. Moreover, the Emperor sat in majesty upon his throne, according to his custom, and did not rise to give the kiss to the Duke, or anyone. But the Duke, together with his men, bowed with bended knees to kiss so glorious and great an Emperor. When at last all had received the kiss, according to their rank, he spoke to the Duke in these words: "I have heard that you are the most mighty knight and prince in your land, a man most prudent and of perfect trust. In the presence of this multitude and more to come, I, therefore, take you for my adopted son; and all that I possess I place in your power, that through you my empire and lands may be saved and freed."

The Duke, appeased and seduced by these friendly and lofty words of the Emperor, not only recognized himself as his son, according to the custom of the country, but, likewise, giving him his hand, declared himself his vassal, together with the princes then present, who followed the Duke in the ceremony. Nor was there delay. Invaluable gifts of all kinds were brought from the treasury of the Emperor, both gold and silver, purples, mules, and horses, and all that he held valuable. So, indeed, the Emperor and the Duke were bound by the indissoluble bond of perfect faith and friendship, from the time of the Nativity of the Lord, when the agreement took place, even to a few days before Pentecost. Every week, four men, bearing gold besants, with ten measures of money called tartaron, were sent from the palace of the Emperor to the Duke to provide sustenance for the soldiers. Wonderful to relate! All, that the Duke distributed to his men from the gifts of the Emperor was forthwith returned to the treasury of the Emperor in exchange for food. Nor is this to be wondered at, for none but the Emperor's wares (such as wine, and oil, as well as grain, barley, and every kind of food) were in that whole kingdom. And thus the treasury of the Emperor was always filled with gold and could not be emptied by any extravagance.

After peace and concord between the Emperor and the Duke had been made on the conditions we have named, the Duke, still more certain of the Emperor's faith and friendship, returned to lodge in the buildings on the Strait and sent back with honor the Emperor's son, who had remained a hostage up to this time. On the day following, it was announced through the entire army, by order of the Duke, that peace and honor should be shown to the Emperor and to all in his command, and that justice should be preserved in transactions of buying and selling. Similarly, the Emperor proclaimed in all his realm that no one, under penalty of death, should harm or defraud any one of the army, but that they should sell all things with just weight and measure to the pilgrims, and, indeed, should lessen the price.

After these events, at the beginning of Lent, the Emperor summoned the Duke into his presence and begged him, on his pledge of friendship, to cross the sea and pitch his tents in Cappadocia, on account of the buildings which his incorrigible people were destroying. The Duke graciously assented to this, and, after crossing the river and pitching camp, he and his people tarried on the plains of Cappadocia.

After this, everything was gradually sold more dearly to the pilgrims, but, nevertheless, the gifts of the Emperor to the Duke were not at all diminished, for he feared him greatly. But the Duke, seeing the difficulty of buying necessaries and unable to endure the clamor of his people, went often by ship to the Emperor and complained to him about the high price of food stuffs. Then the Emperor, as though unaware of this, and unwilling to have it occur, again lightened the burden for all the pilgrims.

(*Anna.*) At that time, too, came Count Godfrey, who had crossed the sea with the other counts and was accompanied by an army of 10,000 knights and 70,000 foot-soldiers. He established his force about the Propontis, his camp extending from the bridge which was opposite Cosmidion up to *St. Phocas*. While the Emperor urged him to cross the strait of the Propontis, he went on from day to day contriving one excuse or another and put off the matter. The real reason, to state the matter simply, was that he was awaiting the arrival of Bohemund and the other counts. For, though in the beginning Peter had aroused this great expedition to adore the Holy Sepulchre, the other counts, Bohemund above all, were cherishing in mind the old grudge against the Emperor and were awaiting a favorable opportunity to take vengeance on him for the splendid victory which he had gained over Bohemund when the latter engaged him in battle at Larissa. And dreaming that if they were of one mind they could take Constantinople itself, they had combined with the same thought and purpose of which we have often made mention above. Thus, apparently they were making an expedition to Jerusalem; in reality, however, they wanted to divest the Emperor of his kingdom and take Constantinople. But the Emperor, long since acquainted with their wiles, by letter ordered forces of Gentiles with their leaders to be stationed by squadrons from the Athyras river up to Philea, a seaport on the Black Sea. (He also ordered them) to watch in ambush for anyone sent, perchance, by Godfrey to Bohemund and the rest of the counts who were following, or by these, in turn, to him, and to deny these messengers all passage.

In the meantime, while this was going on, the following incident occurred, somewhat in this way. The Emperor had summoned before him some of the counts who had come with Godfrey, in order to urge that they consent to persuade Godfrey to carry out the promise which he had made under oath. While the time was thus being dragged out longer (than expected), for the reason that the Latin race is by nature exceedingly garrulous and wordy, there was reported to these people the false rumor that the counts had been taken into custody at the Emperor's command. Thereupon, the Latin legions surged together in a huge crowd and moved upon Byzantium and without delay utterly destroyed the palaces which are situated toward the swamp called *Argyra*. At the same time they tried the walls of the city, not with siege machines, for they were not at hand, but, trusting in their multitude, they resorted to a piece of insolence: they dared to set fire to the lower gate of the palace located near the Temple, which had been built in olden times by one of the Emperors under the invocation of Nicolaus, the greatest of the holy pontiffs.

At the sight of the Latin legions, not only did all of the basest class, the foolish and the unwarlike, groan, cry out, and beat their breasts in their fear, not knowing what else to do; but even the zealous adherents of the Emperor, mindful of that Friday on which the seizure of the city had formerly taken place,[12] feared the present day lest vengeance should fall violently upon them for the deeds committed at that time. However, all who had any acquaintance with military practice and skill poured in at the regal palace, each man coming by himself. But the Emperor neither armed his sides with breastplate of scale-armor, his left hand with a shield, his right with a spear, nor girded himself about with a sword;

but, clothed in royal raiment, he seated himself upon the imperial throne, as though secure. Thus, on the one hand, he reassured all, injecting courage into their hearts by his happy look, and, on the other, he discussed with his advisers and military leaders plans for coming events. First of all, he absolutely refused to have any armed band led outside of the walls against the Latins, this for a twofold reason: First, because this was the most sacred of days, for it was Friday of the greatest, of Holy, Week, when the Saviour had undergone ignominious death for all. In the second place, he refused to engage in civil war between Christians. Therefore, by means of frequent messengers to the Latins he wished to bring about the cessation of the undertaking which they had begun, saying: "Remember that on this day there died for us the Lord, who for the sake of our salvation did not fear to endure the cross, nails and the lance, punishments befitting criminals. But if your desire for a fight is so great, we, too, will stand ready after the coming day of the Lord's resurrection."

But the Latins were so far from yielding to him that they closed their ranks and threw missles in such profusion that they struck across the chest one of the men standing near the Emperor's throne. At the sight of this, most of those who were standing near fell back, here and there, from the Emperor, while he, meanwhile, remained on his throne, not only without any sign of fear, but likewise reassuring them and chiding them greatly for their fear. All admired his presence of mind.

Finally, when he saw that the Latins, bereft of all shame, were invading the walls of the city and scorning his useful counsel, he first summoned his son-in-law, Nicephorus,[13] and commanded him to take with him the strongest men and those skilled in shooting arrows and go to the top of the wall. He advised him, at the same time, to hurl down weapons on the Latins as frequently as possible, but, for the most part, harmlessly, with bad aim, in order to frighten them, not to kill them. For, as was said above, the Emperor respected the religious significance of the day and did not wish to engage in civil war between Christians. At the same time, he ordered some other chosen leaders (each with his cohorts, most of them provided with bows, but some armed with long lances) to charge forth suddenly from the gate which is close to St. Romanus, thus presenting the appearance of violence to the enemy. The battle line was so arranged that each spearman should march protected on each side by bowmen armed with shields. Thus arrayed, they were ordered to advance against the enemy at a slow pace, and archers, instructed to turn about frequently here and there, were sent ahead to wound the Gauls at close quarters. Now, when the two lines were a slight distance apart, they were then to order those bowmen who had spearmen at their side to use their bows carefully, aiming at the horses of the enemy, sparing the riders; and it was further ordered that the spearmen should charge with loose reins upon the Latins and with the full weight of their horses. He gave that order with this in mind, that when their horses were wounded, the violence of the Gallic attack would languish and the Romans would not easily be pursued by the knights; and this, also, which he especially desired, that as little Christian blood as possible should be shed. These men with ready courage did what they had been commanded by the Emperor, and, after the gates had been suddenly opened, they rushed against the enemy, now giving free rein to their horses, now checking them. Thus they killed many of the enemy; a few of our men were wounded in this affair that day. . . . At length the Emperor sent in his own forces and scattered and routed the legions of the Latins.

On the next day, Hugh set out to meet Godfrey and counselled him to make peace with the Emperor, if he did not want to try the warlike skill of the latter anew, to his own hurt, but especially to pledge that he would keep inviolate his faith to the Emperor. Godfrey received him very bitterly saying, "Have not you, who came from home in the spirit and surroundings of a king, with great forces and wealth, now debased yourself from highest dignity to the condition and lot of a humble client? And then, as if this were some great and distinguished deed, you have come to urge me, too, to this same fate!" In reply to him Hugh said, "In the first place, we ought not to have departed from our own lands, and we ought to have stayed away from those of others; but after we have come hither to this place, where we may have necessities by the benevolent care and providence of him who rules here, our business will not turn out happily unless we accede to his counsels and demands."

When Hugh had returned, the matter only made worse, the Emperor, informed through other sources that the rest of the counts who were following Godfrey at a distance were already near, sent chosen leaders with their forces to the army of Godfrey with orders to persuade him, but, if necessary, to compel him to cross the Strait. When the Latins saw them coming, without delay or even question of what was wanted, they sprang up immediately to blows and battle. There occurred a most bitter conflict between them, in which many on both sides fell. Those of our men who rushed too boldly into the fray were wounded, but, as the Romans were conducting themselves valiantly, the Latins turned their backs. And thus, at length, Godfrey after a short time obeyed the Emperor. He came to him and in solemn manner took the oath which was demanded of him: that whatever cities, lands, or fortresses he should thenceforth capture from the barbarians (which cities, lands, or fortresses had formerly belonged to the Emperor) he would in good faith hand over to the military leaders or prefects who should be sent by the Emperor for this very purpose. When this had been confirmed by oath, Godfrey was enriched with great gifts by the Emperor; he was received in the imperial palace and magnificently dined at the royal table. He then crossed the Strait and pitched his camp at *Pelecanum*,[14] the Emperor seeing to it that an ample supply of necessities was provided everywhere.

4. *Alexius and the minor leaders.* (February-April, 1097?)

(*Anna.*) After this, there arrived shortly a count who was called Raoul.[15] He encamped with the counts of his following near the Propontis, close to the monastery called the Patriarch's; the rest of his forces he spread out even to Sosthenium itself. Moreover, as he, like Godfrey, was putting off the day of crossing, awaiting the arrival of the other forces and counts who were yet to come, the Emperor, conjecturing rightly about the future, feared that they would arrive and took care with every act and counsel to hasten the transportation of these men. For this task he summoned Opus, a man second to none in valor, prudence, and military knowledge, and ordered him to go with other valiant troops by land to the camp of Raoul. He commanded him to use every means which necessity should demand to compel him and all his men to cross the Strait. When Opus saw that Raoul was by no means ready to obey the Emperor, nay, was even insolent and haughty, offering many threats against the Emperor, he made ready his arms and drew up a line of battle, hoping, perchance, to terrify the barbarians with this sight and thus to induce them to cross to the other shore. But Raoul and his Gauls drew up their lines quicker than the word and immediately entered into a great battle with Opus. By chance Pegasius arrived at that very time with ships in which to take the forces to Asia. Watching the fight on shore from the sea, and seeing that the Gauls were charging the Roman army too fiercely, he disembarked and attacked the Gauls from the rear. Hence, many were killed, and very many were wounded. Thus it was brought about that those who survived the battle now sought passage over to the other side. But the Emperor, with his most farsighted caution, foresaw that when Raoul's knights should tell Godfrey what had befallen them, they would arouse the latter against himself. So he very freely granted their request, but when they had been placed on ship, he took them by sea to the Sepulchre of the Lord, the very thing which they especially sought. He likewise sent messages to those counts who were even then expected and held forth words of good-will, bidding them expect every good; and so, when they came to Constantinople, they did with alacrity all that was demanded of them. But so much for Count Raoul.

Following the latter closely came an innumerable multitude gathered from almost all the provinces and lands of Gaul, together with the kings, dukes, counts, and even bishops, who led them. The Emperor sent his men out to meet them and received them with words full of grace, for he was conspicuous for his foresight of what was to happen and for seizing with dexterity upon the means useful for the occasion. In addition, he bade men appointed for this purpose see that there was an abundance of food-stuffs and needed articles ready everywhere for the coming armies, lest any occasion, or pretext, be afforded them for venturing upon any hostile act whatsoever. However, as they flowed together at Constantinople, one might have likened them to the stars of the sky, or to the sands which have been cast up on shores of the sea. Truly, as Homer said, there were as many heads of men as there are leaves and flowers that fall in the autumn. All these were hastening to reach the city of Constantine. Nay, even though I desire to report the names of their leaders themselves, I cannot bring them to mind to set down; for my tongue becomes dumb, partly at the barbarous names, which it is not possible to pronounce because of their unexplained sound, and partly, as I look back, at the huge number of them. But what would be gained by taking the trouble to write the names of such a multitude, the very sight of whom wearied those who were there?

The armies which reached the city at the same time were located by the Emperor's command near the monastery of Cosmidion, the camp extending so widely that it touched the Temple itself. Not nine heralds restrained this throng by shouting, as in ancient times they restrained the Greeks, but valiant sturdy knights, who followed the multitude of Latins in sufficient number, gave ample assurance that they would heed the commands of the Emperor. He desired them to subscribe to the same oath by which Godfrey had bound himself and called them before him, one by one, to discuss with them separately what he wished. Those whom he found more amenable he used as intercessors in overcoming the reluctance of the more obstinate. Nevertheless, since those who were awaiting the impending arrival of Bohemund were not won over, but were thinking up new demands to be made from the Emperor and adding additional demands to those already made, the Emperor very easily frustrated the designs which were concealed by them. Approaching them in various ways, he at length compelled them to yield to the oath of Godfrey, who had been summoned across the water from *Pelecanum* in order to be present at the taking of the solemn oath.

When all were assembled for this purpose, Godfrey likewise present, and the oath had already been taken, a certain one of the counts, a noble, forsooth, mounted the Emperor's throne and seated himself on it. The Emperor refrained from saying anything against the man, for he had long been sufficiently acquainted with the unwonted arrogance of the Latins. Count Baldwin, however, approached and, grasping the man by the hand, shook him and, with much cursing, said: "You are not permitted on solemn oath to do anything like this here, especially after you have professed service to the Emperor, for it is not customary for Roman Emperors to let their subjects share their throne. Sworn servants, moreover, should observe the customs of the land in which they are." Upon hearing this, the man said nothing, indeed, to Baldwin, but gazing on the Emperor with angry eyes, he muttered to himself in his native tongue words like these, "Behold, how boorish a person sits here alone, while such dukes as we stand about him!" The motion of the Latin man's lips did not escape the Emperor, who immediately called an interpreter acquainted with his tongue. When he learned the meaning of the speech, he said nothing to the Latin then, but kept his words in mind. When the ceremony was over and the counts were saying farewell to the Emperor, one by one, as they were about to leave, he had the very arrogant and impudent Latin summoned and asked him who, and whence he was, and of what race he was born.

He answered: "I am a pure Frank of noble birth. Moreover, I know one (thing). In the section of the country where I was born stands a temple, built long ago, in which any person who wishes to engage in battle with someone, and does not hesitate to give his name freely in professing this boldness, is wont to implore the aid of the saint, delaying there until an adversary appears who dares to join hands with him. In this meeting place I remained for a long time, awaiting someone to contend with me; but there was never anyone who dared."

The Emperor, hearing these things, replied: "Well, if in your quest of an adversary you did not then find one, the time is now at hand which will afford you more than enough opponents. However, I advise you not to place yourself either among those who bring up the rear line of battle or among those who precede the standards, but that you take a place between the first and last ranks. For I know from long experience the manner of fighting among the Turks."

And he gave this salutary advice not only to him, but also to all the others, to whom he told what was about to happen, urging strongly that they should not pursue the Turks too eagerly, since by the will of God they would conquer these barbarians anyway. He urged, also, that they should look out for ambushes, lest they fall into them and be killed. So much may be said about Godfrey and Raoul and the others following them.

5. *Bohemund and the Emperor.* (April 10-May, 1097.)

(*Gesta.*) When the Emperor heard that the most honorable man, Bohemund, had come to him, he commanded that he be received with honor and carefully lodged outside the city. When he had been so lodged, the evil Emperor sent for him to come to speak with him in secret. Thither, also, came Duke Godfrey with his brother, and at length the Count of St. Gilles approached the city. Then the Emperor in anxious and fervid rage was pondering some way by which they might seize these knights of Christ adroitly and by fraud. But Divine Grace disclosing (his plans), neither time nor place was found by him, or his men, to do them ill. At last, all the noble leaders who were at Constantinople were assembled. Fearing lest they should be deprived of their country, they decided in their counsels and ingenious calculations that our dukes, counts, or all the leaders, ought to make an oath of fealty to the Emperor. These absolutely refused and said: "It is indeed unworthy of us, and, furthermore, it seems to us unjust to swear an oath to him." Perchance we shall yet often be deceived by our leaders. In the end, what were they to do? They say that under the force of necessity they humiliated themselves, willy-nilly, to the will of the most unjust Emperor. To that most mighty man Bohemund, however, whom he greatly feared because in times past he (Bohemund) had often driven him from the field with his army,[16] the Emperor said that, if he willingly took the oath to him, he would give him, in return, land in extent from Antioch fifteen days journey, and eight in width. And he (the Emperor) swore to him in such wise that, if he loyally observed that oath, he would never pass beyond his own land.[17] Knights, so brave and so sturdy, why did they do this? For the reason that they were constrained by much necessity. The Emperor also gave to all our men a pledge of security. He likewise took oath that he, together with his army, would come with us, by land and by sea; that he would afford us faithfully a market by land and sea, and that he would diligently make good our losses; in addition, that he did not wish, and would not permit, any of our pilgrims to be disturbed or come to grief on their way to the Holy Sepulchre.

(*Anna.*) But when Bohemund had arrived at Apri with his companions, realizing both that he was not of noble birth, and that for lack of money he had not brought with him a large enough army, he hastened, with only ten Gauls, ahead of the other counts and arrived at Constantinople. He did this to win the favor of the Emperor for himself, and to conceal more safely the plans which he was concocting against him. Indeed, the Emperor, to whom the schemes of the man were known, for he had long since become acquainted with the hidden and deceitful dealings of this same Bohemund, took great pains to arrange it so that before the other counts should come he would speak with him alone. Thus having heard what Bohemund had to say, he hoped to persuade him to cross before the others came, lest, joined with them after their coming, he might pervert their minds.

When Bohemund had come to him, the Emperor greeted him with gladness and inquired anxiously about the journey and where he had left his companions. Bohemund responded to all these things as he thought best for his own interests, affably and in a friendly way, while the Emperor recalled in a familiar talk his bold undertakings long ago around Durazzo and Larissa and the hostilities between them at that time. Bohemund answered, "Then I confess I was your enemy, then I was hostile. But, behold, I now stand before you like a deserter to the ranks of the enemy! I am a friend of your Majesty." The Emperor proceeded to scrutinize the man, considering him cautiously and carefully and drawing out what was in his mind. As soon as he saw that Bohemund was ready to consent to swear an oath of fealty to him, he said, "You must be tired from the journey and should retire to rest. We will talk tomorrow about anything else."

So Bohemund departed to Cosmidion, where hospitality was prepared for him, and he found a table richly laden with an abundance of food and condiments of all kinds. Then the cooks came and showed him the uncooked flesh of animals and birds, saying: "We have prepared this food which you see on the table according to our skill and the custom of this region; but if, perchance, these please you less, here is food, still uncooked, which can be prepared just as you order." The Emperor, because of his almost incredible tact in handling men, had commanded that this be done and said by them. For, since he was especially expert in penetrating the secrets of minds and in discovering the disposition of a man, he very readily understood that Bohemund was of a shrewd and suspicious nature; and he foresaw what happened. For, lest Bohemund should conceive any suspicion against him, the Emperor had ordered that raw meats be placed before him, together with the cooked, thus easily removing suspicion. Neither did his conjecture fail, for the very shrewd Bohemund took the prepared food, without even touching it with the tips of his fingers, or tasting it, and immediately turned around, concealing, nevertheless, the suspicion which occurred to him by the following ostentatious show of liberality. For under the pretext of courtesy he distributed all the food to those standing around; in reality, if one understood rightly, he was dividing the cup of death among them. Nor did he conceal his cunning, so much did he hold his subjects in contempt; for he this day used the raw meat which had been offered to him and had it prepared by his own cooks after the manner of his country. On the next day he asked his men whether they were well. Upon their answering in the affirmative, that they were indeed very well, that not even one felt even the least indisposed, he disclosed his secret in his reply: "Remembering a war, once carried on by me against the Emperor, and that strife, I feared lest perchance he had intended to kill me by putting deadly poison in my food."

Such a man was Bohemund. Never, indeed, have I seen a man so dishonest. In everything, in his words as well as in his deeds, he never chose the right path; and when anyone deviates from the moderation of virtue, it makes little difference to whatsoever extreme he goes, for he is always far from honesty.

For the rest, the Emperor then summoned Bohemund and exacted from him the usual oath of the Latins. The latter, knowing well his own resources, and realizing that he was neither of noble birth nor well supplied by fortune with wealth, for he had no great force, but only a moderate number of Gauls with him, and being, besides, dishonest in character, readily submitted himself to the will of the Emperor.

After this, the Emperor saw to it that a room in the palace was so filled with a collection of riches of all kinds that the very floor was covered with costly raiment, and with gold and silver coins, and certain other less valuable things, so much so that one was not able even to walk there, so hindered was he by the abundance of these things. The Emperor ordered the guide suddenly and unexpectedly to open the doors, thus revealing all this to Bohemund. Amazed at the spectacle, Bohemund exclaimed: "If such riches were mine, long ago I would have been lord of many lands!" The guide answered, "And all these things the Emperor bestows upon you today as a gift." Most gladly Bohemund received them and with many gracious thanks he left, intending to return to his rest in the inn. But changing his mind when they were brought to him, he, who a little before had admired them, said: "Never can I let myself be treated with such ignominy by the Emperor. Go, take those things and carry them back to him who sent them." The Emperor, knowing the base fickleness of the Latins, quoted this common saying, "Let the evil return to its author." Bohemund having heard this, and seeing that the messengers were busily bringing these things back to him, decided anew about the goods which he had sent back with regret, and, like a polypus, changed in a moment, he now showed a joyous countenance to the bearers. For he was quick, and a man of very dishonest disposition, as much surpassing in malice and intrepidity all the Latins who had crossed over as he was inferior to them in power and wealth. But even though he thus excelled all in great cunning, the inconstant character of the Latins was also in him. Verily, the riches which he spurned at first, he now gladly accepted. For when this man of evil design had left his country in which he possessed no wealth at all (under the pretext, indeed, of adoring at the Lord's Sepulchre, but in reality endeavoring to acquire for himself a kingdom), he found himself in need of much money, especially, indeed, if he was to seize the Roman power. In this he followed the advice of his father and, so to speak, was leaving no stone unturned.

Moreover, the Emperor, who understood fully his wicked intention and perverse mind, skillfully managed carefully to remove whatever might further Bohemund's ambitious designs. Wherefore, Bohemund, seeking a home for himself in the East and using Cretan scheming against Cretans, did not obtain it. For the Emperor feared lest, after obtaining power, he would use it to place the Latin counts under obligation to him, finally thus accomplishing easily what he wished. But since he did not want Bohemund to surmise that he was already discovered, the Emperor misled him by this hope: "Not yet," he said, "has the time come for the thing which you say; but after a little it shall come about by your fortitude and trust in me."

After the Emperor had bestowed upon the Gauls promises, gifts, and honors of every kind, the next day he solemnly took his seat on the imperial throne. Summoning Bohemund and all the counts, he talked about the things which would happen to them on the journey. He wanted, likewise, to show what methods and means of warfare the Turks were wont to employ, and to give directions how the line of battle should be drawn up against them, how ambushes should be set, and how they ought not to follow the fleeing Turks too far. And so, both by gifts of money and by flattering speeches, he soothed the rude nature of the people, and, after giving useful advice, he persuaded them to pass over the sea. . . .

6. *Raymond and the Emperor* (April 21-May 16, 1097.)

(*Raymond.*) Although events have lightly accompanied the writer so far with happy and favorable step, they now follow with so great a weight of bitterness and sorrow that it grieves me to have begun what I have vowed to finish. What, indeed, is the most important and first matter that I shall proceed to mention? The most false and detestable deceit of the Emperor's admonition? Or the most base flight and unthinkable desperation of our army? Or shall I leave a monument of perpetual sorrow by enumerating the deaths of such great princes? Let any one who desires to know this, however, seek it rather from others than from me. This one very memorable event I consider to merit excuse from silence. When our men thought of abandoning the camp, taking flight, deserting their fellows, and leaving everything that they had brought along from such distant regions, they were brought back by the saving deeds of penance and fast to such staunch fortitude that only shame at their former desperate condition and flight most deeply affected them. So much may be said about this.

Accordingly, when the Count had been received most honorably by the Emperor and his princes, the Emperor demanded of the Count homage and the oath which the other princes had made to him. The Count replied that he had not come hither to make another his lord or to fight for any other than the One for whom he had left his country and his possessions. Nevertheless, if the Emperor would go to Jerusalem with the army, he would commit himself and his men and all his goods to him. But the Emperor excused himself from the journey by saying that he greatly feared lest the Germans, Hungarians, Cumans, and other wild peoples would devastate his empire, if he made the journey with the pilgrims. Meanwhile the Count, upon hearing of the flight and death of his men, believed that he had been betrayed, and through certain of our princes he vehemently charged the Emperor with having committed treason. But Alexius said that he did not know that our men had devastated his kingdom, and that he and his men had suffered many injuries; that there was nothing of which the Count could complain, except that while the army of the Count in its usual manner was devastating the villages and towns, it took to flight upon seeing his (the Emperor's) army. Nevertheless, he promised that he would give satisfaction to the Count and offered Bohemund as a hostage for the satisfaction. They went to trial; the Count, according to law, was compelled to give up his hostage.

Meanwhile, our army came to Constantinople; and after this the Bishop, whom the army had left ill at Durazzo, followed us with his brother. Alexius asked (homage) again and again and promised that he would give much to the Count if he would do him the desired homage as the other princes had done. The Count, however, was constantly meditating how he might avenge the injury to his men, and drive away from himself and his followers the disgrace of such great infamy. But the Duke of Lorraine, the Count of Flanders, and the other princes deprecated such action, saying that it would be very foolish to fight with Christians when the Turks were threatening. Bohemund, indeed, promised that he would aid the Emperor, if the Count made any attempt against the Emperor, or if he no longer refused homage and oath. Thereupon, the Count took counsel with his men and swore that neither in person nor through another would he sully the life or honor of Alexius. And when asked about homage, he replied that he would not do it at the risk of his head, wherefore the Emperor gave him few gifts.

(*Gesta.*) The Count of St. Gilles, however, was lodged outside the city in a suburb, and his force had remained behind. Accordingly, the Emperor bade the Count do homage and fealty to him, as the others had done. And while the Emperor was making these demands, the Count was meditating how he might take vengeance on the army of the Emperor. But Duke Godfrey and Robert, Count of Flanders, and the other princes said to him that it would be unjust to fight against Christians. The wise man, Bohemund, also said that if the Count should do the Emperor any injustice, and should refuse to do him fealty, he himself would take the part of the Emperor. Accordingly, the Count, after receiving the advice of his men, swore that he would not consent to have the life and honor of Alexius sullied either by himself or by anyone else. When he was called upon for homage, he answered that he would not do this at the risk of his head.

Then the host of Lord Bohemund approached Constantinople. Tancred, indeed, and Richard of Principati, and almost the whole of Bohemund's force with them, crossed the Strait by stealth, to avoid the oath to the Emperor. And now the army of the Count of St. Gilles approached Constantinople. The Count remained there with his own band. Therefore the illustrious man, Bohemund, stayed behind with the Emperor, in order to plan with him how they might provide a market for the people who were beyond the city of Nicaea.

(*Anna.*) One of them especially, the Count of St. Gilles, he particularly favored because he saw in him superior prudence, tested sincerity, candor of bearing, and, finally, such great zeal for truth that he never placed anything before it. He was as far superior to all the other Latins in all virtues as the sun is above the other stars. For this reason, therefore, the Emperor kept him near him for the time being.

When at the wish of the Emperor all had crossed over the Propontis and had arrived at *Damalium*, Alexius, thus relieved from care and trouble, had the Count of St. Gilles summoned and in talks showed him very distinctly what he thought might happen to the Latins on the way. At the same time, he disclosed to him what suspicions he was cherishing about the intentions and plans of the Gauls. He often spoke freely about them with the Count of St. Gilles, opening the doors of his heart to him, as it were, and making everything clearly known to him. He sometimes warned him, also, to keep close watch against the malice of Bohemund, so as to check him immediately if he should try to break his agreement, and to strive in every way to destroy his schemes. The Count of St. Gilles replied: "Since Bohemund has inherited perjury and deceit, as it were, it would be very surprising if he should be faithful to those promises which he has made under oath. However, I will try to carry out what you command, in so far as I can." Then at the wish of the Emperor he departed, joining himself to the forces of the united Gauls. . . .

7. *Robert of Normandy and Stephen at the Emperor's court.* May 14-May 28, 1097.)

(*Fulcher.*) We could not enter that city, for the Emperor, fearing that possibly we would do some damage to him, did not wish to let us. So it was necessary that we buy our daily supplies outside the walls. These, by the order of the Emperor, the citizens brought to us. We were not allowed to enter the city many at a time. Only five or six per hour were permitted; thus, while some were leaving, others were then entering to pray in the churches.

Oh, what a great and beautiful city is Constantinople! How many churches and palaces it contains, fashioned with wonderful skill! How many wonderful things may be seen even in the streets or courts! It would be too tedious to enumerate what wealth there is there of every kind, of gold, of silver, of every kind of robes, and of holy relics. There traders at all times bring by boat all the necessities of man. They have, I judge, about twenty thousand eunuchs constantly living there.

Then, after we were sufficiently rested, our leaders, having taken counsel, made under oath a treaty with the Emperor at his own instigation. This treaty Bohemund and Duke Godfrey, who had preceded us, had already made. But Count Raymond then refused to subscribe to it. The Count of Flanders, though, took the oath like the rest. For it was essential that all establish friendship with the Emperor, since without his counsel and aid we would not be able to make the journey easily, nor would those who were to follow us along the same route. The Emperor himself supplied them with as much as they wished from his treasury and his wardrobe; and he gave them horses and money, of which they were much in need for completing such a journey. When this had been accomplished, we crossed the sea which is called the Arm of St. George and hastened then to the city of Nicaea.

(*Stephen.*) Count Stephen to the Countess Adele, most sweet friend, his wife; whatever more sweet or pleasing greeting her mind can conceive.

Be it known, to your delight, that, after a successful journey to Romania, I continue in all honor and bodily health. I took pains to send you, by letter from Constantinople, a detailed account of the course of my life and pilgrimage, but, lest some misfortune befall that messenger, I am re-writing the letter to you.

I arrived at Constantinople with great joy, by the grace of God. The Emperor, verily, received me with dignity and honor and with the greatest affection, as if I were his own son, and he loaded me with most bountiful and precious gifts. And in the whole of our army of God there is neither duke, nor count, nor other person of power whom he trusts or favors more than myself. Verily, my beloved, his Imperial Highness has very often urged, and urges, that we commend one of our sons to him; he promises, moreover, that he will accord him so great and such distinguished honor that he (the boy) will not in the least envy our own (position). In truth, I say to you there is no man today like him under heaven, for he is enriching all our princes most bountifully, is relieving all our knights with gifts and refreshing all the poor with feasts. Near the city of Nicaea there is a fortress, Civitote by name, near which runs an arm of the sea. Through this the pious Emperor's own ships rush by night and day to Constantinople, whence they carry food to the camp, where it is distributed daily among the countless poor. Also, in our times, as it seems to us, there has not been a prince so distinguished for general integrity of character. Your father, my beloved, gave many and large gifts, but he was almost as nothing in comparison with this man.[18] I have taken pleasure in writing these little things about him to you, that you may know a little what kind of man he is.

8. *Siege and capture of Nicaea.* (May 14-June 19, 1097.)

(*Gesta.*) And thus Duke Godfrey went first to Nicomedia, together with Tancred and all the rest, and they were there for three days. The Duke, indeed, seeing that there was no road open by which he could conduct these hosts to the city of Nicaea, for so great an army could not pass through the road along which the others had passed before, sent ahead three thousand men with axes and swords to cut and clear this road, so that it would lie open even to the city of Nicaea. They cut this road through a very narrow and very great mountain and fixed back along the way iron and wooden crosses on posts, so that the pilgrims would know the way. Meanwhile, we came to Nicaea, which is the capital of all Romania, on the fourth day, the day before the Nones of May, and there encamped. However, before Lord Bohemund had arrived, there was such scarcity of bread among us that one loaf was sold for twenty or thirty *denarii*. After the illustrious man, Bohemund, came, he ordered the greatest market to be brought by sea, and it came both ways at the same time, this by land and that by sea, and there was the greatest abundance in the whole army of Christ.

Moreover, on the day of the Ascension of the Lord we began to attack the city on all sides, and to construct machines of wood, and wooden towers, with which we might be able to destroy towers on the walls. We attacked the city so bravely and so fiercely that we even undermined its wall. The Turks who were in the city, barbarous horde that they were, sent messages to others who had come up to give aid. The message ran in this wise: that they might approach the city boldly and in security and enter through the middle gate, because on that side no one would oppose them or put them to grief. This gate was besieged on that very day—the Sabbath after the Ascension of the Lord—by the Count of St. Gilles and the Bishop of Puy. The Count, approaching from another side, was protected by divine might, and with his most powerful army gloried in terrestrial strength. And so he found the Turks coming against us here. Armed on all sides with the sign of the cross, he rushed upon them violently and overcame them. They turned in flight, and most of them were killed. They came back again, reinforced by others, joyful and exulting in assured (outcome) of battle, and bearing along with them the ropes with which to lead us bound to Chorosan. Coming gladly, moreover, they began to descend from the crest of the mountain a short distance. As many as descended remained there with their heads cut off at the hands of our men; moreover, our men hurled the heads of the killed far into the city, that they (the Turks) might be the more terrified thereat. Then the Count of St. Gilles and the Bishop of Puy took counsel together as to how they might have undermined a certain tower which was opposite their tents. Men were assigned to do the digging, with *arbalistae*[19] and bowmen to defend them on all sides. So they dug to the foundations of the wall and fixed timbers and wood under it and then set fire to it. However, evening had come; the tower had already fallen in the night, and because it was night they could not fight with the enemy. Indeed, during that night the Turks hastily built up and restored the wall so strongly that when day came no one could harm them on that side.

Now the Count of Normandy came up, Count Stephen and many others, and finally Roger of *Barneville*. At length Bohemund, at the very front, besieged the city. Beside him was Tancred, after him Duke Godfrey, then the Count of St. Gilles, next to whom was the Bishop of Puy. It was so besieged by land that no one dared to go out or in. There all our forces were assembled in one body, and who could have counted so great an army of Christ? No one, as I think, has ever before seen so many distinguished knights, or ever will again!

However, there was a large lake on one side of the city, on which the Turks used to send out their ships, and go back and forth and bring fodder, wood, and many other things. Then our leaders counselled together and sent messengers to Constantinople to tell the Emperor to have ships brought to Civitote, where there is a fort, and that he should order oxen to be brought to drag the ships over the mountains and through the woods, until they neared the lake. This was done forthwith, and he sent his Turcopoles with them. They did not want to put the ships on the lake on the very day that they were brought across, but under cover of night they launched them on the lake itself. (The boats were) filled with Turcopoles well decorated with arms. Moreover, at earliest daybreak the ships stood in good order and hastened through the lake against the city. The Turks marvelled upon seeing them, not knowing whether they were manned by their own forces or the Emperor's. However, after they recognized that it was the host of the

Emperor, they were frightened even to death, weeping and lamenting; and the Franks were glad and gave glory to God.

The Turks, moreover, seeing that they could have no further aid from their armies, sent a message to the Emperor that they would willingly surrender the city, if he would permit them to go entirely away with their wives and children and all their substance. Then the Emperor, full of vain and evil thinking, ordered them to depart unpunished, without any fear, and to be brought to him at Constantinople with great assurance (of safety). These he cared for zealously, so that he had them prepared against any damage or hindrance from the Franks. We were engaged in that siege for seven weeks and three days. Many of our men there received martyrdom, and, glad and rejoicing, gave back their happy souls to God. Many of the very poor died of hunger for the name of Christ, and these bore triumphantly to heaven their robes of martyrdom, crying with one voice, "Avenge, Lord, our blood which has been shed for Thee, who are blessed and praiseworthy forever and ever. Amen." In the meanwhile, after the city had been surrendered and the Turks had been conducted to Constantinople, the Emperor, more and more rejoiced because the city had been surrendered to his power, ordered the greatest alms to be distributed to our poor.

(*Raymond*.) Thereupon, we crossed the sea and went up to Nicaea. For the Duke, Bohemund, and the other princes had preceded the Count and were engaged in the labors of the siege. The city of Nicaea is very strongly fortified by nature, as well as by art. It has on the west a very large lake flowing up to the wall; on the remaining three sides is a moat filled with the overflow of certain little streams; in addition, it is encircled by walls so high that neither the assaults of men nor the attacks of any machine are feared. Indeed, the *ballistae*[20] of the neighboring towers are so turned with reference to one another that no one can approach without danger; however, if anyone wants to approach nearer, he is easily overwhelmed from the top of the towers without being able to retaliate.

Accordingly, this city, such as we have described, was besieged by Bohemund from the north, by the Duke and the Alemanni from the east, by the Count and Bishop of Puy from the middle, for the Count of Normandy was not yet with us. But we believe this one incident should not be passed over:—that when the Count was about to encamp there with his men, the Turks, descending from the mountains in two squadrons, attacked our army. Their plan, indeed, was that while one party of the Turks assailed the Duke and the Alemanni who were on the east, the other party, entering the middle gate of the city and passing out through another, would easily drive our men from the camp at a time when they were not expecting such an attack. But God, who is wont to reverse the plan of the impious, so altered their preparations that, as if it had been arranged, He sent the Count, who was preparing to encamp with his men, upon the squadron of Turks which was now about to enter the city. He put them to flight at the first charge and, after killing several, pursued the rest to the top of the mountain. The other party of Turks which wanted to attack the Alemanni was put to flight in the same way and destroyed. After this, machines were constructed and the wall attacked in vain, for it was very firm against us and was valiantly defended by arrows and machines. So we fought five weeks with no result. At length, through God's will, some men of the household of the Bishop and the Count dangerously enough approached the corner tower which faced the east, and having made a testudo,[21] they began, after a struggle, to undermine one of the towers and by digging threw it to the ground. Thus the city would have been taken, had not the shadows of night prevented. However, the wall was rebuilt during the night, and this rendered our former labor vain. At length the city, terrified with fear, was compelled to surrender. One reason was that the ships of the Emperor which had been dragged over the land were let down into the lake. They therefore gave themselves up to the Emperor, since they now expected no further aid and saw the army of the Franks increasing daily, while they were cut off from their forces. The Count of Normandy had come. Alexius had promised the princes and the people of the Franks that he would give them all the gold, silver, horses, and goods within (the city), and that he would establish there a Latin monastery and hospice for the poor Franks; besides, that he would give to each one of the army so much of his own possessions that they would always want to fight for him. Accordingly, the Franks, placing faith in these promises, approved the surrender. And so, when Alexius had received the city, he afforded the army such an example of gratitude that as long as they live the people will curse him and proclaim him a traitor.

We recognized, then, that the Emperor had betrayed Peter the Hermit, who had long before come to Constantinople with a great multitude. For he compelled him, ignorant of the locality and of all military matters, to cross the Strait with his men and exposed them to the Turks. Moreover, when the Turks from Nicaea saw that unwarlike multitude, they cut them down without effort and delay to the number of sixty thousand. The rest, indeed, fled to a certain fortified place and escaped the swords of the Turks. The Turks, made bold and haughty by this, sent the arms and the captives which they had taken there to the Saracens and the nobles of their own race, and they wrote to the peoples and cities far off that the Franks were of no account in battle.

(*Fulcher.*) Since the middle of May, Lord Bohemund and Duke Godfrey and Count Raymond and the Count of Flanders had already been besieging this city. It was then in possession of Turks from the East, a valiant race of very expert archers. These, indeed, had crossed the Euphrates river from Persia fifty years before and had subjected to themselves the whole land of Romania, as far as the city of Nicomedia. Oh, how many severed heads and bones of the dead we then found beyond Nicomedia, lying upon the plains near the sea! These people, inexperienced in the use of the arrow, the Turks had annihilated. Moved by pity at this sight, we shed many tears.[22]

When, as has been said, those who were already besieging Nicaea heard that our leaders had arrived, namely the Count of Normandy and Stephen of Blois, they gladly came out to meet them and us and escorted us to the place before the city on the southern side, where we pitched our tents. Once already the Turks had prepared to unite, hoping to drive the besiegers from the city, if they could, or at least to fortify the city more securely with their soldiers. But they were fiercely repulsed by us, and about two hundred of them were killed. When, moreover, they saw the Franks, so spirited, and so strong in brave warfare, they retreated in haste into the interior, awaiting an opportune time for attacking. It was in the first week in June that we came, last of all, to the siege.

Then, one army was formed of the many, which those skilful in numbers estimated to be 600,000 strong.[23] Of these 100,000 were armed for battle with leathern corslets and helmets. Besides the army were those unarmed, namely clerics, monks, women, and children. What further then? If all who had departed from their homes on the pious journey had been present there, without doubt there would have been six million soldiers. But at Rome, in Apulia, in Hungary, or in Dalmatia, some, unwilling to undergo hardships, returned to their homes; in many different places thousands were killed; and some who went with us fell sick and died. Many graveyards were to be seen along the roads, on the plains, in the places where our pilgrims were buried.

Be it known that as long as we besieged the city of Nicaea, food for sale was brought to us in ships, by order of the Emperor. Then our leaders ordered machines of war to be made, rams, scrapers, wooden towers, and slings. Arrows were shot from the bows, and destructive stones were hurled. Our enemy fired at us, and we at them, each doing his best in these encounters. With our machines we often assailed the city, but because a strong wall resisted us, the attack failed. Turks often perished, struck by arrows or stones, and Franks likewise. Truly, you would have grieved and sobbed in pity, for when they slew one of our men before the wall in any way, they let down iron hooks by means of ropes and took the body up. They snatched it away, and none of us dared, or was able, to wrest it from them. After stripping the corpse, they threw the body outside.

Then, with the aid of oxen and ropes, we dragged some small boats from Civitote over land to Nicaea and launched them in the lake to guard the approach to the city, lest it be supplied with provisions. But while we were wearying the city with siege for five weeks and had often terrified the Turks with our attacks, a council had meantime been held, and through ambassadors to the Emperor the inhabitants secretly surrendered to him the city, which was already hard pressed by our forces and skill. Then the Turks admitted into it the Turcopoles sent thither by the Emperor. They took possession of the city, with all the money in it, in the name of the Emperor, just as he had commanded. Wherefore, after all this money was taken, the Emperor ordered gifts to be presented to our leaders, gifts of gold, and silver, and raiment; and to the foot-soldiers he distributed brass coins, which they call tartarons. On the day of the siege and the surrender of Nicaea, the month of June had reached the solstice.

(*Anselm.*) To his reverend lord, Manasses, by grace of God Archbishop of Rheims, Anselm of Ribemont, his liege-man and humble servant in the Lord; greeting.

Inasmuch as you are our lord, and as the kingdom of the whole of France is especially dependent upon your care, we are notifying you, father, of the events which have befallen us; how, forsooth, the army of the Lord is bearing itself. In the first place, we are aware that a disciple is not above his master, nor a servant above his lord; yet, may it be pardoned us, we advise and beseech you in the Lord Jesus to consider what you are, what also is the priestly and pontifical duty. Provide, therefore, for our land, so that both the nobles live in concord among themselves, and the people labor in security on that which is theirs, and the ministers of Christ, leading a quiet and peaceful life, be free to devote themselves to the Lord. I likewise pray you and the canons of the Holy Mother

THE FIRST CRUSADE

Church of Rheims, my fathers and lords, to be mindful of us, not only of me and these who are still sweating in the service of God, but also of those of the army of the Lord who have fallen in arms, or died in peace.

But these matters aside, let us return to our promise. Accordingly, after our army arrived at Nicomedia and we were placed at the gates of the land of the Turks, leaders, as well as followers, cleansed by confession, fortified ourselves by partaking of the body and blood of the Lord. Moving our camp thence, we set siege to Nicaea on the second day before the Nones of May. When, moreover, we had been attacking the city for some days with many machines and various instruments of war, the cunning of the Turks, as it had so often done, deceived us much. For one day when they had promised to surrender themselves, Soliman and all the Turks, seeking to attack us unawares, gathered together from regions far and near and fell upon us. However, the Count of St. Giles, making an attack upon them with some of the Franks, killed countless numbers of them; all the others fled in confusion. Our men, moreover, returning with victory, and bearing many heads fixed upon spikes and spears, offered a spectacle joyful to the people of God. This occurred on the seventeenth day before the Kalends of June. At length the enemy, beset and routed in attacks by day and night, surrendered the city, willy-nilly, on the thirteenth day before the Kalends of July. Then the Christians, advancing through the walls with the crosses and imperial standards, regained the city for the Lord, the Greeks and Latins within and without the walls crying out together, "Glory to Thee, O Lord!" When this had been accomplished, the princes of the army went to meet the Emperor, who had come to render thanks. And having received from him gifts of inestimable value, they returned, some with kindly feelings, some otherwise.

(*Stephen.*) But, after ten days, during which time he kept me in his company with the greatest respect, I separated from him as from a father. He, however, commanded that ships be made ready for me, by means of which I crossed very quickly the peaceful arm of the sea which surrounds the city. Some people are wont to say that the arm of the sea at Constantinople is raging and perilous, which is false; for one need feel no more uncertainty at all on it than on the Marne or Seine. Thence we came to that other Strait which is called the Arm of St. George. Along this we ascended, since we could by no means find enough ships. We directed our march to Nicomedia, where the aforesaid arm of the sea has its source and head. This city, in which the blessed martyr, Pantaleon,[24] suffered for Christ, has been made desolate by the Turks. From here we hurried on to the very large city of Nicaea, singing praise to God (as we marched).

More than three hundred towers, my beloved, with walls of marvelous construction enclose Nicaea. We found the Turks within it bold fighters; here we discovered that the infinite army of God had now for four weeks been engaged in a death-dealing struggle with the people of Nicaea. Shortly before we came to the army, Soliman, prince of the Turks, had suddenly rushed upon our men with a large army prepared for battle, thinking that by a certain charge he could break into the city to aid his people. This base design, through the compassion of God, turned out otherwise than he thought. For our men, getting themselves ready most quickly, received the Turks with fierce spirit. All the latter turned their backs in flight immediately. Our men, following them very closely, killed many of them and pursued them over a wide space of territory, wounding and killing them; and had not the difficult mountains been unknown to our men, on that same day they would have driven the enemy to great and irremediable destruction. Of our men, no one perished at that time, but afterwards, as our great army together engaged in many most sharp encounters, killing many of the Turks and their leaders with hurling engines and arrows, some of our men were killed, though, truly, not many—no knight of renown except Baldwin of Flanders, Count of Ghent. When our worthy princes of God saw Nicaea so turreted, as we have said above, they constructed with great labor very high wooden towers provided with loop-holes and various engines. The Turks, upon beholding this, were overcome with fear and surrendered the city to the Emperor by envoys, on condition that he permit them to go out of the city naked, under safe conduct, and that they be held alive in captivity by the Emperor.

9. *Alexius at the surrender of Nicaea.* (June 22(?)-June 27, 1097.)

(*Stephen.*) When the Emperor heard this, he came near, almost up to us. However, he dared not enter his own city of Nicaea at all, for fear that the infinite throng of inhabitants, who revered him as their benevolent father, would smother him in their exultation. He established himself on a certain island of the sea near us. All our princes, except myself and the Count of St. Gilles, ran to him to celebrate so great a victory with him, and he received them, as was proper, with very great affection. And, because he heard that I had remained near the city, lest, by chance, a most hostile horde of Turks should overcome our army and the city, he was greatly delighted; indeed, he valued it much more highly and was better pleased that I had remained at such a time than if I had given him a mountain of gold. On that same island on which he was staying the great Emperor so ordered the distribution of the more precious spoils of the city of Nicaea that the knights were to have such things as gold, gems, silver, robes, horses, and the like; all victuals were to be distributed among the foot-soldiers; all the princes he arranged to enrich from his own treasures.

As we have said before, God triumphing, the very large city of Nicaea was surrendered on the 13th day before the Kalends of July. It is read in (the history of) the primitive church that the holy fathers celebrated a synod at Nicaea and, after the Arian heresy had been destroyed, there confirmed by the teaching of the Holy Spirit the faith of the Holy Trinity. And this city, which because of its sins later became a mistress of error, now, by the mercy of God, has been made, through His sinful servants, a disciple of truth. I tell you, my beloved, that in five weeks we will reach Jerusalem from Nicaea, the city so often mentioned, unless Antioch resists us. Farewell.

(*Anna.*) But though the Emperor wished to attach himself to the Gauls and advance with them against the barbarians, yet, fearing their countless multitude, he decided to go to *Pelecanum*, in order that by camping near Nicaea he might learn what was happening to the Gauls, and also learn the undertakings of the Turks outside, as well as the conditions in the city. . . .

The august Emperor tarried about *Pelacanum* for some time, since he desired those Gallic counts who were not yet bound to him also to take the oath of loyalty. To this end, he sent a letter to Butumites, asking all the counts in common not to start upon the journey to Antioch until they had said farewell to the Emperor. If they did this, they would all be showered with new gifts by him. Bohemund was the first to prick up his ears at the mention of money and gifts. Quickly won by these words of Butumites, he strove industriously to force all the others to return to the Emperor—so greatly did cupidity move the man. The Emperor received them on their arrival at *Pelecanum* with magnificence and the greatest show of good-will. At length, when they were assembled, he addressed them thus: "You know that you have all bound yourselves to me by oath; if you do not now intend to ignore this, advise and persuade those of your number who have not yet pledged faith to take the oath." They immediately summoned the counts who had not sworn. All of these came together and took the oath.

Tancred, however, nephew of Bohemund and a youth of most

independent spirit, professed that he owed faith to Bohemund alone, and would serve him even to death. Rebuked by the loud protest of those of his own fellows who stood near, and of the Emperor's retinue, besides, he turned toward the tent in which the Emperor was then dwelling—the largest and most capacious which anyone has ever seen—and, as if to make sport of them, said, "If you give me this (tent) full of money and, in addition, all the other presents which you gave all the counts, I, too, will take the oath." But Palaeologus,[25] full of zeal for the Emperor, could not endure the mocking speech of Tancred and pushed him away with contempt. Then Tancred, very ready with his arms, sprang upon him. Seeing this, the Emperor arose hastily from his seat and stood between them. Bohemund, too, restrained the youth, saying "It is not fitting shamefully to strike the kinsman of the Emperor." Then Tancred, recognizing the disgrace of his insolence toward Palaeologus, and persuaded by the advice of Bohemund and the others, offered to take the oath himself. . . .

10. *The views of Alexius on his relations with the Crusaders.*

How much you have written to my empire, most venerable servant of God, abbot of the monastery of Monte Cassino! I have read your letter which declares honor and praise to my empire. Toward me and my subjects there is, indeed, very great favor from Almighty and Most Merciful God, for many are His blessings. Through His compassion and by His grace He has honored and exalted my empire. However, not only because I have nothing of good within me, but because I sin above all men, I daily pray that His compassion and patience may be sent to sustain my weakness. But you, filled with goodness and virtue, judge me, sinner that I am, a good man, and truly you have the advantage of me. My empire, though it is praised without having work worthy of praise, holds the praise to its own condemnation.

"I beseech you earnestly to furnish aid to the army of Franks," your most thoughtful letters state. Let your Venerable Holiness be assured on that score, for my empire has been spread over them and will aid and advise them on all matters; indeed, it has already coöperated with them according to its ability, not as a friend, or relative, but like a father. It has expended among them more than anyone can enumerate. And had not my empire so coöperated with them and aided them, who else would have afforded them help? Nor does it grieve my empire to assist a second time. By God's grace, they are prospering up to this day in the service which they have begun, and they will continue to prosper in the future as long as good purpose leads them on. A multitude of knights and foot-soldiers have gone to the Eternal Tabernacle, some of which were killed; others died. Blessed, indeed, are they, since they met their end in good intent! Besides, we ought not at all to regard them as dead, but as living and transported to life everlasting and incorruptible. As evidence of my true faith and my kind regard for your monastery, my empire has sent you an *epiloricum,* adorned on the back with glittering gold.

Sent in the month of June, (1098) sixth Indiction, from the most holy city of Constantinople.[26]

CHAPTER IV

From Nicaea To Antioch

(In the march across Asia Minor the Crusaders for the first time encountered their real enemy, the Seljukian Turks. These had previously contented themselves with an effort to slip into Nicaea, their capital, but the odds were too great and the city was allowed to fall. Now, however, with the Crusaders on the march, the superior knowledge of the country enjoyed by the Turks and their swifter horses combined to offset the numerical advantage of the Christians. For the Latins considerably outnumbered the Turks, in spite of the fact that they were so far away from home in the heart of the enemy's territory. The explanation of this anomalous situation lies in the condition of the Turkish and Mohammedan realm. The Caliph of Bagdad had become spiritual head of the Mohammedans. The Caliph of Egypt was head of the Ishmaelite section of the Mohammedans and bitterly opposed to the Caliph of Bagdad. Their fighting ground was Syria. Sixty years before the First Crusade, a new vitality had been injected into the Caliphate of Bagdad by the creation of the Seljuk Sultanate. These Seljuks, who were the most advanced of the Turks, had but recently taken on the Mohammedan faith. With all the zeal of neophytes, they devoted themselves zealously to the spread of their religion. Under their earlier Sultans, they had extended their domain across Western Asia to the very gates of Constantinople. The second of their Sultans to rule Western Asia, Alp Arslan, had won a brilliant victory over the Eastern Empire at Manzikert in 1071, which opened Asia Minor to the Turks. Their ideas of political organization, however, were as rudimentary as those of the peoples of the West, and Asia Minor was given to a relative on the feudal basis of personal loyalty and homage to the Sultan. The vast empire of the Sultans soon became unmanageable. The third Sultan, Malik Shah, found his vassals restless and had to suppress at least one revolt. Upon his death in 1092, quarrels arose among his sons which lasted for more than a generation. During this time, the numerous feudal vassals exercised practical independence. They not only participated in the wars between the rivals, but often warred with one another. It was at this juncture that the Crusaders came. The Turks were so embittered among themselves that they refused to make common cause against the invaders, and, as a result, the Crusaders were able to overcome one after another of their principalities. The first of these, called the Sultanate of Rum (Romania), included practically all of Asia Minor. This had been given to Suliman by Alp Arslan and had been extended by him to Nicaea, which he made his capital. This Suliman was well known and feared by the Greeks. His son, Kilij Arslan Daud, whom the Crusaders called Soliman, was ruling at the time of the Crusade (1092-1106) and led the fighting in Asia Minor against the Christians.

At Nicaea the various bands were formed into one army, and thereafter the different authors serve to correct and corroborate one another in the account of their common experiences. Two exceptions occur; one in regard to the battle of Dorylaeum, when the army was temporarily divided, and the other when Baldwin and Tancred left the main army on journeys of adventure in Cilicia. The division of the army before Dorylaeum was ended by the battle, and the digression of Baldwin to Edessa took him permanently from the main army, while that of Tancred ended when the main army joined him before Antioch. Fulcher, who accompanied Baldwin, therefore ceases at this time to qualify as an eye-witness of events which occurred in the main army. For Tancred's separate acts the account by the Anonymous may be supplemented by that of Raoul de Caen, who probably gained his story from Tancred himself.[1] Events followed one another in such rapid succession as to confuse writers who delayed the composition of their narratives for some time. This is especially true of Raymond, whose story must be carefully checked by the letters and the *Gesta*. On most matters of importance in this chapter the accounts agree. The most notable exception is that of the defection of the Greek commander *Tetigus*, called also *Tatic, Titidus, Tatanus,* and *Statinus*. The divergent view of Anna deserves consideration in view of the increased distrust between the Latins and the Greeks.[2])

1. *Battle of Dorylaeum.* (July 1, 1097.)

(*Gesta.*) Then on the first day after leaving the city, we came to a certain bridge and remained there for two days. On the third day, however, before day had begun to dawn, our men arose. Since it was night, they were unable to keep to one road, but were divided into two lines and, thus divided, proceeded for two days. In one line were the men, Bohemund, Robert of Normandy, the renowned Tancred, and several others; in the other were the Count of St. Gilles, Duke Godfrey, the Bishop of Puy, Hugh the Great, the Count of Flanders, and many others. But on the third day the Turks rushed violently upon Bohemund and those who were with him. Forthwith the Turks began to whistle and chatter and shout at the top of their voices, uttering a diabolical sound, I know not how, in their own tongue. The wise man, Bohemund, seeing innumerable Turks whistling and shouting from afar with demoniacal voices, straightway ordered all the knights to dismount and quickly pitch their tents. Before the tents had been pitched, he spoke again to all the knights: "Seignors and bravest knights of Christ, behold the battle is now close about us on all sides. Therefore, let all the knights advance manfully against the enemy, and let the foot-soldiers spread the tents carefully and very quickly." But after this was all done, the Turks were already encircling us on all sides, slashing, hurling, piercing, and shooting far and wide in wondrous fashion. Though we could not resist them, nor withstand the press of so great an enemy, yet we (held out) there together. Our women, also, were on that day of greatest support to us. They brought drinking water to our fighters, and, furthermore, ever comforted those who were fighting and defending them. Accordingly, the wise man, Bohemund, straightway sent word to the others (to wit, the renowned Count of St. Gilles, the famous Duke Godfrey, Hugh the Great, the most honorable Bishop of Puy, and all the other knights of Christ) to hurry and come to the battle as quickly as possible, saying that, if they wished to fight that day, let them come bravely. They utterly refused (at first), laughing at the messengers and saying, "Surely this is all false!" For we did not believe that those people were so impudent that they already dared to rise up and fight again with us. Finally, Duke Godfrey, bold and brave, and Hugh the Great went ahead with their armies. The Bishop of Puy also followed them with his army, and the Count of St. Gilles after them with the great host.

Our men wondered exceedingly whence had arisen so great a multitude of Turks, Arabs, Saracens, and others whom I know not how to enumerate, for almost all the mountains and hills and valleys and all the level places, within and without, were on all sides covered with that excommunicate race. Accordingly, secret speech was held among us, praising and advising and saying, "Be of one mind in the faith of Christ, and in the victory of the Standard of the Holy Cross, because this day, if it please God, you will all have been made rich." Straightway our lines of battle were formed. On the left side was the wise man, Bohemund, Robert of Normandy, the renowned Tancred, the most honorable Robert of Anse, and the famous Richard of Principati. The Bishop of Puy, indeed, came over another mountain, surrounding the incredulous Turks on all sides. On the left side, also, rode the most mighty knight, Raymond, Count of St. Gilles. On the right wing was the honorable Duke Godfrey, and the most fierce knight, the Count of Flanders, Hugh the Great, and many others whose names I do not know. Immediately, however, upon the arrival of our troops the Turks, Arabs, Saracens, *Agulani*,[3] and all the barbarous nations quickly turned in flight through the mountain passes and over the level places. Moreover, the number of the Turks, Persians, *Publicani*,[4] Saracens, *Agulani* and other pagans was three hundred and sixty thousand, besides the Arabs, whose number no one knows, unless it be God alone. They fled, indeed, very quickly to their tents, but they were not permitted to remain there long. Again they took to flight, and we followed them, killing them one whole

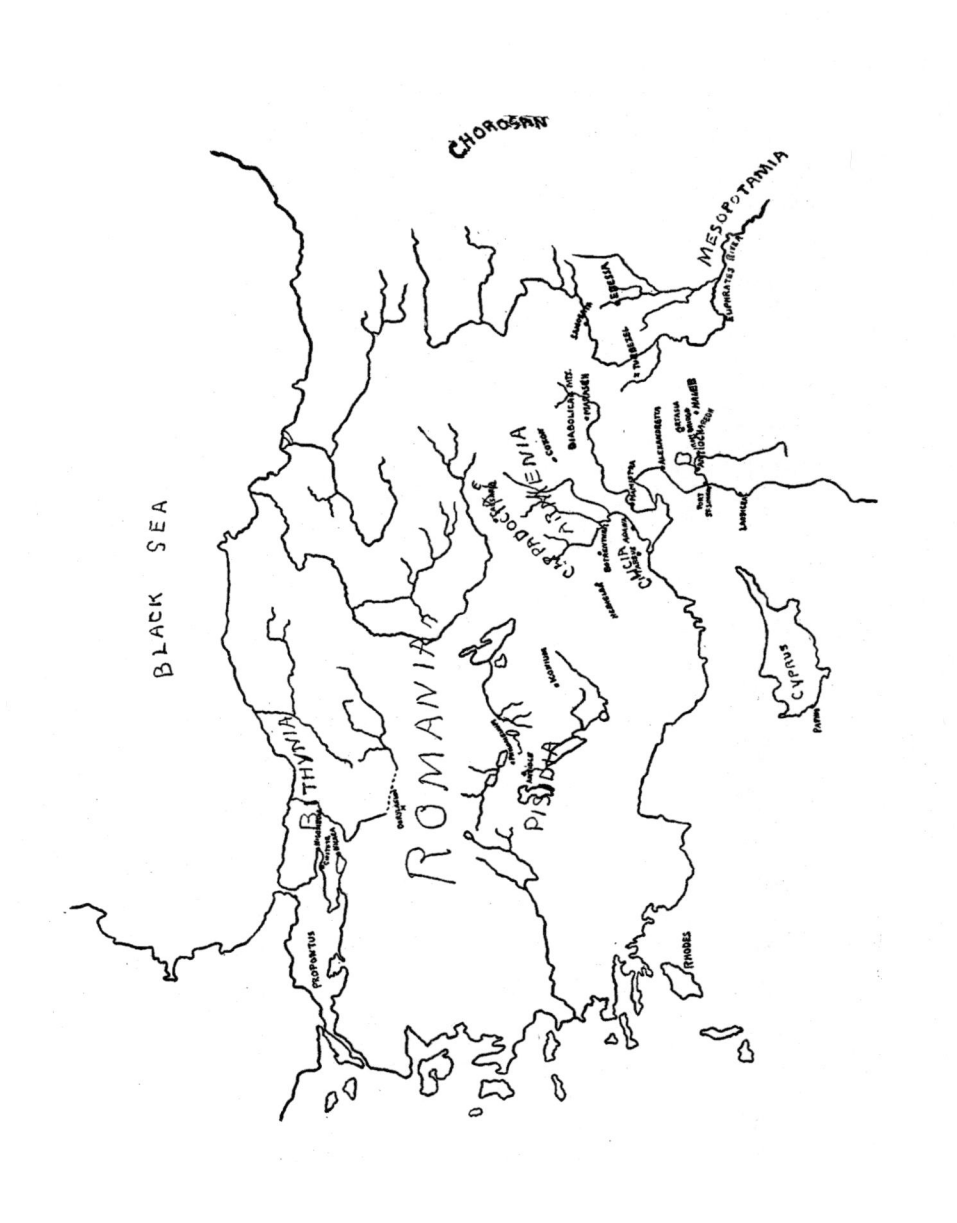

day; and we took much booty—gold, silver, horses, asses, camels, sheep, cattle, and very many other things which we do not know. Had not God been with us in the battle and quickly sent us a second battle line, not one of us would have escaped, for this fight lasted from the third hour even to the ninth. But Almighty God, holy and merciful, who neither permitted His knights to perish nor to fall into the hands of the enemy, hastily sent us His aid. Two honorable knights of ours, Godfrey of Mount Scaglioso, and William, son of Marchisus, brother of Tancred, died there, and (also) other knights and foot-soldiers whose names I do not know.

Whoever will be wise or learned enough to dare to describe the valor, skill, and fortitude of the Turks, who thought to frighten the host of the Franks with the threats of their arrows, just as they frighten the Arabs, Saracens, Armenians, Syrians, and Greeks? But, please God, never will they be so powerful as our men. Indeed, they say that they are of the Frankish race, and that no one ought naturally to be a knight except the Franks and themselves. I shall speak the truth, which no one will dare deny. Certainly, if they had ever been firm in the faith of Christ and holy Christianity, and had been willing to confess the One Lord in Trinity, and that the Son of God was born of a Virgin Mother, suffered, and arose from the dead, and ascended to heaven while His disciples looked on, and then, finally, sent the consolation of the Holy Spirit, and had believed with a right mind and faith in Him, ruling in heaven and on earth, no one could have found more powerful, braver, or more skilful fighters than they. And yet, by the grace of God, they were conquered by our men! This battle was fought on the first day of July.

But after the Turks, enemies of God and holy Christianity, had been entirely beaten, fleeing hither and thither for four days and nights, it happened that Soliman, their Duke, son of the old Soliman, fled from Nicaea. He found ten thousand Arabs who said to him, "O, unhappy and more unhappy than all the Gentiles! why do you flee, terrified?" To them Soliman tearfully replied: "Because just recently, when I had all the Franks beaten and thought them already bound in captivity, and when I would soon have tied them to one another, then, looking back, I saw such an innumerable host of them that, if any of you had been there, you would have thought that all the mountains, hills, valleys, and level places were filled with their multitude. Upon seeing them, we began immediately to take to sudden flight, so amazingly afraid that we hardly escaped from their hands; wherefore we are still in very great terror. And if you wish to believe me and my words, take yourselves hence, because if they can only learn of you, scarcely one of you will any longer remain alive." The enemy, upon hearing such tidings, turned their backs again and spread out through all Romania.

(*Raymond.*) Accordingly, we set out from the city of Nicaea into Romania, and on the second day Bohemund with some of the princes rashly separated from the Count and Bishop and Duke. When on the third day of this digression Bohemund was planning to pitch his tents, he saw a hundred and fifty thousand Turks advancing to battle. And while he was drawing up his lines temporarily and was preparing for battle, he lost several of his army. In the midst of this, he sent word to the Count and Duke to help him, for they were two miles away. Moreover, as soon as the messenger of Bohemund came to the camp, all straightway seized their horses and arms and hastened to go against the enemy. However, when Soliman and those who were with him recognized our army coming to battle against them, they were forced to flee, despairing of victory. And thus he who had taken captives and very many tents from the camp of Bohemund through God's might abandoned his own. A wondrous miracle was reported, but we did not see it; that two knights clad in shining armor and of wonderful appearance advanced before our army and so threatened the enemy that they granted them no chance to fight in any way. Indeed, when the Turks wanted to strike them with lances they appeared invulnerable to them. However, we learned these things which we have stated from those Turks who spurned the companionship of their own people and clung to us. What we add for testimony is as follows: throughout the first and second day we found horses of the enemy, together with their masters, dead along the road.

(*Fulcher.*) When, therefore, our leaders had received the Emperor's permission to depart, we left Nicaea on the third day before the Kalends of July, and, advancing, we came into the interior parts of Romania. But when we had been on the way two days, it was reported to us that the Turks had set ambushes for us and expected to join battle with us in the plains through which they thought we were going to pass. We did not lose courage, however, at this news. But that evening, when our scouts saw many of them a long way off, they at once notified us of it. Therefore, on that night we had our tents protected on all sides by guards. But early in the morning, which was the Kalends of July, we took up our arms, and at the signal of the trumpet we divided into wings, with tribunes and centurians leading the cohorts and centuries. Then with flags flying, we went out against the enemy in good order.

At the second hour of the day, behold, their advance guards approached our scouts. When we had heard this, we pitched our tents near a certain marsh and took off our pack saddles, so that we would be better able to fight.

When this was done, the Emir and chief of the Turks, Soliman, who had held in his possession the city of Nicaea and Romania, gathered together about him the Turks and pagan Persians who, after a journey of thirty days at his command, had come to his aid. There were present with him many chiefs and leaders such as *Admircaradigum, Miriathos*,[5] and many others. Altogether they numbered 360,000 fighters, all on horses and armed with bows, as was their custom. We, on the other hand, had both foot-soldiers and knights. But at that time Duke Godfrey and Count Raymond and Hugh the Great had been two days absent from us. For some unknown reason they had taken a branch road and withdrawn themselves from us with a large number of our men. Therefore an irreparable loss resulted, as much from the number of our soldiers who were killed as from our failure to kill or capture the Turks. And because those absent leaders received our messengers late, they were therefore late in coming to our aid. The Turks crept up, howling loudly and shooting a shower of arrows. Stunned, and almost dead, and with many wounded, we immediately fled. And it was no wonder, for such warfare was new to us all. Already from another part of the marsh, a large column of them rushed violently up to our tents and, entering them, snatched our possessions and killed our people. Then, by the disposition of God, the advance guard of Hugh the Great and Count Raymond and Duke Godfrey came from the rear upon this unhappy scene. When we had been driven up to our tents, those of the enemy who were there fled out, thinking that we had returned to attack them. But what they took for bravery and courage they should have thought great fear.

What further shall I say? We were all huddled together, indeed, like sheep shut in a pen, trembling and frightened, surrounded on all sides by enemies, so that we were unable to advance in any direction. It was clear to us that this befell us as a punishment for our sins. For whomsoever luxury defiles, those, indeed, avarice, or some other vice, corrupts. The air was lashed with a great outcry from men, women, and children, as well as from the pagans, who rushed upon us. Now there was no hope of life left to us. We then confessed that we were debtors and sinners and humbly begged mercy from God. There were present the Bishop of Puy, our patron, and four other prelates. Many priests, vested in white, were also there, who humbly besought God to destroy the power of our enemy and shed upon us the gifts of his mercy. Weeping, they sang, and singing, they wept. Then many, fearing that death was near, ran to the priests and confessed their sins to them. Our leaders, Count Robert of Normandy, and Stephen, Count of Blois, and Robert, Count of Flanders, and Bohemund, also, resisted the enemy with all their might and often tried to charge upon them. They, also, were strongly attacked by the Turks.

But the Lord, no doubt appeased by our supplications,—for He gives victory neither to the splendor of nobility nor to brilliance of arms, but to the pure in heart and to him whose need is piously fortified by divine strength,—little by little restored to us our strength and weakened the Turks more and more. For we saw our allies hastening to our aid from behind. Praising God, we regained our courage and, forming into troops and cohorts, pressed forward to resist them. Oh, how many of our men, coming slowly after us, they killed that day! From the very first hour of the day until the sixth, as I have said, difficulties checked us; but then, little by little, we recovered and were reinforced by our allies. Manifestly Divine Grace was with us, for, as if by sudden impulse, all the Turks turned their backs on us in flight. But we followed them through the mountains and valleys, calling after them loudly. We did not cease pursuing them until our advance guard had come up to their tents. There some of our men loaded horses and camels with their goods and even with the tents which the Turks in their fright had left there. Others followed the fleeing Turks even until night. But because our horses were famished and tired, we kept a few of theirs. It was a great miracle of God that, during the following day and the third, the pagans did not halt in their flight, although no one, unless it were God, followed them further. Exceedingly rejoiced at such a victory, we all gave thanks to God because He did not will that our expedition should be annihilated, but that it should prosper more gloriously than usual, for the honor of His own Christianity. Wherefore, from the East to West its glory shall resound forever.

2. *Hardships of the march through Asia Minor.* (July 3-October, 1097.)

(*Gesta.*) Then we went on pursuing the most iniquitous Turks, who daily fled before us. But they went to all the fortified towns or cities, deceiving and deluding the inhabitants of those lands, saying: "We have conquered all the Christians and have so overcome them that no one of them will ever dare to arise before us;

only let us come in." They destroyed the churches, homes, and everything else, upon entering, and carried off with them the horses, asses, mules, gold, and silver, and whatever they could find. In addition, also, they carried off the children of Christians with them and burned and devastated everything that was convenient or useful, fleeing, greatly frightened, before our faces. Accordingly, we were following them through deserts, and dry and uninhabitable land, from which we scarcely escaped and came out alive. Hunger and thirst pinched us on all sides, and there was absolutely nothing for us to eat, unless, by chance, tearing and grinding grain with our hands, we continued to exist on such food as wretchedly as possible. There most of our cavalry ceased to exist, because (thereafter) many of these became foot-soldiers. For want of horses, our men used oxen in place of cavalry horses, and because of the very great need, goats, sheep, and dogs served as beasts of burden.

Meanwhile we began to enter the best land, filled with bodily nourishment, delicacies, and goods of all kinds, and then we approached Iconium. The inhabitants of that land persuaded and advised us to take along skins filled with water, because there is the greatest lack of water about one day's march from there. We accordingly did so, until we came to a certain river, and there we lodged for two days. However, our scouts began to go on ahead until they came to Heraclea, in which town there was a very large gathering of Turks, waiting and plotting how they could harm and put to grief the knights of Christ. The knights of Almighty God found and boldly attacked these Turks. And thus our enemy was overcome on that day, and they fled as swiftly as an arrow flies when discharged with a mighty pull of string and bow. Our men, accordingly, entered the city immediately and remained there for four days.

(*Fulcher.*) Then, indeed, we continued our journey quietly, one day suffering such extreme thirst that many men and women died from its torments. Whole troops of Turks, fleeing before us, sought refuge by scattering throughout Romania. Then we came to that Antioch which they called the lesser, in the province of Pisidia, and thence to Iconium. In these regions we very often were in need of bread and other foods. For we found Romania, a land which is good and very rich in all products, thoroughly devastated and ravished by the Turks. Still, you would often see this multitude of people well refreshed by whatever little vegetation we found at intervals on this journey throughout barren regions. This happened by the aid of God, who from five loaves and two fishes fed the five thousand. Wherefore, glad and rejoicing, we declared that these were gifts of the mercy of God. Truly, one would not know whether to laugh or to cry from pity, when many of our men without pack-mules, since many of theirs had already perished, loaded sheep, goats, hogs, and dogs with their supplies, such as clothing, and food, and whatever luggage was necessary for pilgrims. The skin of those animals was worn by the weight of the baggage. And knights with their armor sometimes even mounted oxen. But who ever heard such a mixture of languages in one army? There were Franks, Flemish, Frisians, Gauls, Allobroges, Lotharingians, Alemanni, Bavarians, Normans, Angles, Scots, Aquitanians, Italians, Dacians, Apulians, Iberians, Bretons, Greeks and Armenians.[6] If a Breton or Teuton questioned me, I would not know how to answer either. But though we spoke diverse languages, we were, however, brothers in the love of God and seemed to be nearest kin. For if one lost any of his possessions, whoever found it kept it carefully a long time, until, by inquiry, he found the loser and returned it to him. This was indeed the proper way for those who were making this holy pilgrimage in a right spirit.

When we had reached the city of Heraclea, we beheld a certain prodigy in the sky, which, shining in brilliant whiteness, appeared in the shape of a sword with the point towards the East. We did not know what it portended for the future; but we left the present and future to the Lord. Then we arrived at a certain flourishing town which is called Marasch and we rested there for three days.

3. *Baldwin and Tancred depart from the main army.* (Early September, 1097.)

(*Gesta.*) There Tancred, son of Marchisus, and Baldwin, the famous Count, brother of Duke Godfrey, separated from the others, and together went into the valley of *Botrenthrot.*[7] Tancred went to Tarsus alone with his troops. At length, the Turks came out from the city and advanced to meet them; then, gathered together, they hastened to battle against the Christians. As our men approached and fought, our enemy fled, returning rapidly to the city. But Tancred, distinguished and honorable knight of Christ, loosened his breast-plate and encamped before the gate of the city. From another side, thereupon, came the famous man, Count Baldwin, with his army, demanding and praying Tancred, most harsh knight, that with the greatest friendship he would deign to take him most kindly into partnership in the city. To him Tancred said, "I absolutely refuse to take you into partnership." And so when night came, the terrified Turks took to flight in a body. Then the inhabitants of the city came out under the shadows of the night, shouting at the top of their voices, "Run! most invincible Franks, run! For the Turks, driven out by fear of you, are all departing." Moreover at daybreak, the leaders of the city came and willingly surrendered it, saying to those who were quarrelling about this matter among themselves, "Stop, Seignors, stop! for we seek and wish for lord and ruler him who yesterday so bravely fought with the Turks." Baldwin, thereupon, wonderful Count, quarrelled and disputed with Tancred, saying, "Let us enter together, and despoil the city, and let him who is the more able hold it, and him who can, take it." "On the contrary," most brave Tancred said, "I will have none of this, for I am unwilling to despoil Christians. The men of this city have chosen me lord over them, and they desire to have me." Nevertheless the brave man, Tancred, was unable to struggle long with Baldwin, most learned Count, because his army was large. Therefore Tancred left the city, willy-nilly, and manfully withdrew with his army. Immediately there were surrendered to him two very fine cities, Adana and Mamistra, and very many fortified towns.

(*Fulcher*), (Middle of October, 1097.) But when we had traversed a day's journey from there and were now not more than three days from Syrian Antioch, I, Fulcher, withdrew from the main army with Count Baldwin, brother of Duke Godfrey, and turned towards the region of the province which is to the left.

Baldwin was indeed a very fine knight, who sometime before had left the army. With his men he had very boldly taken the city called Tarsus of Cilicia from Tancred, who, with the consent of the Turks, had already sent his men into the city. Leaving guards in it, Baldwin returned to the army.[8] So, trusting in God and in his own strength, he collected a few soldiers and set out towards the Euphrates; and he there took many towns both by force and by strategy. Among those which he captured was a very rich one called Turbezel. The Armenians who dwelt there gave it up peacefully to him; and many others became subject to him.

Since his fame had circulated far and wide, the prince of the city of Edessa sent a delegation to him. Edessa was a most celebrated city and most fruitful in the products of the earth. This city is in Syrian Mesopotamia, about twenty miles beyond the above mentioned Euphrates, and about a hundred or a few more miles from Antioch. Baldwin was asked by the Duke to go there, and to agree that they should be mutual friends as long as they both should live, that they should be like father and son. And if by chance the Duke of Edessa himself should die, Baldwin should immediately come into possession of all his land, just as if he were his own son. Since he had no son or daughter, and since he was unable to defend himself against the Turks, this Greek wished himself and his land to be defended by this Baldwin, for he had heard that both he and his soldiers were most brave fighters.

As soon as Baldwin had heard this offer, and had been persuaded of its truth by the oath of the deputies from Edessa, he set out with his little army of about eighty knights and crossed the Euphrates. After we had crossed this river, we went on very hastily all night and, very much afraid, we passed between the Saracen forts, leaving them on either side of us. When the Turks in the fortified town of Samosata had heard this, they set ambush for us along the way by which they thought we would go. But the following night a certain Armenian most hospitably entertained us in his castle and warned us to guard ourselves from the ambush of the enemy. Wherefore, for two days we remained concealed in this place. But the Turks, wearied by such delay, on the third day, rushed down in a sudden onslaught from their place of hiding and, with flags flying, ran before the stronghold in which we were; and the booty which they found there in the pastures they seized before our eyes. We went out against them; but because we were too few, we were unable to contend with them. They shot arrows, but wounded none of us. However, they left in camp one of their men killed with a lance. His horse was kept by the one who unhorsed him. Then the pagans left, but we stayed there. The following day we resumed our journey and passed in front of the Armenian forts. When they heard that we were going to defend them from the Turks, under whose yoke they had for so long been oppressed, it was wonderful to see how they advanced to meet us, humbly and for the love of God. They carried crosses and banners, and they kissed our robes and our feet.

(February 20, 1098.) At length we reached Edessa where the aforesaid Duke of the city and his wife, together with the citizens, gladly received us; and what had been promised to Baldwin they fulfilled at once. After we had delayed there for fifteen days, the citizens wickedly plotted to kill their prince because they hated him, and to set up Baldwin as ruler over the land in his place. This was suggested; and it was done. Baldwin and his men were much grieved that they were not able to obtain mercy for him. As soon as Baldwin had accepted as a gift from the citizens the principality of this man who had been wickedly murdered, he began a war against the Turks who were in the country. Often he conquered, either killing or taking them prisoners. However, it happened, also, that many of our men were killed by the Turks.

I, Fulcher of Chartres, was chaplain for the same Baldwin. I shall now resume where I left off the narrative about the army of God. . . .

4. *The march through Armenia.* (The third week in October, 1097.)

(*Gesta.*) The greater army, namely, Raymond, Count of St. Gilles, the most learned Bohemund, Duke Godfrey, and the other princes, entered the land of Armenia, thirsting and raging after the blood of the Turks. At length, they came to a certain fortified place which was so strong that they could do nothing to it. There was there, however, a certain man named Simeon, who had been born in that region, and who sought this land that he might defend it against the hostile Turks. To him they willingly gave the land, and he remained there with his people. Then, going from this place, we came happily to Caesarea of Cappadocia. Going out of Cappadocia, however, we came to a certain very beautiful and exceedingly fruitful city, which the Turks had besieged for three weeks before our arrival, but had not conquered. Immediately upon our arrival there, it straightway surrendered into our hands with great pleasure. A certain knight whose name was Peter of the Alps begged this from all the seignors to defend it in fealty to God, the Holy Sepulchre, the seignors, and the Emperor. They granted it to him freely, with great affection. On the following night Bohemund heard that the Turks who had been engaged in the siege of the city were ahead of us in great numbers. Straightway he made himself ready to attack them on all sides with his knights alone, but he could not find them. Then we came to a certain city, *Coxon* by name, in which there was the greatest abundance of all goods which we needed. Thereupon, the Christian inhabitants of that city surrendered immediately, and we remained there three days very well provided for, and our men were greatly refreshed.

When Raymond, Count of St. Gilles, heard that the Turks who were in custody at Antioch had withdrawn, he concluded on his own counsel that he would send thither some of his knights to guard the place diligently. Then he chose those whom he wished to appoint, namely Peter, Viscount of Castillon, William of Montpellier, Peter of *Roasa*, Peter Raymond of Hautpoul, with five hundred knights. They came, accordingly, into a valley near Antioch to a certain fortified place of the *Publicani*, and there they heard that the Turks were in the city and ready to defend it vigorously. Peter of *Roasa* there separated from the others and with the approach of night crossed near Antioch and entered the valley of Rugia. He found Turks and Saracens, fought with them, killed many of them, and pursued the rest closely. The Armenian inhabitants of the land, seeing that he had bravely overcome the pagans, straightway surrendered to him. He immediately took the city of *Rusa*,[9] and very many fortified places.

However, we who had remained, going thence, entered a diabolical mountain, which was so high and steep that none of us dared to step before another through the pass which was open in the mountain. There horses fell headlong, and one pack animal pushed over another. The knights stood there, sad; they beat themselves with their hands for their great grief and sadness, uncertain what they should do about themselves and their arms, selling their shields and their best breast-plates, together with their helmets, for only three or five *denarii*, or whatever they could get. Those who could not sell them threw them away for nothing and marched on. And so we went out of the accursed mountain and came to a city called Marasch. The inhabitants of that city came out rejoicing to meet us, and bringing along the greatest market. There we had all supplies while we waited for Lord Bohemund to arrive. And thus our knights reached the valley in which is situated the regal city of Antioch, the capital of all Syria, which the Lord Jesus Christ handed over to the blessed Peter, chief of the Apostles, to recall to the worship of the true faith—the same Lord Jesus who liveth and reigneth with God the Father, in unity with the Holy Ghost, forever and ever. Amen.

When we had begun to approach the Iron Bridge, our advance guard, who were accustomed to precede us, found innumerable Turks assembled to meet us. They were on their way to give aid to Antioch. Accordingly, our men rushed upon them with one heart and one mind and overcame the Turks. The barbarians were thrown into consternation and fled, and many of them died in the struggle. Our men, therefore, having defeated them by the grace of God, captured great spoils—horses, camels, mules, asses laden with grain and wine. At length our men went and encamped on the bank of the river. Forthwith, the wise man, Bohemund, went with four thousand knights to watch before the gate of the city, (to see) whether, perchance, anyone was leaving or entering the city secretly by night.

(*Raymond.*) And so, after conquering and scattering the Turks, we came peacefully and quickly across Romania up to Antioch. But the Count kept his army a short distance behind because of his illness. A certain incident brought about by divine clemency should not be passed in silence, even though we knew that it would be sufficiently displeasing to the incredulous. There was in our army a certain Count from Saxony, who came to Count Raymond and asserted that he was the envoy of St. Gilles; and said that he had been admonished once and a second time to say to the Count: "Rest secure, you will not die of this illness; I have obtained a truce for you from God; I will always be with you." And though the Count believed this fully, yet he was so affected by this illness that, when he was put down from his bed on the ground, his pulse scarcely throbbed. Therefore, the Bishop of the city of Orange read the offices for him as for one dead, but divine clemency, which preferred him as a leader of his army, there lifted him from death and restored him to health.

When we neared Antioch it was not the advice of many princes to besiege it, especially since winter was at hand, and the army was scattered among the castles and diminished by the stormy weather. They said, likewise, that they ought to await the Emperor's forces and the army which was announced to be coming from France, and thus they urged that we spend the winter up to spring. But others of the princes, among whom was the Count, said: "We have come by the inspiration of God; through His mercy we obtained Nicaea, a very strongly fortified city, and through the same clemency we have obtained victory and security from the Turks; there has been peace and concord in our army. Thus we should commit our lot to Him. We ought not to fear kings, or the chiefs of kings, nor yet places, or times, when God has snatched us from so many dangers." Accordingly, we went to Antioch and pitched our camp so near that the enemy from their towers frequently wounded our men and our horses in the tents.

5. *Beginning of the siege of Antioch.* (October 21(?)-end of November, 1097.)

(*Gesta.*) On the next day, moreover, they came even to Antioch at mid-day on the fourth day of the week, which is the twelfth day before the Kalends of November. In marvelous fashion we besieged three gates of the city, since on the other side there was no place from which to besiege (them), for a very steep mountain constrained us. However, our enemies, the Turks who were within the city, were so afraid of us on all sides that none of them dared to offend any of our men for a space of almost fifteen days. Camping immediately in front of Antioch, we found there every abundance—vines full everywhere, pits full of grain, trees bent down with fruit, and many other goods useful for the body. The Armenians and Syrians who were within the city came out and, pretending that they were fleeing, were with us daily, but their wives were in the city. Indeed, they craftily investigated our condition and strength and reported everything to those excommunicate who were shut up in the city. But after the Turks had been informed of our condition, they began little by little to go out from the city and to harass our pilgrims, not only on one side, but on all sides, for they were in hiding everywhere, from sea to mountain, to meet us.

Moreover, there was at no great distance a certain fortress named Aregh, where many very brave Turks, who frequently disturbed our men, were gathered. Thereupon, when our seignors heard such reports, they were exceedingly sorry, and sent some of the knights to explore carefully the place where the Turks were. When they had found the place where they were concealed, our knights, who were seeking them, encountered them. But while our men were retiring little by little to the place where they knew Bohemund was located with his army, two of them were immediately killed. Bohemund, upon hearing of this, arose with his men, like the bravest athlete of Christ. The barbarians rushed against them, because our men were few; yet, united, they entered battle. Verily many of our enemy were killed, and others, taken captive before the gates of the city, were there beheaded, in order that those who were in the city might become the sadder. Others, indeed, used to come out from the city and climb upon a certain gate and shoot arrows at us, so that their arrows fell into the camp of Lord Bohemund, and one woman was killed by the shot of an arrow. Accordingly, all our leaders assembled and held a council, saying, "Let us build a fortress on the top of Mt. *Maregart*,[10] a mount above the hosts of Bohemund, by means of which we can remain secure and safe from the ar of the Turks." And so when this fortress was built and fortified, all the leaders guarded it in turn.

(*Raymond.*) Since the occasion offers itself to us, we ought to speak about Antioch and its location so that the battles and assaults which were made there may be easily understood by those who have not seen it. There is a certain plain among the mountains of Lebanon which in width is one day's travel, and in length a day and a half. This plain has on it western side a certain swamp; on the east, a river which, after encircling a certain part of this plain, so winds back to the foot of the mountains which are in the middle of that land that there is no passage between the mountains and the stream, and thus it flows into the Mediterranean, which is very close to Antioch. Moreover, Antioch is so situated in those passes which the river, clinging to the aforesaid mountains,

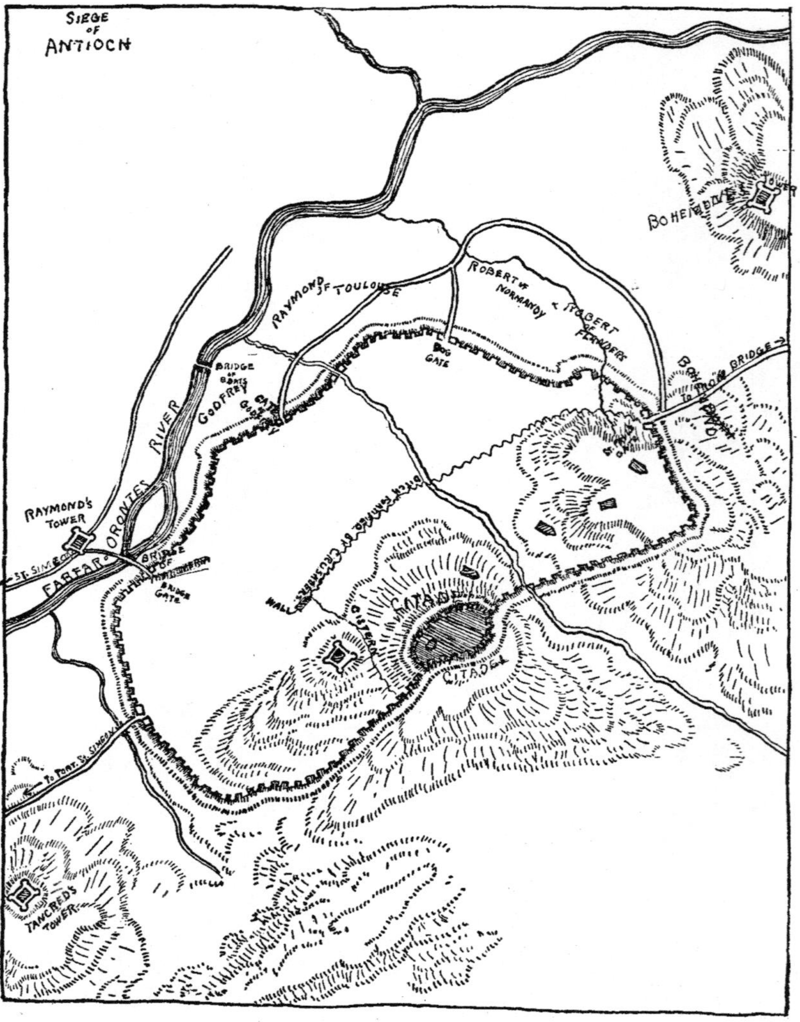

SIEGE OF ANTIOCH
RAYMOND OF TOULOUSE
ROBERT OF NORMANDY
& ROBERT OF FLANDERS
BOHEMOND'S TOWER
BOHEMOND
TO IRON BRIDGE
BRIDGE OF BOATS
GODFREY
DOG GATE
ORONTES
RIVER
RAYMOND'S TOWER
ST. SIMEON
FARFAR
BRIDGE GATE
WALL
CISTERN
CITADEL
TO PORT ST. SIMEON
TANCRED'S TOWER

makes that on the west the river, flowing against the lower wall, leaves a certain portion of land in the form of a bow between it and the city. The city, situated in this manner on the east, rises up toward the east, and within its embrace are enclosed the crests of three mountains. That mountain, indeed, which is located on the north is divided from the others by a very great precipice, so that no access, or rather a most difficult one, is afforded from it to the others. Moreover, on the northern hill there is a certain castle; on the middle hill another castle, which is called in Greek *Colax*, and on the third hill only towers. Moreover, this city, two miles in length, is so fortified by walls, towers, and fore-walls that it fears the attack of no machine and the assault of no man, even if every race of man should come together against it.

This city, such as we have described, this well fortified city, the army of the Franks besieged from the northern side. Nevertheless, though there were one hundred thousand men in the army, they made no assault there except that they pitched their camp near it. There were, furthermore, in the city two thousand of the best knights, and four or five thousand common knights, and ten thousand and more footmen. Indeed, these very lofty walls were fortified by a valley and swamp, so that, the gates being guarded, the rest remained secure. When we first came we pitched camp so rashly that if our practice had been known by the enemy beforehand, any part of our camp could have been destroyed by them, since in our army no regular method of watches or encamping was observed. It happened, also, that all the castles of this region and the neighboring cities had surrendered to our men, not only from fear of our army, but also for the sake of escaping Turkish servitude. This fact scattered our knights widely; for each one, wanting to look after his own affairs most, thought nothing of the common interest. Meanwhile, those who remained in the camp had such an abundance of food that they did not care to eat anything except the thighs and the shoulders of cattle, and only a few were willing to eat the breast; but of grain and wine nothing is to be said, except that they were taken most lightly.

While this was going on in the camp, the enemy at first hid themselves within the walls, so that no one was seen there except the watchmen. However, when they learned that our men, scattered and unarmed, were devastating the villages and fields, the enemy came, I know not whether from Antioch or from another city two days distant, and began to kill our men whom they found thus straggling and unarmed. These acts diminished the food supply in our camp somewhat. The enemy, indeed, beset the roads much too fiercely for any chance of robbery and destruction.

However, since these matters had become clearly known in the camp, Bohemund was chosen to go out against them. Moreover, the Counts of Flanders and Normandy set out with him. They could not lead out more than one hundred and fifty knights, and had not the shame of returning restrained them, they would have turned back because of the few knights. Thus, God urging them, they set forth, found the enemy and pursued them and forced them to destruction in the river. When they had thus gained the victory and spoils, they returned with great exultation to the camp. In the meanwhile the Genoese ships had landed on the coast, which was about ten miles from the camp. That place, moreover, was called the Port of St. Simeon.

And now the enemy, going forth from the city little by little, killed the squires or peasants who were herding the horses and cattle beyond the river, and they took great plunder into the city. For we had placed the tents near the river and had made a bridge of the ships which were found there. However, the city also had a bridge, which was on the lower western corner, and there was a certain little mountain opposite us, where there were two mosques and some *casalia* of tombs. We mention these things, moreover, that the deeds which we will describe as done there will be easily clear. Just as we said, when the boldness of the enemy had somewhat increased, our men going forth from the camp, though frequently fewer than the enemy, were, nevertheless, not afraid to attack them. The Turks, however, though frequently scattered and put to flight, rose up again for battle there, not only because they had the swiftest horses and were nimble and unburdened with arms, other than bows, but also because in the bridge, which we have mentioned, they had a hope of refuge. They looked forward to the chance of shooting arrows at a distance from the little mountain, for their bridge was about one mile distant from our bridge. On the plain, moreover, which lay between the two bridges there were constant assaults and daily fights. It happened, indeed, at the beginning of the siege that the Count and the Bishop of Puy placed their camp near the river, and thus nearer the enemy, they were most frequently attacked by them. And so it came about through assaults of this kind that they lost all their horses, because the Turks, not prepared to fight with lances or swords, but with arrows at a distance, were to be feared while they fled, as well as when they pursued.

6. *Summary of the march to Antioch and the beginning of the siege.* (June 28-November, 1097.)

(*Anselm.*) However, moving camp from Nicaea on the fourth day before the Kalends of July, we kept to the march for three days. On the fourth day, the Turks, with forces gathered from all sides, again attacked a smaller part of our army; moreover, they killed many of our men and drove all the rest within the camp itself. The men in command of this part of the army were Bohemund, Count of the Romans,[11] Count Stephen, and the Count of Flanders. To these in such fearful straits there suddenly appeared the standards of the larger army; in the front rode Hugh the Great, and the Duke of Lorraine, but the Count of St. Gilles, as well as the venerable Bishop of Puy, were following. For they had heard of the battle and were hastening to their aid. Moreover, the Turks are estimated as 260,000, upon whom our men advanced, killing many and forcing the rest to flight. On this day I returned from the Emperor, to whom the princes had sent me for our common interest. From this day our princes, remaining together in one army, did not separate from each other. And while we were thus crossing the regions of Romania and Armenia we found no obstacle, except that after we had passed Iconium our advance guard encountered a few Turks. These were put to flight, and on the twelfth day before the Kalends of November we laid siege to Antioch. Then we took by force the neighboring cities of Tarsus and Laodicaea. One day, however, before we had surrounded the city in siege, we put to flight at the Iron Bridge some Turks who had gone out to devastate the region, and we snatched from them many Christians; moreover, we led back horses and camels (laden) with very great plunder. But after we had surrounded the city in siege, the Turks of the nearest castle were daily killing those of the army going in and out. The princes of our army came upon them in hiding and killed four hundred of them and drove others headlong into a certain river. Some, however, they brought along with them.

Know that we are besieging Antioch with all diligence to take it very shortly, as we think. We are abundantly supplied with grain, wine, oil, and all goods beyond belief. However, I ask you and all to whom this letter shall have come to pray God for us and for our dead. The following are those who have perished in arms: At Nicaea, Baldwin of Ghent, Baldwin *Chalderuns,* who was the first to do battle with the Turks. On the Kalends of July in battle, Robert of Paris, Lisiard of Flanders, Hilduin of Mazingarbe, Ansellus of *Caium,* Manasses of Clermont. The following are those who died in peace at Nicaea: Wido of Vitry, Odo of Varneuil, Hugh of Rheims; at the castle *Sparnum*, the venerable abbot Roger, my chaplain; at Antioch, Alard of *Spiniacum*, Hugh of *Calniacum*.[12] Again and again I urge you, readers of this letter, to pray for us, and you, Lord Archbishop, not to delay recommending the same task to your bishops. And know for a fact that we have acquired two hundred cities and fortresses for the Lord. Let the Mother Church of the West be joyful; she who has borne such offspring to acquire so glorious a name for her and to aid so marvelously the Church of the East. And that you may believe this (to be genuine), know that you have sent me a tapestry through Raymond of Cassel.[13] Farewell.

(*The Crusading Princes.*) Bohemund, son of Robert, and Raymond, Count of St. Gilles, likewise Duke Godfrey and Hugh the Great, to the lords and vassals of the whole world who cherish the Catholic faith in hope of eternal life.

In order that it may be known to all how peace has been made between ourselves and the Emperor, and how it has fared with us in the land of the Saracens since we have come there, we are sending to you this, our legate, who will diligently set forth in order all that has been done by us.

The first matter to be told is that the Emperor, in the middle of May, pledged us his faith and security on oath, giving us, likewise, hostages, namely his nephew and his son-in-law. In addition to this, he added that he would not further attempt to molest any pilgrim to the Holy Sepulchre. Later, he sent his *protopatron*[14] through all his land, sending him even to Durazzo, and commanded that no one should dare to harm any pilgrim; that if any one should violate this command, he would fittingly suffer the penalty of hanging instantly. What more? Let us return now to these matters by which your hearts should be filled with the greatest joy.

At the end of the month of May, indeed, we made a stand to do battle with the Turks. Thanks to God, however, we overcame them. Of them, moreover, thirty thousand are undoubtedly dead; of us but three thousand rest in peace, who are without any doubt glorying in eternal life. There, indeed, all of us gained in countless measure an abundance of gold, silver, and precious garments, as well as armor. We also seized the huge city of Nicaea with great valor, and beyond it we acquired forts and towns along a ten days' journey. After this, however, we engaged in a great battle at Antioch which we bravely won, to such an extent that of their number seventy thousand were killed, but of our own only ten thousand lie dead in peace. Who has seen such joy? For whether we live or die, we are of the Lord! Besides this, know for a fact that the King of the Persians has sent word that he will do battle with us on the feast of All Saints, asserting that if he overcomes us, he, with the King of Babylon and many other pagan kings, will not cease to advance against the Christians; but if he should lose, he has pledged his word that he and all whom he can persuade will become Christians. Wherefore, we urgently pray you all constantly to fast, give alms, and say masses with devotion. Help us especially, however, with many devout prayers and alms on the third day before the festival, which is Friday, on which we will engage mightily in battle, Christ triumphing. Farewell.

I, Bishop of Grenoble, send this letter which was brought to me at Grenoble, to you, Archbishops and Canons of the Holy Church at Tours, that through you it may be made known to all who will gather together for the festival, and through them to the diverse parts of the world to which they shall return. Let some of these aid by just petition, prayers, and alms, but let others hasten to join them with arms.

(*Stephen.*) Count Stephen to Adele, his most sweet and most beloved wife, and to his very dear children and all his vassals, noble and common; the grace and blessing of his whole greeting.

You may believe most certainly, dearest, that this messenger, whom I have sent for your delight, left me before Antioch in good health and unharmed, and, through God's grace, in the greatest prosperity. There, with the chosen army of Christ and in His great might, we had already advanced toward the seat of the Lord Jesus for twenty-three successive weeks. You may know for a fact, my beloved, that I now have twice as much of gold, silver, and other riches as your love assigned me at the time when I parted from you. For all our princes, with the common consent of the whole army, constituted me, even though I was unwilling, their lord and director and governor of all their acts up to the present time.

You have heard (fully) enough that after the capture of Nicaea we had a considerable battle with the treacherous Turks, and that at first, the Lord God aiding us, we defeated them. After this, we acquired the whole region of Romania and later Cappadocia. And we learned that there dwelt in Cappadocia a certain Turkish prince, Assam.[15] Thither we directed our march. We took by storm all his fortresses and pursued him into a very strong castle situated on the top of a cliff. Also, we gave the land of Assam himself to one of our princes, and in order that he might conquer the aforesaid Assam, we left him there with many soldiers of Christ. Then, through the midst of Armenia we routed the unspeakable Turks, who had incessantly followed us, (and pursued them) up to the great Euphrates river and even to the bank of this river, where they dropped all their baggage and pack saddles and fled through the river into Arabia. But the braver of these Turks, entering Syria, hastened by forced marches night and day, in order that they might enter the royal city of Antioch before our arrival. The whole army of God, however, upon learning of this (victory), gave fitting thanks and praise to the Omnipotent Lord.

(*Simeon and Adhemar.*) Simeon, Patriarch of Jerusalem and Adhemar,[16] Bishop of St. Mary of Puy, especially the latter, who received from Pope Urban charge of the Christian army; greeting, peace, and eternal salvation from our God and Lord Jesus Christ.

By common advice we clergy, bishops, and monks, as well as dukes, counts, and other leading laymen are sending (envoys) to you with most urgent prayers for the salvation of your souls. We admonish all who dwell in the northern regions of the West not to delay coming to us. However, let those come above all who desire their salvation and have bodily health and means for the journey. Even though you can come with but little, God Almighty will provide for you so that you may live. We Christians, most beloved brethren, are in Romania. Though with great difficulty, we have, nevertheless, conquered the large city of Nicaea and subjected it to our sway. We have fought three battles; our army has moved from Nicaea to Antioch; and we have taken by storm many other cities and fortresses of the Turks. We have a hundred thousand mounted knights and armored men, but what of it? We are few in comparison with the pagans, but verily God is fighting in our behalf. In this connection, hear, too, brethren, the miracle which the same most holy Patriarch commends to all Christians— how the Lord Himself appeared to him in a vision, promising that each one now engaged in this expedition will march before Him on that awful last day of Judgment wearing a crown. Therefore, since you well know that those who have remained apostate in deed, after having been signed with the cross, are in truth excommunicate, we admonish and beseech you to smite them all with the sword of anathema, if they do not make haste to follow us, so that by next Easter they may be where we are in Romania. Farewell. Be mindful of us who are laboring night and day. Pray for us.

7. *The foraging expedition of Bohemund and Robert of Flanders.*
   (December 28, 1097-January 2(?), 1098.)

(*Gesta.*) Now grain and all food began to be excessively dear before the birthday of the Lord. We did not dare to go outside;

we could find absolutely nothing to eat within the land of the Christians, and no one dared to enter the land of the Saracens without a great army. At last holding a council, our seignors decided how they might care for so many people. They concluded in the council that one part of our force should go out diligently to collect food and to guard the army everywhere, while the other part should remain faithfully to watch the enemy. At length, Bohemund said, "Seignors, and most distinguished knights, if you wish, and it seems honorable and good to you, I will be the one to go out with the Count of Flanders on this quest." Accordingly, when the services of the Nativity had been most gloriously celebrated on Monday, the second day of the week, they and more than twenty thousand knights and footmen went forth and entered the land of the Saracens, safe and unharmed.

There were assembled, indeed, many Turks, Arabs, and Saracens from Jerusalem, Damascus, Aleppo, and other regions, who were on their way to reinforce Antioch. So, when they heard that a Christian host was being led into their land, they made themselves ready there for battle against the Christians, and at earliest daybreak they came to the place where our people were gathered together. The barbarians divided themselves and formed two battle lines, one in front and one behind, seeking to surround us from every side. The worthy Count of Flanders, therefore, girt about on all sides with the armor of true faith and the sign of the cross, which he loyally wore daily, went against them, together with Bohemund, and our men rushed upon them all together. They immediately took to flight and hastily turned their backs; very many of them were killed, and our men took their horses and other spoils. But others, who had remained alive, fled swiftly and went away to the wrath of perdition. We, however, returning with great rejoicing, praised and magnified God, Three in One, who liveth and reigneth now and forever, Amen.

Finally, the Turks in the city of Antioch, enemies of God and Holy Christianity, hearing that Lord Bohemund and the Count of Flanders were not in the siege, came out from the city and boldly advanced to do battle with us. Knowing that those most valiant knights were away, they lay in ambush for us everywhere, more especially on that side where the siege was lagging. One Wednesday they found that they could resist and hurt us. The most iniquitous barbarians came out cautiously and, rushing violently upon us, killed many of our knights and foot-soldiers who were off their guard. Even the Bishop of Puy on that bitter day lost his seneschal, who was carrying and managing his standard. And had it not been for the stream which was between us and them, they would have attacked us more often and done the greatest hurt to our people.

At that time the famous man, Bohemund, advancing with his army from the land of the Saracens, came to the mountain of Tancred,[17] wondering whether perchance he could find anything to carry away, for they were ransacking the whole region. Some, in truth, found something, but others went away empty-handed. Then the wise man, Bohemund, upbraided them, saying: "Oh, unhappy and most wretched people! O, most vile of all Christians! Why do you want to go away so quickly? Only stop; stop until we shall all be gathered together, and do not wander about like sheep without a shepherd. Moreover, if the enemy find you wandering, they will kill you, for they are watching by night and by day to find you alone, or ranging about in groups without a leader; and they are striving daily to kill you and lead you into captivity." When his words were finished, he returned to his camp with his men, more empty-handed than laden.

(*Raymond.*) And since already in the third month of the siege food was bought too dearly, Bohemund and the Count of Flanders were chosen to lead an army into *Hispania*[18] for food, the Count and the Bishop of Puy being left as a guard in the camp. For the Count of Normandy was away at the time, and the Duke was very ill. However, when the enemy learned this, they repeated their customary assaults. The Count, moreover, was compelled to attack them in his usual manner, and, after forming the ranks of the foot-soldiers, he, with some knights, pursued the assailants. He captured and killed two of them on the slope of the little mountain and forced all the enemy to enter by the bridge. As our foot-soldiers saw this, they left their posts and their standards and ran in a mob up to their bridges. And when there, as if already in safety, they cast stones and weapons upon those who were defending the bridge. The Turks, after forming a line, began to rush against our men by the bridge and by a path which was lower down. Meanwhile, our knights chased toward our bridge a certain horse whose master they had overthrown. When our people saw this, thinking our knights in flight, they showed their backs to the attack of the enemy without delay. Then the Turks killed without ceasing those who fled. Even if the knights of the Franks wished to resist and fight for their people, they were caught by the crowd of fleeing footmen, by their arms, and by the manes and tails of the horses, and were either thrown from their horses, or, out of compassion and regard for the safety of their people, were brought to flight. The enemy, indeed, without delay, without pity, slaughtered and pursued the living and despoiled the bodies of the dead. Moreover, it was not enough for our men to leave their arms, take flight, despise shame, but they rushed into the river to be overwhelmed with stones or arrows of the enemy, or to remain under water. If skill and strength in swimming bore anyone across the river, he reached the camp of his companions. However, our flight extended from their bridge to our bridge. They there killed about fifteen of our knights and about twenty foot-soldiers. The standard-bearer of the Bishop was killed there, and his standard was captured. A certain very noble youth, Bernard Raymond of Beziers, died there.

Let the servants of God neither complain nor be angry with us, if our men bequeathed such open shame to the memory of our army; since God, who in this way desired to drive to penance the minds of adulterers and robbers, at the same time gladdened our army in *Hispania*. For a rumor, going forth from our camp, announced to Bohemund and his fellows that all was prosperous, and that the Count had gained a most noble victory. Moreover, this report aroused their spirits no little. After Bohemund had besieged a certain village, he heard some of his peasants suddenly fleeing and shouting, and when he had sent knights to meet them, they saw an army of Turks and Arabs close at hand. Moreover, among those who had set out to determine the cause of the flight and outcry was the Count of Flanders, and with him certain Provençals. For all from Burgundy, Auvergne, Gascony, and all Goths[19] are called Provençals, while the others are called of the Frankish race: that is, in the army; among the enemy, however, all are spoken of as Frankish. This Count of Flanders, as we have said, however, thinking it a disgrace to report about the enemy before attacking them, rushed impetuously against the phalanxes of the Turks. The Turks, indeed, unaccustomed to conduct battles with swords, took to flight for refuge. Nor did the Count sheathe his sword until he had removed a hundred of the enemy from life. When he was now returning to Bohemund as victor, he saw twelve thousand Turks coming behind him, and rising up on the nearest hill toward the left he saw a countless multitude of foot-soldiers. Then, after communicating his plan to the rest of the army, he took a number of men back with him and violently attacked the Turks. Bohemund, indeed, followed at a distance with the rest and guarded the rear lines. For the Turks have this custom in fighting: even though they are fewer in number, they always strive to encircle their enemy. This they attempted to do in this battle also, but by the foresight of Bohemund the wiles of the enemy were prevented. When, however, the Turks and the Arabs, coming against the Count of Flanders, saw that the affair was not to be conducted at a distance with arrows, but at close quarters with swords, they turned in flight. The Count followed them for two miles, and in this space he saw the bodies of the killed lying like bundles of grain reaped in the field. The ambushes which Bohemund had encountered were scattered and put to flight in the same way. But the countless horde of foot-soldiers, of which we spoke above, slipped away in flight through places impassable to horses. I would dare, I say, were it not arrogant to judge, to place this battle ahead of the fights of the Maccabees, since if Maccabaeus with three thousand felled forty-eight thousand of the enemy, more than sixty thousand of the enemy were here turned in flight by a force of forty knights. I do not, indeed, belittle the valor of the Maccabees, nor exalt the valor of our knights, but I say that God, then marvelous in Maccabaeus, was now more marvelous in our troops.

A (strange) result of this achievement was that after the enemy had been put to flight the courage of our men decreased, so that they did not dare to pursue those whom they saw headlong in flight. Accordingly, when the army returned victorious and empty-handed, there was such famine in the camp that two *solidi* were scarcely enough to keep one man in bread for a day, nor were other things to be obtained less dearly.

8. *Sufferings in camp before Antioch.* (January-March, 1098.)

(*Gesta.*) When the Armenians and Syrians, however, saw that our men were returning utterly empty-handed, they counselled together and went away through the mountains and places of which they had previous knowledge, making subtle inquiry and buying grain and other bodily sustenance. This they brought to the camp, in which hunger was great beyond measure, and they sold a single ass-load for eight *perpre*, which is worth one hundred and twenty *solidi* of *denarii*. There, indeed, many of our men died because they did not have the means wherewith to buy at such a dear price.

William Carpenter and Peter the Hermit secretly left because of the great sorrow and misery. Tancred pursued and caught them and brought them back in disgrace. They gave him a pledge that they would return willingly to camp and render satisfaction to the seignors. Then William lay all that night, like an evil thing, in the tent of Bohemund. On the next day at early dawn he came shamefacedly and stood in the presence of Bohemund, who, addressing him, said, "O, the misfortune and infamy of all France, the disgrace and villainy of Gaul! O, most evil of all whom the earth endures! Why did you so vilely flee? Was it, perchance, for the reason that you wished to betray these knights and the host of Christ, as you betrayed others in *Hispania?*" He was entirely silent and no speech proceeded from his mouth. Almost all those of Frankish race gathered together and humbly asked Lord Bohemund not to let anything worse befall him. He nodded, with calm countenance, and said, "To this I willingly consent for love of you, if he will swear to me with his whole heart and mind that he will never withdraw from the march to Jerusalem, whether for good or evil; and if Tancred will agree not to let anything untoward befall him, either through him or his men." When William had heard these words, he willingly agreed, and Bohemund forthwith dismissed him. Later, indeed, Carpenter, caught in the greatest villainy, slipped away by stealth without long delay. This poverty and wretchedness God meted out to us because of our sins. Thus in the whole army no one could find a thousand knights who had horses of the best kind.

Meanwhile the hostile *Tetigus*, upon hearing that the army of the Turks had come upon us, said that he was afraid, thinking that we would all perish and fall into the hands of the enemy. Fabricating all the falsehoods which he could industriously scatter, he said: "Seignors and most illustrious men, you see that we are here in the greatest need, and aid is coming to us from no side. So permit me now to return to my country of Romania, and I will, for certain, cause many ships to come hither by sea, laden with grain, wine, barley, meat, butter, and cheese, and all the goods which you need. I shall also cause horses to be brought for sale, and a market to be brought hither in the fealty of the Emperor. So I will swear all this loyally to you and attend to it. Also, my servants and my tent are still in camp, from which you may believe firmly that I will return as quickly as possible." And so he concluded his speech. That foe went and left all his possessions in the camp, and he remains, and will remain, in perjury.

Therefore in this way the greatest need came upon us, because the Turks pressed us on all sides, so that none of us dared now to go out of the tents, for they constrained us on one side, and excruciating hunger on the other; but of succour and help we had none. The lesser folk, and the very poor fled to Cyprus, Romania, and into the mountains. Through fear of the most evil Turks we dared not go to the sea, and the way was never made open to us.

Accordingly, when Lord Bohemund heard that an innumerable host of Turks was coming against us, he went cautiously to the others, saying: "Seignors, most illustrious knights, what are we going to do? For we are not so great that we can fight on two sides. But do you know what we may do? Let us make two lines of ourselves; let a portion of the foot-soldiers remain together to guard the pavilions, and by feinting they will be able to resist those who are in the city. Let the other portion, however, consisting of knights, go with us to meet our enemy, who are lodged here near us in the fortress Aregh beyond the Iron Bridge." Moreover, when evening came the famous man, Bohemund, advanced with the other most illustrious knights and went to lie between the river and the lake. At earliest daybreak he straightway ordered scouts to go out and see how many squadrons of Turks there were, where (they were) and definitely what they were doing. They went out and began to inquire craftily where the lines of the Turks were hidden. Then they saw innumerable Turks, divided into two battle lines, coming from the side of the river, with their greatest valor marching in the rear. The scouts returned very quickly, saying, "Behold! See, they come! Be prepared, therefore, all of you, for they are already near us." And the wise man, Bohemund, spoke to the others, "Seignors, most invincible knights, array yourselves for battle, each one for himself." They answered: "Wise and famous man! Great and magnificent man! Brave and victorious man! Arbiter of battles, and judge of disputes! Make arrangements for us and yourself." Thereupon, Bohemund commanded that each one of the princes should himself form his line in order. They did so, and six lines were formed. Five of them went out together to attack them (the enemy). Bohemund, accordingly, marched a short distance in the rear with his line.

Thus, when our men were successfully united, one band urged on the other. The clamor resounded to the sky. All fought at the same time. Showers of weapons darkened the air. When their troops of greatest valor, who had been in their rear, came up, they attacked our forces sharply, so that our men fell back a little. As the most learned man, Bohemund, saw this, he groaned. Then he commanded his constable, that is to say Robert, son of Girard, saying: "Go as quickly as you can, like a brave man, and remember our illustrious and courageous forefathers of old. Be keen in the service of God and the Holy Sepulchre, and bear in mind that this battle is not carnal, but spiritual. Be, therefore, the bravest athlete of Christ. Go in peace. The Lord be with you everywhere." And so that man, fortified on all sides with the sign of the cross, went into the lines of the Turks, just as a lion, famished for three or four days, goes forth from his cave raging and thirsting for the blood of beasts and, rushing unexpectedly among the herds of sheep, tears them to pieces as they flee hither and thither. So violently did he press upon them that the tips of his renowned standard flew over the heads of the Turks. Moreover, as the other lines saw that the standard of Bohemund was so gloriously borne before them, they went back to the battle again, and with one accord our men attacked the Turks, who, all amazed, took to flight. Our men, therefore, pursued them even to the Iron Bridge and cut off their heads. The Turks, however, rushed hastily back to their camps and, taking everything they could find there, despoiled the whole camp, set it on fire, and fled. The Armenians and Syrians, knowing that the Turks had utterly lost the battle, went out and watched at the narrow places, where they killed and captured many of them. And so by the favor of God our enemy was overcome on that day. Moreover, our men were sufficiently rewarded with horses and many other things which they greatly needed. And they carried the heads of one hundred dead before the gate of the city, where the envoys of the Emir of Babylon,[20] who had been sent to the princes, were encamped. During the whole day those who had remained in the tents had fought before the three gates of the city with those who were inside. This battle was fought on the Wednesday before the beginning of Lent, on the fifth day before the Ides of February, with the favor of our Lord Jesus Christ, who, with the Father and the Holy Ghost, liveth and reigneth God forever and ever. Amen. Our men returned triumphant and joyful from the victory which, under God's guidance, they had obtained on that day over their defeated enemy. The enemy, entirely beaten, fled, ever roaming and wandering hither and thither. Some (at length) went to Chorosan, but others entered the land of the Saracens.

(*Raymond*). And so the poor began to leave, and many rich who feared poverty. If any for love of valor remained in camp, they suffered their horses to waste away by daily hunger. Indeed, straw did not abound; and fodder was so dear that seven or eight *solidi* were not sufficient to buy one night's food for a horse. Another calamity also befell the army, for Bohemund, who had become most distinguished in *Hispania* said that he would leave; that he had come for honor, and (now) beheld his men and horses perishing for want; and he (further) said that he was not a rich man whose private resources would suffice for so long a siege. We found out afterwards that he had said this for the reason that he was ambitiously longing to become head of the city of Antioch.

Meanwhile, there was a great earthquake on the third day before the Kalends of January, and we beheld a very marvelous sign in the sky. For in the first watch of the night the sky was so red in the north that it seemed as if dawn had arisen to announce the day. And though in this way God chastised His army, so that we were intent upon the light which was rising in the darkness, yet the minds of some were so blind and abandoned that they were recalled neither from luxury nor robbery. At this time the Bishop prescribed a fast of three days and urged prayers and alms, together with a procession, upon the people; moreover, he commanded the priests to devote themselves to masses and prayers, the clerics to psalms. Thereupon, the merciful Lord, remembering His compassion, put off the punishment of His children, lest the arrogance of their adversaries increase.

There was, besides, in our army a certain member of the Emperor's household whom he had given to us in his place, *Tatius* by name, mangled in nose and all virtue. I had almost forgotten him, since he deserved to be abandoned to oblivion forever. This man, however, was daily whispering in the ears of the princes that they should scatter to the neighboring camp, and thence assail the people of Antioch by frequent assaults and ambush. However, as all this was made clear to the Count (for he had been sick since the day when he was forced to flee at the bridge), he called his princes and the Bishop of Puy together. After holding a council, he gave them fifty marks of silver on this condition, truly, that if any of his knights lost a horse, it should be restored to him out of those fifty marks and other (resources) which had been given to the brotherhood. Moreover, this kind of coöperation was of great profit at that time, since the poor of our army, who wanted to cross the river to gather herbs, feared the frequent assaults of the enemy, and since very rarely did any care to go against the enemy, because their horses were starved and weak, and, in addition, so few that scarcely one hundred could be found in the whole army of the Count and Bishop. A similar lot had befallen Bohemund and the other princes. Accordingly, for this reason our knights were not afraid to meet the enemy, especially those who had bad or weak horses, since they knew that if they lost their horses they would obtain better ones. Moreover, something else occurred, namely that all the princes except the Count promised the city to Bohemund, provided it was taken. So Bohemund and the other princes swore to this agreement, that they would not withdraw from the siege of Antioch for seven years, unless the city was taken.

While these matters were happening in the camp, rumor also announced that the army of the Emperor was coming. It was reported to have been assembled from many peoples; namely, Slavs and Patzinaks and Cumans and Turcopoles. For they are called

Turcopoles who either were reared among the Turks, or were born of a Turkish father and a Christian mother. These peoples, moreover, because they had hurt us on the march confessed that they were afraid to meet us. All this, however, that mangled *Tatius* had made up, and he had made such comments in order to be able to get away. This man, after heaping up not only (these) statements, but even the very greatest insults, betrayal of his companions, and perjury, slipped away in flight, after having granted to Bohemund two or three cities, *Turso*,[21] Mamistra, Adana. Accordingly, after acquiring everlasting shame for himself and his people in this way, he feigned a journey to the army of the Emperor, and, leaving his tents and his servants, he set out with the curse of God.[22]

It was announced to us at this time that the chief of the Caliph was coming to the help of Antioch with a large army, which he was leading from Chorosan. On this account, after a council had been held in the house of the Bishop, it was decided that the foot-soldiers should guard the camp and the knights should go out of the camp against the enemy; for they said that if the many unwarlike and fearful in our army saw a multitude of Turks, they would afford examples of fright, rather than of boldness. Our men, therefore, set forth at night, lest those in the city should notice (their departure) and report it to those who were coming to aid them, and hid themselves among the little mountains about two leagues distant from our camp.

However, when it became morning, the enemy appeared with the sun. Let them hearken, let them hearken, I beg, who have at one time and another tried to hurt the army, so that, when they recognize that God enlarges His compassion among us, they may hasten to make restitution by lamentations of penance. Accordingly, after the knights had been formed in six squadrons, God multiplied them so much that they who had scarcely seemed to number seventy before the formation, after it were sworn to number more than two housand in each squadron. What, indeed, shall I say of their boldness, when the knights even sang the military songs so festively that they regarded the coming battle as if it were a game? Moreover, the battle happened to be fought in this place where the swamp and river are a mile apart. This, however, prevented the enemy from spreading out, so that they could not encircle us in their usual manner. For God, who had given us other things, afforded us six successive valleys for advancing to battle. In one hour after going forth the field was taken, and while the sun shone brightly, the battle was committed to arms and shields. Our men, moreover, at first advanced a little, while the Turks, though they scattered to shoot with their bows, yet made a move to retreat. But our men suffered very much until the first ranks of the Turks were pushed into the rear, for as we learned from their deserters, there were said to be not less than twenty-eight thousand horsemen in this battle. And when the first line of the Turks was sufficiently mixed up with the following lines, the Franks called upon the Lord and charged. Nor was there delay; the Lord, strong and mighty in battle, was present. He protected His children, and hurled down the enemy. So the Franks pursued them even to their very strongly fortified camp, which was about ten miles from the place of battle. But the custodians of the camp, upon seeing this, set fire to it and fled. We were, however, so rejoiced and exultant at this, that we hailed as a second victory the burning of the camp.

And thus on that same day the light in the camp was so great that there was no place toward the city where fighting was not going on. For the enemy had arranged that, while we were most fiercely engaged by the besieged, we should be overwhelmed by their unexpected aid from the rear. But God, who granted victory to our knights, fought among our foot-soldiers (also). And on that day we obtained no less a triumph over the besieged than our knights reported over the helpers. Accordingly, after the victory and the spoils had been won, the several heads of the dead were brought to the camp. And that we might cause fear among the enemy by the evidence of the (fate of) their scattered allies, the heads that had been brought along were suspended on stakes. This we believed later to have been done by the disposition of God. For when the standard of the Blessed Mary had been captured, they put it point downward in the ground, as if to shame us. And thus it happened that they were restrained from taunting us by the sight of the uplifted heads of their men.

At this time there were in our camp envoys from the King of Babylon, who, upon seeing the wonders which God was working through His servants, glorified Jesus, the son of the Virgin Mary, who through His poor had ground to dust their mightiest tyrants. These envoys, moreover, promised us favor and good will with their king; besides, they told of very many good deeds of their king toward the Egyptian Christians and our pilgrims. Thereupon, our envoys were sent back with them to enter upon a treaty and friendship with the King.[23]

9. *Call for reinforcements.*

(*Simeon and the bishops*). The Patriarch of Jerusalem and the bishops, Greek as well as Latin, and the whole army of God and the Church to the Church of the West; fellowship in celestial Jerusalem, and a portion of the reward of their labor.

Since we are not unaware than you delight in the increase of the Church, and we believe that you are concerned to hear matters adverse as well as prosperous, we hereby notify you of the success of our undertaking. Therefore, be it known to your delight that God has triumphed in forty important cities and in two hundred fortresses of His Church in Romania, as well as in Syria, and that we still have one hundred thousand men in armor, besides the common throng, though many were lost in the first battles. But what is this? What is one man in a thousand? Where we have a count, the enemy have forty kings; where we have a company, the enemy have a legion; where we have a knight, they have a duke; where we have a foot-soldier, they have a count; where we have a camp, they have a kingdom. However, confiding not in numbers, nor in bravery, nor in any presumption, but protected by justice and the shield of Christ, and with St. George, Theodore, Demetrius, and Basil,[24] soldiers of Christ, truly supporting us, we have pierced, and in security are piercing, the ranks of the enemy. On five general battle-fields, God conquering, we have conquered.

But what more? In behalf of God and ourselves, I, apostolic Patriarch, the bishops and the whole order of the Lord, urgently pray, and our spiritual Mother Church calls out: "Come, my most beloved sons, come to me, retake the crown from the hands of the sons of idolatry, who rise against me—the crown from the beginning of the world predestined for you. Come, therefore, we pray, to fight in the army of the Lord at the same place in which the Lord fought, in which Christ suffered for us, leaving to you an example that you should follow his foot-steps. Did not God, innocent, die for us? Let us therefore also die, if it be our lot, not for Him, but for ourselves, that by dying on earth we may live for God. Yet it is (now) not necessary that we should die, nor fight much, for we have (already) sustained the more serious trials, but the task of holding the fortresses and cities has been heavily reducing our army. Come, therefore, hasten to be repaid with the twofold reward—namely, the land of the living and the land flowing with milk and honey and abounding in all good things. Behold, men, by the shedding of our blood the way is open everywhere. Bring nothing with you except only what may be of use to us. Let only the men come; let the women, as yet, be left. From the home in which there are two, let one, the one more ready for battle, come. But those, especially, who have made the vow, (let them come). Unless they come and discharge their vow, I, apostolic Patriarch, the bishops, and the whole order of the orthodox, do excommunicate them and remove them utterly from the communion of the Church. And do you likewise, that they may not have burial among Christians, unless they are staying for suitable reasons. Come, and receive the two-fold glory! This, therefore, also write.

10. *The erection of a fortress.   Fights with the Turks.* (March 5—end of May, 1098).

(*Gesta*). However, when our leaders saw that those of our enemy who were in the city were doing us damage and harassing us, watching and lying in ambush wherever they could hurt us, they assembled together and said, "Before we lose our people, let us build a fort at the mosque which is before the gate of the city, where the bridge is; and there, perchance, we will be able to harass our enemy." All agreed, and approved it as a good thing to be done. The Count of St. Gilles spoke first and said, "Help me build the fort, and I will fortify and guard it." Bohemund answered, "If it is your desire and the other lords approve, I will go with you to the Port of St. Simeon diligently to fetch those men who are there for this work. Let the others, who are to remain, fortify themselves on all sides, lest, perchance, the enemies of God and ourselves should go out from the city, and let all be gathered at the place which we have pointed out." And thus it was done. So the Count and Bohemund went forth to the Port of St. Simeon. We who remained in one body began (to build) the fort, until the Turks prepared themselves and came out of the city for battle against us. And thus they rushed upon us and put us to flight and killed several of us, whereat we were exceedingly sad. On the next day, when the Turks saw that our leaders were absent and that on the day before they had gone to the Port, they made themselves ready and went out to meet them (Bohemund and Raymond) as they came from the Port. Then, as they saw the Count and Bohemund coming and escorting that host, they began immediately to whistle, and chatter, and shout with the most violent outcry, encircling us on all sides, hurling, shooting, wounding (our men), and cruelly cutting them down with the sword. For so fiercely did they attack our forces that the latter took to flight over the top of the mountain, and wherever a passageway was open. He who could advance at rapid pace escaped alive, but he who could not flee met death. There were martyred on that day more than a thousand of our knights and footmen, who, we believe, ascended joyfully to heaven. Clothed in white and wearing the robe of martyrdom that they had received, they there glorified and magnified our Lord God, Three in One, in whom they happily triumphed, crying aloud with one voice, "Wherefore didst thou not defend our blood which to-day was shed for Thy name?"

Bohemund, therefore, did not hold to the road which they had taken, but with a few knights came more quickly to us who were gathered together. Then, angered at the killing of our men, we called upon the name of Christ, and putting our trust in the march to the Holy Sepulchre, together went out against them for battle and attacked them with one heart and one mind. The enemies of God and ourselves stood thoroughly astounded and greatly terrified, thinking that our men would conquer and kill them, just as they themselves had done the people of the Count and Bohemund. But Almighty God did not accord them this end. Therefore the true knights of God, armed on all sides with the sign of the cross, rushed fiercely upon them and attacked them violently, but they fled quickly by means of the narrow bridge to their entrance. Those who could not cross the bridge alive, because of the multitude of people and horses there, received eternal death and yielded their unhappy souls to the devil and the ministers of Satan. And so we overcame them, driving and hurling them down into the river. The water of the rapid stream seemed to flow everywhere red with the blood of the Turks. And if, perchance, any of these wished to crawl upon the columns of the bridge, or by swimming tried to reach the land, he was wounded by our men, who stood all around on the bank of the river. Furthermore, the noise and outcry of both our forces and theirs sounded to the sky. Showers of javelins and arrows covered the sky and (obscured) the clearness of the day; voices (shrieked) within and without the city. Christian women of the city came to the windows of the wall, where they beheld the wretched fate of the Turks and stealthily applauded with their hands, as was their custom. The Armenians and Syrians, willing or unwilling, shot arrows out at us by order of the Turkish leaders. Likewise, there were killed in body and soul at that battle twelve Emirs of the Turkish horde, and others of the foremost and braver knights who took a leading part in the defense of the city. The number (of these) was fifteen hundred. The rest who remained alive dared no longer shout or chatter by night or by day, as they had formerly been wont to do. And so night alone overcame all of them and us, and night prevented both sides from fighting, hurling, piercing, and shooting. Thus our enemies were overcome by the valor of God and the Holy Sepulchre, and they could no longer have such strength, either in voice or deed, as they had before. And thus on that day we were bountifully supplied with their horses and many other things which were necessary enough for us.

On the next day, at earliest dawn, other Turks went out from the city, and, collecting all the fetid corpses of the dead Turks which they could find on the bank of the river, except those which lay hidden in the sand of the same river, they buried them at the mosque which is across the bridge in front of the city gate. At the same time they buried with them their garments, gold besants, bows, arrows, and very many other instruments which we were unable to name. And so, when our men heard that the Turks had buried their dead, all made preparation and came in haste to the diabolical temple and ordered the bodies to be exhumed, the tombs broken open, and the corpses dragged forth from the sepulchre. They cast all the cadavers into a ditch and carried off the severed heads to our tents, in order to find out their number exactly—all the heads, that is, except those loaded upon the four horses of the envoys of the Emir of Babylon and sent to the sea. The Turks grieved exceedingly upon beholding this, and were sad even to death; grieving daily, they did nothing else except weep and lament.

But the third day we began with joined forces to construct the above-mentioned fortress of stone, which we took from the tombs of the Turks. And so, when the fort was finished, we forthwith began to press our enemies from every side. Their arrogance was now reduced to nothing. We, however, roamed in security hither and thither, to the Port and to the mountains, praising and glorifying our Lord God, whose honor and glory is forever and ever, Amen.

Now nearly all the roads were forbidden and closed to the Turks on every side, except on that part of the river where there was a fort and a certain monastery. If this fortress had been thoroughly guarded by us, not one of these people would have dared to go out of the gate of the city. At length our leaders held a council and with unanimous accord said, "Let us select one of us to hold that fort sturdily and close to our enemies the mountains and plains, the entrance and exit of the city." But most of them refused to be installed there themselves, unless there were many in a body (with them). Tancred was the first to offer himself before the others, saying: "If I knew what it would profit me, I would carefully strengthen the fort with my men alone, and I would energetically deny our enemy the road by which too frequently they are wont to rage against us." They straightway promised him four hundred marks of silver. Tancred did not tarry; although alone, he went forth with his most renowned knights and servants and immediately shut off on all sides the road and pass from the Turks. As a result, none of them, already terrified by fear of him, now dared to go out either for fodder, wood, or any other necessities. Tancred remained there with his men and began violently to harass the city on all sides. That same day a very large party of Armenians and Syrians, who were bringing food to the Turks in the city, came down from the mountains in fancied security. Tancred, coming upon them, seized them with all that they carried—grain, wine, barley, oil, and other things of this kind. He conducted himself so stoutly and successfully there that he now held all the roads and paths closed to the Turks until the capture of Antioch.

(*Raymond*). At the same time it seemed best to our princes to erect a fortified camp on the hill above the tents of Bohemund, so that if the enemy should come against us again, they could in no way attack our tents. When this had been done, our camp would be so strong that, like a city, we would be protected on all sides by craft as well as by nature. For we had this fortress on the east; on the south, the walls of the city and the swamp which fortified the walls likewise protected us, and did not give the people of the city a chance to fight us, unless they came out through the gates. On the west, there was the river; on the north, a certain old wall which, descending from the mountain, extended up to the river. The people, likewise, approved (the idea) that another fortress should be established on the little mountain which was above their bridge. Engines, too, were constructed in the camp to attack the walls of the city; but this was in vain.

And when now in the fifth month of the siege our ships landed at our port with provisions, the Turks of the city began to besiege the roads to the sea and to kill the bearers of supplies. Our princes at first only endured this; the Turks, however, unpunished for their villainy and hoping for plunder, pressed us by day and by night. At length, it was agreed to establish a camp toward their bridge. But since many of our people had gone away to the Port, the Count and Bohemund were chosen to bring them back from there, together with mattocks and other instruments with which the wall of the new castle might be made. And when it was found out in the city that the Count and Bohemund were away, they began their customary attacks. Our men, moreover, advancing too rashly and without order, were basely scattered and put to flight.

And on the fourth day when the Count and Bohemund were returning from the Port with a very great multitude they were watched by the Turks. Our men thought themselves secure by their numbers alone. But why do I grieve over many matters?

It came to a fight, and our men turned their backs. Indeed, we lost up to three hundred men, but how much booty and how many arms it is impossible to say. While we were being slaughtered and pressed together like cattle among the mountains and precipices, the men from the camp began to advance against the enemy. And so it happened that they (the Saracens) were recalled from a slaughter of the fugitives. Why thus, Lord God? They in the camp were beaten, and these two greatest princes in Thy army were also beaten outside the camp! Should we flee to the camp? Or those from the camp to us? Arise and aid us, for Thy name's sake! Because if it had been learned back in the camp that the princes were beaten, or if it had chanced that we knew of the flight of those in the camp, all would have fled together. The Lord God thus arose as our helper at the opportune time, and those whom He had previously terrified, He now aroused to be first in battle.

When *Gracianus*,[25] ruler of the city, saw the spoils taken from our men, and the victory of his people, and that some of the men were still bold, he sent all his knights and foot-soldiers out; and, led on by hope of victory, he ordered the gates of the city to be shut behind his men, ordering his knights to conquer or to die. Meanwhile, our men advanced a short distance at command; the Turks, however, withdrew, shot with their bows, and charged our men very boldly. But our men suffered it for a while, until they could attack them in mass; nor did they yield at the charge of the enemy. There was, indeed, such lamentation and outcry to God in the camp that you would have thought the mercy of God must descend at the flowing of their tears. When they were about to come to close quarters, a certain knight, Ysoard of Ganges, a most noble Provençal with one hundred and fifty foot-soldiers, called upon God on bended knees. Then, encouraging his companions by saying, "On, soldiers of Christ!" he rushed upon the enemy. Our other lines attacked likewise. Thereupon, the arrogance of the enemy is disturbed. The gate is shut, the bridge is narrow, but the river is very wide. What result? The enemy in panic are knocked down and killed and overwhelmed with stones in the river; no avenue of escape, moreover, lies open. And had not *Gracianus* opened the gate of the city, we would on that day have had peace from Antioch. I have heard from many who were there that with boards taken from the bridge they destroyed twenty Turks and more in the river. The Duke of Lorraine gained much glory there, for he checked the enemy at the bridge and divided them in two as they were climbing up.

Thereupon, when the victory had been achieved, our men returned to camp with great rejoicing, many horses, and much booty. A certain memorable incident occurred there, which would that those who follow our vows could had seen! For, while a certain horseman of the enemy through fear of death was rushing headlong into the depths of the stream, he was caught by many of his own people and cast down from his horse and brushed off in the middle of the stream, together with that multitude which had caught him. It was worth the trouble to have seen some of the poor returning from the victory, for some of them, riding about among the tents on Arabian horses, displayed to their companions the relief of their poverty; others, moreover, dressed in two or three silken garments, magnified God, the Giver of victory and reward; still others, protected by three or four shields, eagerly showed the evidence of their triumph. And while by these and other displays they persuaded us to a belief in the magnificent victory, they could not persuade us of the number killed. Since the victory had been obtained at evening, the heads of the dead were not carried to camp. And the next day, when the fortress was to be erected before the enemy's bridge, some of the Turks were found in the ditch, for that hill was used as a burial ground of the Saracens. Thereupon, the poor, provoked at the remains of these people, broke open all their tombs. And thus when the Turks had been exhumed, no one had a doubt how great had been the victory, for about fifteen hundred were counted. I am not speaking now about those buried in the city and those carried off by the river. However, when the unbearable stench oppressed those who were at work on the fortress, the corpses were cast forth into the river. The sailors, indeed, who had been scattered and wounded in the flight of the Count and Bohemund, were still dubious, because of their fright, about the extent of the victory. However, when they saw so great a multitude of dead, as though made well thereby, they began to magnify God, who is wont to correct and gladden His children. Therefore it had been so arranged by the disposition of God that those who had given to the wild beasts and birds the bearers of provisions destroyed on the coast and on the banks of the river should themselves become food for the beasts and the birds in the same places. Accordingly, when the victory had been recognized and celebrated and the fortress constructed, the city of Antioch was besieged from north and south.

Consultation was held at this time as to who of the princes could go to garrison the fortress. Verily, a matter of common responsibility is frequently neglected, since each one thinks that it is being looked after by others. And while some of the princes, as if for a price, sought from the others the privilege of guarding it, the Count took over the custody of the fortress against the will of his men, both to avoid the charge of sloth and avarice, and to show the path of energy and valor to the torpid. For during the past summer he had been tried by a severe and protracted illness and had been so weak during the whole winter that he was said to be ready neither to fight nor to pay. Although he had done many things, yet because it was believed he could do more, he was proclaimed a nobody. Accordingly, having come upon this difficulty, that is, a question of his valor, he suffered such great hatred from all that he was almost cut off from his own people. In the meantime, while the Count was ignoring this, hoping that the enemy, oppressed on most sides, would flee thither from the city, he was early one morning surrounded by the enemy. There shone forth then a great miracle of divine protection, for sixty of our men sustained the attack of seven thousand Saracens; all the more wonderful, since the heavy showers of the past days had moistened the forest earth, filling the moat of the new fortress. And thus no lack of ways, but the valor of God alone checked the enemy. I do not think, however, that I should pass over the distinguished bravery of some of the knights, who, cut off by the enemy while they were guarding the bridge, could not return to the fortress for refuge, since it was a bowshot away. Thereupon, these knights, after making a circle in the multitude of the enemy, reached the corner of a neighboring house, and there stoutly and without fear sustained the attacks of the enemy, the rage of arrows, and the cloud of stones from all sides. Meanwhile, the sound of battle heard in the camp aroused our men. Thus the fortress was freed from the enemy, and though they abandoned the siege when they saw aid coming from afar, and though their bridge was very near, yet the last of them were cut off. Thereupon, when the moat and the walls of the fortress had been restored, the bearers of provisions could go back and forth from the Port in security. Accordingly, the hatred which the Count had borne was so lightened that he was called by all the father and preserver of the army. From this time, therefore, the fame of the Count increased, because he had borne the attacks of the enemy alone.

When, therefore, the bridge and the gate of the bridge were besieged, the Turks began going out by another gate, which faced the south, beside the river; and they sent their horses out to a certain retreat between the mountains and the river, which was a very fine pasture. Thereupon, when the place had been discovered by our men, they encircled the city by a difficult mountain at the close of the day and came to that pasture. Others, crossing by a ford, led from there two thousand horses, not counting the mules which were recovered; for in time past on the journey from the sea the enemy had taken many mules from us, which were now captured, recognized by their masters, and given to their former owners.

After this, Tancred fortified a certain monastery across the river, for which the Count gave him one hundred marks of silver, and the other princes whatever they could; for this fortress constrained the enemy much. Therefore we were pleased to wait; the fewer we were in number, the braver the grace of God made us.

11. *Capture of Antioch.* (End of May—June 3, 1098).

(*Gesta*). I can not enumerate all the things which we did before the city was captured, because there is no one in these regions, whether cleric or layman, who can at all write or tell just how things happened. Nevertheless, I will say a little.

There was a certain Emir of the race of the Turks, whose name was *Pirus*,[26] who took up the greatest friendship with Bohemund. By an interchange of messengers Bohemund often pressed this man to receive him within the city in a most friendly fashion, and, after promising Christianity to him most freely, he sent word that he would make him rich with much honor. *Pirus* yielded to these words and promises, saying, "I guard three towers, and I freely promise them to him, and at whatever hour he wishes I will receive him within them." Accordingly, Bohemund was now secure about entering the city, and, delighted, with serene mind and joyful countenance, he came to all the leaders, bearing joyful words to them in this wise: "Men, most illustrious knights, see how all of us, whether of greater or less degree, are in exceeding poverty and misery, and how utterly ignorant we are from what side we will fare better. Therefore, if it seems good and honorable to you, let one of us put himself ahead of the rest, and if he can acquire or contrive (the capture of) the city by any plan or scheme, by himself, or through the help of others, let us with one voice grant him the city as a gift." They absolutely refused and spurned (the suggestion) saying, "This city shall be given to no one, but we will hold it equally; since we have had equal effort, so let us have equal reward from it."

Bohemund, upon hearing these words, laughed a bit to himself and immediately retired. Not much later we listened to messages concerning (the approach of) an army of our enemy, Turks, *Publicani, Agulani*, Azimites, and very many other gentile nations that I know not how to enumerate or name. Immediately all our leaders came together, and held a council, saying: "If Bohemund can acquire the city, either by himself, or with the help of others, let us give it to him freely and with one accord, on condition that if the Emperor comes to our aid and wishes to carry out every agreement, as he swore and promised, we will return it to him by right. But if he does not do this, let Bohemund keep it in his power." Immediately, therefore, Bohemund began meekly to beseech his friend in daily petition, holding out most humbly the greatest and sweetest promises in this manner: "Behold, we have now truly a fit time to accomplish whatever good we wish; therefore, now, my friend *Pirus,* help me." Greatly pleased at the message, he replied that he would aid him in every way, as he ought to do. Accordingly, at the approach of night, he cautiously sent his son to Bohemund as a pledge, that he might be the more secure about his entrance to the city. He also sent word to him in this wise: "Tomorrow sound the trumpets for the Frankish host to move on, pretending that they are going to plunder the land of the Saracens, and then turn back quickly over the mountain on the right. With alert mind, indeed, I will be awaiting those forces, and I will take them into the towers which I have in my power and charge." Then Bohemund ordered a certain servant of his, Malacorona by name, to be called, and bade him, as herald, to admonish most of the Franks faithfully to prepare themselves to go into the land of the Saracens. This was so done. Thereupon Bohemund entrusted his plan to Duke Godfrey, and the Count of Flanders, also to the Count of St. Gilles and the Bishop of Puy, saying, "The grace of God favoring, Antioch will this night be surrendered to us."

All these matters were at length arranged; the knights held the level places and the foot soldiers the mountain. All the night they rode and marched until dawn, and then began to approach the towers which that person (*Pirus*) was watchfully guarding. Bohemund straightway dismounted and gave orders to the rest, saying, "Go with secure mind and happy accord, and climb by ladder into Antioch which, if it please God, we shall have in our power immediately." They went up the ladder, which had already been placed and firmly bound to the projections of the city wall. About sixty of our men climbed up it and were distributed among the towers which that man was watching. *Pirus,* upon seeing that so few of our men had ascended, began to tremble with fear for both himself and our men, lest they fall into the hands of the Turks. And he said, *"Micro Francos echome*—There are few Franks here! Where is most fierce Bohemund, that unconquered knight?" Meanwhile a certain Longobard servant descended again, and ran as quickly (as possible) to Bohemund, saying, "Why do you stand here, illustrious man? Why have you come hither? Behold, we already hold three towers!" Bohemund was moved with the rest, and all went joyfully to the ladder. Accordingly, when those who were in the towers saw this, they began to shout with happy voices, "God wills it!" We began to shout likewise; now the men began to climb up there in wondrous fashion. Then they reached the top and ran in haste to the other towers. Those whom they found there they straightway sentenced to death; they even killed a brother of *Pirus*. Meantime the ladder by which we had ascended broke by chance, whereupon there arose the greatest dismay and gloom among us. However, though the ladder had been broken, there was still a certain gate near us which had been shut on the left side and had remained unknown to some of the people, for it was night. But by feeling about and inquiring we found it, and all ran to it; and, having broken it open, we entered through it.

Thereupon, the noise of a countless multitude resounded through all the city. Bohemund did not give his men any rest, but ordered his standard to be carried up in front of the castle on a certain hill. Indeed, all were shouting in the city together. Moreover, when at earliest dawn those in the tents outside heard the most violent outcry sounding through the city, they rushed out hurriedly and saw the standard of Bohemund up on the mount, and with rapid pace all ran hastily and entered the city. They killed the Turks and Saracens whom they found there, except those who had fled into the citadel. Others of the Turks went out through the gates, and by fleeing escaped alive.

But *Cassianus*, their lord, fearing the race of the Franks greatly, took flight with the many others who were with him and came in flight to the land of Tancred, not far from the city. Their horses, however, were worn out, and, taking refuge in a certain villa, they dashed into a house. The inhabitants of the mountain, Syrians and Armenians, upon recognizing him (*Cassianus*), straightway seized him, cut off his head, and took it into the presence of Bohemund, so that they might gain their liberty. They also sold his sword-belt and scabbard for sixty *besants*. All this occurred on the third day of the incoming month of June, the fifth day of the week, the third day before the Nones of June. All the squares of the city were already everywhere full of the corpses of the dead, so that no one could endure it there for the excessive stench. No one could go along a street of the city except over the bodies of the dead.

(*Raymond*). Meanwhile, messengers began to come very

frequently, saying that aid was coming to the enemy. Moreover, this report came to us not only from the Armenians and the Greeks, but was also announced to us by those who were in the city. When the Turks had obtained Antioch fourteen years before, they had converted Armenians and Greek youths, as if for want of servants, and had given them wives. When such men as these had a chance to escape, they came to us with horses and arms. And when this report became frequent, many of our men and the Armenian merchants began to flee in terror. Meanwhile, good knights who were scattered among the fortresses came and brought arms, fitted, and repaired them. And when the gradually lessening swelling (of pride) had flowed from our army, and courage, ever ready to undergo dangers with brothers and for brothers, had come (in its place), one of the converted who was in the city sent word to our princes through Bohemund that he would surrender the city to us.

Accordingly, when the plan had been communicated, the princes sent Bohemund and the Duke of Lorraine and the Count of Flanders to try it out. And when they had come to the hill of the city at midnight, an intermediary sent back by him who was surrendering the city said, "Wait until the light passes." For three or four men went along the walls of the city with lamps all night, arousing and admonishing the watchers. After this, however, our men approached the wall, raised a ladder, and began to ascend it. A certain Frank, Fulger by name, brother of Budellus of Chartres, was the first boldly to ascend the wall; the Count of Flanders, following, sent word to Bohemund and the Duke to ascend; and since all hurried, each to go ahead of the other, the ladder was broken. But those who had climbed up went down into the city and opened a certain little postern. Thus our men went in, and they did not take captive any of those whom they found. When the dawn of day appeared, they shouted out. The whole city was disturbed at this shout, and the women and small children began to weep. Those who were in the castle of the Count, aroused at this outcry since they were nearer (it), began to say to one another, "Their aid has come!" Others, however, replied, "That does not sound like the voice of joyful people." And when the day whitened, our standards appeared on the southern hill of the city. When the disturbed citizens saw our men on the mountain above them, some fled through the gate, others hurled themselves headlong. No one resisted; in truth, the Lord had confounded them. Then after a long time, a joyful spectacle was made for us, in that those who had so long defended Antioch against us were now unable to flee from Antioch. Even if some of them had dared to take flight, yet they could not escape death. A certain incident occurred there, joyful and delightful enough for us. For when some Turks strove to flee among the cliffs which divide the hill in two from the north, they encountered some of our men, and when the Turks were forced to go back, the repulsed fugitives went with such rapidity that they all fell over the precipice together. Our joy over the fallen enemy was great, but we grieved over the more than thirty horses who had their necks broken there.

How great were the spoils captured in Antioch it is impossible for us to say, except that you may believe as much as you wish and then add to it. Moreover, we cannot say how many Turks and Saracens then perished; it is, furthermore, cruel to explain by what diverse and various deaths they died. When those foes who guarded the castle on the middle hill saw the destruction of their men and that our men were refraining from besieging them, they kept their castle. *Gracianus*, however, who had gone out by a certain postern, was captured and beheaded by some Armenian peasants, and his head was brought to us. This, I believe, was done by the ineffable disposition of God, that he who had caused many men of this same race to be beheaded should be deprived of his head by them. The city of Antioch was captured on the third day before the Nones of June; it had been besieged, however, since about the eleventh day before the Kalends of November.

12. *Summary of the siege of Antioch.* (End of October 1097—June 3, 1098).

(*Stephen*). Hastening to the aforesaid city of Antioch with great joy, we placed it in siege and there we very often had many conflicts with the Turks. Seven times, in truth, we fought with the inhabitants of Antioch, and with innumerable allies advancing to their aid, whom we chanced to meet. We fought them with fiercer spirits, Christ leading, and in all the seven aforesaid battles, the Lord God coöperating, we were victorious; and most truly we killed numbers of them beyond all count. But in these same battles, and in very many attacks made against the city, they killed many of our brothers who worship Christ, whose souls have truly gone to the joys of Paradise.

Moreover, we found Antioch a city great beyond belief, very strong and unassailable. And too, more than five thousand bold Turkish knights had collected within the city, not to mention the Saracens, *Publicani*, Arabs, Turcopoles, Syrians, Armenians, and various other peoples, of whom an infinite multitude had come together there. Thus, in the work of besieging these enemies of God and of ourselves, by the grace of God we have endured up to this time many trials and countless afflictions. Likewise, many have already consumed all their substance in this most holy passion. Very many of our Frankish-born, indeed, would have undergone temporal death through hunger, had not the clemency of God and our wealth come to their aid. Furthermore, through the whole winter we have endured excessive cold for the Lord Christ, and an immoderate abundance of rain. What some say, that in all Syria one can scarcely endure the heat of the sun, is false, for winter among them is like our western winter.

Moreover, when *Caspianus*, Emir of Antioch, that is, its prince and lord, saw himself so closely pressed by us, he sent his son, *Sensadolus*[27] by name, to the prince who holds Jerusalem, and to Rodoan, Prince of Aleppo and to *Docap*, Prince of Damascus. He likewise sent him into Arabia for *Bolianuth* and into Chorosan for *Hamelnuth*.[28] These five emirs, with twelve thousand chosen Turkish knights, suddenly came to aid Antioch. But unaware of all this, we had sent many of our knights among the cities and fortresses. We have, indeed, one hundred and sixty-five towns and fortresses throughout Syria within our own dominion. But a short time before they came to the city, we, with seven hundred knights, went out three leagues to meet them at a certain plain near the Iron Bridge. God, moreover, fought for us, His faithful, against them; for on this day, with the might of God, we were victorious in fighting them, and we killed large numbers of them, God ever fighting in our behalf. We likewise brought back to the army more than two hundred of their heads, so that Christ's people might derive great joy therefrom. Moreover, the Emperor of Babylon[29] sent his Saracen envoys with letters to us in camp, and by this means he established peace and concord with us.

I love to tell you, dearest, what befell us this Lent. Our princes decided to erect a fort before a certain gate which was situated between our camp and the sea. The Turks, passing out through this gate daily, used to kill our men on their way to the sea, for the city of Antioch is five leagues distant from the sea. On this account they sent the distinguished Bohemund and Raymond, Count of St. Gilles, with a company of only sixty knights, to the sea, thence to fetch sailors to aid in this work. However, when they were returning to us with these sailors, an army of Turks, which had assembled, came upon our two unsuspecting princes and drove them into perilous flight. In this rout, unexpected, as we have said before, we lost more than five hundred foot-soldiers to the glory of God; of our knights, we lost only two for certain. Moreover, on that very day we went out along the road to receive our brothers with joy, knowing nothing of their misfortune.

But while we were approaching the aforesaid gate of the city, a horde of knights and foot-soldiers from Antioch, bearing themselves in a triumphant manner, rushed likewise against us. Upon seeing them, we sent word to the Christian camp that all should follow us ready for battle. While our men were still assembling, the separated princes—namely Bohemund and Raymond, with the remainder of their army—came up and recounted the great misfortune which had befallen them. At this very bad news, our men, inflamed with anger against the sacrilegious Turks, and ready to die for Christ, went into battle for the loss of their brothers. However, the enemy of God and of ourselves fled before us in haste and tried to enter their city, but by the grace of God the affair turned out far otherwise. For when they wanted to cross over the river by the bridge which ended at a mosque, we, following them closely, killed many of them before they reached the bridge; many we hurled off into the river, all of whom were killed; moreover, we killed many on the bridge and likewise very many before the entrance to the city. Verily I tell you, my beloved, and you may believe most truly, that in that same battle we killed thirty emirs, that is, princes, and three hundred other noble Turkish knights, not to mention the other Turks and pagans. Indeed, the dead Turks and Saracens are reckoned 1230 in number! Of our men, however, we lost not one single man.

Moreover, on the day following Easter, while my chaplain, Alexander, was writing this letter with the greatest haste, a portion of our men who were lying in wait for the Turks had a victorious battle with them, the Lord leading, and they killed sixty of their knights, whose heads they brought back to the army.

These things which I am writing to you, dearest, are indeed few of the many (that have happened), and since I cannot express to you all that my heart holds, dearest, I (only) bid you do well and make excellent arrangement for your land, and treat your children and your vassals with honor, as befits you, for you will surely see me as soon as I can possibly come. Farewell.

(*Anselm*). In the name of the Lord!

To his lord and father, Manasses, by grace of God venerable Archbishop of Rheims, Anselm of Ribemont, his loyal vassal and humble servant; greeting.

Let your Eminence, reverend father and lord, know that, even though absent and not present, we are daily asking aid in our hearts from you—not only from you, but, also, from all the sons of the Holy Mother Church of Rheims, in whom we have the greatest faith. Likewise, inasmuch as you are our lord, and the counsel of the whole kingdom of France is especially dependent upon you, we are keeping you, father, informed of whatever happy and adverse events have happened to us. Let the others, moreover, be informed through you, that you may share equally in our sufferings, and rejoice with us in our success.

We have informed you how we fared in the siege and capture of Nicaea, in our departure thence and our journey through all Romania and Armenia. It now remains for us to tell you a little about the siege of Antioch, the many kinds of danger we there tasted, and the innumerable battles which we fought against the King of Aleppo, the King of Damascus, and against the adulterous King of Jerusalem.[30]

Antioch has been besieged by the army of the Lord since the thirteenth day before the Kalends of November with exceeding valor and courage beyond words. What unheard of battles you might have perceived there at a certain gateway to the west! How marvelous it would seem to you, were you present, to see them daily rushing forth through six gates—both they and ourselves fighting for safety and life! At that time our princes, seeking to enclose the city more and more closely, first besieged the eastern gate, and Bohemund, having built a fort there, stationed a part of his army in it. However, since our princes then felt somewhat elated, God, who chasteneth every son whom he loveth, so chastened us that hardly seven hundred horses could be found in our army; and thus, not because we lacked proven and valiant men, but from lack of horses, or food, or through excessive cold, almost all were dying. The Turks, moreover, supplied with horses and all necessities in abundance, were wont daily to ride around our camp, a certain stream which lay between serving as a wall. There was likewise a castle of the Turks almost eight miles away; and these Turks were daily killing many of our men, who were going back and forth from our army. Our princes went out against them and with God's help put them to flight and killed many of them. Therefore the ruler of Antioch, seeing himself afflicted, called the King of Damascus to his aid. By God's providence, this King met Bohemund and the Count of Flanders, who had gone to find food with a part of our army, and, God's help prevailing, he was defeated and routed by them. The ruler of Antioch, still concerned about his safety, sent to the King of Aleppo and aroused him with promises of very great wealth, to the end that he should come with all his forces.

Upon his arrival, our princes went forth from camp, and that day, God being their helper, with seven hundred knights and a few foot-soldiers they defeated twelve thousand Turks with their King, put them to flight, and killed many of them. Our men regained not a few horses from that battle, and returned rejoicing with victory. Growing stronger and stronger, therefore, from that day our men took counsel with renewed courage as to how they might besiege the western gate which cut off access to the sea, wood, and fodder. By common agreement, therefore, Bohemund and the Count of St. Gilles went to the coast to fetch those who were staying there. Meanwhile, those who had remained to look after the possessions, seeking to acquire a name for themselves, went out incautiously one day after breakfast, near that western gate from which they were ingloriously repulsed and put to flight. On the third day after this, Bohemund and the Count of St. Gilles, on their way back, sent word to the princes of the army to meet them, (intending) together to besiege the gate. However, since the latter delayed for a short time, Bohemund and the Count of St. Gilles were beaten and put to flight. Therefore all our men, grieving and bewailing their disgrace, as well, for a thousand of our men fell that day, formed their lines and defeated and put to flight the Turks, who offered great resistance. On this day, moreover, almost fourteen hundred of the enemy perished both by weapons and in the river, which was swollen with winter rains.

And so, when this had been accomplished, our men began to built the fortress, which they strengthened, also, with a double moat and a very strong wall, as well as with two towers. In it they placed the Count of St. Gilles with machine men and bowmen. Oh, with what great labor we established the fortress! One part of our army served the eastern front, another looked after the camp, while all the rest worked on this fortress. Of the latter, the machine men and bowmen kept watch on the gate; the rest, including the princes themselves, did not stop in the work of carrying stones, and building the wall. Why recount the trials of many kinds, which, even if passed over in silence, are sufficiently evident in themselves—hunger, intemperate weather, and the desertion of faint-hearted soldiers? The more bitter they were, the more ready our men were in enduring them. Yet, indeed, we think that we should by no means pass in silence the fact that on a certain day the Turks pretended that they would surrender the city and carried the deception so far as to receive some of our men among them, and several of their men came out to us. While this was going on in this manner, they, like the faithless people that they were, set a trap for us in which Walo, the Constable, and others of them as well as of us were destroyed. A few days after this, moreover, it was announced to us that *Corbara*,[31] chief of the army of the king of the Persians, had sworn to our death, and had already crossed the great Euphrates river with an innumerable army. God, however, who does not desert those who place their trust in Him, did not abandon His people, but on the Nones of June compassionately gave to us the city of Antioch, which three of its citizens betrayed. We, however, devastated the city, and on that same day killed all the pagans in it, except some who were holding out in the castle of the city.

(*The Crusading Princes*). To the venerable lord Pope Urban, Bohemund and Raymond, Count of St. Gilles, Godfrey, Duke of Lorraine, Robert, Count of Normandy, Robert, Count of Flanders and Eustace, Count of Boulogne; greeting and loyal service and, as sons of their spiritual father, true subjection in Christ.

We all wish and desire that it be made known to you how, by the compassion of God and by His most manifest assistance, Antioch has been captured by us, and how the Turks, who had hurled many insults at our Lord Jesus Christ, have been captured and killed: how we, pilgrims of Jesus Christ on our way to Jerusalem, have avenged the wrong against Most High God; how we, who were at first besieging the Turks, were later besieged by Turks coming from Chorosan, Jerusalem, Damascus, and many other lands; and how, by the compassion of Jesus Christ, we have been liberated.

Accordingly, when, after the capture of Nicaea, we had defeated that very great multitude of Turks which met us, as you have heard, in the valley of Dorylaeum on the Kalends of July, and had put that great Soliman to flight, despoiled his land and all his possessions, and had acquired and pacified all Romania, we went to besiege Antioch. In this siege we suffered very many ills, especially from battles with the neighboring Turks and pagans, who rushed upon us so often, and in such numbers, that we might more truly have been spoken of as besieged by those whom we were besieging in Antioch. Nevertheless, when we had won all these battles, the Christian faith being greatly exalted by their outcome, I, Bohemund, by an agreement made with a certain Turk, who betrayed the city itself to me, shortly before daybreak, placed scaling ladders against the wall with the help of many soldiers of Christ. Accordingly, on the third day before the Nones of June, we took the city, which before this time was resisting Christ. *Cassianus* himself, the tyrant of the city, we killed, together with many of his soldiers, and we kept their wives, children, and servants, together with their gold, silver, and all possessions. The citadel, however, which had been previously fortified by the Turks, we could not obtain.

(*People of Lucca*). To the primates, archbishops, bishops, and other rectors, and to all the faithful of the lands of Christ anywhere; the clergy and people of Lucca (send) greeting full of peace and gladness in the Lord.

To the praise and glory of the Redeemer, our Lord Jesus Christ, we are truly and faithfully making known to all (the news) which we received truly and faithfully from participants in the affairs themselves—at what time, with what great triumph, the most mighty right hand of Christ gave complete victory over the pagans to our brethren, His champions, after trial and perils. A certain citizen of ours, Bruno by name, known and very dear to all of us, in the year preceding this, went with the ships of the Angles even to Antioch itself. There, as a partner in work and danger, sharer of triumph and joy, he fought along with the fighters, starved with the starving and conquered, also, with the conquering; and when the complete victory had already been achieved, and he had rejoiced three weeks there with all, he returned to us, after a happy voyage. Placing him in our midst, we received from him the pure and simple truth of the matter—lo! in his own account, as follows:

"When we who were voyaging by sea had come to Antioch, the army, which had gathered together from everywhere by land, had already surrounded the city in siege, though not very well. On the following day, our princes proceeded to the sea, for the sake of visiting us. They urged us to get together an abundant supply of wood for the construction of war engines, which we did at great expense. On the third day, moreover, before the Nones of March, that is the first Friday, our princes decided to erect a fortress at the western gate of the city. This fortress, a very short ballista-shot away (from the city), is now called by the name of the Blessed Mary. There, on that same day, in an attack of the Turks, in which they killed 2,055 of our men, we killed 800 of the enemy. From the third day, morever, when the fortress had been erected, until the third day before the Nones of June, our men endured many hardships, and, weakened by hunger and the sword, they toiled there at great cost. However, on this day the city was captured in the following manner: Four brothers, noble men of Antioch, on the second day of June promise to surrender the city to Bohemund,

Robert Curtose,[32] and Robert, Count of Flanders. These, however, with the common assent of all our princes, at nightfall conduct the whole army to the wall of the city, without the knowledge of the Turks. And in the morning, when the citizens of Antioch open the gates to receive the three named princes alone, according to promise, all of our men suddenly rush in together. There is the greatest clamor: our men obtain all the fortified places, except the very high citadel; the Turks—these they kill, those they hurl to destruction over the precipice."

CHAPTER V.

Kerbogha and the Finding of the Lance.

(When the Crusaders entered Syria, the Mohammedans whom they dispossessed fled as refugees to Bagdad. Their pitiable flight and their pleas moved the Caliph deeply. He sent a personal embassy to the warring Sultans begging them to unite against the common foe, but they did not heed him. Many of the lesser Turkish princes did respond, however, and a considerable army was brought together, which the Caliph placed in charge of Kerbogha as general. Kerbogha wasted three whole weeks before Edessa and then moved on to Antioch, which he reached just as the Crusaders had entered it—two days too late. The whole First Crusade forms an unpleasant chapter in Saracen history, one which their historians do not love to describe. They did not treat of it at length until the more favorable turn of events under Nured-din and Saladin affords them the opportunity of contrasting the period with the happier conditions of their own times. Hence, eye-witness accounts of the First Crusade by Mohammedan writers do not exist. Later Mohammedan authors have charged Kerbogha with incapacity and ill treatment of his subordinate officers as an explanation of his failure to relieve Antioch and destroy the Christian army. However, Baldwin's fortunate presence at Edessa, which served to delay Kerbogha, and the astonishing discovery of the Holy Lance, with its marvelous effect upon the discouraged Latins in Antioch, must be counted as no mean factors in that result. It is interesting to note the practically unanimous belief of the writers and Crusaders in the Lance at this time).

1. *Kerbogha lays siege to the Crusaders in Antioch.* (June 5, 1098).

(*Gesta*). Some time before, *Cassianus,* Emir of Antioch, had sent a message to *Curbara,* chief of the Sultan of Persia, while he was still at Chorosan, to come and help him while there was yet time, because a very mighty host of Franks was besieging him shut up in Antioch. If the Emir would aid him, he (*Cassianus*) would give him Antioch, or would enrich him with a very great gift. Since *Curbara* had had a very large army of Turks collected for a long time, and had received permission from the Caliph, their Pope, to kill the Christians, he began a long march to Antioch. The Emir of Jerusalem came to his aid with an army, and the King of Damascus arrived there with a very large host. Indeed, *Curbara* likewise collected countless pagan folk, Turks, Arabs, Saracens, *Publicani,* Azimites,[1] Kurds, Persians, *Agulani* and countless other peoples.

The *Agulani* were three thousand in number and feared neither lances, arrows, nor any kind of arms, because they and all their horses were fitted with iron all around, and they refused to carry any arms except swords into battle. All of these came to the siege of Antioch to disperse the gathering of Franks.

And when they neared the city, *Sensadolus,* son of *Cassianus,* Emir of Antioch, went to meet them, and straightway rushed in tears to *Curbara,* beseeching him with these words: "Most invincible chief, I, a supplicant, pray thee to help me, now that the Franks are besieging me on every side in the city of Antioch; now that they hold the city in their sway and seek to alienate us from the region of Romania, or even yet from Syria and Chorosan. They have done everything that they wished; they have killed my father; now nothing else remains except to kill me, and you, and all the others of our race. For a long time now I have been waiting for your help to succor me in this danger."

To him *Curbara* replied: "If you want me to enter wholeheartedly into your service and to help you loyally in this danger, give that town into my hands, and then see how I will serve you and protect it with my men."

Sensadolus replied, "If you can kill all the Franks and give me their heads, I will give you the town, and I will do homage to you and guard the town in your fealty."

To this *Curbara* answered: "That won't do; hand over the town to me immediately." And then, willy-nilly, he handed the town over to him.

But on the third day after we had entered the town, *Curbara's* advance guard ran in front of the city; his army, however, encamped at the Iron Gate. They took the fortress by siege and killed all of the defenders, whom we found in iron chains after the greater battle had been fought.

On the next day, the army of the pagans moved on, and, nearing the city, they encamped between the two rivers and stayed there for two days. After they had retaken the fortress, *Curbara* summoned one of his emirs whom he knew to be truthful, gentle, and peaceable and said to him: "I want you to undertake to guard this fortress in fealty to me, because for the longest time I have known you to be most loyal; therefore, I pray you, keep this castle with the greatest care, for, since I know you to be the most prudent in action, I can find no one here more truthful and valiant."

To him the Emir replied: "Never would I refuse to obey you in such service, but before you persuade me by urging, I will consent, on the condition that if the Franks drive your men from the deadly

THE FIRST CRUSADE

field of battle and conquer, I will straightway surrender this fortress to them."

Curbara said to him: "I recognize you as so honorable and wise that I will fully consent to whatever good you wish to do." And thereupon *Curbara* returned to his army.

Forthwith the Turks, making sport of the gatherings of Franks, brought into the presence of *Curbara* a certain very miserable sword covered with rust, a very worn wooden bow, and an exceedingly useless lance, which they had just recently taken from poor pilgrims, and said, "Behold the arms which the Franks carry to meet us in battle!" Then *Curbara* began to laugh, saying before all who were in that gathering, "These are the warlike and shining arms which the Christians have brought against us into Asia, with which they hope and expect to drive us beyond the confines of Chorosan and to wipe out our names beyond the Amazon rivers, they who have driven our relatives from Romania and the royal city of Antioch, which is the renowned capital of all Syria!" Then he summoned his scribe and said: "Write quickly several documents which are to be read in Chorosan."

"To the Caliph, our Pope, and to our King, the Lord Sultan, most valiant knight, and to all most illustrious knights of Chorosan; greeting and honor beyond measure.

Let them be glad enough and delight with joyful concord and satisfy their appetites; let them command and make known through all that region that the people give themselves entirely to exuberance and luxury, and that they rejoice to bear many children to fight stoutly against the Christians. Let them gladly receive these three weapons which we recently took from a squad of Franks, and let them now learn what arms the Frankish host bears against us; how very fine and perfect they are to fight against our arms which are twice, thrice, or even four times welded, or purified, like the purest silver or gold. In addition, let all know, also, that I have the Franks shut up in Antioch, and that I hold the citadel at my free disposal, while they (the enemy) are below in the city. Likewise, I hold all of them now in my hand. I shall make them either undergo sentence of death, or be led into Chorosan into the harshest captivity, because they are threatening with their arms to drive us forth and to expel us from all our territory, or to cast us out beyond upper India, as they have cast out all our kinsmen from Romania or Syria. Now I swear to you by Mohammed and all the names of the gods[2] that I will not return before your face until I shall have acquired with my strong right hand the regal city of Antioch, all Syria, Romania, and Bulgaria, even to Apulia, to the honor of the gods, and to your glory, and to that of all who are of the race of the Turks." And thus he put an end to his words.

The mother of the same *Curbara*, who dwelt in the city of Aleppo, came immediately to him and, weeping, said: "Son, are these things true which I hear?"

"What things?" he said.

"I have heard that you are going to engage in battle with the host of the Franks," she replied.

And he answered: "You know the truth fully."

She then said, "I warn you, son, in the names of all the gods and by your great kindness, not to enter into battle with the Franks, because you are an unconquered knight, and I have never at all heard of any imprudence from you or your army. No one has ever found you fleeing from the field before any victor. The fame of your army is spread abroad, and all illustrious knights tremble when your name is heard. For we know well enough, son, that you are mighty in battle, and valiant and resourceful, and that no host of Christians or pagans can have any courage before your face, but are wont to flee at the mention of your name, as sheep flee before the wrath of a lion. And so I beseech you, dearest son, to yield to my advice never to let it rest in your mind, or be found in your counsel, to wish to undertake war with the Christian host."

Then *Curbara*, upon hearing his mother's warning, replied with wrathful speech: "What is this, mother, that you tell me? I think that you are insane, or full of furies. For I have with me more emirs than there are Christians, whether of greater or lesser state."

His mother replied to him: "O sweetest son, the Christians cannot fight with your forces, for I know that they are not able to prevail against you; but their God is fighting for them daily and is watching over them and defending them with His protection by day and night, as a shepherd watches over his flock. He does not permit them to be hurt or disturbed by any folk, and whoever seeks to stand in their way this same God of theirs likewise puts to rout, just as He said through the mouth of the prophet David: 'Scatter the people that delight in wars,' and in another place: 'Pour out Thy wrath upon the nations that know Thee not and against the kingdoms that call not upon Thy name.'[3] Before they are ready to begin battle, their God, all powerful and potent in battle, together with His saints, has all their enemies already conquered. How much more will He now prevail against you, who are His enemies, and who are preparing to resist them with all your valor! This, moreover, dearest, know in very truth: these Christians, called 'sons of Christ' and by the mouth of the prophets 'sons

THE FIRST CRUSADE

of adoption and promise,' according to the apostle are the heirs of Christ to whom He has already given the promised inheritance, saying through the prophets, 'From the rising to the setting of the sun shall be your border and no one shall stand before you.'[4] Who can contradict or oppose these words? Certainly, if you undertake this battle against them, yours will be the very greatest loss and disgrace, and you will lose many of your faithful knights and all the spoils which you have with you, and you will turn in flight with exceeding fear. However, you shall not die now in this battle, but, nevertheless, in this year, because God does not with quick anger immediately judge him who has offended Him, but when He wills, He punishes with manifest vengeance, and so I fear He will exact of you a bitter penalty. You shall not die, now, I say, but you shall perish after all your present possessions."

Then *Curbara,* deeply grieved in his heart at his mother's words, replied: "Dearest mother, pray, who told you such things about the Christian folk, that God loves only them, and that He restrains the mightiest host from fighting against Him, and that those Christians will conquer us in the battle of Antioch, and that they will capture our spoils, and will pursue us with great victory, and that I shall die in this year by a sudden death?"

Then his mother answered him sadly: "Dearest son, behold the times are more than a hundred years since it was found in our book and in the volumes of the Gentiles that the Christian host would come against us, would conquer us everywhere and rule over the pagans, and that our people would be everywhere subject to them. But I do not know whether these things are to happen now or in the future. Wretched woman that I am, I have followed you from Aleppo, most beautiful city, in which, by gazing and contriving ingenious rhymes, I looked back at the stars of the skies and wisely scrutinized the planets and the twelve signs, or countless lots. In all of these I found that the Christian host would win everywhere, and so I am exceedingly sad and fear greatly lest I remain bereft of you."

Curbara said to her: "Dearest mother, explain to me all the incredible things which are in my heart."

Answering this, she said: "This, dearest, I will do freely, if I know the things which are unknown to you."

He said to her: "Are not Bohemund and Tancred gods of the Franks, and do they not free them from their enemies, and do not these men in one meal eat two thousand heifers and four thousand hogs?"

His mother answered: "Dearest son, Bohemund and Tancred are

mortals, like all the rest; but their God loves them greatly above all the others and gives them valor in fighting beyond the rest. For (it is) their God, Omnipotent is His name, who made heaven and earth and established the seas and all things that in them are, whose dwelling-place is in heaven prepared for all eternity, whose might is everywhere to be feared."

Her son said: "(Even) if such is the case, I will not refrain from fighting with them." Thereupon, when his mother heard that he would in no way yield to her advice, she returned, a very sad woman, to Aleppo, carrying with her all the gifts that she could take along.

But on the third day *Curbara* armed himself and most of the Turks with him and went toward the city from the side on which the fortress was located. Thinking that we could resist them, we prepared ourselves for battle against them, but so great was their valor that we could not withstand them, and under compulsion, therefore, we entered the city. The gate was so amazingly close and narrow for them that many died there from the pressure of the rest. Meanwhile, some fought outside the city, others within, on the fifth day of the week throughout the day until the evening.

(*Raymond*). In the meantime, while our men, engaged in counting and identifying their spoils, had desisted from the siege of the upper fortress, and, while listening to the pagan dancing girls, had feasted in splendor and magnificence, not at all mindful of God who had granted them so great a blessing, they were besieged by the pagans on the third day, on the Nones of the same June. And so it was brought about that they who by the mercy of God had so long besieged the Turks in Antioch were through His disposition in turn besieged by the Turks. And that we might be the more fearful, the upper fortress which is a kind of citadel, was in the hands of the enemy. Our men, accordingly, under the stress of fear, took up the siege of the fortress.

Corbaga, however, lord of the Turks, expecting the battle to take place there, fixed his tents at a distance of about two miles from the city and, with ranks arrayed, came up to the bridge of the city. Our men, however, had strengthened the fortress of the Count on the first day, fearing that if they proceeded to battle it would be seized by the enemy who were in the citadel, or, if they deserted the fortress which was before the bridge and the enemy occupied it, that the enemy would shut us off from a chance to fight and block our exit.

There was in the army a knight most distinguished and very dear to all, *Roger of Barneville* by name, who, while pursuing the army of the retiring enemy, was captured and deprived of his head. Fear and grief, accordingly, assailed our men, so that many were led to the desperate hope of flight. Thereupon, when the Turks had once and again suffered a repulse in fighting, they besieged the fortress on the third day; and the fighting was carried on there with such violence that the might of God alone was believed to defend the fortress and resist the adversaries. For when the Turks were already prepared to cross the moat and destroy the walls, they were taken with fright, I know not why, and rushed headlong into flight. Then, seeing no reason for their flight, they returned to the siege after they had run a short distance, blaming their own timidity; and, as if to atone for the disgrace of the flight they had made, they attacked more violently and again were more violently terrified by the might of God. Therefore the enemy returned to their camp on that day. On the next day, however, they returned to the fortress with a very great supply of siege machinery, but our men set fire to the fortress and thrust themselves within the walls of the city. And thus, as the fear of the Franks was increased, the boldness of the enemy grew; forsooth, we had nothing outside the city, and the fortress, which was the head of the city, was held by our foes. The Turks, emboldened by this, arranged to enter against us by the fortress. Our men, however, relying on their favorable and lofty location, fought against the enemy and at the first attack overthrew them; but, forgetful of the threatening battle and intent upon plunder, they (in turn) were most vilely put to flight. For more than a hundred men were suffocated in the gate of the city, and even more horses. Then the Turks who had entered the fortress wanted to go down into the city. For the valley between our mountain and their fortress was not large, and in the middle of it was a certain cistern and a little level place. Nor did the enemy have a path down into the city except through our mountain; wherefore they strove with every intent and all their might to drive us out and remove us from their path. The battle was waged with such force from morning to evening that nothing like it was ever heard of. There was a certain frightful and as yet unheard of calamity befell us, for amidst the hail of arrows and rocks, and the constant charge of javelins, and the deaths of so many, our men became unconscious. If you ask for the end of this fight, it was night.

2. *Dire straits of the Crusaders.* (June, 1098).

(*Gesta*). In the midst of this, William of Grandmesnil, his brother Alberic, Wido *Trursellus*, and Lambert the Pauper, all of them frightened by yesterday's battle which had lasted until evening, secretly slipped away by night and fled over the wall on foot to the sea, so that nothing remained either on their hands or feet, except bone alone. Many others whose names I do not know fled with them. Accordingly, when they came to the ships which were at the Port of St. Simeon, they said to the sailors: "Why do you stay here, wretched men? All of our men are dead, and we barely escaped with our lives, for the army of the Turks is besieging the rest in the city on all sides." But when those men heard this, they stood stupefied and, terrified with fear, rushed to the boats and put out to sea. Then the Turks came up and killed all whom they found, burned the ships which rested on the bed of the river, and took off their spoils. We who remained could no longer withstand the force of their arms. We made a wall between them and ourselves, which we guarded day and night. Meanwhile, we were oppressed by such need that we ate our horses and asses.

Then the Turks who were up in the castle pressed us on all sides so closely that on a certain day they shut three of our knights in a tower which was before their castle. For the Gentiles had gone out and rushed upon the knights so fiercely that they could not resist their force. Two of the knights went out from the tower wounded, but the third manfully defended himself from the attack of the Turks throughout the whole day with such skill that on that day he stretched out two Turks over the entrance to the tower with their spears broken. Thus, three were that day shattered in his hands. But the Turks suffered the sentence of death. The knight's name was Hugh de *Forcenez* of the army of Gosfrid of Mt. Scaglioso. However, when that venerable man, Bohemund, saw that he could not again lead the people up into the fortress to battle (for of those who were shut up in the houses, some feared starvation and others the Turks), he was greatly angered and ordered fire to be placed immediately throughout the city on that side where the palace of *Cassianus* was located. When those who were in the city saw this, they left their homes and everything that they had, and fled, some to the castle, and others to the gate of the Count of St. Gilles, others to the gate of Duke Godfrey—each one to his own people.

Then a very severe storm so suddenly arose that no one could guide himself aright. Thereupon, that wise man, Bohemund, was exceedingly sad, fearing for the churches of St. Peter and St. Mary and other churches. This fury lasted from the third hour even to midnight, and almost two thousand churches and homes were burned. However, at the approach of midnight all the fury of the fire suddenly fell. Thereupon, the Turks who lived in the castle fought with us inside the city day and night, and nothing else separated us from our arms. However, when our men saw that they could not long endure this, because whoever had bread was not allowed (time) to eat it, and whoever had water did not get a chance to drink it, they built a fortress and machines, that they might be more secure. A part of the Turks, however, remained in the castle, keeping up battle with us, but the other portion was lodged near the castle in a valley. When the night came, forsooth, a fire from heaven appeared, coming from the west; and, drawing near, it fell within the army of the Turks, whereat both our men and the Turks marvelled. Moreover, when it became morning, the Turks, terrified by fear of the fire, all fled before the gate of Bohemund and were there lodged. But that part (of the Turks) in the castle kept up battle with us by day and night, shooting, wounding, and killing. The other part, however, beset the city everywhere on all sides, so that none of us dared go out or in, except at night, and (then) stealthily. Thus were we besieged and oppressed by these pagans, enemies of God and Christianity, whose number was innumerable.[5]

These profane enemies of God held us so inclosed in the city of Antioch that many died of hunger because a little loaf of bread sold for a *besant*. Of wine I won't speak. They sold and ate horse and ass-flesh; they also sold a cock for fifteen *solidi*, an egg for two *solidi*, and a nut for a *denarius*. Thus everything was very dear. They cooked and ate the leaves of the fig tree, grapevine, and thistle, and of all trees, so tremendous was their hunger. Others cooked the dry hides of horses, camels, asses, cattle or buffalos and ate them. These and many such troubles and straits which I cannot name, we suffered for the name of Christ, and to free the way to the Holy Sepulchre. Such tribulation, famine, and fears we endured for twenty-six days.

Then the base Stephen, Count of Chartres, whom all our nobles had chosen to be our leader, and who had feigned very great illness before Antioch was captured, basely withdrew to another fortified place called Alexandretta. Therefore, we who had been shut up in the city without saving aid daily besought him to come to our relief. But after he heard that a host of Turks was surrounding and besieging us, he stealthily climbed upon the mountain nearest to Antioch and saw the countless tents. Seized with a most violent fear, he turned and fled hastily with his army. Then coming to his own fortress, he despoiled it and withdrew at rapid pace. But after he came upon the Emperor at Philomelium, he called him apart and said secretly: "Know for a truth that Antioch has been captured, but the citadel has not been taken; all our men are besieged with great pressure and, as I think, have now been killed by the Turks. Go back, therefore, as quickly as you can, lest they find you and this people which you are leading with you."

Then the Emperor, terrified with fear, secretly called Wido, brother of Bohemund, and certain others and said to them: "Seignors, what shall we do? Behold, all our men have been held in close siege, and perchance at this hour have all been killed by the Turks, or led into captivity, just as that ill-favored Count, who is basely fleeing, reports. If you wish, let us turn back at a quick pace, lest we, too, should die a sudden death, even as they, also, are dead." When Wido, a knight most honorable, heard such falsehoods, he began to weep with all the rest, and to complain with most violent outcry. With one voice all exclaimed: "O true God, Three and One, why hast Thou permitted this to come to pass? Why hast Thou permitted the people who followed Thee to fall into the hands of the enemy, and so quickly abandoned them who wished to free the way of Thy journey and Sepulchre? Surely, if this word which we have heard from these most iniquitous men be true, we and the other Christians will depart from Thee, and no more remember Thee, and not one of us will again dare to call upon Thy name." And there was this most gloomy talk in the whole army, so that none of them, whether bishop, abbot, cleric, or lay, dared to call upon the name of Christ for several days.

And no one could console Wido, who wept and beat himself with his hands and broke his fingers and said: "Woe is me! My lord Bohemund, honor and glory of the world, whom all the world was wont to fear and love! Alas, what sadness is mine! I did not deserve in grief to see your most honorable face, I who desired to see nothing else more. Who will let me die for you, sweetest friend and lord? Why was I not dead, as I came from the womb of my mother? Why did I come to this sad day? Why was I not drowned in the sea? Why did I not fall from my horse to meet sudden death from a broken neck? Would that I had gained a happy martyrdom with you, so that I might behold you receiving a most glorious end!" When all had run to him to console him, so as to bring an end to his grief, he turned away and said to himself: "Perchance you believe this grizzled, shameless knight? Truly, I have not ever heard mention of any campaign which he has made. But basely and dishonorably he turns back, like a most iniquitous and ill-favored man, and whatever that wretch reports you may know to be false."

Meanwhile, the Emperor commanded his men, saying: "Go and

lead all of the men of this land into Bulgaria, and seek out and devastate all places, so that when the Turks come they will be able to find nothing." Willy-nilly our men turned back, grieving most bitterly even to death, and many of the pilgrims died. Failing in strength, and unable vigorously to follow the army, they stopped and died along the way. But all the rest returned to Constantinople.[6]

(*Raymond*). In the night, however, when our men should have expected the mercy of God, many began to despair and let themselves down headlong from the top of the walls by ropes. Others, moreover, withdrawing from the battle into the city, announced to everybody that the general beheading of all had come; and, to increase their fears, while some were urging others to resist bravely, these same men turned in flight. . . .

In the meanwhile, there was such famine in the city that a horse's head without the tongue was sold for two or three *solidi*, the intestines of goats for five, a cock for eight or nine. What shall I say about bread, five *solidi's* worth of which was not enough to satisfy the hunger of one person? This was not astonishing, nor when they had abundant gold and silver and clothes could it have weighed heavily upon those who bought at such a price. However, these things were (now) so dear because the consciences of the soldiers, troubled with crimes, were bereft of courage. Moreover, they plucked unripe figs from the trees, cooked them, and sold them very dearly. Indeed, the hides of cattle and horses and other things which they had disregarded for a long time they now slowly cooked and sold so dearly that any one could eat the worth of two *solidi*. Most of the knights lived on the blood of their own horses; awaiting the mercy of God, they did not yet want to kill them. Moreover, these and many other evils difficult to enumerate threatened and besieged. Another very serious calamity happened in that some of our men fled to the Turks and told them of the misery in the city. The Turks, emboldened by this and other occurrences, threatened us most violently. Moreover, one day at mid-day about thirty Turks climbed into one of our towers, whereat our men became exceedingly terrified. Nevertheless, because of the danger, they fought with the help of God, killed some, and forced the others to flee precipitately. For this reason, accordingly, all promised obedience to Bohemund for fifteen days after the battle, so that he might arrange about the battle and the custody of the city. For the Count was very ill, also the Bishop; and Count Stephen, whom the other princes had chosen as ruler before the capture of the city, had fled when he heard rumors of the battle.

3. *Revelation of the Lance.* (June 4, 1098.)

(*Gesta*). But one day as our leaders, sad and disconsolate, were standing back before the fortress, a certain priest came to them and said: "Seignors, if it please you, listen to a certain matter which I saw in a vision. When one night I was lying in the church of St. Mary, Mother of God, our Lord Jesus Christ, the Saviour of the world, appeared to me with His mother and St. Peter, prince of the apostles, and stood before me and said, 'Knowest thou me?'

"I answered, 'No.' At these words, lo, a whole cross appeared on His head.

"A second time, therefore, the Lord asked me 'Knowest thou me?'

"To Him I replied: 'I do not know Thee except that I see a cross on thy head like that of Our Saviour.'

"He answered, 'I am He.'

"Immediately I fell at His feet, humbly beseeching that He help us in the oppression which was upon us. The Lord responded: 'I have helped you in goodly manner and I will now help you. I permitted you to have the city of Nicaea, and to win all battles, and I conducted you hither to this point, and I have grieved at the misery which you have suffered in the siege of Antioch. Behold, with timely aid I sent you safe and unharmed into the city, and lo! (you are) working much evil pleasure with Christian and depraved pagan women, whereof a stench beyond measure arises unto heaven.'

"Then the loving Virgin and the blessed Peter fell at His feet, praying and beseeching Him to aid His people in this tribulation, and the blessed Peter said: 'Lord, for so long a time the pagan host has held my house, and in it they have committed many unspeakable wrongs. But now, since the enemy have been driven hence, Lord, the angels rejoice in heaven.'

"The Lord then said to me: 'Go and tell my people to return to Me, and I will return to them, and within five days I will send them great help. Let them daily chant the response *Congregati sunt,* all of it, including the verse.'

"Seignors, if you do not believe that this is true, let me climb up into this tower, and I will throw myself down, and if I am unharmed, believe that this is true. If, however, I shall have suffered any hurt, behead me, or cast me into the fire." Then the Bishop of Puy ordered that the Gospel and the Cross be brought, so that he might take oath that this was true.

All our leaders were counselled at that time to take oath that not one of them would flee, either for life or death, as long as they were alive. Bohemund is said to have been the first to take the oath, then the Count of St. Gilles, Robert of Normandy, Duke Godfrey, and the Count of Flanders. Tancred, indeed, swore and promised in this manner: that as long as he had forty knights with him he would not only not withdraw from that battle, but, likewise, not from the march to Jerusalem. Moreover, the Christian assemblage exulted greatly upon hearing this oath.

There was a certain pilgrim of our army, whose name was Peter, to whom before we entered the city St. Andrew, the apostle, appeared and said: "What art thou doing, good man?"

Peter answered, "Who art thou?"

The apostle said to him: "I am St. Andrew, the apostle. Know, my son, that when thou shalt enter the town, go to the church of St. Peter. There thou wilt find the Lance of our Saviour, Jesus Christ, with which He was wounded as He hung on the arm of the cross." Having said all this, the apostle straightway withdrew.

But Peter, afraid to reveal the advice of the apostle, was unwilling to make it known to the pilgrims. However, he thought that he had seen a vision, and said: "Lord, who would believe this?" But at that hour St. Andrew took him and carried him to the place where the Lance was hidden in the ground. When we were a second time situated in such (straits) as we have stated above, St. Andrew came again, saying to him: "Wherefore hast thou not yet taken the Lance from the earth as I commanded thee? Know, verily, that whoever shall bear this lance in battle shall never be overcome by an enemy." Peter, indeed, straightway made known to our men the mystery of the apostle.

The people, however, did not believe (it), but refused, saying: "How can we believe this?" For they were utterly terrified and thought that they were to die forthwith. Thereupon, this man came forth and swore that it was all most true, since St. Andrew had twice appeared to him in a vision and had said to him: "Rise, go and tell the people of God not to fear, but to trust firmly with whole heart in the one true God and they will be everywhere victorious. Within five days the Lord will send them such a token that they will remain happy and joyful, and if they wish to fight, let them go out immediately to battle, all together, and all their enemies will be conquered, and no one will stand against them." Thereupon, when they heard that their enemies were to be overcome by them, they began straightway to revive and to encourage one another, saying: "Bestir yourselves, and be everywhere brave and alert, since the Lord will come to our aid in the next battle and will be the greatest refuge to His people whom He beholds lingering in sorrow."

Accordingly, upon hearing the statements of that man who reported to us the revelation of Christ through the words of the apostle, we went in haste immediately to the place in the church of St. Peter which he had pointed out. Thirteen men dug there from morning until vespers. And so that man found the Lance, just as he had indicated. They received it with great gladness and fear, and a joy beyond measure arose in the whole city.

(*Raymond*). And so, as we said, when our men were in a panic and while they were on the verge of despair, divine mercy was at hand for them; and that mercy which had corrected the children when they were wanton, consoled them when they were very sad, in the following way. Thus, when the city of Antioch had been captured, the Lord, employing His power and kindness, chose a certain poor peasant, Provençal by race, through whom He comforted us; and He sent these words to the Count and Bishop of Puy:

"Andrew, apostle of God and of our Lord Jesus Christ, has recently admonished me a fourth time and has commanded me to come to you and to give back to you, after the city was captured, the Lance which opened the side of the Saviour. To-day, moreover, when I had set out from the city with the rest to battle, and when, caught between two horsemen, I was almost suffocated on the retreat, I sat down sadly upon a certain rock, almost lifeless. When I was reeling like a woe-begone from fear and grief, St. Andrew came to me with a companion, and he threatened me much unless I returned the Lance to you quickly."

And when the Count and Bishop asked him to tell in order the apostolic revelation and command, he replied: "At the first earthquake which occurred at Antioch when the army of the Franks was besieging it, such fear assailed me that I could say nothing except 'God help me.' For it was night, and I was lying down; nor was there anyone else in my hut to sustain me by his presence. When, moreover, the shaking of the earth had lasted a long time, and my fear had ever increased, two men stood before me in the brightest raiment. The one was older, with red and white hair, black eyes, and kindly face, his beard, indeed, white, wide, and thick, and his stature medium; the other was younger and taller, handsome in form beyond the children of men. And the older said to me 'What doest thou?' and I was very greatly frightened because I knew that there was no one present. And I answered, 'Who art thou?'

"He replied, 'Rise, and fear not; and heed what I say to thee. I am Andrew the Apostle. Bring together the Bishop of Puy and the Count of St. Gilles and Peter Raymond of Hautpoul, and say these words to them: "Why has the Bishop neglected to preach and admonish and daily to sign his people with the cross which he bears before them, for it would profit them much?"' And he added, 'Come and I will show thee the Lance of our father, Jesus Christ, which thou shalt give to the Count. For God has granted it to him ever since he was born.'

"I arose, therefore, and followed him into the city, dressed in nothing except a shirt. And he led me into the church of the apostle of St. Peter through the north gate, before which the Saracens had built a mosque. In the church, indeed, were two lamps, which there gave as much light as if the sun had illuminated it. And he said to me, 'Wait here.' And he commanded me to sit upon a column, which was closest to the stairs by which one ascends to the altar from the south; but his companion stood at a distance before the altar steps. Then St. Andrew, going under ground, brought forth the Lance and gave it into my hands.

"And he said to me 'Behold the Lance which opened His side, whence the salvation of the whole world has come.'

"While I held it in my hands, weeping for joy, I said to him, 'Lord, if it is Thy will, I will take it and give it to the Count!'

"And he said to me 'Not now, for it will happen that the city will be taken. Then come with twelve men and seek it here whence I drew it forth and where I hide it.' And he hid it.

"After these things had been so done, he led me back over the wall to my home; and so they left me. Then I thought to myself of the condition of my poverty and your greatness, and I feared to approach you. After this, when I had set forth for food to a certain fortress which is near Edessa, on the first day of Lent at cock-crow, St. Andrew appeared to me in the same garb and with the same companion with whom he had come before, and a great brightness filled the house. And St. Andrew said 'Art thou awake?'

"Thus aroused, I replied 'No, Lord; my Lord, I am not asleep.'

"And he said to me 'Hast thou told those things which I bade thee tell some time ago?'

"And I answered 'Lord, have I not prayed thee to send some one else to them, for, fearful of my poverty, I hesitated to go before them?'

"And he said 'Dost thou not know why the Lord led you hither, and how much He loves you and why He chose you especially? He made you come hither (to rebuke) contempt of Him and to avenge His people. He loves you so dearly that the saints already at rest, fore-knowing the grace of Divine arrangements, wished that they were in the flesh and struggling along with you. God has chosen you from all peoples, as grains of wheat are gathered from the oats. For you excel in favor and rewards all who may come before or after you, just as gold excels silver in value.'

"After this they withdrew, and such illness oppressed me that I was about to lose the light of my eyes, and I was arranging to dispose of my very meagre belongings. Then I began to meditate that these things had justly befallen me because of my neglect of the apostolic command. Thus comforted, I returned to the siege. Thinking again of the handicap of my poverty, I began to fear that if I went to you, you would say that I was a serf and was telling this for the sake of food; therefore, I was silent instead. And thus in the course of time, when at the Port of St. Simeon on Palm Sunday I was lying down in the tent with my lord, William Peter, St. Andrew appeared with a companion. Clad in the same habit in which he had come before, he spoke thus to me, 'Why hast thou not told the Count and Bishop and the others what I commanded thee?'

"And I answered 'Lord, have I not prayed thee to send another in my place who would be wiser and to whom they would listen? Besides the Turks are along the way and they kill those who come and go.'

"And St. Andrew said 'Fear not that they will harm thee. Say also to the Count not to dip in the river Jordan when he comes there, but to cross in a boat; moreover when he has crossed, dressed in a linen shirt and breeches, let him be sprinkled from the river. And after his garments are dry, let him lay them away and keep them with the Lance of the Lord.' And this my lord, William Peter, heard, though he did not see, the apostle.

"Thus comforted, I returned to the army. And when I wanted to tell you this, I could not bring you together. And so I set out to the port of Mamistra. There, indeed, when I was about to sail to the island of Cyprus for food, St. Andrew threatened me much if I did not quickly return to you and tell you what had been commanded me. And when I thought to myself how I would return to camp, for that port was three days distant from the camp, I began to weep most bitterly, since I could find no way of returning. At length, admonished by my lord and my companions, we entered the ship and began to row to Cyprus. And although we were borne along all day by oar and favoring winds up to sunset, a storm then suddenly arose, and in the space of one or two hours we returned to the port which we had left. And thus checked from crossing a second and a third time, we returned to the island at the

Port of St. Simeon. There I fell seriously ill. However, when the city was taken, I came to you. And now, if it please you, test what I say."

The Bishop, however, thought it nothing except words; but the Count believed it and handed over the man that had said this to his chaplain, Raymond, to guard.

Our Lord Jesus Christ appeared on the very night which followed to a certain priest named Stephen, who was weeping for the death of himself and his companions, which he expected there. For some who came down from the fortress frightened him, saying that the Turks were already descending from the mountain into the city, and that our men were fleeing and had been defeated. For this reason the priest, wishing to have God witness of his death, went into the church of the Blessed Mary in the garb of confession and, after obtaining pardon, began to sing psalms with some companions. While the rest were sleeping, and while he watched alone, after having said, "Lord, who shall dwell in Thy tabernacle, or who shall rest in Thy holy hill?"[7] a certain man stood before him, beautiful beyond all, and said to him, "Man, who are these people that have entered the city?"

And the priest answered "Christians."

"Christians of what kind?"

"Christians who believe that Christ was born of a Virgin and suffered on the Cross, died, and was buried, and that He arose on the third day and ascended into heaven."

And that man said "And if they are Christians, why do they fear the multitude of pagans?" And he added, "Dost thou not know me?"

The priest replied "I do not know thee, but I see that thou art most beautiful of all."

And the man said, "Look at me closely."

And when the priest intently scrutinized him, he saw a kind of cross much brighter than the sun proceeding from his head. And the priest said to the man who was questioning him, "Lord, we say that they are images of Jesus Christ which present a form like thine."

The Lord said to him, "Thou hast said well, since I am He. Is it not written of me that I am the Lord, strong and mighty in battle? And who is the Lord in the army?"

"Lord," replied the priest, "there never was in the army but one Lord, for rather do they put trust in the Bishop."

And the Lord said, "Say this to the Bishop, that these people have put me afar from them by evil doing, and then let him speak to them as follows: 'The Lord says this: "Return to me, and I will return to you."' And when they enter battle, let them say this 'Our enemy are assembled and glory in their own bravery; destroy their might, O Lord, and scatter them, so that they may know that there is no other who will fight for us except Thee, O Lord,' And say this also to them 'If ye do whatever I command you, even for five days, I will have mercy upon you!'"

Moreover, while He was saying this, a woman of countenance radiant beyond measure approached and, gazing upon the Lord, said to him, "Lord, what are thou saying to this man?"

And the Lord said to her, "I am asking him about these people who have entered the city, who they are."

Then the Lady replied, "O, my Lord, these are the people for whom I entreat thee so much."

And when the priest shook his companion who was sleeping near him, so that he might have a witness of so great a vision, they had disappeared from his eyes.

However, when morning came the priest climbed the hill opposite the castle of the Turks, where our princes were staying, all except the Duke, who was guarding the castle on the north hill. And thus, after assembling a gathering, he told these words to our princes, and, in order to show that it was true, he swore upon the Cross. Moreover, wishing to satisfy the incredulous, he was willing to pass through fire, or to jump from the top of the tower. Then the princes swore that they would neither flee from Antioch nor go out, except with the common consent of all; for the people at this time thought that the princes wanted to flee to the fort. And thus many were comforted, since in the past night there were few who stood steadfast in the faith and did not wish to flee. And had not the Bishop and Bohemund shut the gates of the city, very few would have remained. Nevertheless, William of Grandmesnil fled, and his brother, and many others, cleric and lay. It befell many, however, that when they had escaped from the city with the greatest danger, they faced the greater danger of death at the hands of the Turks.

At this time very many things were revealed to us through our brethren; and we beheld a marvelous sign in the sky. For during the night there stood over the city a very large star, which, after a short time, divided into three parts and fell in the camp of the Turks.

Our men, somewhat comforted, accordingly, awaited the fifth day which the priest had mentioned. On that day, moreover, after the necessary preparations, and after every one had been sent out of the Church of St. Peter, twelve men, together with that man who had spoken of the Lance, began to dig. There were, moreover, among those twelve men the Bishop of Orange, and Raymond, chaplain of the Count, who has written this, and the Count himself, and Pontius of *Balazun,* and Feraldus of Thouars. And after we had dug from morning to evening, some began to despair of finding the Lance. The Count left, because he had to guard the castle; but in place of him and the rest who were tired out from digging, we induced others, who were fresh to continue the work sturdily. The youth who had spoken of the Lance, however, upon seeing us worn out, disrobed and, taking off his shoes, descended into the pit in his shirt, earnestly entreating us to pray God to give us His Lance for the comfort and victory of His people. At length, the Lord was minded through the grace of His mercy to show us His Lance. And I, who have written this, kissed it when the point alone had as yet appeared above ground. What great joy and exultation then filled the city I cannot describe. Moreover, the Lance was found on the eighteenth day before the Kalends of July.

On the second night, St. Andrew appeared to the youth through whom he had given the Lance to us and said to him "Behold, God has given to the Count that which he never wished to give to anyone and has made him standard-bearer of this army, as long as he shall continue in His love."

When the youth asked mercy from him for the people, St. Andrew replied to him that verily would the Lord show mercy to His people. And, again, when he asked the same saint about his companion, who it was he had so often seen with him, St. Andrew answered, "Draw near and kiss His foot."

And so, when he was about to draw near, he saw a wound on His foot as fresh and bloody as if it had just been made. When, however, he hesitated to draw near because of the wound and blood, St. Andrew said to him:

"Behold, the Father who was wounded on the Cross for us, whence this wound. The Lord likewise commands that you celebrate that day on which He gave you His Lance. And since it was found at vespers, and that day cannot be celebrated, celebrate the solemn festival on the eighth day in the following week, and then each year on the day of the finding of the Lance. Say, also, to them that they conduct themselves as is taught in the Epistle of my brother, Peter, which is read to-day." (And the Epistle was this: "Humble yourselves under the mighty hand of God.")[8] "Let the clerics sing this hymn before the Lance: *Lustra sex qui jam peracta tempus implens corporis.* And when they shall have said,

Agnus in cruce levatus immolandus stipite, let them finish the hymn on bended knees."

When, however, the Bishop of Orange and I, after this, asked Peter Bartholomew if he knew letters, he replied, "I do not," thinking that if he were to say "I do," we would not believe him. He did know a little; but at that hour he was so ignorant that he neither knew letters nor had any remembrance of the things he had learned from letters, except the *Paternoster, Credo in Deum, Magnificat, Glory in Excelsis Deo,* and *Benedictus Dominus Deus Israel.* He had lost the others as if he had never heard them, and though he was able afterwards to recover a few, it was with the greatest effort.

4. *Defeat of Kerbogha.* (June 28, 1098.)

(*Gesta*). From that hour we took counsel of battle among ourselves. Fortwith, all our leaders decided upon the plan of sending a messenger to the Turks, enemies of Christ, to ask them with assured address: "Wherefore have you most haughtily entered the land of the Christians, and why have you encamped, and why do you kill and assail servants of Christ?" When their speech was already ended, they found certain men, Peter the Hermit and Herlwin, and they told them as follows: "Go to the accursed army of the Turks and carefully tell them all this, asking them why they have boldly and haughtily entered the land of the Christians and our own?"

At these words, the messengers left and went to the profane assemblage, saying everything to *Curbara* and the others as follows: "Our leaders and nobles wonder wherefore you have rashly and most haughtily entered their land, the land of the Christians? We think, forsooth, and believe that you have thus come hither because you wish to become Christians fully; or have you come hither for the purpose of harassing the Christians in every way? All our leaders together ask you, therefore, quickly to leave the land of God and the Christians, which the blessed apostle, Peter, by his preaching converted long ago to the worship of Christ. But they grant, in addition, that you may take away all your belongings, horses, mules, asses, camels, sheep, and cattle; all other belongings they permit you to carry with you, wherever you may wish."

Then *Curbara,* chief of the army of the Sultan of Persia, with all the others full of haughtiness, answered in fierce language: "Your God and your Christianity we neither seek nor desire, and we spurn you and them absolutely. We have now come even hither because we marvelled greatly why the princes and nobles whom you mention call this land theirs, the land we took from an effeminate people.

Now, do you want to know what we are saying to you? Go back quickly, therefore, and tell your seignors that if they desire to become Turks in everything, and wish to deny the God whom you worship with bowed heads, and to spurn your laws, we will give them this and enough more of lands, castles, and cities. In addition, moreover, (we will grant) that none of you will longer remain a foot-soldier, but will all be knights, just as we are; and we will ever hold you in the highest friendship. But if not, let them know that they will all undergo capital sentence, or will be led in chains to Chorosan, to serve us and our children in perpetual captivity forever."

Our messengers speedily came back, reporting all this most cruel race had replied. Herlwin is said to have known both tongues, and to have been the interpreter for Peter the Hermit. Meanwhile, our army, frightened on both sides, did not know what to do; for on one side excruciating famine harassed them, on the other fear of the Turks constrained them.

At length, when the three days fast had been fulfilled, and a procession had been held from one church to another, they confessed their sins, were absolved, and faithfully took the communion of the body and blood of Christ; and when alms had been given, they celebrated mass. Then six battle lines were formed from the forces within the city. In the first line, that is at the very head, was Hugh the Great with the Franks and the Count of Flanders; in the second, Duke Godfrey with his army; in the third was Robert the Norman with his knights; in the fourth, carrying with him the Lance of the Saviour, was the Bishop of Puy, together with his people and with the army of Raymond, Count of St. Gilles, who remained behind to watch the citadel for fear lest the Turks descend into the city; in the fifth line was Tancred, son of Marchisus, with his people, and in the sixth line was the wise man, Bohemund, with his army. Our bishops, priests, clerics, and monks, dressed in holy vestments, came out with us with crosses, praying and beseeching the Lord to make us safe, guard us, and deliver us from all evil. Some stood on the wall of the gate, holding the sacred crosses in their hands, making the sign (of the cross) and blessing us. Thus were we arrayed, and, protected with the sign of the cross, we went forth through the gate which is before the mosque.

After *Curbara* saw the lines of the Franks, so beautifully formed, coming out one after the other, he said: "Let them come out, that we may the better have them in our power!" But after they were outside the city and *Curbara* saw the huge host of the Franks, he was greatly frightened. He straightway sent word to his Emir, who had everything in charge, that if he saw a light burn at the head of the army he should have the trumpets sounded for it to retreat, knowing that the Turks had lost the battle. *Curbara* began immediately to retreat little by little toward the mountain, and our men followed them little by little. At length the Turks divided; one party went toward the sea and the rest halted there, expecting to enclose our men between them. As our men saw this, they did likewise. There a seventh line was formed from the lines of Duke Godfrey and the Count of Normandy, and its head was Reinald. They sent this (line) to meet the Turks, who were coming from the sea. The Turks, however, engaged them in battle and by shooting killed many of our men. Other squadrons, moreover, were drawn out from the river to the mountain, which was about two miles distant. The squadrons began to go forth from both sides and to surround our men on all sides, hurling, shooting, and wounding them. There came out from the mountains, also, countless armies with white horses, whose standards were all white. And so, when our leaders saw this army, they were entirely ignorant as to what it was, and who they were, until they recognized the aid of Christ, whose leaders were St. George, Mercurius, and Demetrius.[9] This is to be believed, for many of our men saw it. However, when the Turks who were stationed on the side toward the sea saw that that they could hold out no longer, they set fire to the grass, so that, upon seeing it, those who were in the tents might flee. The latter, recognizing that signal, seized all the precious spoils and fled. But our men fought yet a little while where their (the Turks) greatest strength was, that is, in the region of their tents. Duke Godfrey, the Count of Flanders, and Hugh the Great rode near the water, where the enemy's strength lay. These men, fortified by the sign of the cross, together attacked the enemy first. When the other lines saw this, they likewise attacked. The Turks and the Persians in their turn cried out. Thereupon, we invoked the Living and True God and charged against them, and in the name of Jesus Christ and of the Holy Sepulchre we began the battle, and, God helping, we overcame them. But the terrified Turks took to flight, and our men followed them to the tents. Thereupon, the knights of Christ chose rather to pursue them than to seek any spoils, and they pursued them even to the Iron Bridge, and then up to the fortress of Tancred. The enemy, indeed, left their pavilions there, gold, silver, and many ornaments, also sheep, cattle, horses, mules, camels, asses, grain, wine, butter, and many other things which we needed. When the Armenians and Syrians who dwelt in those regions heard that we had overcome the Turks, they ran to the mountain to meet them and killed as many of them as they could catch. We, however, returned to the city with great joy and praised and blessed God, who gave the victory to His people.

Thereupon, when the Emir who was guarding the citadel saw that *Curbara* and all the rest had fled from the field before the army of the Franks, he was greatly frightened. Immediately and with great haste he sought the standards of the Franks. Accordingly, the Count of St. Gilles, who was stationed before the citadel, ordered his standard to be brought to him. The Emir took it and carefully placed it on the tower. The Longobards who were there said immediately: "This is not Bohemund's standard!" Then the Emir asked and said: "Whose is it?" They answered: "It belongs to the Count of St. Gilles." Thereupon, the Emir went and seized the standard and returned it to the Count. But at that hour the venerable man, Bohemund, came and gave him his standard. He received it with great joy and entered into an agreement with Bohemund that the pagans who wished to take up Christianity might remain with him (Bohemund), and that he should permit those who wished to go away to depart safe and without any hurt. He agreed to all that the Emir demanded and straightway sent his servants into the citadel. Not many days after this the Emir was baptized with those of his men who preferred to recognize Christ. But those who wished to adhere to their own laws Lord Bohemund had conducted to the land of the Saracens.

This battle was fought on the fourth day before the Kalends of July, on the vigil of the apostles Peter and Paul, in the reign of our Lord Jesus Christ, who has honor and glory forever and ever. Amen. And after our enemies had now been completely conquered, we gave fitting thanks to God, Three and One, and the Highest. Some of the enemy, exhausted, others, wounded in their flight hither and thither, succumbed to death in valley, forest, fields, and roads. But the people of Christ, that is, the victorious pilgrims, returned to the city, rejoicing in the happy triumph over their defeated foes.

(*Raymond*). As we have said, when our men were beaten, discouraged, and in narrow straits, divine aid appeared. And the blessed Andrew taught us through the youth who had spoken of the Lance how we ought to conduct ourselves before the battle and in the battle:—

"You have all offended deeply, and you have been deeply humbled; and you have cried out to the Lord, and the Lord has heard you. And now let each one turn himself to the Lord because of his sins, and let him give five alms because of the five wounds of the Lord.

If he cannot do this, let him say the *Paternoster* five times. When this has been done, begin battle in the name of the Lord by day or by night, as the judgment of the princes deems best, because the hand of God will be with you. If anyone has doubt of victory, let the gates be opened for him, and let him go forth to the Turks, and he will see how their God will save him. Moreover, if anyone shall refuse to fight, let him be classed with Judas, the betrayer of the Lord, who deserted the apostles and sold his Lord to the Jews. Let them fight in the faith of St. Peter, holding in mind that God promised him that after the third day He would arise and appear to him, and for this reason, also, because this land is justly St. Peter's, and not the pagans'. And let your battle-cry be 'God help us!' and verily God will help you. All your brothers who died since the beginning of the expedition are present with you in this fight; you have only to storm the tenth part of the enemy, because they will assail nine parts in the might and command of God. And do not put off the battle, because (if you do), the Lord will lead as many enemies from the other sides as you have on this side, and He will keep you shut up here until you devour one another. But know certainly that those days are at hand which the Lord promised to the Blessed Mary and to His apostles, saying that He would raise up the kingdom of the Christians, after the kingdom of the pagans had been cast down and ground into dust. But do not turn to their tents in search of gold and silver."

Then the power of God was disclosed, in that He who had commanded the above words to be preached to us through His apostle so comforted the hearts of all that each one in faith and hope seemed to himself already to have triumphed over his enemy. They urged on one another, and in urging regained courage for fighting. The crowd, too, which in the past days seemed to be consumed with want and fright, now reproached the princes and complained of the delay of the battle. However, when the day for battle had been fixed, our princes sent word by Peter the Hermit to *Corbara,* leader of the Turks, to give up the siege of the city, because it was by right the property of St. Peter and the Christians. That proud leader replied that, rightly or wrongly, he was going to rule over the Franks and the city. And he compelled Peter the Hermit, who was unwilling to bow, to kneel to him.

The question was raised at this time as to who should guard the city against those who were in the citadel, while the rest went forth to fight. They built a stone wall and ramparts on our hill against the enemy; these they fortified with many rocks, finally leaving Count Raymond, who was deathly ill, and about two hundred men there.

The day of the fight had come. In the morning all partook of communion and gave themselves to God, to death, if He willed, or to the glory of the Roman church and the race of the Franks. Moreover, they decided about the battle as follows: that two double lines should be made of the Count's and Bishop's people, so that the foot-soldiers went before the knights and halted at the command of the princes; and the knights were to follow them and guard them from the rear. Similar arrangement was made of the people of Bohemund and Tancred; the like of the people of the Count of Normandy and the Franks; likewise, of the people of the Duke and the Burgundians. Moreover, trumpeters went through the city shouting that each man should stay with the princes of his people. It was likewise ordered that Hugh the Great, the Count of Flanders, and the Count of Normandy should advance to the battle first, then the Duke, the Bishop after the Duke, and Bohemund after the Bishop. They assembled, each man to his own standard and kinfolk, within the city before the gate of the bridge.

Oh, how blessed is the people whose Lord is God! Oh, how blessed the people whom God has chosen! Oh, how unaltered His face! How changed the army from sadness to eagerness! Indeed, during the past days princes and nobles went along the city streets calling upon the aid of God at the churches, the common people (walked) with bare feet, weeping and striking their breasts. They had been so sad that father did not greet son, nor brother brother, upon meeting, nor did they look back. But now you could see them going forth like swift horses, rattling their arms, and brandishing their spears, nor could they bear to refrain from showing their happiness in word and deed. But why do I grieve about many matters? They were given the power to go forth, and what had been agreed upon by the princes was fulfilled in order.

Meanwhile *Corbara*, leader of the Turks, was playing at chess within his tent. When he received the message that the Franks were advancing to battle, he was disturbed in mind because this seemed beyond expectation, and he called to him a certain Turk who had fled from Antioch, Mirdalin by name, a noble known to us for his military prowess. "What is this?" he said? "Didn't you tell me the Franks were few and would not fight with us?" And Mirdalin replied to him, "I did not say that they would not fight, but come, and I will look at them and tell you if you can easily overcome them."

And now the third line of our men was advancing. When he saw how the lines were arrayed, Mirdalin said to *Corbara*, "These men can be killed; but they cannot be put to flight."

And then *Corbara* said "Can none of them be driven back at all?"

And Mirdalin replied, "They will not yield a footstep, even if all the people of the pagans attack them."

Then, although disturbed in mind, he drew up his many and multiple lines against us. And when at first they could have prevented our exit, they allowed us to go out in peace. Our men, however, now directed their lines toward the mountains, fearing that the Turks might surround them from the rear. However, the mountains were about two long miles from the bridge. We were advancing in open file as the clergy are wont to march in processions. And verily we had a procession! For the priests and many monks, dressed in white robes, went in front of the lines of our knights, chanting and invoking the aid of the Lord and the benediction of the saints. The enemy, on the contrary, rushed against us and shot arrows. *Corbara,* now ready to do what he had just recently refused, likewise sent word to our princes (proposing) that five or ten Turks should do battle with a like number of Franks, and that those whose knights were conquered should peacefully yield to the others. To this our leaders replied, "You were unwilling when we wanted to do this; now that we have advanced to fight, let each fight for his right."

And when we had occupied the whole plain, as we said, a certain portion of the Turks remained behind us and attacked some of our foot-soldiers. But those foot-soldiers, turning about, sustained the attack of the enemy vigorously. When, indeed, the Turks could in no way drive them out, they set fire around them, so that those who did not fear the swords might at all events be terrified by fire. And thus they forced them to give way, for that place had much dry hay.

And when the lines had gone forth, the priests, with bare feet and garbed in their priestly vestments, stood on the walls of the city, calling upon God to defend His people, and through the victory of the Franks in this battle to afford a testimony hallowed by His blood. Moreover, as we were advancing from the bridge up to the mountain, we met with great difficulty because the enemy wanted to surround us. In the midst of this, the lines of the enemy fell upon us who were in the squadron of the Bishop, and though their forces were greater than ours, yet, through the protection of the Holy Lance which was there, they there wounded no one; neither did they hit any of us with arrows. I beheld these things of which I speak and I bore the Lance of the Lord there. If anyone says that Viscount Heraclius, the standard-bearer of the Bishop, was wounded in this battle, let him know that he handed over this standard to another and fell behind our line some distance.

When all our fighting men had left the city, five other lines appeared among us. For, as has already been said, our princes had drawn up only eight, and we were thirteen lines outside the city. In the beginning of the march out to battle the Lord sent down upon all His army a divine shower, little but full of blessing. All those touched by this were filled with all grace and fortitude and, despising the enemy, rode forth as if always nourished on the delicacies of kings. This miracle also affected our horses no less. For whose horse failed until the fight was over, even though it had tasted nothing except the bark or leaves of trees for eight days? God so multiplied our army that we, who before seemed fewer than the enemy, were in the battle more numerous than they. And when our men had thus advanced and formed in line, the enemy turned in flight without giving us a chance to engage in battle. Our men pursued them until sunset. There the Lord worked marvelously as well in the horses as in the men; forsooth, the men were not called away from battle by avarice, and those pack horses which their masters had led into battle, after a scant feeding, now very easily followed the sleekest and swiftest horses of the Turks.

But the Lord did not wish us to have this joy only. For the Turks who were guarding the citadel of the city gave up hope upon seeing the headlong flight of their people; some, on the pledge of their lives alone, surrendered themselves to us, and the rest fled headlong. And though this battle was so terrible and frightful, yet few knights of the enemy fell there; but of their foot-soldiers scarcely any escaped. Moreover, all the tents of the enemy were captured, much gold and silver, and the greatest amount of spoils—grain and cattle and camels without measure or number. And that incident of Samaria[10] about the measures of wheat and barley which were bought for a shekel was renewed for us. Moreover, these events occurred on the vigils of St. Peter and Paul, through which intercessors was granted this victory to the pilgrim church of the Franks by the Lord Jesus Christ, who liveth and reigneth God through all ages. Amen.

5. *Summary of events.* (June 5— beginning of July 1098).

(*Anselm.*) But on the following day *Corbara* approached with the King of Damascus, Duke *Baldach*,[11] the King of Jerusalem, and very many others and laid siege to the city. Accordingly, we were both besieged by them, and (were ourselves) besieging the aforesaid few in the castle of the city, and we were thus driven to eat the flesh of horses and asses. Moreover, on the second day after their arrival they killed Roger of *Barneville*.[12] On the third day, they attacked the fortress which we had erected against the Antiochenes, but accomplished nothing. However, they did inflict a wound upon Roger, chatelain of Lille, from which he died. Seeing that they were accomplishing nothing on that side, they ascended the hills. However, when we went out against them, we were beaten and put to flight. Then they entered inside the wall, and that day and the following night we were only a stone's throw from each other. On the following day at daybreak they called upon *Baphometh*[13] at the top of their voices, but we, calling upon our God in our hearts, made a charge upon them and drove them all outside the walls of the city. There Roger of *Betheniville* died. But they moved their camp and set siege to all the gates of the city, seeking to compel our surrender through lack of food.

Thereupon, when His servants had been placed in such tribulation, God stretched forth His right hand in aid and mercifully revealed the Lance with which the body of Christ was pierced. It lay buried, moreover, to a depth of two men's stature beneath the floor in the church of St. Peter. So, when this precious gem was found, all our spirits were revived.

On the vigil of the apostles Peter and Paul,[14] (our princes), after taking counsel among themselves, sent envoys to *Corbara* to say: "The army of the Lord sends this message: 'Leave us and the inheritance of St. Peter, or, otherwise, thou shalt be put to flight by arms!'" When he heard this, *Corbara* unsheathed his sword and swore by his kingdom and throne that he would defend himself from all the Franks; and he further said that he himself owned the land and would possess it, justly or unjustly. For, he answered, they would hear no word from him until, abandoning Antioch, they denied Christ and professed the law of the Persians.[15] When this message was heard, the Christians, cleansed by confession, and stoutly armed by partaking of the body and blood of Christ, went out from the gate ready for battle. The first to go forth was Hugh the Great, with his Franks; next the Count of the Normans and the Count of Flanders; after them, the venerable Bishop of Puy and the battle line of the Count of St. Gilles; after him, Tancred; and last of all, unconquered Bohemund. When, accordingly, the lines had been formed, with the Lance of the Lord and the Cross before them, they began battle with the greatest confidence. God helping, they turned in flight the Turkish princes, who were confused and utterly beaten, and killed countless numbers of them. Returning, therefore, with victory, we gave thanks to the Lord and celebrated the festival of the apostles with the greatest rejoicing. On that day the citadel was surrendered to us, the son of the King of Antioch having fled with *Corbara*. The King himself had been killed by peasants while fleeing in the mountains on the day that the city was surrendered.

We have sent this news to you, father, that you may take pleasure in the rescue of the Christians and the liberation of Antioch, and that you may pray God with greater devotion for all of us. For we place great faith in your prayers, and all that we accomplish we ascribe, not to our merit, but to your prayers. Now we pray you to keep our land in peace, and to defend the churches and the poor from the hands of tyrants. We pray, likewise, that you take counsel about the false pilgrims, either that they again take up the sign of the saving cross with penance, and resume the journey of the Lord, or that they undergo the peril of excommunication. Know for certain that the door of the land has been opened to us, and that, among our other good fortunes, the King of Babylon, by envoys sent to us, has said that he will obey our will. Farewell. We beseech in the name of the Lord Jesus that all whom this letter reaches pray God for us and our dead.

(*The People of Lucca*). "One day later, however, an innumerable army of Turks was at hand. They immediately besieged all the gates of the city; they shut us off from all exit or entrance. Those of our men, moreover, who were stationed at the sea coast, they destroyed by fire and sword.

"And, too, with this wretchedness of living and distress of dying, a great famine began to afflict us extremely. Moreover, Count Stephen, William, Bohemund's relative,[16] and very many others, terrified with fear at this, went down to Constantinople. As a result, anyone who heard that these men had thus withdrawn abandoned the expedition which he had begun, thinking that the whole army had perished. In the city, moreover, bread now failed those whom the greatest famine was wasting; then the flesh of horses and asses failed, and, finally, every means of subsistence.

"But the holy and merciful Lord was moved to pity at their lamentations, wailing, and tears and granted this favor. For there was a certain man, the poorest and nearly the most abject of all, a Provençal by birth, to whom St. Andrew appeared most clearly and, taking him by the hand, led him to the church of St. Peter and, pointing out a place with his finger, said: 'Here lies buried the Lance with which the Lord was wounded as He hung upon the Cross; go to the princes of the army of the Lord and tell them what thou hast seen.' That poor man was frightened and unwilling to go. Warned a second time, he went and set forth the vision. The faithful dug and found it; then, rejoicing and certain of the compassion of God, they glorified Christ. Moreover, after a fast of three days had been prescribed, they devoted themselves to prayer, confessed what wrongs they had done, and marched around the churches with bared feet. After this was done, each army equipped itself for battle.

"On the vigils of the apostles Peter and Paul, our men, after invoking the name of Christ, marched out of the city. The Bishop of St. Mary of Puy preceded, bearing the Cross and the triumphal Lance of the Saviour. The priests and many clerics followed, dressed in white vestments. And when they had advanced thus for about three miles to the field, they beheld a wonderful standard, white and exceeding high, and with it a countless host of knights. At the same time a wind and cloud of dust arose and drove the Turks into such flight that the fugitives cast away their arms, and even their very garments. And thus, God scattering them, they melted away never more to appear to us. Marvelous it is to relate, for no one was certain whence came either the standard or those who were with it. And so, our men, collecting the equipment and huge plunder of the fugitives, went into the city, exulting with great joy. Moreover, on that day the Lord gave them a greater abundance of food and other supplies than we have at home in harvest time. And now they possess freely the stronghold of the city, and all the region about, even to upper Nicaea."

This Bruno faithfully explained in the presence of all. We, moreover, dearest brethren, pray and beseech you who are in charge of the people to recount and explain to your sons the victory of Christ, and by admonishing and enjoining remission of sins to prevail upon all who are fit, paupers and women excepted, to go and join their brothers. And do you also devote yourselves assiduously to psalms, vigils, and prayers, that, fortified by the merits of intercessors as well as by the arms of warriors, they may lead a safe and tranquil life along the way which they are to take among barbarous nations. We also make it known to you that Lord Pope Urban holds a council at Bari, considering and arranging (matters) with many senators of the land (who are) soon to take the road to Jerusalem. Farewell.

(*Crusading Princes*). But when we wished to attack the citadel on the next day, we saw overrunning all the fields an infinite multitude of Turks, whose coming we had been expecting for many days, while outside the city. These besieged us on the third day, and more than one hundred of their soldiers entered the citadel; for they wanted to break through the gate into the portion of the city located below the citadel, common to both ourselves and them.

But taking a stand on another hill opposite the citadel, we guarded the road passing between the two armies down to the city, lest many more of them break in upon us. Fighting night and day, within and without, we forced them to enter the gates of the citadel which led them to the city, and to return to their camp. Accordingly, when they saw that they could do no harm on that side, they surrounded us all about, so that none of our men could go out or come to us. As a result of this, we were all so destitute and afflicted that many of our men, dying of starvation and many other wants, killed and ate our famished horses and asses.

But meanwhile, by the most kind compassion of Almighty God, who comes to our aid, and is watchful in our behalf, we found the Lance of the Lord by which the side of our Saviour was pierced at the hands of *Longinus*.[17] St. Andrew the apostle thrice appeared to a certain servant of God and pointed out where the Lance lay buried in the church of St. Peter, chief of the apostles. We were so comforted and strengthened by finding it, and by many other divine revelations, that we, who before had been afflicted and timid, were then most boldly and eagerly urging one another to battle.

Accordingly, on the vigil of the apostles, Peter and Paul, after we had been besieged for three weeks and four days, we placed our trust in God and, having confessed all our iniquities, sought the gates of the city from which we went out with the whole army, ready for battle. We were so few that they were sure that we were not fighting against them, but rather fleeing. However, when all our men were ready, and the lines of foot-soldiers, as well as of knights, had been definitely formed, we boldly sought out with the Lance of the Lord (the points) where their valor and endurance was greatest; and from the first stand of battle we forced them to flee. However, as is their custom, they began to scatter themselves everywhere, and, by occupying hills and seizing roads wherever they could, they wanted to encircle us. But the grace and mercy of God so aided us, who had been instructed against their wiles and stratagems by many battles, that we, who were very few in comparison with them, forced them all together into one body; and God's right hand fighting with us, we forced them, so gathered, to flee and abandon their camp with all that was in it. When we had conquered them, after pursuing them all day and killing very many of their knights, we returned to the city, happy and rejoicing. Moreover, a certain Emir who was in the aforesaid citadel with a thousand men surrendered to Bohemund, and at his hand they unanimously yielded to the Christian faith. And thus our Lord Jesus Christ has bound the city of Antioch to the Roman religion and faith.

CHAPTER VI

Dissension Among the Leaders

(With the overthrow of Kerbogha all pressing danger from the Seljukian Turks and the Caliph of Bagdad was ended for several years at least. Henceforth the most serious obstacle from the Mohammedan side consisted in the Fatimite Caliph of Egypt. The latter, however, had entered into negotiations with the Crusaders, so that there was little cause to worry on that score. All Syria was now at the disposal of the Christians, and the fear of immediate danger was removed. But this situation threatened even greater perils to the cause of the Crusaders. For the main incentive for close cooperation and harmony was lost with the removal of danger from common foes. The death of Adhemar, papal vicar, at this juncture aggravated the state of affairs, for it took away the only leader who had claims upon the allegiance of them all. As a result, the leaders quarrelled and all but fought with each other. On one pretext and another the journey to Jerusalem was postponed to satisfy their selfish ambitions. The amazing pressure exerted at length by the common knights and foot-soldiers for some unity of action and adhesion to the original vow deserves much greater attention in the history of feudal organization than has usually been accorded it. Count Raymond's use of Peter Bartholomew to support his personal plans was undoubtedly the chief cause for questioning the Lance, on which Peter's reputation was primarily based. Mediaeval history affords few instances of the trial by the ordeal of fire so stringent or so graphically described, and the varied account of the outcome betrays what intense feeling had sprung up among the parties since the capture of Antioch. The elaborate version by Raymond, in marked contrast with the absolute silence of the Anonymous, necessitates the addition of the less direct testimony of Raoul de Caen and Fulcher. The question continued a subject of debate for years in the West, as well as in the East, but for the time being the Ordeal made united action again possible.)

1. *Disorganization of the Army.* (June-November 1, 1098.)

(*The Crusading Princes.*) But since some sorrow is ever wont to occur in the midst of happiness, that Bishop of Puy whom you committed to us as your vicar died on the Kalends of August, after the battle in which he had taken an honorable part was over and the city pacified. Now, therefore, we, your sons, bereft of the father committed to us, bid you, our spiritual father, who started this expedition, who, by your sermons, caused us all to leave our lands and all that was on those lands, commanded us to take up the cross to follow Christ, and admonished us to exalt the Christian name—we bid you complete the task which you urged; come to us and persuade all whom you can to come with you. For here the blessed Peter was enthroned in the church which we see daily, and those who before were called Galileans[1] were here first in general called Christians. What in the world, therefore, can seem more proper than that you, who stand forth as the father and head of the Christian religion, should come to the first and chief city of the Christian name, and complete on your part the war which is your own? For we have driven out the Turks and pagans; the heretics, however, Greeks and Armenians, Syrians, and Jacobites,[2] we cannot expel. We bid you, therefore, again and again, our most beloved father, come as father and head to the place of your fatherhood, and, as the vicar of St. Peter, take your seat in his church and have us as your obedient sons in well doing. Root out and destroy all heresy of whatever kind by your authority and our valor, and thus complete the expedition of Jesus Christ, begun by us, and preached by yourself. And, likewise, open to us the gates of both Jerusalems, make free the Sepulchre of the Lord and exalt the Christian name above every name. For, if you will come to us, and with us finish the expedition begun by you, all the world will be obedient to you. May He Himself cause you to do this, Who liveth and reigneth God for ever and ever. Amen.

A matter has been related to me which, indeed, is very much against God and all worshippers of Christ; namely, that persons signed with the cross hold permission from you to remain among Christians. I marvel greatly at this, because, since you are the instigator of this holy journey, those who put off that journey ought to receive neither counsel nor anything good from you until they have fulfilled the journey which they began. And it is not only our concern that you thus disturb the good which you have begun but, also, that you should strengthen us by the coming of yourself and all whom you can lead with you. For it is fitting that we, who by God's help and your pious prayers are possessors of all Romania, Cilicia, Asia, and Syria, should have you, after God, as our aid and succour. Moreover, most holy father, you ought to separate us, sons obedient to you in all things, from the unjust Emperor who has made us many good promises, but has not at all carried them out. For he has caused us all the ill and hindrance which he could.

This document was written on the 11th day of the beginning of September, Fourth Indiction.

(*Gesta.*) Immediately all our leaders, Godfrey, Raymond, Count of St. Gilles, Bohemund, Lord Robert, Count of Normandy, the

Count of Flanders, and all the rest sent the most noble knight Hugh the Great to the Emperor at Constantinople (with a message) to come and receive the town and fulfil the agreements which he had with them. He went and never afterward returned. After all this had been done, all our leaders assembled and held a council as to how they could successfully lead and rule over this multitude until they should have accomplished the march to the Holy Sepulchre, for which they had already up to this point suffered so many dangers. It was decided in the council that they should not yet dare to enter the land of the pagans, because in the summer time it is very dry and has no water, and so they agreed to wait until the Kalends of November. Then the leaders separated, and each one set out into his own land, (to wait) until the time for going. And the princes had the trumpets sounded throughout the whole city, announcing that if any needy person without gold and silver wished to remain with them, he would be gladly maintained by them, upon making an agreement.

There was a certain knight of the army of the Count of St. Gilles, whose name was Raymond Piletus. He retained very many vassals, knights, and foot-soldiers. He went out with this assembled army and entered the land of the Saracens and, setting out beyond two cities, came to a certain fortified place, the name of which was *Talamania*. The inhabitants of the place, Syrians, immediately surrendered to him of their own accord. And when all had been there for eight days, messengers came to him saying: "There is near us here a fortress filled with a multitude of Saracens." To this camp went the pilgrim knights of Christ and attacked it on all sides, and it was straightway captured by them with the aid of Christ. Thereupon, they took all the inhabitants of this place and killed those who were unwilling to receive Christianity. And when this had been accomplished, our Franks returned with great joy to their former camp.

But on the third day they went out and came to a certain city near them, Marra by name. Moreover, there were gathered there many Turks and Saracens from the city of Aleppo, and from all the cities and towns which were around it. The barbarians, accordingly, came out against us to do batle, and our men, thinking to struggle with them in fighting, forced them to flight; but they, returning, attacked our men from time to time throughout the whole day, and their attack lasted up to evening. The summer being hot beyond measure, our men were already unable to endure such great thirst because they could nowhere find water to drink; nevertheless, they wished to return in safety to their fortress. But because of their sins the Syrians and the poor people, seized with great fear, began immediately to take the way back again. As the Turks saw them coming back, they began at once to pursue them, and victory ministered strength to them; thus many of these people gave up their souls to God for love of whom they had there assembled. This slaughter occurred on the fifth day in the month of July. However, the Franks who had remained returned to their camp, and there Raymond lingered with his people for several days. But the others who had remained in Antioch stayed in the city with great joy and gladness.

Their guide and shepherd was the Bishop of Puy, who at the nod of God was taken with a serious illness and, as it was the will of God, departed from this earth and, resting in peace, slept in the Lord on the festival of St. Peter which is called Ad Vincula.[3] As a result, there was great anguish, tribulation, and very great grief in the whole Christian army, because he had been a support to the poor, counsel to the rich, and he had ordained clergy. He had preached and admonished the leaders saying: "No one of you can be saved, unless he respects and refreshes the poor. You cannot be saved without them, they cannot live without you; it is fitting, therefore, that they pray God in daily supplication for your sins, because you offend Him daily in many ways. Therefore, I ask you for the love of God to cherish them and sustain them as much as you can."

Not long after this, the venerable man, Raymond, Count of St. Gilles, went out, and, entering the land of the Saracens, he came to a certain city called Barra, which he attacked with his army and straightway captured. He killed all the Saracen men and women, noble and common, whom he found there. After he held it in his power, he recalled it to the faith of Christ. He then sought counsel from his wisest men, that he might have a bishop most devoutly ordained in this city, to recall it loyally to the worship of Christ and out of the house of the devil to consecrate a temple and altars of the saints to the true and living God. They straightway chose a certain honorable and very wise man and conducted him to Antioch to be consecrated, and this was done. The rest, however, who had remained in Antioch were there with great joy and gladness.

(*Raymond.*) After this victory it happened that our princes, Bohemund, the Count, the Duke, and the Count of Flanders, received the fortress of the city; but Bohemund took the highest towers, already at that time plotting the wiles by which he caused an injustice. For he next drove the men of the Duke, of the Count of Flanders, and of the Count of St. Gilles violently from the citadel, saying that he had given oath to that Turk who had surrendered the city that he alone would hold it. On this account, too, since he had done this with impunity, he began to seek the castles and gates of the city which the Count, Bishop, and Duke had guarded during the time that we were besieged. All gave in to him, except the Count. For, though ill, he was yet unwilling to give up the gate of the bridge either for prayer, promises, or threats. Discord at this time not only disturbed our princes, but it also so destroyed harmony among the people that there were few who did not quarrel with their companions or servants about matters of theft or plunder. Nor was there in the city any judge who could, or would, settle these disputes, but as much injustice as he could bear befell each man. Moreover, the Count and Bishop were very ill and could not in the least protect their men from wrong. But why do we delay over these matters? Forsooth, our men, once more enjoying ease and riches against the command of God, put off to the Kalends of November the journey on which account they had come, although at this time the cities of the Saracens were so terrified and beset with fear at the flight of the Turks that if our Franks had ridden forth then we believe there would not have been a city, even to Jerusalem, which would have thrown a stone at them.

Meanwhile Lord Bishop, Adhemar of Puy, beloved of God and men, a man dear in everything to all, passed in peace to the Lord on the Kalends of August. So great was the grief of all the Christains at his death that, when we undertook to describe it, we who saw it could not at all comprehend it because of its magnitude. How useful he had been to the princes and the army of God was manifest after his death when the princes were divided among themselves, Bohemund going back to Romania and the Duke of Lorraine setting out toward Edessa.

On the second night after the Bishop had been buried in the church of St. Peter at Antioch, the Lord Jesus Himself, together with St. Andrew and the same Bishop, stood before that Peter Bartholomew who had spoken of the Lance, in the chapel of the Count where the Lance of the Lord was. And the Bishop spoke to him, saying:

"Thanks be to God, to Bohemund, and to all of you, my brothers, who have delivered me from hell. For I had sinned gravely after the Lance of the Lord was found. On this account I was led down into hell and there most severely punished, and my head and face were burned, as you can see. My soul was there from the hour in which it went forth from my body until my poor body was given to the dust. The Lord gave to me amidst the burning flames the garment that you see, because when I received the order of the episcopate I gave it in the name of God to a certain poor man. And though Gehenna was exceedingly hot and the ministers of Tartarus raged against me, yet they could do no harm beneath it. Nothing of all that I brought from my fatherland has been of such value to me as this candle which my friends offered here for me and those three *denarii* which I offered to the Lance, for these have restored me when, suffering in hell, I was near unto death. Lord Bohemund said that he would bear my body to Jerusalem. Let him know that it is to his advantage not to move me, for the blood of the Lord who accompanies me is still there. But if he doubts this which I say, let him open my tomb and he will see my head and face burned. I have committed my following to my lord the Count; let it comfort him that God bestows His mercy upon him and fulfils what He has promised him. And let my brothers not grieve that I have finished life, since I never was so useful as I will now be, if they are willing to observe the commands of God. For I shall dwell with them and likewise all my brothers who, like myself, have ended this life; and I shall appear and shall counsel them much better than hitherto. And you, my brothers, be mindful of the punishments of hell which are so severe and so dreadful. Accordingly, serve God who can deliver you from these and other evils. How well-born is he who shall know not the punishments of hell! This the Saviour can grant to those who observe His precepts. Keep what remains of this candle in the morning. And let the Count, together with those he may wish, choose a bishop in my place, since it is not just for the Blessed Mary to have no bishop after my death. Give one of my cloaks to the church of St. Andrew."

And the blessed Andrew knelt down to Him. After this, St. Andrew, sitting nearer, spoke as follows: "Let all hear what the Lord speaks through me: Be mindful, Count, of that gift which the Lord gave to thee; strive to work in His name, that the Lord may direct thy deeds and words, and heed thy prayer. The first gift which the Lord conferred upon thee, Nicaea, has been turned from Him. God gave thee His city and took it from His enemies and afterwards was not recognized there. If anyone invoked the name of the Lord, he was beaten there, and the deeds of the Lord were not done there. But because of His kindness the Lord has not willed to refuse that which thou seekest, and even more than thou hast dared to ask. For he gave thee the Lance which wounded His body, whence the blood of our redemption flowed forth. But He did not give it thee to do with as thou didst with the other; thou canst see that the Lord has given thee this because of thy deserts. The Lord commands thee, O Count, to find out who will be willing to make himself lord of this city over the others; and to seek from him what kind of dominion he shall wish to establish for the sake of the Lord. If thou and thy brothers to whom God gave this city know that he is faithful and wishes to maintain the justice of God, let him have it. And if he is unwilling to do and hold justice and judgment, but wishes to keep the city through his might, do thou alone, and through thy brothers, ask advice of God, and He will give it thee. And those men who have followed the right path, or whom God cherishes, will not fail thee; let those, however, who are unwilling to keep the right way, turn to him who is unwilling to execute justice, and it will be seen how God will save them. For they shall have the same curse from God and His Mother which Lucifer had when he fell from heaven. And do you, if you are all of one mind, ask advice in prayer and God will give it to you. And if there is concord among you, take counsel about a patriarch who is of your law. Moreover, do not loose those men who have come to you from captivity to keep your law. Do not receive those who have wandered into Chorosan to adore the God of the Turks, but hold them as Turks and send two or three of them to prison and they will betray the rest to you. Moreover, after the deeds above named have been done, seek advice from the Lord about the journey because of which you came, and He will advise you. Jerusalem is ten days from you, and if you are not willing to keep the above written commands, you shall not go into Jerusalem in ten years. And after ten years I will lead back the infidels in honor, and a hundred of them shall prevail against a thousand of you. Do you, men of Christ, seek from the Lord the petition which the apostles sought. And just as He gave it to them, so also will He now give it to you. You, Count and Bohemund, go to the church of St. Andrew, and he will give you the best counsel from God. And that which God shall place in your hearts (to do), do. And after St. Andrew has visited you, visit him and have your brothers visit him. Between you, Count and Bohemund, let there be concord and love of God and neighbor. And if, indeed, you have fortunately come to agreement, nothing will be able to separate you. It is well to show first the justice which you ought to maintain. According as the men are followers of their individual bishops, let them profess their wealth; let them aid the poor of their kind just as they can, and as there shall be need. Moreover, about other matters do as you shall agree. If any are unwilling to do this and other justice, constrain them. And if anyone shall wish to retain any other city of those which God shall give you, make him conduct himself according to the above directions. If, however, they are unwilling to do this, let the Count with the children of God punish them."

These words, at first believed, were then forgotten, for some said, "Let us return the city to the Emperor." Others, however, said not.

When, indeed, Peter was pressed by death at the siege of Archas, he called the Count to him and said, "When you have reached Jerusalem, have the army ask God to prolong your life and continue it, and God will prolong it as much as you have already lived. However, when you shall have returned, place the Lance of God five leagues from the church of St. Trophim, and have a church built there, and let there be a medal which you shall swear is not falsified, and do not allow anything else to be falsified there. That place will be called the Mount of Joy. Let these things be done within Provence, for St. Peter promised to his disciple, St. Trophim,[4] that he would send the Lance of God to him."

And thus through discord and seditions of this kind the property of the poor was wiped out. Of this advice which the princes received from St. Andrew nothing came.

Meanwhile, the Turks of the Caliph besieged a certain fortified place called *Asa*. Therefore the afflicted Turks who were within sent word to the Duke, who was in that region, to receive their fortress; that they then wished to have no lord except one of the race of the Franks. On this account, therefore, the Duke, returning to Antioch, summoned together the Count, who had already convalesced from his illness, and all his knights and foot-soldiers, for the sake of the poor to lead them into *Hispania* for plunder. He urged greatly that the Count, for God, for the glory of the race of the Franks, and for himself, should aid the Turks who were calling upon God, adding that the besieged Turks held forth the Cross against the machines of the besieging Turks. After these and many other prayers of this kind, the Count set out with the Duke. However, when this was found out by the Turks, they withdrew from the siege. As our army came to *Asa*, the Duke received hostages from the fortress for fealty thereafter, and the Count, with a heavy expense to his army, returned to Antioch. Again the Count assembled his army to lead the poor people into *Hispania* because they were failing from hunger and illness at Antioch.

However, St. Andrew appeared to Peter Bartholomew, this time at Rugia, in a tent where the Bishop of Agde was staying and the chaplain of Count Raymond and another chaplain, Simon by name. This Simon, moreover, hearing them speaking together, that is,

St. Andrew with Peter Bartholomew, lent his ears, and, as he said, heard very many things, but remembered only this: "Lord, I say."

But the Bishop of Agde said: "I know not whether it was in a dream or not. A certain old man dressed in a white cloak and holding in his hand the Lance of the Lord stood before me and said to me, 'Dost thou believe that this is the Lance of Jesus Christ?'

"And I replied, 'I believe, Lord.'

"And when he had thus questioned me a second and a third time, I said 'Verily I believe, Lord, that this is the Lance which drew forth from the side of Jesus Christ the blood whence we all have been redeemed.'"

And after this, the Bishop violently aroused me, who was sleeping near. When I looked out, I saw an unwonted splendor, and, feeling a certain grace of spirit, I began to ask of those who were present whether they had noticed any disturbance among the people. And all began to say, "Not at all." But when we said to one another the things which we said above, that Peter to whom this revelation had been made replied, "And truly enough did you here see a grace-giving splendor, since the Father from whom all grace proceeds stood here for some time."

When, moreover, we asked him to make clear what had been told him, he said this to us and the Count:

"On this night the Lord and St. Andrew came here in the form in which they have been wont to come before, together with a certain third person with a very long beard whose stature was slight and who was dressed in linen. Then St. Andrew threatened me much because I had left in an unworthy place the relics of his body which were found in his church at Antioch, and said 'When I was hurled headlong from a mountain near Antioch by the infidels, I broke two of my fingers, and after my death this man took them and brought them to Antioch. But thou, when thou didst find them, neglected them; one thou hast permitted to be taken away from thee, the other thou hast unworthily neglected.' And he showed his hand without the fingers. Then, Count, he complained much about you, for, although you have received the ineffable reward granted to no one else by the Lord, you do not fear to sin gravely and wickedly in the sight of God. Therefore the Lord showed you this sign. For five days ago when you offered a candle on the festival of the blessed Fidus[5] large enough to last for three days and nights, it did not even give light, but melted away immediately and was destroyed on the ground. Moreover, tonight you offered a candle so little that it could scarcely last till cockcrow, and it is now day, and it still lasts, nor has a third part of it been burned. Besides this, the Lord sends you word to begin nothing, unless you have first done penance; otherwise you and whatever you do will sink, like the melted candle, into the ground. And he says that if you do penance, all that you begin in the name of the Lord God will perfect and finish, and as you see this little candle last a long time, so will the Lord make great whatever you shall undertake, even though it be small."

And when the Count denied that he had sinned so gravely, Peter also narrated the sin to him, and the Count thus confessed and did penance.

And again Peter said to the Count, "St. Andrew complains of your counsellors, that they knowingly advise many evil things. Wherefore he commands that you do not admit them to your counsel. Hear also, Count: the Lord commands you not to delay, because, unless Jerusalem is first captured, you shall have no aid. When, however, you shall draw near Jerusalem, let no one ride closer than two leagues; if you do this, God will give the city to you. After this, St. Andrew thanked me much because I had caused the church which was built in his name to be consecrated. St. Andrew said this and other things to me about which it is not now the place to speak. After this they disappeared, he and his companions."

Accordingly, the Count set out with the poor people and a few knights into Syria and took by storm the first city of the Saracens, Barra by name; and he killed there many thousands of Saracens and many thousands were led back to Antioch to be sold. But he permitted those to go away free who, for fear of death, gave themselves up to him while they were being besieged. Then, after taking counsel with his chaplains and leaders, he there very laudably and honorably chose a certain priest as Bishop. When all who were there with him had been assembled, the chaplain of the Count mounted a wall and made clear the desire of the Count to the whole assemblage. And when the people were very insistent that the election should be made, the same chaplain of the Count began to seek if there was there any cleric to receive the vows of the faithful and to serve God and his brothers there, as much as he could, in resisting the pagans. And when all were silent, we urged a certain Peter, Narbonne by race, to whom we held forth the work of the episcopate in the presence of all the Council, begging that he should not hesitate to accept it for God and his brothers, if he had it in mind to prefer to die rather than leave that city. When he professed this, all the people unanimously approved him and offered great thanks to God that through the administration of this man He wished to have a Roman bishop in the Oriental church. The Count granted to the Bishop one half of the city and its land.[6]

2. *Disputes between Raymond and Bohemund.* (November 1, 1098-January 13, 1099.)

(*Gesta.*) But as the time set approached, that is the Feast of All Saints, all our leaders returned to Antioch and together began to seek how they might accomplish the journey to the Holy Sepulchre, saying: "Since the time set for going has arrived, there is not time for further quarrelling." Bohemund, however, daily sought (confirmation of) the agreement which all the leaders had long ago made with him to give him the city.[7] But the Count of St. Gilles wished to commit himself to no agreement with Bohemund, because he feared to perjure himself with the Emperor. Nevertheless, they often assembled in the Church of St. Peter to do what was just. Bohemund recited his agreement and presented his reckoning. The Count of St. Gilles, likewise, laid bare his words and the oath which he had made to the Emperor on the advice of Bohemund. The bishops, Duke Godfrey, the Count of Flanders, the Count of Normandy, and the other leaders separated from the rest and entered (the space) where the chair of St. Peter stands, there to decide upon a judgment between the two. But fearing later that the journey to the Holy Sepulchre might be interrupted, they were unwilling to make public their judgment. Then the Count of St. Gilles said: "Rather than see the way to the Holy Sepulchre (unachieved), if Bohemund will consent to go with us, I will faithfully agree to whatever our peers (to wit, Duke Godfrey, the Count of Flanders, Robert of Normandy, and the other seignors) approve, saving fealty to the Emperor."[8] Bohemund approved of all this, and both promised in the hands of a bishop that the journey to the Holy Sepulchre would in no way be disturbed by them. Then Bohemund took counsel with his vassals, how with men and provisions he might fortify the citadel on the high mountain. The Count of St. Gilles, likewise, took counsel with his men, how he might fortify with men and provisions enough for a long time the palace of *Cassianus,* and the tower which is above the gate of the bridge, on the side toward the Port of St. Simeon.

This city of Antioch is indeed very beautiful and glorious, since within its walls are four very large and exceedingly high mountains. On the higher one has been built a castle, wonderful and exceedingly strong. Down below is the city glorious, near at hand and adorned with honors of all kinds, since many churches have been built within it. It contains three hundred and sixty monasteries, and the Patriarch holds under his sway one hundred and fifty-three bishops.[9] The city is enclosed by two walls; the greater one, furthermore, is very high and marvelously wide, and constructed of great stones, on which have been arranged four hundred and fifty towers. The city is beautiful in every way. On the east it is enclosed by four mountains, on the west beside the walls flows a certain stream, Orontes by name. So they were unwilling foolishly or senselessly to give up the regal city of Antioch, which was of such great authority that it held seventy-five kings under its sway. The chief of these was King Antiochus,[10] from whom it is called Antioch. The Franks besieged that city for eight months and a day, and afterwards were shut up in it for three weeks by the Turks and other pagans, than whose number there has never been a greater gathering of men, whether Christians or Pagans. Nevertheless, after those people had been defeated by God's Christians, with the aid of God and the Holy Sepulchre, we rested in Antioch with great joy and gladness for five months and eight days.

When these things had been fulfilled, Raymond, Count of St. Gilles, left Antioch with his army in the month of November and came to a city called Rugia and to another which is called Barra. But at the end of the fourth day of outgoing November he came to the city of Marra, in which a very great multitude of Saracens, Turks, Arabs, and other pagans had been assembled, and the Count himself attacked it on the next day. Not much later, Bohemund with his army followed the Counts[11] and joined them on the day of the Lord.

On the second day of the week they attacked the city vigorously on all sides, so fiercely and so powerfully that their ladders were set up against the wall. But so very great was the valor of the pagans that on that day they could do them no hurt or offense. However, when our leaders saw that they could accomplish nothing and were laboring in vain, Raymond, Count of St. Gilles, caused a certain wooden fortress to be made strong and high. This fortress was contrived and built on four wheels. On (the top of) it were stationed many knights and Everard the Hunter, who sounded his trumpet loudly, but below were armed knights who took the fortress up to the very wall of the city, near a certain tower. When the pagan people saw this, they immediately constructed a machine by means of which to cast great stones on the fortress, so that they almost killed our knights. They also threw Greek fire on the fortress, expecting it to burn and be destroyed. But Almighty God was unwilling to burn the fortress in this fashion, for it towered over all the walls of the city. Accordingly, our knights who were in the upper compartment, William of Montpellier and many others, hurled great stones upon those who were standing on the wall of the city and thus struck them over their shields, so that enemy and shield fell down into the city to death. So were these men doing; but the rest held glorious banners on their spears, and with lances and iron hooks planned to drag the enemy to them. Thus they fought until evening. The priests and clerics, dressed in their sacred vestments, stood behind the fortress, praying and beseeching God to defend His people, exalt Christianity, and cast down paganism. On the other side, however, our knights fought with the pagans daily and raised ladders to the wall, but their valor was so great that our men could accomplish nothing. Godfrey of Lastour was the first to climb up the ladder to the wall, but the ladder was immediately broken by the multitude of the others. Yet he climbed onto the wall with a few, and those who had ascended cleared the wall close about them. The others, too, found another ladder and quickly set it up against the wall, and many knights and foot-soldiers, ascending by it, immediately climbed over the wall. Thereupon the Saracens so stoutly attacked them from the wall and from the ground by shooting arrows and hurling spears everywhere that many of our men in terror let themselves down from the wall. For a long time those most illustrious men who remained on the wall bore the attack of the enemy, as long as the rest beneath the fortress were undermining the wall of the city. But when the Saracens saw that our men had undermined the wall, they were overcome with fright and immediately fled into the city. All this happened on the Sabbath day, toward the hour of vespers, at sunset on the eleventh day of incoming December.[12]

Bohemund, thereupon, had it proclaimed through an interpreter to the leaders of the Saracens that they might place themselves, with their wives and children and other possessions, in a palace near the gate, and that he would defend them from the sentence of death. But all our men entered the city, and whatever goods they found in the houses and in the pits each one appropriated as his own. However, when day came they killed many of them, whether man or woman, wherever they found them. No corner of the city was free from corpses of the Saracens, and we could scarcely go anywhere in the city without stepping on the Saracen dead. At length, Bohemund seized those whom he had commanded to enter the palace and took from them all they had: to wit, gold, silver, and other ornaments. Some he had killed; others, however, he ordered to be taken to Antioch for sale.

Moreover, the delay of the Franks in that city was for one month and four days, during which time the Bishop of Orange died. There were some of our men who did not find it there to their taste, not only because of the long stay, but also because of the pressure of hunger, since they could find nothing outside to take. But they burned the bodies of the dead because they found gold besants hidden in their stomachs, while others cut the flesh of the bodies to pieces and cooked them for food.

However, Bohemund could not get the Count of St. Gilles to agree to this matter that he sought and returned in anger to Antioch. Accordingly Count Raymond, without long delay, sent (word) through his legates at Antioch to Duke Godfrey, the Count of Flanders, Robert the Norman, and Bohemund that they should come to the city of Rugia to speak with him. All the leaders went there and held a council as to how they could honorably continue the journey to the Holy Sepulchre, for the sake of which they had been aroused and had come hither to this place. They could not bring Bohemund into accord with Raymond, unless Count Raymond gave Antioch to him. The Count refused to agree to this because of the pledge which he had made to the Emperor. The Counts and the Dukes then returned to Antioch with Bohemund, but Count Raymond returned to Marra, where the pilgrims were. He also bade his knights strengthen the palace and castle which was over the gate of the bridge to the city.

(*Raymond.*) And now the Kalends of November was pressing, the day on which all the princes had promised to convene at Antioch and begin the journey because of which they had come. Moreover, Barra was about two days distant from Antioch. Accordingly, the Count left his army at Barra and, with his Bishop-elect and many captives and much booty, returned to Antioch with great exultation. All the princes assembled there except Baldwin, brother of the Duke. But this Baldwin, who had set out before the capture of Antioch toward the Euphrates, had obtained Edessa, a very wealthy and famous city; and he had successfully fought many battles with the Turks.

But before we go on to the rest, this one incident about the Duke of Lorraine should not be passed over. When he was coming to Antioch at this time with twelve knights, he met one hundred and fifty Turks. Thereupon, after taking up his arms and urging on his knights, he bravely attacked the enemy. However, when the Turks saw that the Franks preferred death in fighting to flight with safety, a certain portion of the Turks dismounted so that the other portion might fight in greater security, since they would know that their companions, having left their horses, would not withdraw from the battle. And thus, since the battle, once begun, was lasting long and severely, the Duke's knights, who equalled the number of the twelve apostles and regarded their lord as the vicar of God, encouraged one another and fearlessly attacked the lines of the Turks. There God granted so great a victory to the Duke that he killed almost thirty of the enemy and took the same number captive; and, pursuing the rest in the swamps and the river which were nearby, he forced some to be destroyed, some drowned. And so he came to Antioch with a great victory, for he caused several heads of the dead to be carried by the living Turks, a sight joyful enough for us.

And so, when all the princes had come together into the church of St. Peter, they began to talk about our journey. Then some who held castles and revenues in the region of Antioch said: "What will be done about Antioch? Who will keep it? The Emperor will not come. For when he received the message that the Turks were besieging us, he fled, trusting neither his own courage nor the multitude of men which he had with him. Shall we still wait for him? Surely he will not come to our aid, he who forced our brothers, on their way to the aid of God and ourselves, to turn back! And if we leave this city, and the Turks occupy it, the end will be worse than before. But let us all grant it to Bohemund, since he is wise and will guard it very well; and his name is great among the pagans."

But the Count and the others said on the contrary, "We swore to the Emperor upon the Cross of the Lord, and the Crown of thorns, and upon many other holy objects, that we would not retain without his will any city or fortress of all that belonged to his Empire."

And thus, with some contradicting the others in this way and that, the princes suffered such discord that they almost came to blows. The Duke and the Count of Flanders regarded the city of Antioch lightly; for though they wished Bohemund to have it, yet they dared not approve giving it to him for fear of incurring the infamy of perjury.[18] In this way, accordingly, the matter of the journey and other things pertaining to the journey and to the poor were put off. However, when the people saw this, each one began to say to his companion and neighbor, then openly to all: "Since the princes, either from fear or because of their oaths to the Emperor, are unwilling to lead us to Jerusalem, let us choose some brave knight in serving whom loyally we can be safe, and, if it is the will of God, we will arrive in Jerusalem with this same knight as leader. Alas! is it not enough for the princes that we have been here a year, and two hundred thousand armed men have been wasted? Let them who wish to have the Emperor's gold have it, and those who wish to have the revenues of Antioch, likewise. Let us, however, take up our march with Christ as leader, for whom we have come. Let those who want to hold Antioch perish miserably, as its inhabitants recently perished. If this great dispute about Antioch is continued longer, let us tear down its walls, and the peace which held the princes together before the city was taken will unite them after it has been destroyed. Nay, before we waste away utterly here from starvation and disease, we ought to return to our own homes." For these and other reasons the Count and Bohemund made discordant peace between themselves. So when the day had been fixed, the people were ordered to prepare for the avowed journey.

Accordingly, when the necessary preparations had been made and the day fixed, the Count of St. Gilles and the Count of Flanders set out with the people into Syria, and there they besieged Marra, a very rich and populous city. Marra was about eight miles from Barra. Its citizens were so haughty, because, at one time in a certain fight they had killed many of our men, that they cursed our army and maligned the princes, and, to provoke us most, they placed crosses upon the walls and plied them with insults. For this reason, therefore, on the second day after our arrival, we assailed them so fiercely that if we had had four more ladders the city would have been taken: but since we had only two, and those so short and fragile that one climbed upon them timidly, it was decided that machines, hurdles, and mounds be constructed, by means of which the wall could be forced, undermined, and levelled. In the meantime, Bohemund came with his army and besieged it from the other side. Again, without having prepared the machines which we spoke of above, as if because of the encouragement of Bohemund, who had not been present at the former assault, we wished to attack the city by filling the moat. But this was in vain, for we then fought much worse than we did before. After this, there was such famine in the army that, pitiful to say, you could see ten thousand men going about the fields like cattle, digging and looking (to see) if by chance they might find grains of wheat, or barley, or beans, or the grains of any other legume. In the meanwhile, though the machines of which we spoke above were being prepared to take the city by storm, nevertheless some of our men, upon seeing the misery of our people and the boldness of the Saracens, despaired of God's mercy and fled.

But God, who has concern for His followers, did not permit His people whom He saw placed in extreme tribulation to suffer too far. Therefore He sent word to us through His blessed apostles

Peter and Andrew, through whom we should both learn His will and be able to satisfy His stern will towards us. Accordingly, they came into the chapel of the Count about midnight and aroused Peter to whom they had recently shown the Lance. When he then suddenly saw them clothed in ill-shapen garb, standing near the chest where the relics were, he believed them to be some paupers who wanted to steal something from the tent. For there was St. Andrew, dressed in an old shirt torn at the shoulders and in a cloak ripped at the opening of his left shoulder; there was nothing over the right shoulder and he was vilely shod. Peter wore only a coarse and long shirt down to his ankles.

Then Peter Bartholomew said to them, "Who are you, Sirs? What do you want?"

And St. Peter replied, "We are envoys of God. I am Peter, and this is Andrew. But we wished to appear to thee in this garb, in order that thou shouldst see how much it profiteth to serve God devoutly. In this season and garb, as thou seest us, we came to God, and such we now are."

And at this word nothing was brighter than they, nothing more beautiful. Peter, indeed, who saw this, terrified at the bright light, fell to the earth as if dead, and, sweating from excessive anguish, he moistened the earth upon which he had fallen. Then St. Peter raised him and said to him, "Thou didst fall easily."

And he replied, "It is so, Lord."

Again St. Peter (spoke): "So fall all who are in unbelief, or who transgress the commands of God. But if they are penitent for their evil deeds, and call out to God, the Lord raises them just as I raised thee when thou hadst fallen. And just as thy sweat remains on the ground, so God will take up and bear away the sins of those who cry out to Him. Tell me, how is the army?"

And he replied, "Indeed, Sire, they are in great fear of hunger and all wretchedness."

And then St. Peter said: "And verily can they be in great fear who had deserted Almighty God! They do not remember the dangers from which He rescued them to give Him any thanks. For when you were all beaten and humbled at Antioch, you cried out to the Lord so that we who were in heaven heard. The Lord heeded you and gave you His Lance as a token of victory; then He caused you miraculously and gloriously to triumph over your enemies who besieged you. And now to which Lord do you entrust your safety, you who have gravely offended God? Will the high mountains or the caves protect you? For even if you should be on a very high and strong place and have abundance of all the necessaries of life, yet you could not be secure, since a hundred thousand adversaries would threaten each one of you. Among you is killing and rapine and theft, no justice, and very much adultery, when it would please God if you should all take wives. But concerning justice, the Lord commands thus; that if any one shall do violence to a poor man, all that is in the house of the oppressors shall be made public (property). Of the tithes the Lord says that, if you render them, He Himself is ready to give whatever is necessary. But whenever you wish to besiege it, he will give you that city out of His compassion and not for your deserts; without doubt it will be taken."

Moreover, when Peter announced this to the Count in the morning, the Bishops of Orange and Barra assembled the people, and we made known to them what has been written. The faithful, thus led on to the greatest hope of taking the city, offered most generous alms and prayers to Almighty God to free His poor people for His name alone. After this, ladders were swiftly built, and a wooden tower erected, and hurdles joined, and at the close of the day the fight was begun. Those who were inside the city threw stones with hurling engines, javelins, fire, wood, beehives with bees, and slack lime upon our men who were undermining the wall; but by the valor and compassion of God, these things hurt none, or few, of them. However, this fight lasted from sunrise to sunset so marvelously that no rest was ever given, and yet there was doubt of victory. At length, all cried out to God with one voice to be more favorable to His people, and to fulfil the promises of His apostles. The Lord was present there and gave us the city, according to the words of the apostles. Godfrey of Lastours was the first to scale (the wall); more followed him and invaded the wall and some towers of the city. Then night came down which cut off the battle. The Saracens still retained some towers and a part of the city. On this account the knights, expecting that the Saracens would not surrender even in the morning, kept guard outside the city, lest any should escape. But those to whom life was not very dear, whom long fasting had led to contempt of self, were not afraid to attack the Saracens amidst the shadows of the night. And thus the poor gained both the spoils and houses of the city. Moreover, when morning came the knights went into the city and found few things which they might take for themselves. The Saracens, indeed, concealed themselves in underground caves, and none, or few, appeared. When our men had carried off all that they found above ground, thinking that everything else was with the Saracens, they searched out the caves with fire and sulphur smoke; and because they did not find much booty there, in hopes of spoils they tortured to death the Saracens whom they could find. It happened, however, to some of our men that when they led the Saracens through the city for spoils, the Saracens conducted them to cisterns, and suddenly hurled themselves into them, choosing death rather than to be willing to reveal their own or other's property. Wherefore, all fell down dead; and they were cast forth among the swamps of the city and outside the walls. And so not much booty was taken in the city.

Meanwhile, a quarrel arose between Bohemund's men and those of the Count for the reason that, though the knights of Bohemund had not taken much part in the siege, they obtained the largest number of towers, houses, and captives. The Lord performed a miracle in the capture of Marra. Before it was taken, although we expounded to the people the commands of the apostles Peter and Andrew, just as was written above, Bohemund and his companions laughed at us. Therefore, neither he nor those with him were present at the fight, but rather were absent. And since they now had the greatest share of the spoils, some of the Count's following bore it unworthily. At length, a disagreement arose between the leaders themselves, because the Count wished to give the city to the Bishop of Barra, and Bohemund was unwilling to let go the towers which had surrendered to him, saying, "Unless the Count gives up to me the towers at Antioch, I will not agree with him in anything."

Meanwhile, the knights and people began to ask about the journey, when it would please the princes to begin it. For though the march had started long time ago, yet it seemed to us merely to begin the journey, since it was not yet ended. Bohemund said that he would put it off to Easter, and it was then the Christmas time. Many, likewise, despaired because there were few horses in the army, and the Duke was absent, and many of the knights went away to Baldwin of Edessa. Therefore many turned back. At length the Bishop of Albara and some nobles met with the poor people and summoned the Count. When the Bishop had finished his preaching, the knights and all the people knelt before the Count. With many tears they prayed him to whom the Lord had given the Lance to become their leader and lord of this same army, adding that he had especially merited the Lance of the Lord for the reason that if the other princes failed, he himself, indebted for so great a blessing of the Lord, would not fear to go forward in security with the people. Otherwise, he should give the Lance to the people, and the people would go to Jerusalem with the Lord Himself as leader. However, the Count hesitated because of the absence of the other princes, fearing that if he alone should determine the day of the journey, the others would not go because of envy of him. Why say much? The Count, overcome by the tears of the poor, named the fifth or sixth day to be announced through the city for the journey, and after this he returned to Antioch.

The Count with the Bishop sought a way to retain the city, and who and how many men they could leave there as a garrison for it. Meanwhile, the Count sent word to the Duke of Lorraine and to the others who were not present at Marra to assemble in one place and deal with the matters which would be necessary for the march. And so they assembled at *Rusa*, which was about midway between Antioch and Marra. There a colloquy was held and all the princes behaved worse (than usual). For the princes excused themselves from the journey, and many others because of them. Nevertheless, the Count wished to give the Duke ten thousand *solidi*, an equal amount to Robert of Normandy, six thousand to the Count of Flanders, and five thousand to Tancred, and to the other princes accordingly.

In the midst of this, when the news came to the poor who had remained at Marra that the Count wanted to leave many knights and foot-soldiers of the army in the city of Marra as a garrison, they said to one another, "Oho! quarrels about Antioch and quarrels about Marra! In every place which God shall give us will there be contention among the princes, and a lessening of the army of God? Surely there will be no further argument about this city! Come, and let us destroy its walls, and peace will be made between the princes and security for the Count, lest he lose it."

Thereupon, the weak and sick arose from their beds, and, armed with clubs they went to the walls. After those stones which three or four yoke of oxen could scarcely drag had been rolled back, a serf easily pushed them far out from the walls. But the Bishop of Albara and other intimates of the Count went around the city complaining and forbidding this to be done in any way. When, however, those guardians had passed, those who had hidden themselves and climbed down at the approach of the Bishop and his companions, immediately returned to the work begun. And those who dared not destroy by day, or could not, being otherwise engaged, applied themselves (to the task) at night. There was scarcely anyone of the people too weak or ill to tear down the wall.

Meanwhile, there was such famine in the army that the people ate most greedily the already fetid bodies of the Saracens which they had cast into the swamp of the city two weeks and more ago. These events frightened many of our people, as well as others. On this account very many of our men turned back, despairing of the journey without the help of the Frankish people. But the Saracens and the Turks said on the contrary: "And who can resist these people, who are so obstinate and cruel that for a whole year they could not be turned from the siege of Antioch by famine, sword, or any other dangers, and who now live on human flesh?" These and other very cruel practices the pagans said existed among us. For God gave fear of us to all people, but we did not know it.

The Count, meanwhile having returned to Marra from the colloquy, was exceedingly angry at the people about the destruction of the wall. But when it was explained to him that neither the Bishop nor other princes could move the people, either by threats or blows, from the destruction of the walls, he learned thereby that it was divine and ordered the foundations of the wall to be destroyed. Meanwhile, the famine grew daily more severe. And now when the day proposed for the journey was at hand, we commanded the people to offer to God alms and prayers for the journey. But when the Count saw that none of the leading princes came to him, and he perceived almost all his people wasting away, he commanded the people to go into interior *Hispania* for food, and (he said that) he himself with his knights would precede them. But this did not please some of his intimates. For they said, "In the army there are scarcely three hundred knights, and there is not a large number of other armed men, and yet will some go on the expedition and others stay here within the destroyed city, which is without fortification?" And they enlarged upon the very great fickleness of the Count.

Nevertheless, in the end the Count set forth because of the poor and gained many castles and captives and great spoil. When he was returning with great exultation and victory after very many of the Saracens had been killed, six or seven of our poor were captured and killed by the pagans. All these dead, however, had crosses on their right shoulders. Moreover, when the Count and those with him saw this, they thanked Almighty God, who was mindful of His poor, as much as possible, and for this reason they were greatly comforted. And thus that they might satisfy all who had remained with the baggage at Marra, they brought along one of the killed who was still breathing. Verily, we beheld a miracle in that man, who, though he scarcely had a whole place where his soul could hide, lingered for seven or eight days without food, bearing witness that Jesus, to whose judgment he was to go, without doubt, was God the Author of this cross. Therefore, comforted by the favorable turn of events and by the (sign of the) cross, they left their spoils in a certain fortified place called Cafardan, a journey four leagues distant from Marra, and those who had companions at Marra returned with the Count.

3. *Raymond finally starts for Jerusalem. Archas.* (January 13-March, 1099.)

(*Gesta.*) When Raymond, moreover, saw that because of him none of the leaders would go upon the way to the Holy Sepulchre, he went out with bare feet from Marra on the thirteenth day of incoming January and came up to Cafardan and remained there for three days. There the Count of Normandy joined Count Raymond. Moreover, the King of Caesrea had very often sent word by his messengers to the Count at Marra and Cafardan that he wished to have peace with him and would give him a tribute from his own (possessions), and that he would cherish the Christian pilgrims. He would make a pledge that the pilgrims would not suffer the least offence, as far as his sway extended, and he would joyfully supply a market of horses and bodily nourishment.

Our men, moreover, left and went to lodge near Caesarea, above the river Orontes. And when the King of Caesarea saw the camp of the Franks lodged so near his city, he was grieved in spirit and ordered the market to be denied them, unless they withdrew from the neighborhood of the city. But on the next day he sent along with them two Turks, his messengers, to show them the ford of the river, and to conduct them where they could find something to take. Finally they came to a valley below a certain fortress, and there they took plunder of more than five thousand animals and enough grain and other goods with which the whole army of Christ was greatly refreshed. At length, that fortress surrendered to the Count and gave him horses and the purest gold, and they swore by their law that no evil would henceforth be done to the pilgrims. We were there for five days.

Departing thence, we came to a lodge at a certain Arab fortress. Thereupon, the lord of the place came out and made an agreement with the Count. Going on from this place, we came to a certain very beautiful city located in a valley filled with goods of all kinds—Raphania by name. But when the inhabitants of the place heard that the Franks had come, they abandoned the city, gardens filled with olives, and houses full of food, and fled. On the third day we went forth from the city and, passing over a high and immense mountain, entered the valley of *Desem*, in which there was the greatest abundance of all goods, and we were there for about fifteen days.

This was near a certain fortified place in which there was gathered a very large multitude of pagans. Our men attacked this place and would have conquered it bravely, had not the Saracens driven out immense herds of animals. Our men returned, carrying goods of all kinds to their tents. At the break of dawn, however, we folded our tents and went to besiege their fortified place. We expected to pitch our camp there, but the pagan host took to flight and left the place empty. However, when our men entered they found there every abundance of wine, butter, oil, and everything that they needed. There we very devoutly celebrated the festival of the Purification of the Virgin Mary. Envoys came to us there from the city of *Camela*. For the King of that place sent horses and gold to the Count and made an agreement with him that he would not hurt Christians in any way, but would cherish and honor them. Moreover, the King of Tripoli sent word to the Count that he would faithfully enter into an agreement with him and keep friendship, if it pleased him, and he sent him ten horses, four mules, and gold. But the Count said that he would in no wise accept peace with him, unless he became a Christian.

After leaving this very fine valley, we came to a certain fortified town called Archas on Monday noon, the second day of the week in the middle of February, and around it we pitched our tents. This town was filled with a countless host of pagans, Turks, Saracens, Arabs, and *Publicani,* who had fortified the town marvelously and were defending themselves bravely. At that time fourteen of our knights went against the city of Tripoli, which was near us. Those fourteen found about sixty Turks and certain others, who had collected in front of them some men and more than five hundred animals. Strengthened with the sign of the cross, they attacked the Turks and, with the help of God, wonderfully overcame them, killed six of them, and captured six horses. Furthermore, Raymond Piletus and Raymond, Viscount of Turenne, went out from the army of Count Raymond, and, coming before the city of Tortosa, they strongly attacked it, fortified, as it was, by a very great multitude of pagans. But since night had already come, they withdrew to a certain retired place and camped there; then they built countless fires, as if the whole host was there. Indeed, the pagans, terrified with fear, fled secretly by night and left the city filled with goods of all kinds. It also contained a very fine port on the sea. On the next day our men went to attack it on all sides and found it empty. They entered and lived in it as long as the siege before Archas lasted. There is near it another city called Maraclea. The Emir who ruled over it made an agreement with our men and let our men and our standards into the city.

(*Raymond.*) On the day fixed they burned the city and set forth. But the count, his clerics, and the Bishop of Albara went unshod, invoking the compassion of God and the protection of the saints. Tancred followed us with forty knights and many foot-soldiers. When the kings of that land heard this, they sent Arab nobles with many entreaties and gifts to the Counts, (promising) now and thereafter to be their tributaries, and to bring provisions free and for sale. After receiving security from them on oath, as well as foods for the journey, we continued further. Moreover, we had guides from the King of Caesarea who led us badly on the first day, as it seemed to us, for in that camp we were in want of everything except water. Then on the second day these same guides imprudently led us into a certain valley where the cattle of the King and the whole region had fled for fear of us. At that time the King, having known long before that we would come there, had commanded all his Saracens to flee before us; but if he had commanded that all of that region should oppose us, it would not have turned out so well. Raymond of Lille and his companions caught a Saracen this day with letters of the King, which he was bearing to all of that region, (saying) to flee before us. When this became known to the King, he said, "I had ordered my men to flee before the Franks as fast as they could, and (instead) they came to them. I see that God has chosen this people; besides, whatever they do, I will not harm them." Then the King himself blessed God, who provides sufficient necessaries for those who fear Him.

However, when our knights saw such sudden and so great abundance, they and the sturdier people took up all their money and went to Caesarea and *Camela* to buy fat horses there, saying, "Since God has taken concern about our food, we will take care of His poor and His army." Thus it came about that we had about a thousand very fine chargers. The poor daily grew better; the knights were daily comforted; the army seemed daily to be multiplied, and the farther we proceeded the greater benefits God provided for us. Although everything was coming to us in sufficient quantities, yet some bent the Count to this plan, that he should want to go off the route a bit for the sake of Gibellum, which is a city on the sea-coast. But Tancred and many other brave men and good brought it about that this did not happen in any way, saying: "God has visited the poor and ourselves, and ought we to depart from the journey? The past labors at Antioch, the misery of battle, cold, hunger, and every kind of suffering are enough for us. Why should we alone besiege the whole world, and kill all the inhabitants of the world? Behold of one hundred thousand knights we have scarcely one thousand, and of two hundred thousand foot-soldiers and more, there are not five thousand now in our army! Shall we wait until all are destroyed? Why will they come from our land when they hear that Antioch and Gibellum and the other cities of the Saracens have been captured? But let us go to Jerusalem for which we came, and, verily, God will give it to us. And then through fear alone of those who will come from our land and other lands, these cities, Gibellum, Tripoli, Tyre, and Acre, which are on our march, will be abandoned by the inhabitants."

While we were thus proceeding forward, some Turks and Arabs were following the army, killing and despoiling the poor, who, because of their long illness, remained behind the army. And when they had done this once and again, the Count remained in hiding on the next day until all the army had passed. The enemy, in hope of plunder and without fear, followed our army in their usual manner. But when they had already pased the ambush, our knights, coming forth from their hiding place with the Count, attacked the column of the enemy, routed them, and threw them into confusion. Then they killed them and led their very fine horses to the army with great exultation. After this, no enemy followed our army, because the Count with an armed multitude of knights went behind our people. Moreover, other armed knights with the Count of Normandy, Tancred, and the Bishop of Albara went ahead in great numbers, so that the enemy might not unexpectedly disturb us from either rear or front. For the Count, since he had few knights with him when he set forth from Marra, asked the Bishop, after he had placed a guard at Barra, to come with him. The Bishop, hearing of a certain knight of his, William, son of Peter of *Cumiliacum,* by name, left him there with seven knights and thirty foot-soldiers. He was a man faithful and devoted to God and increased the property of the Bishop by the help of God ten-fold in a short time. And he soon had seventy men, instead of thirty, and sixty knights and more.

It was decided at this time about our journey that we should leave the road which led by Damascus and turn to the sea-coast, because if our ships which we had left at Antioch should come toward us, we would have trade with the people of the Isle of Cyprus and the other islands. And when we started upon the route agreed upon, the inhabitants of the land abandoned cities, fortified places, and villages full of all goods. Thus, after encircling great mountains, we came into a certain very rich valley, where some peasants, arrogant because of their numbers and the strength of their fortress, were willing neither to send to us for peace nor to abandon their fortress, and, in addition, attacked our squires and foot-soldiers, who were unarmed and were running through the villages for food. After having killed some, they took the spoils into their fortress. Our men, therefore, went to the fortress in anger. The peasants, however, hesitated to come against us at the foot of the mountain on which the fortress was located. Then our men, after taking counsel, drew up ranks of foot-soldiers and knights, and, climbing to the top of the mountain from three sides, they forced the body of peasants to flee. There were about thirty thousand Saracens, and their fortress was on the slope of a certain very high mountain; besides, when they wished, they sought refuge in the castle, and some higher up on the mountain. So they resisted us for a little while. At length, we shouted out the cry usual in our straits, "God help us! God help us!" Our enemy were so disturbed that at the entrance of their castle upwards of a hundred fell dead without wounds, because of fear and the rush of their companions. There was, moreover, very great plunder of cattle, horses, and sheep outside the castle where our people were engaged. And while the Count and some knights were intent upon the battle, our poor, after taking plunder, began to return, one after the other. Next the poor foot-soldiers took the way, after them the poor knights. Moreover, our tents were some distance from the castle, about ten miles. Meanwhile the Count ordered the knights and the people to encamp. Then, when the Saracens who had climbed higher on the mountain and those in the fortress saw that the greatest portion of our men had left, they began to urge one another in turn to join forces. But the Count overlooked this and found himself almost abandoned by his knights. For the hill on which the fortress stood was very steep and stony, and the path was a difficult one in which one horse could scarcely follow another. Thereupon, when the Count was caught in this difficulty, he began to advance with his companions, as if to fight against those who were coming down from higher up the mountain. The Saracens at first hesitated at the approach of the Count; then our men changed their route and descended into the valley, as if secure. Upon seeing themselves frustrated, and that our men descended in security, the Saracens from both the fortress and the mountain together attacked our forces. Therefore, some of our men under compulsion dismounted from their horses, and others went headlong over the steep rocks. So with the greatest danger some escaped death, but others died fighting bravely. This one fact we learned for certain: that the Count never was in greater danger of his life. Therefore, angry at himself and at his men, he called a council upon returning to the army and complained much that the knights had gone away without permission and had left him in danger of death. All promised that they would not withdraw from the siege of the castle until, by the grace of God, the foundation had been overturned. But God, who was guiding them so that they should not be hindered by evils of any kind whatsoever, so terrified the keepers of the fortress through the night that they not even gave their dead burial, so headlong was their flight. Moreover, when it became morning we went there and found only spoils and a fortress empty of men.

This time there were with us envoys from the Emir of *Camela* and from the King of Tripoli. When these beheld the boldness and bravery of our men, they begged of the Count permission (to leave), saying that they would return as quickly as possible. Accordingly, when those envoys were allowed to leave with our envoys, they returned in a short time with great gifts and many horses. For the siege of that fortress had frightened the whole region, because it could never before be taken by any people. Besides, the inhabitants of that region sent to the Count with many entreaties and gifts, praying that when he had caused their cities and fortress to be taken over, he would send them his standards and his seals. For it was the custom in the army that if the standard of any Frank was found on a city or fortress, it was not thereafter besieged by anyone. Wherefore the King of Tripoli placed the standards of the Count on his castles.

The name of the Count was at this time so great that it seemed more than equal to that of any former leader. And when our knights who had been sent as envoys to Tripoli saw the regal wealth, most rich kingdoms, and that populous city, they persuaded the Count to besiege Archas, a fortress very strongly fortified and unassailable by human might, in order to obtain from the King of Tripoli after the fourth or fifth day as much gold and silver as he should desire. And so at their wish we besieged the fortress where our brave men endured such trials as they never had before. And besides, most bitter to tell, we lost so many and such great knights. There was killed Pontius of *Balazun* with a stone from a petrary, at whose prayers I am writing for all the orthodox, especially those across the Alps, and for you, revered head of Viviers, this work which I have undertaken to compose.

Now, however, I shall strive with the inspiration of God, who did all this, to write what remains with the same charity with which I began. I beg, therefore, and beseech everyone to believe that these things which they are to hear are true. And if I have applied to anyone, through zeal or hate for anyone, anything beyond belief or probability, may God apply to me all the tortures of hell, and erase me from the book of life! For though I am ignorant of many things, this one I know: that since I have been promoted to the priesthood on God's expedition, I ought to obey God in witnessing the truth, rather than to weave lies, striving for reward or money from anyone else. But since, according to the apostle, "charity vaunteth not itself," I want to proceed with the same charity. May God give me aid!

While we were delaying somewhat in pressing this siege, our ships came to us from Antioch and Laodicaea, also many other ships of the Venetians[14] and Greeks with grain, wine, and barley, pork, and other things for sale. But since this castle was about a mile from the sea, the ships could not remain in port, and the sailors returned to the port of Laodicaea and to the port of Tortosa. This Tortosa, a very strongly fortified place, built with walls and forewalls, and filled with many good things, had been abandoned by its Saracen inhabitants for fear of our army alone. For God had established such great dread of us among the Arabs, and Saracens of that region that they believed we could accomplish everything and that we wanted to destroy all that we could. But this was before the siege of Archas.

However, this siege which we had set chiefly for other causes contrary to justice than for God, God was unwilling to promote, but there did everything against us. And since our men had been prompt and ready for all other battles and assaults, it was wonderful that they were found sluggish and useless for this. If any fervent spirits wanted to do anything, they were either wounded or what they had begun came to naught. There Anselm of Ribemont gloriously departed. When he arose in the morning, he called the priests to him, and, having confessed his negligences and his sins, he begged mercy from God and from them, announcing to them that the end of his life was imminent. They were amazed at this, since they beheld him well and unhurt, and he said to them:

"Do not wonder, but rather listen. This night I saw Lord Engelrand of St. Paul, who was killed at Marra. I was not asleep, but awake, and I said to him, 'What is this? For thou hast suffered death and, lo! thou art now alive!'

"And he answered, 'Indeed those who end their lives in the service of Christ do not die.'

"When I asked him again about his beauty, which was very great, whence it had happened to him, he answered me, 'Thou shouldst not wonder about my beauty, when I dwell in so splendid a home.'

"And straightway he showed me his home in heaven, so beautiful that I could believe nothing more beautiful. Seeing that I was stunned at the splendor of his home, he said to me, 'A much more beautiful one is being prepared for thee to-morrow.' And with these words he disappeared."

Moreover, it happened on the same day on which Anselm had recounted this to several people that he was proceeding to battle against the Saracens. They had gone out secretly from the fortress and wanted to come up to our tents to steal something there, or to hurt someone. But when this fight had grown great on both sides and Anselm was resisting bravely, he was struck on the head by a stone from a hurling engine; and thus he departed from this world to the place prepared for him by God.

Here a legate came to us from the King of Babylon, who along with him had sent back to us our legates whom he had held captive for a year. He was hesitating whether to make friendship with us or with the Turks. We were willing to agree with him in this way: If he would give us help from Jerusalem, or if he would give us Jerusalem with what pertained to it, we would give him all his cities which the Turks had taken from him, when we should capture them. The other cities of the Turks, however, which were not of his kingdom, we would divide between us, if they were taken with his help. But the Turks, as it was related to us, were willing to do this for him: If he would come with them to battle against us, they would worship Ali,[15] who is the race of Mohammed, whom he worshipped. They would also accept his coins and would pay a certain tribute, and they would do many other things for him which we did not fully know. He learned about us that we were few, and that the Emperor Alexius was hostile to us to death; concerning this, we found letters of the Emperor Alexius written about us in the tent of the same King, after the battle with the King of the Babylonians had been fought at Ascalon. For these and other reasons, therefore, the Emir had detained our envoys as captives for a year in Babylon. But now, when he heard that, having entered his lands, we were devastating villages, fields, and all, he sent word to us that we should go without arms in groups of two hundred or three hundred to Jerusalem, and that, after adoring the Lord, we should return. But we laughed at this, expecting God's mercy, and announced that unless he freely gave us Jerusalem we would sue him for Babylon. For the Emir at this time held Jerusalem. When he heard that the Turks had been beaten by us at Antioch, he went to besiege Jerusalem, knowing that the Turks, so often scattered and put to flight by us, would not face him in battle. At length, after giving very large gifts to those who were defending it, he received the city of Jerusalem and offered candles and incense to the Sepulchre of the Lord on Mt. Calvary. But let us now return to the siege.

4. *Continued quarrels among the leaders. The trial of the Lance.* (March-April 20, 1099.)

(*Gesta.*) Duke Godfrey, Bohemund, and the Count of Flanders went up to the city of Laodicaea. Bohemund separated from them and returned to Antioch, but they went and besieged a certain city whose name is Gibellum. Thereupon, when Raymond, Count of St. Gilles, heard that an innumerable host of pagans was rushing upon us for battle, he held a council there with his men, in order to send (word) to the leaders who were at the siege of Gibellum to come to his aid. When they heard this, they straightway made an agreement with the Emir, making peace with him, and they received horses and gold and left the city and came to our aid. But the enemy did not come to battle against us. Thereupon, the aforesaid Counts lodged beyond the river and there besieged that fortress. Not long after this, our men rode against Tripoli and found outside the city Turks, Arabs, and Saracens, whom our men attacked and put to flight and killed the greatest part of the nobles of the city. So great was the slaughter of pagans and shedding of blood that even the water which flowed in the city seemed to grow red and to flow into their cisterns, whereat the rest were exceedingly sad and sorrowful. Indeed, they were now so terrified with fear that none of them dared to go out of the city gate. On the next day, our men rode beyond *Desem* and found cattle and sheep and asses and many other animals, and they carried off, also, almost three thousand camels.

We besieged the aforesaid town for three months, less one day, and there celebrated Easter on the fourth day before the Ides of April. While we were engaged in that siege, our ships, forsooth, came to a certain port near us bearing the greatest market—grain, wine, meat, cheese, barley, and oil, whereof there was now the greatest abundance throughout the whole army. At length, several of our men happily received martyrdom, namely Anselm of Ribemont, William the Picard, and several others whose names I do not know. The King of Tripoli, also, often sent envoys to the leaders with word to leave the fortress and make peace with him. Accordingly, when our leaders, Godfrey, and Raymond, Count of St. Gilles, Robert the Norman, and the Count of Flanders, heard this, and when they saw that new fruit had grown (for we were eating new beans in the middle of March, and even grain in the middle of

April), they held a council and said: "It is very good to carry out the march to Jerusalem with the new fruits."

(*Raymond.*) When, as we said, our army was laboring greatly in the siege of Archas, it was announced to us that the Pope of the Turks was coming to battle against us; and since he was of the race of Mohammed, innumerable people followed him. Accordingly, the army was commanded that all should prepare themselves for battle. So they sent the Bishop of Albara to the Duke and the Count of Flanders, who were besieging Gibellum. This is a fortress above the sea, about half way between Antioch and the fortress of Archas, two days distant from both. When they had received the message, they gave up the siege and came quickly to us. Meanwhile (the report) was found to be false. The Saracens had made it up so that, while our men were thereby terrified, the besieged might be able to gain a little rest.

So when our armies had been joined, the men of the Count's party began to show the sleek horses and the riches which God had given them in the regions of the Saracens because they had exposed themselves to death for God; but the others held forth their poverty. At this time it was preached that the people should give a tithe of all they had taken, because there were many poor in the army and many sick. It was commanded that they should render a fourth part to their priests whose masses they attended, a fourth part to the Bishop, and the other two parts to Peter the Hermit, whom they had placed in charge of the poor of both clergy and people. And thus he received two parts; to wit, one part for those who were of the clergy, and the other for those who were of the people. Therefore God so multiplied our army in horses, mules, camels, and the other necessities of life that it became a marvel to us and a dream. And thus from the wealth of possessions there arose a dispute and arrogance among the princes, so that those who loved God dearly desired much more that want and fearful battles should threaten.

The King of Tripoli wished to give us fifteen thousand gold coins of Saracen minting, besides horses, mules, and many robes, and then tributes each year much greater than this. One gold coin, forsooth, was at this time worth eight or nine *solidi* of our money. This was our money: *Pictavini, Cartenses, Manses, Luccenses, Valanzani, Melgorienses,* and *Pogesi,* two of which (were offered) for one of the others.[16] But that lord of Gibellum, afraid that he might again be besieged, sent to our princes five thousand gold coins, horses, mules, and much wine; then we had food enough. And not only did these send us gifts, but also those from many cities and castles. Some of the Saracens, too, were baptized either out of zeal or from fear of our law, renouncing Mohammed and all his offspring. For these reasons, therefore, one of our princes sent envoys to the cities of the Saracens with letters announcing that he was lord of the whole army. Thus did our princes conduct themselves at this time! And Tancred, especially, stirred up the affair. Although he had received five thousand *solidi* and two very fine horses on the agreement that he would remain in the Count's service up to Jerusalem, he now wanted to withdraw and be with the Duke of Lorraine. On this account many quarrels were held. At length, ill enough, he withdrew from the Count.

Many revelations were made known to us at this time, which were sent to us from God. The following is one of these, which is written under the name of him who saw it.

"In the year of the Lord 1099, in the seventh Indiction, twenty-sixth Epact, fifth Concurrence, on the night of the Nones of April,[17] when I, Peter Bartholomew, lay in the chapel of the Count of St. Gilles at the siege of Archas, I began to meditate on the priest to whom the Lord appeared with the Cross when we were besieged by the Turks in Antioch. And when I marvelled much that He had never appeared to me with the Cross, I saw the Lord entering with His apostles, Peter and Andrew, and a certain other, large and heavy, of dark complexion, nearly bald, and with large eyes.

"And the Lord said to me 'What art thou doing?'

"I replied, 'Lord, I am standing here.'

"And the Lord spoke again, 'Thou hast barely escaped being submerged (in sin) with the rest. But of what art thou now thinking?'

"And I replied, 'Lord, Father, I was thinking about a priest to whom Thou didst appear with the Cross.'

"The Lord answered, 'I know that.' And then: 'Believe that I am the Lord for whom thou hast come hither and who suffered for sinners on the Cross at Jerusalem, just as thou wilt now behold.'

"And at that very hour I saw there a cross made of two black and round planks, neither polished nor fitted, except that in the middle the beams were notched and supported each other in turn.

"The Lord said to me, 'Behold the Cross, since it is the Cross which thou seekest.' And on that Cross was the Lord extended and crucified as at the time of the Passion. Peter, moreover, supported His head from the right; Andrew from the left bore it on his neck; that third person supported it from the rear with his hands.

"And the Lord said to me, 'Say to My people that thou hast seen

Me thus. Dost thou see these, My five wounds? Thus do you consist of five ranks. The first rank is the rank of those who do not fear javelins and swords, or any kind of engine. That rank is like unto Me; for I went to Jerusalem and did not fear swords and lances, cudgels and staves, or, in addition, the Cross. They die for Me; and I died for them; and I am in them, and they in Me. When such as these die, they are placed on the right hand of God, where after the resurrection I sat, having ascended to heaven. The second is the rank of those who are a help to the first; but they guard them from the rear, and to them the former also come for refuge; verily, these are like the apostles who followed Me and ate with Me. The third is the rank of those who bring stones and javelins to the first; they are like those who, when they saw Me placed on the Cross, bemoaning my Passion, beat their breasts, proclaiming that wrong had been done Me. The fourth, indeed, is the rank of those who, upon seeing the battle surge, push themselves into houses and turn to their own affairs, trusting that victory rests not in My might, but in human worth. They are like those who said "He is worthy of death; let Him be crucified; since He makes Himself a king and says that He is the Son of God." The fifth, however, is the rank of those who, when they hear the shout of battle, look on from afar, asking the cause of the outcry, and afford examples of cowardice, not of bravery, and are unwilling to undergo dangers not only for Me, but, likewise, for their brothers. Under the form of avoiding (danger), they want others to fight, or bring arms to the fighters, and they feast at looking on; they are like Judas the Betrayer and Pontius Pilate, the judge.'

"Moreover, the Lord was naked upon the Cross, encircled only with a linen cloth from knees to loins, and the linen cloth was of a color midway between red and black. And about His ears He had a white, red, and green head-band. Later, when the Cross had been taken away, the Lord remained in the garb which He wore before.

"And I said to Him, 'Lord, God, if I say this, they will not believe me.'

"The Lord replied to me, 'Dost thou want to recognize those who will not believe this?'

"And I said, 'Yea, Lord.'

"And the Lord answered, 'Let the Count assemble the princes and people, and let them make arrangements about the battles, or when it shall be time for the siege of the fortress. Let the most renowned herald proclaim "God help us!" thrice, and let him strive to carry out the arrangements. Then as I have told thee, thou wilt see these ranks: and together with the others who believe this thou wilt distinguish the unbelievers.'

"And I said, "What are we to do about the incredulous?'

"The Lord, answered, 'Spare them not, kill them; for they are my betrayers, brothers of Judas Iscariot. But give their possessions to those who are of the first rank, according to their needs. If you do this, you will find the right way, which you have thus far gone around. And just as the other things which thou hast prophesied happened unchanged in the future, this also will occur. Dost thou know which people I love especially?'

"And I replied, 'The race of the Jews.'

"The Lord said, 'These people I hold in hate, because they were unbelievers and I have placed them below all peoples. See, therefore, that you are not unbelievers. Otherwise I will take up other peoples, while you remain with the Jews; and through them I will fulfil what I promised you. Say this also to them (the army): "Why do you fear to do justice? And what is better than justice?" I want them to keep the following justice. Let them place judges by families and relatives. When, moreover, anyone shall offend another, let him who suffered the wrong say: "Brother, dost thou wish it to be done thus with thee?" After this, unless the offender shall desist, let the other oppose him in the name of his authority. Then let the judge freely take all his goods from the malefactor, and the half of all that has been taken let him give to the one who suffered this wrong, the remaining part to the authorities. If, however, the judge should defer this for any reason, go to him and say that if he does not correct himself, he will not be absolved even at the last day, unless thou dost release him. Dost thou know how serious a matter it is to be forbidden? For I forbade Adam to touch the tree of good and evil knowledge; he transgressed my prohibition and both he and his posterity were in wretched captivity until I came in the flesh and redeemed them by dying the death of the Cross. Verily, some have done well about the tithe, because they gave it as I commanded. Therefore, I will multiply them, and I will make them known among the others.'

"Moreover, when the Lord had said this, I began to ask Him out of His kindness to give back the knowledge of letters which He had recently taken from me.

"And the Lord said to me, 'Are the things that thou knowest not enough to tell this? And yet thou desirest to know as much as possible!'

"And forthwith I seemed to myself so wise that I would ask nothing further.

"Then the Lord said, 'Is what thou knowest enough for this?'

"I replied, 'It is.'

"The Lord again said, 'What have I said to thee? Answer.'

"And I knew nothing. When He pressed me to answer some of the things which He had said, I replied, 'Lord, I know nothing.'

"And the Lord said, 'Go and tell what thou knowest, and what thou knowest will be sufficient for thee.'

"When, however, I would have made this known to the brethren, some began to say that they would never believe that God spoke to such a man, that He passed our princes and bishops and revealed Himself to a peasant man; whence they likewise doubted about the Lance. Wherefore we called together those brethren to whom the Lance had been revealed at one time and another, and after this, Arnulf, chaplain of the Count of Normandy who was, as it were, the head of the unbelievers;[18] and we asked him why he doubted.

When he said that the Bishop of Puy had doubted it, a certain priest by the name of Peter Desiderius replied, "I saw the Bishop of Puy after his death and St. Nicholas with him. After many other things the Bishop said this to me, 'I am in the choir with St. Nicholas, but because I, who should have believed most, doubted the Lance of the Lord, I was led into hell where my hair from the right side of my head and my beard were burned; and though I am not in punishment, yet I will not clearly see the Lord until my hair and beard grow out as they were before.'" This and many other things that priest told us, which afterwards occurred; but these things can be told in their place.

A certain other priest, Ebrard by name, came and said: "At the time when the Turks were besieging our army in Antioch, I was at Tripoli. For before Antioch was taken I had come there for the necessaries of life. When I heard that Antioch had been taken, and that our men in the city were held in such a stage of siege that none of them dared to go in or out, except by stealth, and that many other evils threatened the besieged (mostly false reports which the Saracens and Turks added to the true evils), I was doubtful of my secular life, and fled to a certain church where I knelt before the majesty of the Mother of God. With tears and prayers I began to appeal through her for the mercy of God; and I did this for some days, remaining without food and saying to her: 'O dearest Lady, these are pilgrims who have left all their little ones, their wives, and all their dear ones for the name of thy Son and for thee. They have come hither from distant regions and are fighting for thy Son; have pity on them! And, O Lady, what will be said of thy Son and of thee in their lands, if thou givest them over into the hands of the Turks?'

"And when I had in anger and lament too often repeated this

and other statements like it, a certain Syrian, who was a Christian, said to me 'Be of good spirit, and see that you weep no longer. Recently I was before the doors of the church of the Blessed Mary, Mother of the Lord, and a cleric, clothed in white garments, appeared to me. When I asked him who he was, or whence he came, he replied, "I am Mark, the evangelist, and I come from Alexandria; and I turned hither because of the Church of the Blessed Mary." And again when I asked him where he was going, he said, "Our Lord is at Antioch and has sent word to all His disciples to come there, since the Franks are due to fight with the Turks, and we will be their protection."' And when he had said this, he went away!

"But since I would place little faith in these words, nor cease from grief or tears, the same Syrian said to me, 'Know, in the Gospel of the blessed Peter it is written that the Christian host which shall take Jerusalem shall first have been shut up in Antioch. Nor can they thence go forth until they shall have found the Lance of the Lord.'"

And the priest added, "If you doubt any of this, let the fire be built; and in the name of God and with the witness of these people, I will go through the midst of it."

Then another priest, Stephen, surnamed Valentine, a man of great integrity and good life, came forth and said, "The Lord Jesus Himself spoke to me in the very midst of the suffering which was at Antioch, and promised in the presence of His most Blessed Mother, the Virgin Mary, that on the fifth day to come He would be merciful to His people and complete their different undertakings, if they would return to Him with their whole heart. And on that day the Holy Lance was found; therefore I believe that the promises of the Lord were fulfilled. If you doubt any of this, as soon as I saw this vision I offered the Bishop of Puy as proof of it to go through fire in the presence of the whole multitude, if he wished, or to throw myself from the highest tower. And I still make this very offer to you."

Moreover the Bishop of Agde, came forth and said, "Whether I saw this in my sleep or not, I know not for certain; God knows. A man, dressed in white, and holding the Lance of the Lord, this Lance, I say, in his hands, came and stood before me and said to me, 'Dost thou believe this to be the Lance of the Lord?'

"And I replied: 'I do, Lord.'

"I had hesitated somewhat about it, but after he had sternly exacted this (answer) from me a second and a third time, I said to him: 'I believe, Lord, that this is the Lance of my Lord Jesus Christ.' And after this he left me."

And I who have written this, in the presence of the brethren and the Bishop said this there: "I was present while the digging took place; and before all of the Lance appeared above the ground, I kissed the point. And there are several in the army who were with me." And I added, "There is a certain other priest, Bertrand of Puy by name, who was a servant of the Bishop of Puy during his life. Moreover, this priest was sick unto death in Antioch; and when he had already given up hope of his life, there came before him the Bishop of Puy with his standard bearer, Heraclius, who, in the greatest fight made at Antioch was wounded in the face by an arrow while he was fearlessly launching forth against the lines of the Turks, and as a consequence ended his life.

"And Heraclius said, 'Lord, he is ill.'

"The Bishop replied, 'He is ill because of his unbelief.'

"And the priest thereupon said: 'Lord, do I not believe in the Lance of the Lord, just as also the Passion of the Lord?'

"Then the Bishop said to him, 'And thou must yet believe many other things.'"

And though this does not pertain to this matter, nevertheless, since it is worthy, I will add something for the sake of good men. When the priest had reseated himself before the Bishop and his lord Heraclius, for he was sick and could not stand, he beheld in the face of his lord the wound from which he had ended the labors of his mortal life. And the priest said to him, "Sire, we believed that thy wound had already healed. Why is this?"

Heraclius answered, "Well hast thou asked this question. When I came before my Lord, I begged him that this wound might never be closed, since because of it I ended my life. And this the Lord granted me." This and much else the Bishop and Heraclius said to the priest, which are not now necessary (to relate).

When he had listened to these and many other men, Arnulf believed and confessed; and he promised the Bishop of Albara that he would do penance in the presence of all the people for his unbelief. However, on the appointed day when Arnulf had come, summoned to council, he began to say that he would place full faith in it (the Lance), but that he wished to speak with his lord before doing penance. But when Peter Bartholomew heard this, he was exceedingly angry, and like a plain man, and one who has well known the truth, he said, "I wish and beg that a very large fire be built; and I will pass through the midst of it with the Lance of the Lord. If it is the Lance of the Lord, I will pass through the fire unhurt, but if it is not, I will be burned in the fire. For I see that neither signs nor witnesses are believed."

All this pleased us; and having commanded him to fast, we said that the fire would be built on the day on which the Lord was wounded on the Cross with it (the Lance) for our salvation. And after the fourth day, then was the day of preparation. So when the appointed day shone, the fire was made ready after midday. Princes and people to the number of sixty thousand men assembled there; priests were there in bare feet and dressed in their priestly vestments. The fire was made of dry olive branches and had a length of thirty feet; and there were four feet in the height of the piles. After the fire had burned violently, I, Raymond, said before the whole multitude, "If Almighty God spoke face to face with this man, and St. Andrew showed him the Lance when he was on watch, let him pass through the fire unhurt. If, however, it is a falsehood, may he be burned, together with the Lance which he will carry in his hand!" And all upon bended knees responded, "Amen!"

The fire was so hot that it filled the air for thirty cubits. Verily, no one could go near it. Then Peter Bartholomew, dressed only in an undergarment, knelt down before the Bishop of Albara and called God as his witness that he had seen Him face to face upon the Cross, and had heard from Him what has been written above, and also from St. Peter and Andrew; and that he had not made up any of the things which he had reported in the name of St. Peter, or St. Andrew, or of the Lord Himself; and that if he had told any lie, he should never pass through the present fire. (He prayed) that God would forgive him the other (sins) which he had committed, both against God and his neighbor, and that the Bishop and all the other priests and the people who had gathered to witness the test would pray for him. After this, when the Bishop had placed the Lance in his hand, he knelt and, after invoking the sign of the cross upon himself, went forth boldly and without fear into the fire. He stopped for a brief moment in the midst of the fire, and thus by the grace of God passed through.

There are, moreover, to this day some who saw this miracle there, that, before he had escaped destruction, a bird flew over head and, after encircling the fire, plunged into it. Ebrard the priest, he of whom we made mention above, and who later remained at Jerusalem for the sake of the Lord, saw this; and William, son of William the Good, an excellent knight, of good reputation, from the region of Arles, bears witness that he saw this. A certain other honorable knight of the people of Beziers, William *Maluspuer* by name, saw a man dressed in priestly garb, except that he had a robe folded back over his head, advance into the fire before Peter went into the flames. When he saw that (this man) did not come forth, thinking that it was Peter Bartholomew, he began to weep, believing that he had been destroyed in the fire. There was a multitude of men there and they could not see everything. And many other things were revealed to us and done which we do not wish to write for fear of tiring the readers—since three suitable witnesses are sufficient for any question. Let us not pass over this one occurrence. After Peter Bartholomew had passed through the fire, though much fire was still burning, yet the people so eagerly gathered brands and coals, together with ashes, that in a short space of time none of it remained. In the faith of those people the Lord afterwards worked many good deeds through these relics.

But as Peter came forth from the fire, with his shirt unburned and with no sign of any hurt on that very fine cloth with which the Lance of the Lord was wound, all the people welcomed him when he had signalled to them, holding the Lance in his hand, and had shouted at the top of his voice, "God help us!" They welcomed him, I say, and dragged him along the ground and almost that whole multitude stepped upon him, each one wishing to touch him, or to take some piece of his garment, and each one believing him near someone else. And thus they made three or four wounds on his legs, cutting off the flesh; and trampling upon his back-bone, they broke it. And there Peter would have breathed out his soul, as we believe, had not Raymond Piletus, a most noble and brave knight, supported by a crowd of companions, rushed into the mass of the confused mob and freed him by fighting even to death. But now from concern and anguish we cannot write more about this.

When Raymond Piletus had brought Peter to our house and his wounds had been bound up, we asked him why he had stopped in the fire. To this he replied, "The Lord met me in the midst of the flames and, taking me by the hand, said to me, 'Since thou didst doubt the finding of the Lance when St. Andrew showed it to thee, thou shalt not pass through unhurt, but thou shalt not see hell.' And having said this, He left me. Look, therefore, if you wish, at my burns." And there was a slight burn on his legs but not much; the wounds, however, were large.

After this we called together all who had doubted the Lance to come and see his face, head, hair, and other members. They would find out that what he said of the Lance and other matters was true, since for proof of these things he had not feared to enter such a fire. Therefore many looked, and, upon seeing his face and whole body, they glorified God, saying, "Well can the Lord, who delivered this man from such a flaming fire, protect us amidst the swords of our enemies! Indeed, we did not believe that any arrow could pass unhurt through the fire, as this man passed through!"

After this Peter called the chaplain of the Count, Raymond, by name, to him and said, "Why did you wish me to pass through fire for proof of the Lance of the Lord and other things that I reported as from God? I know well that you have thought this way and that."

And he told me what he had thought. But when Raymond denied that he had so thought, Peter Bartholomew replied, "You can not deny it to me, since I know it for certain, because the other night the most Blessed Virgin Mary was here and the Bishop of Puy, through whom I learned the things which you deny. Since you did not doubt the words of the Lord and His apostles, I wonder, indeed, why you should wish, at my risk, to hold trial about these matters alone."

Then Raymond, seeing his thought detected and himself culpable before God, broke forth most bitterly in tears. And Peter thereupon said: "Do not despair for the most Blessed Virgin Mary and St. Andrew will obtain pardon for you with God. But you must be more zealous in beseeching them."

Meanwhile, so many and such great disputes arose between the leaders of our army that almost the whole army was divided. But God, who was our Guide and Master, forbade such (an end) to befall His good work. The city of Tripoli was not far from our camp. Accordingly, when the lord of this city learned of the discord between our princes, he replied as follows to our men who called upon him about paying tribute: "And who are the Franks? And what kind of knights are they? And how great is their power? Behold it is now the third month since the army of the Franks besieged Archas, and I have seen neither an assault of theirs nor any armed man, and yet they are only four leagues away. But let them come hither, and let us see them and prove their military skill. Why should I become tributary to these men whose faces I have not seen, and whose bravery I do not know?" As this was reported to our army, some said to one another, "Behold what we have gained by our quarrels and discord! God is blasphemed and we are despised!" For this cause, therefore, our princes came to agreement and decided that the Bishop of Albara should guard the camp with a part of the army; and, as was their manner of fighting, that the princes with the ranks of foot-soldiers and knights should attack the walls of the city.

However, on the appointed day when our men thus set forth, the people of Tripoli, relying on the multitude of their number, came forth to meet our men, ready to fight with them. There is a very strong and high wall of an acqeduct into the city, between which and the sea there is not much space; for the sea encircles Tripoli on three sides. Accordingly, the Saracens fortified this wall of the aqueduct, which we have mentioned, so that if any misfortune befell them they could go forth and return, as though from castle to castle. And thus when our men saw this multitude, relying upon the place of their arms, they called upon God, and with upraised spears the foot-soldiers and knights went up to them in a body, as if in a procession, so that if you had seen our men you would have believed or said that they were friends, not enemies. The land is now polluted with the blood of the Moors, and the aqueduct filled with their dead bodies. Such fear did the Lord cast down upon the enemy that scarcely any of them could flee after the first blows. It was indeed very delightful to behold the stream of the aqueduct bear the beheaded corpses of nobles and people swiftly into the city. One or two of our men fell there; but of the enemy, we heard that as many as seven hundred had fallen.

And thus, upon returning with a great victory and many spoils, our princes said to the people, "This day the King of Tripoli saw us, and we saw the roads to the city and have considered its approaches. And now, if you approve, we have decided that tomorrow the king may find out what kind of knights we are." When, therefore, they returned on the next day, they found no one outside the wall. After this moreover the King of Trpioli sent word to our princes that if they would desist from the siege of Archas, he would give them fifteen thousand gold coins, horses, mules, raiment, and food, and that he would afford a market of all goods for all the people; in addition to this, that he would return all our people whom he held captive.

At this time envoys from the Emperor Alexius came to us with very great complaints against Bohemund, because he was retaining the city of Antioch against the oaths which he had made to the Emperor. Bohemund was holding Antioch at this time, for upon hearing that the Count had set forth from Marra into the interior of Syria, he violently expelled the Count's men from the towers of Antioch which they were guarding. Alexius further sent word to our princes that he would give them much gold and silver and would come with them to Jerusalem, and that they should wait for him until the Festival of St. John.[19] Easter was then at hand.

Many, among whom was the Count, for this reason said: "Let us wait for the Emperor and we will gain both his gifts and himself. He will cause a market to come by land and by sea, and we will be in accord under him as leader. All the cities will surrender to him, and he will invest those he wishes, and destroy those he wishes. Besides, if these people of ours, assailed by long and daily trials, should come to Jerusalem, they would wish to go home, perchance, after having seen it from the outside. Consider carefully the dangers and very great dangers which remain for those who desire to finish the journey. Besides this, moreover, let us besiege the fortress of Archas, and it will surrender within a month, or be captured by force. When people at a distance learn of this siege, if we abandon it as impossible, our army, which hitherto has undertaken nothing that it has not finished, will be much despised."

But others said on the other hand, "The Emperor has always done us hurt, has always lied, has always plotted against us. And now because he sees that he can do nothing, and that we are victorious through the grace of God, he zealously strives to draw us off from the proposed journey, lest those who will hear of it arrange to follow our example. But now let those whom he has so often hurt by word and deed take care not to place trust in him in vain. Putting our faith, therefore, in Christ our Leader, who has delivered us from so many dangers beyond expectation, and who has preserved us against all the efforts and wiles of the Emperor, let us proceed on the journey for which we came; and by God's promise we will easily accomplish what we wish. When the Emperor shall hear that Jerusalem has been captured and the road is free, he will fulfil in deed what he has feigned in words. It will be likewise with the gifts." The people approved this opinion most. But because the friends of the Count were many, the Count would surely have exposed himself with his people to death without the other princes, and he would have given large individual gifts to many, had not the counsel of the princes and the votes of the people prevented.

At this time we preached a fast, prayers, and alms to the people, that Almighty God, who had led them hither from so many regions, should deign to breathe into them which of these (opinions) was pleasing in His sight. And thus the prayers of the faithful easily obtained from God what they sought. For the Bishop of Puy appeared to Stephen Valentine, whom we mentioned above, the one who saw the Lord with the Cross, and, beating him with a switch as he was returning to his home by night, said to him, "Stephen." He replied, "Sire," and looking back, he recognized him.

The Bishop said, "Why hast thou time and again neglected what I said to thee about the Cross of the Lord and our Mother, Virgin Mary? I commanded that the Cross which I was accustomed to have carried before me be brought to the army. And what sign is better than the Cross? Or has that Cross not been stoned enough for you? Or has it not led you truly to the Lance of the Lord? And now Our Lady and Blessed Virgin Mary says that unless you keep that Cross, you will not be able to obtain counsel."

And the priest said immediately, "O, dearest Lord, where is the Blessed Mary?" And straightway the Bishop showed her to him. About nine or ten cubits distant from him was the Blessed Mary, exceedingly wonderful in face and adornment; and by her was St. Agatha and another virgin, bearing two wax candles.

Then the priest said to the Bishop who stood by her, "Sire, how many things are said of thee in the army, that thy hair and beard were burned in hell, and many other things which are not believed! And now I beg thee to give me one of those candles to take to the Count, as proof of these things which thou sayest."

Then said the Bishop to him, "Look and see my face. Is it not burned?" After this, the Bishop approached the Blessed Virgin Mary and, upon learning her will, he returned to the priest and said to him, "That which thou asketh cannot be obtained by thee; but this ring that thou hast on thy finger is of no use to thee, nor is it right for thee to wear it. Go and give it to the Count, saying, 'Most Holy Virgin Mother sends this ring to thee; and as often as thou shalt fail in any matter, remember the Lady who sent it to thee, and appeal to her and the Lord will aid thee.'"

Again, when the priest asked him what he wished his brother to do, the Bishop replied to him, "Let him strongly urge the Bishop-elect to celebrate three masses to the Lord for the souls of our relatives. Our Mother commands that the Lance should not be shown except by a priest clothed in sacred vestments; and that the Cross be borne before it, thus."

And the Bishop held the Cross placed upon a little spear, and a person dressed in priestly garb followed him, holding the Lance in his hands. Then the bishop began this response, *Gaude, Maria Virgo, cunctus haereses sola interemisti.* Hundreds of thousands of voices without number took it up; and so the gathering of saints departed. Moreover, when it became morning, the priest went first to see if we had the Lance; and when he saw it, he began to narrate with many tears what had been heard and seen, as we have told above. Therefore the Count sent William Hugo, brother of the Bishop of Puy, to Laodicaea, where the Cross had been left with the hood of the same Bishop.

Meanwhile, Peter Bartholomew, distressed with illness from his beating and wounds, summoned the Count and his princes and said to him, "The end of my life approaches; and I know well enough that I will be judged before God for all that I have done, or said, or thought evilly. In your presence and in the sight of God, I this day call Him to witness that I made up nothing of what I announced to you as from God and His apostles, and I say this to you now. And as you have seen fulfilled the things which I announced to you, so without doubt will you see these things which I tell you now, if indeed you serve God faithfully." After this Peter departed in safety and peace in the Lord at the hour appointed for him by God, and he was buried in that place where he had passed through the fire with the Lance.

5. *Another view of the revelation and trial of the Lance.*

(*Raoul.*) . . . . . . Permit us to run back to the origin of this hatred, that we may wonder the less when we reach the force of the raging current. While Antioch was still resisting the princes of Gaul, by whom it was enclosed, a quarrel arose between the adherents of Bohemund and Raymond. Men of both parties were sent to gather grain. They found food and a fight at one and the same time, and the grain was divided by the sword. Both parties were wounded, as well as frightened, and both sides returned home wounded. The princes were wrought up at the sight of the blood of their vassal' host, and they inflamed the minds of the wounded men to revenge whenever a similar affair should occur. They commanded that the fire should be covered in camp; outside the flame should be fanned with a raging wind. Their ready ears received this command willingly—a command difficult to revoke. Accordingly, when thereafter a greater band of one party met a smaller one of the other laden with provisions, the burdens of food were put down there, and their necks were loaded with a shower of blows; and thus the one that was stronger enjoyed the spoils. Then, the weaker party, thus despoiled, grieved that they had exerted themselves for others, and not for themselves. He who understood the tongue of either now lashed with it; meanwhile, the innocent were lashed for it. All from Narbonne, Auvergne, Gascony, and all this kind of people were for the Provençals; the remainder of Gaul, especially the Normans, conspired with the Apulians. The Bretons, Swabians, Huns, Ruthenians,[20] and people of this kind were protected by the barbarity of their tongues. All this was going on outside the wall.

In the city, also, the quarrel did not decrease, but rather increased, for when the besieged people were in the throes of famine, as mentioned above, there arose from the army of Raymond a versatile fabricator of lies, Peter, who preached that the salvation of the people had been revealed to him in this way: "St. Andrew, the apostle," he said, "appeared to me, when I was half asleep, and spoke this command in my ear. 'Arise and announce to the people who are laboring that consolation has come from heaven, which the Lance that opened the side of the Lord will confer when it is found. It lies hidden beneath the soil within the church of St. Peter. Break the pavement at such a place (and he pointed out the place), and by digging there you will find the iron mentioned. When the horror of battle threatens, turn that against the enemy, and you will conquer through it.' Terrified, I thought that I had been deceived by a dream; and that I would not disclose it, but would remain silent forever, unless I was warned the second and the third time. The quiet of the next night was again enfolding me when the same apostle again returned, uttering the very statement which he had made before, but like one scolding and in wrath. 'Wherefore,' he said,' didst thou shun me and remain silent? Thou alone art delaying the safety of many. The people have cried out to the Lord and have been heard; and still thy negligence leaves them as if neglected. Hasten, therefore, as quickly as possible to correct this, that thou mayest continue to live.' Frightened at these words, when I had emerged from the sleep, I was at the same time more certain and more troubled; yet, still I hesitated whether to keep the secret or disclose it. In this worry I passed a whole day, and half the night, with prayer and fasting, begging the Lord for the third visit, if the first two had really been from him. The cock had twice acclaimed the morning, when, at length, just before the third crow, sleep bound my tired limbs; then without delay he who had come a first time, who had come a second time, appeared there again, ever more terrible, ever more commanding. 'Rise up, go, lazy brute, mute dog, delayer of safety and victory, menace to your fellows, solace of your enemies. Thou hast trembled with fear where there was no fear; where it is thou hast no fear.' Threats and curses still continued, when my spirit, terrified with fear at the threats, carried me away from sleep; perspiration and trembling coursed over my body at the same time, and if fire was burning one side, the other was stiff with ice. By these steps I came to teach what I had learned; you, however, fathers and brothers, do not stop to test the truth of the matter; it remains for me to point out the place for you to dig."

When this rumor was brought to the ears of Raymond, he called a council and had Peter summoned to the church of St. Peter. When asked about the place, he pointed behind the altar, true to his story, and advised them to dig; and that his words might have weight, he likewise composed his expression. They dug, but without avail; the upturned earth could not return what had not been committed to it, and what it had not received. However, the man had secreted about him an Arabic spear point, from the chance finding of which he had contrived material for his deception. Therefore, seizing the hardened, worn, and aged point, which was in form and size unlike those which we used, he was encouraged thereby to believe that people would put faith in his new creations. Accordingly, when the time for the deception came, he took a spade, jumped into the pit and, turning to a corner, said, "Here we must dig. Here lies hidden what we seek. Here it will come forth." Then, multiplying blow on blow, often and more often, he pulled forth from the dug up ground the spear which had been fraudulently dropped by him. The darkness conspired in the deception; likewise, the throng of people with the darkness, and the narrowness of the pit with the throng. But when the sound of metal striking upon metal was heard, this same fabricator of lies held out the iron and filled the excited ears of the simple with these words: "Lo, behold! Heaven promised what the earth preserved; the apostle revealed what the prayer of the people obtained!" Scarcely had he said this when they went outside and, following the trophy with hymns and chants, showered it with gifts and wrapped it up in cloth of gold.

This Raymond and those who supported him had fittingly arranged, but the men of other parties, too, in their rude simplicity, paid devotion to it with gifts. Before victory earnestly, after it much more earnestly, the Provençals said that the glory of the triumph should be ascribed to the Lance, which was borne ahead in battle, as if it were a trophy. And so, the treasury of Raymond was enlarged, his spirit exalted, and his army became insolent. Some of the princes whom he had joined to himself, partly by flattery and partly by deference, sided with him.

But Bohemund, since he was no fool, scrutinized the matter in detail. For who was that dreamer? In what vagaries had he involved the people? What place had he pointed out to the diggers? In the fact that he himself had leaped into it, had dug and found it, Bohemund immediately detected a trick. He decided that the finding was invalid and proved the inventor false by keen conjectures: "Beautifully," said he, "was it contrived that St. Andrew should appear to a man who, I hear, frequents taverns, roams the streets, is a friend to vanities and ingrained with folly! The holy apostle chose a fine person to whom to disclose the secret of heaven! For to whom would that trick not be evident? If a Christian had hidden it, why did he pass over the nearest altar for a hiding place, or if a

Gentile, or a Jew, why was it hidden within the walls of a church? Why near an altar? If it is ascribed to neither, but to chance, in what historical account is Pilate found to have come to Antioch? Surely we knew that it was the lance of a soldier, and a soldier of Pilate. But what follows is delightful! I hear that the finder leaped in, after the diggers had been laboring in vain, and that was granted to one man in the darkness which had been denied many in the open. Oh, boorish foolishness! Oh, boorish credulity! Oh, credulity, easily won! So be it! His integrity corroborates the man, and nearness to the crucifixion the place. Is this most recent fraud of that man not evident enough? If he had walked purely, simply, in the way of God; if he had trusted in the apostle who appeared to him, he himself would not (alone) bear witness to this discovery but would obtain another's testimony. But why do I devote so much scorn to that person? Because the Provençals ascribe our victory, which is from above, like light from the Father, to their piece of iron. Let that grasping Count and stupid rabble regard it as their own! We, however, have won and shall win in the name of our Lord Jesus Christ!" This said Bohemund, and with him those who looked more deeply below the surface, the Counts of Normandy and Flanders, and the vice-prelate, Arnulf, and Tancred.

Accordingly, Raymond, wounded by the sharp points of Bohemund's arguments, sought vengeance by a thousand arts, or a thousand ways. Then, withdrawing, without a mediator, he said, "Either I will die soon, or I will avenge the insults of the son of Guiscard. If the meeting does not occur openly, let it come secretly. Let the dagger prevail, where the Lance will not! *Dolus, an virtus, quis in hoste requirat?*[21] Since the custody of the city is mine, then the citadel on the hill, the chief palace, the market place, the bridge, and the gates belong to me; also the Lance and most of the people are subject to me. What remains, except that, with Bohemund out of the way, I shall gain the principality?"

While he was turning this and much more over in his mind, he decided first of all that an uprising should be stirred up among the people, so that Bohemund would be overwhelmed from head to foot. In the beginning, oaths would be hurled back and forth in the market place; the clamor would rise to disturb the people; the leaders from both sides would bring aid to their men; and every arrow, every javelin, would be aimed at Bohemund. While Raymond was digesting this plot in his heart, like a lion, God willed that this injustice should not be concealed, and it was disclosed to Arnulf, and through him to Bohemund. Thus the plot was thwarted and the soul of a man, whose life had already been of the greatest advantage to those seeking Jerusalem, and was yet to be of great advantage, was saved from death.

Thus their anger had its beginning; thus began the kindling of their hate. . . . While their arms were idle and ease shut out warlike cares, the question of the finding of the above mentioned spear point was to be put to test, for division was disturbing the people. These favored the Lance, those condemned it, neither party at all reasonable. As a result, the chief leaders agreed that he who had been the beginning of the difficulty should himself end it, and should prove the matter in question by the ordeal of fire. Accordingly, when Peter had been brought in to the council, they decided that he should take nine steps hither and thither through the midst of burning, flaming branches, that by this test the finding would be proved true, if he were unhurt, or false, if he were burnt. A period of three days was set aside for a fast, and proper provision was made for prayer and virgil. So they separated. But soon, on the third day, they met again. Branches were set afire in a double row. Peter, dressed in a shirt and breeches, otherwise naked, proceeded through the midst of it, fell burned at the other end, and died on the following day. The people, upon seeing what was done, confessed that they had been deceived by his wordy guile, were sorry that they had erred, and testified that Peter was a disciple of Simon, the magician.[22]

But Raymond and his Provençal accomplices defended the accused with obstinate minds,[23] proclaimed him a saint, threatened Arnulf, as the chief discoverer of the fraud which had been revealed and, finally, sent an armed band against him to overwhelm him unexpectedly at his house. Had he not previously warned the Count of Normandy, in whose service he was, he would have come to an early death. The Count was eating, with him the Count of Flanders, and both were reclining. When they heard the cause of the commotion, their session was broken off. The Counts separated, each to his own forces, and both sent arms to oppose the armed men. But frightened by the commotion of the Normans which they heard, they tried to cover up the matter, making believe that they were looking for something else and had some other intent. By this artifice they saved themselves; otherwise those whom flight spared would have grieved, not that they had taken up arms in vain, but that they had done so unfortunately.

CHAPTER VII

THE CAPTURE OF JERUSALEM

(The last quarrel between the leaders at Archas apparently cleared the minds of all. Their attitude thereafter seemed one of grim determination to fulfil their vow as quickly as possible. The description of the siege and the capture of Jerusalem offers very graphic testimony as to the degree of civilization attained by eleventh century Europe. With Jerusalem in their possession, the Crusaders were still threatened by the vacillating ruler of Egypt, or Babylon, as they called it. Jerusalem had been surrendered to the Saracens of Egypt by its Seljuk rulers when the Crusaders were at Antioch. The inability of the Caliph to send an army to the relief of the city while it was being besieged is sufficient evidence of his weakness. The ease with which the Crusaders disposed of Al-Afdhal's host, while it confirms this weakness, also affords eloquent testimony to the prestige which Western courage and skill had won among the Mohammedans.)

1. *March to Jerusalem.* (May 13—June 7, 1099.)

(*Gesta.*) Accordingly, we left the fortified town and came to Tripoli on the sixth day of the week on the thirteenth day of incoming May, and we stayed there for three days. At length, the King of Tripoli made an agreement with the leaders, and he straightway loosed to them more than three hundred pilgrims who had been captured there and gave fifteen thousand *besants* and fifteen horses of great value; he likewise gave us a great market of horses, asses, and all goods, whence the whole army of Christ was greatly enriched. But he made an agreement with them that if they could win the war which the Emir of Babylon was getting ready against them and could take Jerusalem, he would become a Christian and would recognize his land as (a gift) from them. In such manner it was settled.

We left the city on the second day of the week in the month of May and, passing along a narrow and difficult road all day and night, we came to a fortress, the name of which was Botroun. Then we came to a city called Gibilet near the sea, in which we suffered very great thirst, and, thus worn out, we reached a river named Ibrahim. Then on the eve of the day of the Ascension of the Lord we crossed a mountain in which the way was exceedingly narrow, and there we expected to find the enemy lying in ambush for us. But God favoring us, none of them dared to appear in our way. Then our knights went ahead of us and cleared the way before us, and we arrived at a city by the sea which is called Beirut, and thence we went to another city called Sidon, thence to another called Tyre, and from Tyre to the city of Acre. But from Acre we came to a fortified place the name of which was Cayphas, and then we came near Caesarea. There was celebrated Pentecost on the third day of outgoing May. Then we came to Ramlah, which through fear of the Franks the Saracens had left empty. Near it was the famous church in which rested the most precious body of St. George,[1] since for the name of Christ he there happily received martyrdom from the treacherous pagans. There our leaders held a council to choose a bishop who should have charge of this place and erect a church. They gave tithes to him and enriched him with gold and silver, and with horses and other animals, that he might live the more devoutly and honorably with those who were with him.[2] He remained there with joy.

(*Raymond.*) Meanwhile the Count and the other princes inquired of the inhabitants of that region how the march to Jerusalem might be better and more easily made. For there are the mountains of Lebanon, in which almost sixty thousand Christian men dwell. The Christians who are near the city of Tyre (now commonly called Sur, whence they are called Surians) have possessed that land and mountains for a long time. But when the Saracens and Turks arose through the judgment of God, those Surians were in such great oppression for four hundred and more years that many of them were forced to abandon their fatherland and the Christian law. If, however, any of them through the grace of God refused, they were compelled to give up their beautiful children to be circumcised, or converted to Mohammedanism; or they were snatched from the lap of their mothers, after the father had been killed and the mother mocked. Forsooth, that race of men were inflamed to such malice that they overturned the churches of God and His saints, or destroyed the images; and they tore out the eyes of those images which, for lack of time, they could not destroy, and shot them with arrows; all the altars, too, they undermined. Moreover, they made mosques of the great churches. But if any of those distressed Christians wished to have an image of God or any saint at his home, he either redeemed it month by month, or year by year, or it was thrown down into the dirt and broken before his eyes. In addition, too harsh to relate, they placed youths in brothels, and, to do yet more vilely, exchanged their sisters for wine. And their mothers dared not weep openly at these or other sorrows. Why do we say much about them? Surely that people had conspired against the Holy of Holies and His inheritance! Except by the command and direction of God, the people of the Franks would have encountered these ills, had not God straightway armed brute animals against their enemies, as He did once in our presence.[3] And so much for this.

When those Surians who, as we said above, came to the Count, were asked about the better route, they replied: "The way through Damascus is level and full of vituals; but you will not find water for two days. The other way through the mountains of Lebanon is safe enough and well watered, but it is very hard for the pack animals and camels. There is another way along the sea, where there are so many and such narrow passes that if fifty or a hundred Saracens want to hold them, they can do so against all mankind. And yet it is contained in the Gospel of St. Peter, which we have, that if you are the people who are to take Jerusalem, you will pass along the sea-coast, though because of the difficulty it seems impossible to us. Moreover, there is written in that Gospel among us not only what you have done, but also what you ought to do about this march and many other things."

While some were urging in this and other ways, and others were contradicting, William Hugo of Monteil returned with the Cross of which we spoke above.[4] Moreover, when the friends of the Count likewise beheld this Cross, they became so eager for the march that, except for the counsel of the Count and the other princes, the servants of the Count would have burned their huts and been the first to leave the siege of Archas. Thereupon, the Count was disturbed to tears and even to hatred of himself and his people. But the Duke of Lorraine especially wished this journey and admonished the people to it. Accordingly, having set forth from that detestable and hateful siege of Archas, we came before Tripoli. Even then Count Raymond with prayers and gifts urged all the nobles to besiege the city of Tripoli, but all opposed him.

At this time, St. Andrew appeared to Peter Desiderius, of whom we have made mention above, and said to him, "Go and speak to the Count, saying: 'Do not molest thyself or others, for unless Jerusalem shall first have been taken, thou shalt have no help. Do not trouble thyself about the unfinished siege of Archas; let it not weigh upon thee that this city, or others which are on the journey, are not taken at present, because a fight will soon come upon thee in which these and many other cities shall be captured. Furthermore, do not trouble thyself or thy men, but distribute freely in His name whatever God shall grant to thee, and be a companion and loyal friend to thy vassals. If thou shalt do this, God will grant thee Jerusalem and Alexandria and Babylon. But if thou dost not do this, thou shalt neither acquire the things promised by God nor have a message, until thou art placed in such straits that thou knowest not how to escape!'" So the Count accepted the words of the priest; he accepted them, truly, in words, but he refused them in deeds. For when he had received great wealth from the King of Tripoli, he was never willing to give anyone any of it, but he even daily afflicted his people with blows and insults. Not only this, however, did that priest tell us, but also many other things, some of which we have added to this work.

For once, when we wanted to set out from Antioch, that priest came to me, Raymond, and said to me that a certain person had appeared to him in a vision who said to him, "Go into the church of St. Leontius, and thou wilt find there the relics of four saints; take them with thee and carry them to Jerusalem." And he showed him in that vision the relics and locations of the relics, and he taught him the names of the saints. When that priest had awakened, not fully believing in his vision, he began to urge God with prayers and entreaties to make known to him a second time if this vision was from Him. Several days later the same saint stood before him in a vision and threatened him much because he had neglected the command of God, and (said that) unless he had taken those relics away by the fifth day of the week, it would be a great hurt to him and his lord, Count Ysoard. Ysoard, Count of Die, was a man loyal to God as far as he knew, and helpful to all of us for his wisdom and uprightness.

When the priest had narrated this to me, Raymond, I told it to the Bishop of Orange and to the Count of St. Gilles and to some others. We took candles and went to the church of St. Leontus, We offered the candles and vows to God and to the saints of the same church, (praying) that Almighty God, who had sanctified them, might give them to us as companions and helpers; and that those saints might not spurn the company of pilgrims and exiles for God, but, rather, out of charity might join us and link us with God. When it became morning, we went with the priest to the places where the relics were kept, and we found everything just as it had been foretold. Moreover, these are the names of the saints: Cyprian, *Omechios*, Leontius, John Chrysostom.[5] And, furthermore, at the place where the relics were kept we found a little chest filled with relics. When he asked a priest about these, of which saint they were the relics, he replied that he did not know. But when we inquired of the inhabitants if they knew of which saint these were the relics, some said of St. Mercurius, others, however, of other saints. But the priest wished to take them up and put them with the collection of other relics. To him, I, Raymond, said angrily in the presence of all who were there, "If this saint wishes to come with us to Jerusalem, let him make known his name and wish; otherwise let him remain here. Why should we weight ourselves with unknown bones and carry them along?" Therefore on that day those relics were left behind. But when the priest had collected the other relics and had rolled them up in cloths and a covering, on the night which followed, as he lay awake, there appeared to him a youth of about fifteen years, exceedingly beautiful, who said to him, "Why didst thou this day not take any relics with the rest?"

The priest replied to this, "Who art thou?"

"Dost thou not know who is the standard bearer of this army?" he replied.

The priest answered, "I do not, Sire."

When the priest had made the same reply to the same question a second time, the youth threatened the priest terribly, saying, "Tell me the truth."

And then the priest said, "Sire, it is said of St. George that he is the standard-bearer of this army."

He replied, "Thou hast said well. I am he. Take, therefore, my relics and put them with the others."

When, however, the priest had deferred doing this for several days, the same George came to him and commanded the priest sternly, saying, "Do not delay longer than the morning to take up my relics; and near by in a little ampule thou wilt find some of the blood of the virgin and martyr St. Tecla, which likewise take; and after this chant mass." And the priest found all this, and did it.

But before we go on to the remainder, we ought not to pass over these men who did not hesitate, for love of the most holy expedition, to sail through the unknown and very long water of the Mediterranean and the Ocean. For when the Angles heard the name of the Lord's vengeance against those who unworthily occupied the birthplace of Jesus Christ and His apostles, they embarked upon the Anglican Sea. Rounding Spain, crossing the ocean, and thus ploughing through the Mediterranean Sea, with great labor they gained the port of Antioch and the city of Laodicaea, before our army came thither by land.[6] Their ships, as well as those of the Genoese were of advantage to us at this time, for during the siege we had trade with the island of Cyprus and the remaining islands because of these ships and the security which they offered.

Forsooth, these ships passed daily over the sea, and for this reason the ships of the Greeks were safe, since the Saracens feared to encounter them. But when the Angles saw the army setting forth for Jerusalem, and that the strength of their own ships was impaired by the long wait (for though they had thirty ships in the beginning, they now had scarcely nine or ten), some abandoned their ships and exposed them; others, however, burned theirs and hastened with us on the journey.

When our princes were entangled in delay before Tripoli, the Lord sent such great desire of going to Jerusalem that no one could there restrain himself, or another, but, setting out at evening against the decrees of the princes and the custom of our army, we walked along all that night and came on the following day to Beirut. After this, when the narrow passages which are called The Twisted Mouth had been suddenly seized in advance, we came in a few days and without baggage to Acre. The King of Acre, however, afraid that we would besiege his city, and hoping that we would withdraw, took oath to the Count that if we captured Jerusalem, or were in the region of Judaea for twenty days, and the King of Babylon did not meet us in battle, or if we were able to overcome that king, he would surrender himself and his city to us; but that in the meanwhile he would be our friend.

Setting forth from Acre one day at vespers, we pitched camp by the swamps which are near Caesarea. And while, according to custom, some ran here and there below the camp, as need demanded, and while others were inquiring from acquaintances where their companions were lodged, a dove, mortally wounded by a hawk, fell down in the midst of those runnnig about. When the Bishop of Agde took it up, he found a letter which it was carrying. And the sense of the letter was as follows:

"The King of Acre to the Duke of Caesarea: A canine breed, a foolish and troublesome host without order, passed me. As you love your law, try by yourselves and through others to hurt them; this you can easily do, if you wish. Send this likewise to other cities and fortresses."

In the morning, when we were commanding the army to rest, the letter was shown to the princes and to all the people, and (it was manifest) how God had been kind to us, so that not even the birds could cross through the air to harm us, and that He likewise disclosed to us the secrets of our foes. Wherefore, we rendered praise and thank to Almighty God. And thence setting forth securely and willingly, we went forward, frequently in the front rank of the army, and also at the end.

But when the Saracens who lived in Ramlah heard that we had crossed the river near by, they left their fortifications and arms, and much grain in the fields, and crops, which we gathered. And when we came to it on the next day, we found out that God was truly fighting for us. So we offered vows to St. George because he had confessed himself our guide. The leaders and all the people agreed that we should there choose a bishop, since that was the first church which we found in the land of Israel, and, also, in order that St. George might entreat God in our behalf, and might lead us faithfully through the land in which He was not worshipped. Moreover, Ramlah is about fifteen miles from Jerusalem. Therefore, we there held a conference.

Some said, "Let us not go to Jerusalem at present, but towards Egypt; we will obtain not only Jerusalem, but likewise Alexandria and Babylon and very many kingdoms. If we go to Jerusalem and, failing of sufficient water, give up the siege, we will accomplish neither this nor the other afterwards."

But others said in opposition, "There are scarcely fifteen hundred knights in the army, and the number of armed men is not great; and yet it is now suggested that we go to very distant and unknown regions, where we will be able neither to get help from our people nor to place a garrison in a city, if we capture one; nor, even if it should be necessary, would we be able to return thence. But none of this; let us hold to our way, and let God provide for His servants for the siege, for thirst, for hunger, and for other things!"

Accordingly, after leaving a garrison in the fortress of Ramlah with the new Bishop, we loaded our camels and oxen, and then all our baggage animals and horses, and turned our march to Jerusalem. However, the word which Peter Bartholomew had commanded us—that we should not approach Jerusalem except with bared feet—we forgot and held in low regard, each one, from ambition to occupy castles and villas, wishing to go ahead of the next. For it was a custom among us that if any one came to a castle or villa first and placed his standard there with a guard, it was touched by no one else afterward. Therefore, because of this ambition they arose at midnight and, without waiting for companions, gained all those mountains and villas which are in the meadows of the Jordan. A few, however, to whom the command of God was more precious, walked with naked feet and sighed heavily for the contempt of the Divine word; and yet no one recalled a companion or friend from that ambitious chase. Moreover, when by such arrogant procedure we had come near Jerusalem, the people of Jerusalem came forth to meet the first of our men and wounded the horses severely. Of those men three or four fell on that day, and many were wounded.

2. *The Siege.* (June 7—July 15, 1099.)

(*Gesta.*) Rejoicing and exulting, we reached the city of Jerusalem on Tuesday, on the third day of the week, the eighth day before the Ides of June, and began to besiege the city in a marvelous manner.[7] Robert the Norman besieged it from the north side, near the church of St. Stephen, which was built on the very spot where that first martyr won eternal happiness by being stoned in Christ's name. Next to the Norman Count was Robert, Count of Flanders, while Duke Godfrey and Tancred besieged the city from the west. The Count of St. Gilles located himself on the south, on Mount Zion, near the church of St. Mary, the mother of the Lord, where Christ once supped with His disciples.

On the third day some of our men, namely Raymond Piletus and Raymond of Turenne, went out on a foraging expedition. They encountered a force of two hundred Arabs, and the soldiers of Christ fought these unbelievers. With the Lord's help, they fought so valiantly that they killed many of the enemy and captured thirty horses. On the second day of the following week, we made an attack on the city, and so bravely did we fight that, if scaling ladders had been ready for our use, the city most certainly would have fallen into our hands. As it was, we pulled down the outer wall and placed one ladder against the main wall, upon which some of our men ascended and fought hand to hand with swords and lances against the Saracen defenders of the city. Many of our men were killed in this attack, but more of the enemy.

For a period of ten days during the siege we were not able to buy bread at any price, until a messenger came announcing the arrival of our ships. We also suffered greatly for thirst. In fear and terror we were forced to water our horses and other animals at a distance of six miles from camp. The Pool of Siloam, at the foot of Mount Zion, sustained us, but, nevertheless, water was sold among us very dearly.

When the messenger arrived from our ships, the leaders took counsel and decided that armed men should be sent to guard the ships and sailors at the port of Joppa. So one hundred men from the army of Raymond, Count of St. Gilles, under Raymond Piletus, Achard of Montemerle, and William of Sabran,[8] left camp in the early dawn and started confidently toward Joppa. Thirty of these knights separated themselves from the rest of the band and met seven hundred Arabs, Turks, and Saracens from the army of the Emir. The soldiers of Christ boldly attacked the enemy, whose force was so superior to ours that they soon surrounded us. Achard and some of the poor footmen were killed. While this band was completely surrounded, and all believed that they would be killed, a messenger was sent to Raymond Piletus, who said, "Why do you stand here with these knights? Lo, all of our men are in serious danger from the Arabs, Turks, and Saracens, and may all be dead by this time. Hasten to them and aid them." As soon as they heard this, our men hastened to the scene of battle. When the pagans saw the rest of our knights approaching, they formed themselves into two lines. Our men rushed upon the unbelievers, shouting the name of Christ, each determined to bring down his man. The enemy soon realized that they would not be able to withstand the bravery of the Franks, so they turned their backs and fled in terror. Our men, pursuing them a distance of four miles, killed many of them, but kept one alive to give them information. One hundred and three horses were captured.

During this siege we were so distressed with thirst that we sewed up skins of oxen and buffalos and in these carried water for a distance of six miles. Between fetid water and barley bread we were daily in great want and suffering. Moreover, the Saracens hid in ambush at the watering places and either killed and wounded our animals or drove them away to caverns in the hills.

(*Raymond.*) Duke Godfrey and the Count of Flanders and the Count of Normandy besieged the city from the north side, that is from the church of St. Stephen, located in the center of the city, southward to the angular tower next to the tower of David. Count Raymond and his army, however, settled down on the West and besieged Jerusalem from the camp of the Duke to the foot of Mount Zion. But since his men could not come close to besiege the wall because of a gully which intervened, the Count wished to move his camp and change his position. One day, while he was reconnoitering, he came to Mount Zion and saw the church which is located on the Mount. When he heard of the miracles that God had performed there, he said to his leaders and companions, "If we neglect to take this sacred offering, which the Lord has so graciously offered us, and the Saracens there occupy this place, what will become of us? What if through hatred of us they should destroy and pollute these sacred things? Who knows that God may not be giving us this opportunity to test our regard for Him? I know this one thing for certain: unless we carefully protect this sacred spot, the Lord will not give us the others within the city." And so Count Raymond, against the wishes of the leaders of his army, ordered his tents to be moved to that spot. As a result, he incurred such great hatred from his men that they were neither willing to encamp with him nor to do guard duty during the night; each stayed

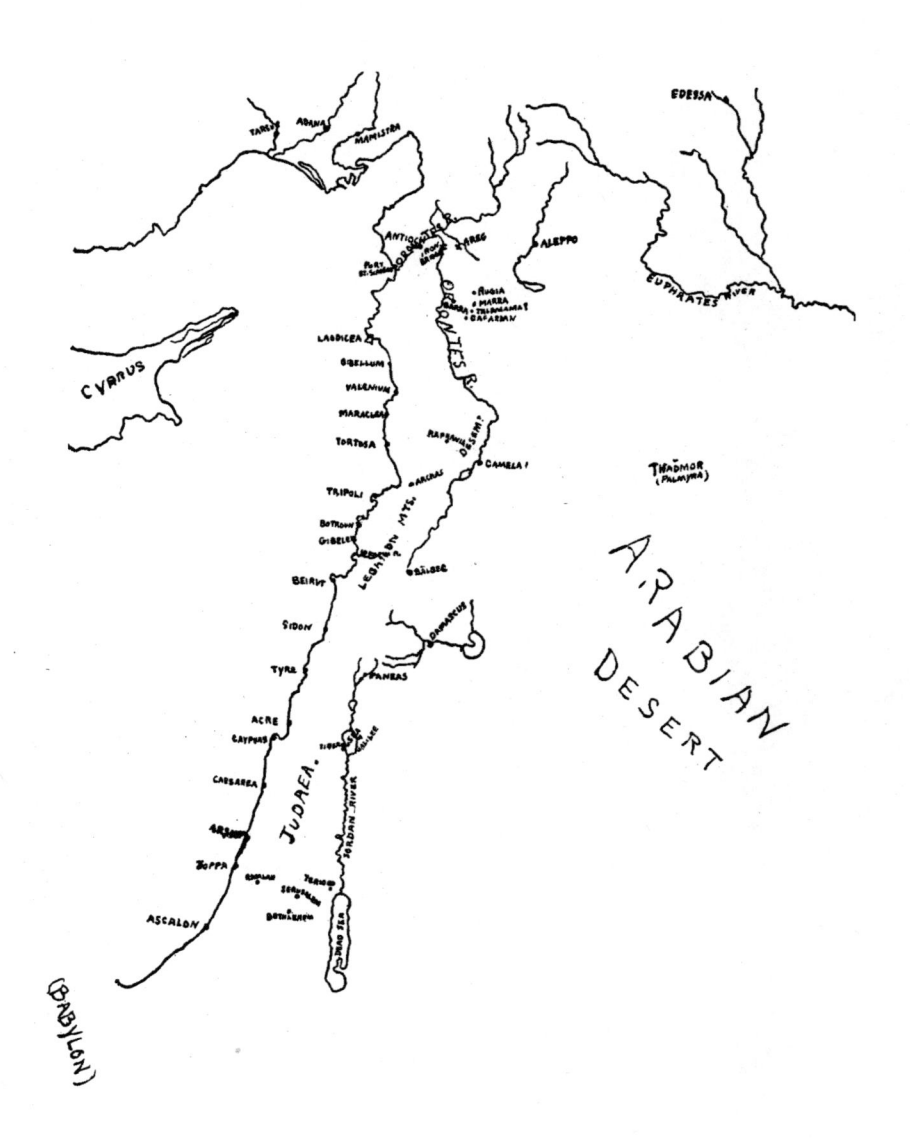

where he had first pitched his tent, with the exception of a few who accompanied the Count. However, by great rewards the Count daily induced knights and footmen to guard his camp. There are in that church these sacred treasures—the tombs of the kings, David and Solomon, as well as that of the first martyr, St. Stephen. There the Blessed Mary departed from this world; the Lord supped there and, after rising from the dead, appeared there to His disciples and to Thomas. On this spot, also, the disciples were filled with the Holy Spirit.

Thereupon, when the siege had been set, it happened one day that some of the leaders of the army met a hermit on the Mount of Olives, who said to them, "If you will attack the city tomorrow till the ninth hour, the Lord will deliver it into your hands." They replied, "But we do not have the necessary machinery for storming the walls." The hermit replied: "God is all powerful. If He wills, He will storm the walls even with one ladder. The Lord aids those who labor for the Truth." So, with such machinery as could be constructed during the night, an attack was made on the city in the early morning, and it lasted till the third hour. The Saracens were compelled to retreat behind the inner walls, for the outer wall was broken down by our men, some of whom even climbed to the top of the inner walls. Now when the city was about to be captured, in the confusion of desire and fear the attack was interrupted, and we then lost many men. On the next day no attack was attempted.

After this, the whole army scattered throughout the surrounding country to collect provisions, and nothing was even said of the necessity of preparing the machines that were needed to capture the city. Each man was serving his mouth and stomach; what was worse, they did not even ask the Lord to free them from such great and manifold evils, and they were afflicted even unto death. Just before our arrival, the Saracens had filled up the springs, destroyed the cisterns, and dammed up the brooks from the springs. And the Lord Himself had turned rivers into wilderness and watersprings into thirsty ground for the wickedness of them that dwell therein.[9] Therefore water was obtained with great difficulty. There is a fountain at the foot of Mount Zion, which is called the Pool of Siloam. Indeed, it is a large spring, but the water flows forth only once in three days, and the natives say that formerly it emptied itself only on Saturdays; the rest of the week it remained stagnant. We do not know how to explain this, except that the Lord willed it to be so. But when, as we have said, the water did flow forth on the third day, it was consumed with such great crowding and haste that the men pushed one another into it, and many baggage animals and cattle perished in it. And so when the pool was filled with the crowd and with the bodies of dead animals, the stronger, even at the price of death, forced their way to the very opening in the rocks through which the water flowed, while the weak got only the water which had already been contaminated. Many sick people fell down by the fountain, with tongues so parched that they were unable to utter a word; with open mouths they stretched forth their hands toward those who had water. In the field were many horses, mules, cattle, and sheep, most of the animals without strength enough to move. And when they had become parched and died because of extreme thirst, they rotted where they had long stood, and there was a most sickening stench throughout the camp. Because of such affliction it was necessary to fetch water a distance of two or three leagues, also to drive the cattle to distant watering places. When the Saracens noticed that our people were going unarmed to the watering places through the dangerous passes in the hills, they lay in wait for them in ambush. They killed many of them and drove away the flocks and herds. The situation was so bad that when any one brought foul water to camp in vessels, he was able to get any price that he cared to ask, and if any one wished to get clear water, for five or six *nummi*[10] he could not obtain enough to satisfy his thirst for a single day. Wine, moreover, was never, or very rarely, even mentioned. In addition, the heat, the dust, and the wind increased their thirst, as though this was not bad enough in itself. But why say so much about these troubles? None, or few, were mindful of the Lord, or of such work as was needed to capture the city; nor did they take heed to beseech the Lord's favor. And thus we did not recognize God in the midst of our affliction, nor did He show favor to the ungrateful.

Meanwhile, messengers came to camp, announcing that our ships had arrived at Joppa and that the sailors demanded that a guard be sent to hold the tower of Joppa and to give them protection at the port; for the town of Joppa had been destroyed except the castle, and that was nearly in ruins, with the exception of one tower. However, there is a harbor there, and it is the one nearest to Jerusalem, being about one day's journey distant. All of our people rejoiced when they heard the news of the ships, and they sent out Count Galdemar, surnamed *Carpinellus*, accompanied by twenty knights and about fifty footmen. Later, they sent Raymond Piletus with fifty knights and William of Sabran with his followers.

As Galdemar and his contingent approached the plains that are on this side of Ramlah, they encountered a force of four hundred chosen Arabs and about two hundred Turks. Galdemar, because of the small number of his men, arranged his knights and bowmen in the front ranks and, trusting in the Lord, advanced upon the enemy without hesitation. The enemy, however, thought that they would be able to crush this band, and, rushing upon them and shooting arrows, they encircled them. Three or four of Galdemar's knights were killed, including Achard of Montemerle, a noble youth and renowned knight; others were wounded, and all our bowmen fell. However, many of the enemy were also killed. Nevertheless, the attack of the enemy did not slacken on account of all this, nor did the courage of our knights, nay God's knights, falter; though oppressed by wounds and death itself, they stood up to their enemies all the more fiercely, the more they suffered from them. But when our leaders, rather from weariness than from fear, were about to withdraw, a cloud of dust was seen approaching. Raymond Piletus was rushing headlong into the fight with his men. Moreover, his men raised so much dust that the enemy thought there were very many knights with him. Thus, by the grace of God, our men were delivered. The enemy scattered and fled, about two hundred of them were killed, and much plunder was taken. It is the custom of this people, when they flee and are hard pressed by the enemy, first to throw away their arms, then their clothes, and lastly their saddle bags. Thus it happened in this fight that our few knights continued killing the enemy until they were worn out, and they kept the spoils obtained from the rest, even of those whom they did not kill.

After the pursuit was over our men assembled, divided the spoils, and then marched to Joppa. The sailors received them with great joy and felt so secure after their arrival that they forgot their ships and neglected to place watches on the sea, but entertained the crusaders with a feast of bread, wine, and fish from their ships. The sailors, careless of their security, failed to post lookouts for the night, and in the darkness they were suddenly surrounded by enemies from the sea. When dawn came, they realized that the enemy was too strong to be resisted, and they abandoned their ships, carrying only the spoils. Thus our knights returned to Jerusalem after winning one battle and losing another. However, one of our ships which had gone on a plundering expedition was not captured. It was returning to port with the greatest plunder when it saw the rest of our ships surrounded by so great a fleet of the enemy. By the use of oars and sail it made its escape to Laodicaea and told our friends and companions at that port what had been happening at Jerusalem. We knew that we had deserved this misfortune, for we had refused to place faith in the words sent to us by the Lord. Despairing of God's mercy, the men went to the plain of the river Jordan, collected palms, and were baptized in its waters. They did so chiefly with the intention of abandonng the siege, having seen Jerusalem, and of going to Joppa, thence to return home by whatever means they could. But the Lord looked after the ships for His unfaithful.

About this time a public assembly was held, for the leaders of the army were quarreling with each other. There was dissatisfaction because Tancred had occupied Bethlehem and had placed his standard over the church of the Nativity, as though it was an ordinary house. An effort was also made to elect one of the princes king to have custody of the city, lest what had been achieved in common should be destroyed in common for want of anyone to take care of the city, if God should give it to us. The bishops and clergy replied (to this suggestion), "You ought not to choose a king where the Lord suffered and was crowned. For if a David, degenerate in faith and virtue, should say in his heart, 'I sit upon the throne of David and hold his kingdom,' the Lord would probably destroy him and be angry with place and people. Besides, the prophet proclaims, saying, 'When the Holy of Holies shall come, unction shall cease, because it will be manifest to all peoples that He has come.'[11] But there should be an advocate to guard the city and divide the tributes and rents of the region among the guardians of the city." For this and many other reasons the election was stopped and put off until the eighth day after the capture of Jerusalem. Not in this matter alone, but in other ways, our affairs did not prosper, and the troubles of the people increased every day. Nevertheless, the merciful and propitious Lord, both for His name's sake and lest our enemies should insult His law and say, "Where is their God?" sent word to us through the Bishop of Puy, Lord Adhemar,[12] how we could placate His anger and obtain His mercy. We, however, preached that this be done without mentioning the command of God, lest if the people transgressed this command of the Lord, they should be especially afflicted, as they would then be the more culpable. For the Lord was so kind to us that He had sent His messengers to us often, but because they were our brothers we had not heeded them.

The Bishop (Adhemar) appeared before Peter Desiderius, saying; "Speak to the princes and all the people, and say to them: 'You who have come from distant lands to worship God and the Lord of hosts, purge yourselves of your uncleanliness, and let each one turn from his evil ways. Then with bare feet march around Jerusalem invoking God, and you must also fast. If you do this and then make a great attack on the city on the ninth day, it will be captured. If you do not, all the evils that you have suffered will be multiplied by the Lord?'"

When the priest had said this to William Hugo, the brother of the Bishop, to his lord, Count Ysoard, and to certain of the clergy, they assembled the princes and the people and addressed them. "Brothers, you know why we undertook this expedition, and what we have suffered, and that we are acting negligently in that we are not constructing the machines that are needed to capture the city. Likewise, we are not careful to reconcile the Lord to us, for we offend Him in many ways and through our evil deeds have driven Him from us. Now, if it seems right to you, let each one become reconciled to his brother whom he has offended, and let brother graciously forgive brother. After this, let us humble ourselves before God; let us march around Jerusalem in bare feet and, through the patronage of the saints, invoke the mercy of the Lord, so that Almighty God, who for us, His servants, laid aside the form of His Godhead, assumed the flesh, and humbly rode into the city on an ass to suffer death on the Cross for our sins, may come to our aid. If we make this procession around the walls, for the honor and glory of His name, He will open the city to us and give us judgment upon His enemies and ours, who now with unjust possession contaminate the place of His suffering and burial, the enemy who seek to deny us the great blessing of the place of God's humiliation and our redemption."

These words were pleasing to both princes and people, and it was publicly commanded that on the next Friday the clergy should lead the procession with crosses and relics of the saints, while the knights and all able-bodied men, with trumpets, standards, and arms, should follow them, barefooted. All this we did according to the commands of God and the princes. When we reached the spot on the Mount of Olives whence the Lord had ascended into heaven after the resurrection, the following exhortation was made to the people: "Now that we are on the very spot from which the Lord made His ascension and we can do nothing more to purify ourselves, let each one of us forgive his brother whom he has injured, that the Lord may forgive us." What more? All were reconciled to each other, and with generous offerings we besought the mercy of God, that He should not now desert His people, whom He had led so gloriously and miraculously to this goal. Thus the mercy of God was obtained, since every thing that had been against us was now favorable.

Although we have passed over many matters, this one we ought to record. While we marched around the city in procession, the Saracens and Turks made the circuit on the walls, ridiculing us in many ways. They placed many crosses on the walls in yokes and mocked them with blows and insulting deeds. We, in turn, hoping to obtain the aid of God in storming the city by means of these signs, pressed the work of the siege day and night.

3. *Final assault and capture.* (July 15, 1099.)

(*Gesta.*) At length, our leaders decided to beleaguer the city with siege machines, so that we might enter and worship the Saviour at the Holy Sepulchre. They constructed wooden towers and many other siege machines. Duke Godfrey made a wooden tower and other siege devices, and Count Raymond did the same, although it was necessary to bring wood from a considerable distance. However, when the Saracens saw our men engaged in this work, they greatly strengthened the fortifications of the city and increased the height of the turrets at night. On a certain Sabbath night, the leaders, after having decided which parts of the wall were weakest, dragged the tower and the machines to the eastern side of the city. Moreover, we set up the tower at earliest dawn and equipped and covered it on the first, second, and third days of the week. The Count of St. Gilles erected his tower on the plain to the south of the city.

While all this was going on, our water supply was so limited that no one could buy enough water for one *denarius* to satisfy or quench his thirst. Both day and night, on the fourth and fifth days of the week, we made a determined attack on the city from all sides. However, before we made this assault on the city, the bishops and priests persuaded all, by exhorting and preaching, to honor the Lord by marching around Jerusalem in a great procession, and to prepare for battle by prayer, fasting, and almsgiving. Early on the sixth day of the week we again attacked the city on all sides, but as the assault was unsuccessful, we were all astounded and fearful. However, when the hour approached on which our Lord Jesus Christ deigned to suffer on the Cross for us, our knights began to fight bravely in one of the towers—namely, the party with Duke Godfrey and his brother, Count Eustace.[13] One of our knights, named Lethold, clambered up the wall of the city, and no sooner had he ascended than the defenders fled from the walls and through the city. Our men followed, killing and slaying even to the Temple of Solomon, where the slaughter was so great that our men waded in blood up to their ankles.

Count Raymond brought his army and his tower up near the wall from the south, but between the tower and the wall there was a very deep ditch. Then our men took counsel how they might fill it, and had it proclaimed by heralds that anyone who carried three stones to the ditch would receive one *denarius*. The work of filling it required three days and three nights, and when at length the ditch was filled, they moved the tower up to the wall, but the men defending this portion of the wall fought desperately with stones and fire. When the Count heard that the Franks were already in the city, he said to his men, "Why do you loiter? Lo, the Franks are even now within the city." The Emir who commanded the Tower of St. David surrendered to the Count and opened that gate at which the pilgrims had always been accustomed to pay tribute. But this time the pilgrims entered the city, pursuing and killing the Saracens up to the Temple of Solomon, where the enemy gathered in force. The battle raged throughout the day, so that the Temple was covered with their blood. When the pagans had been overcome, our men seized great numbers, both men and women, either killing them or keeping them captive, as they wished. On the roof of the Temple a great number of pagans of both sexes had assembled, and these were taken under the protection of Tancred and Gaston of *Beert*. Afterward, the army scattered throughout the city and took possession of the gold and silver, the horses and mules, and the houses filled with goods of all kinds.

Later, all of our people went to the Sepulchre of our Lord, rejoicing and weeping for joy, and they rendered up the offering that they owed. In the morning, some of our men cautiously ascended to the roof of the Temple and attacked the Saracens, both men and women, beheading them with naked swords; the remainder sought death by jumping down into the temple. When Tancred heard of this, he was filled with anger.

(*Raymond.*) The Duke and the Counts of Normandy and Flanders placed Gaston of *Beert* in charge of the workmen who constructed machines. They built mantlets and towers with which to attack the wall. The direction of this work was assigned to Gaston by the princes because he was a most noble lord, respected by all for his skill and reputation. He very cleverly hastened matters by dividing the work. The princes busied themselves with obtaining and bringing the material, while Gaston supervised the work of construction. Likewise, Count Raymond made William *Ricau* superintendent of the work on Mount Zion and placed the Bishop of Albara in charge of the Saracens and others who brought in the timber.

The Count's men had taken many Saracen castles and villages and forced the Saracens to work, as though they were their serfs. Thus for the construction of machines at Jerusalem fifty or sixty men carried on their shoulders a great beam that could not have been dragged by four pair of oxen. What more shall I say? All worked with a singleness of purpose, no one was slothful, and no hands were idle. All worked without wages, except the artisans, who were paid from a collection taken from the people. However, Count Raymond paid his workmen from his own treasury. Surely the hand of the Lord was with us and aided those who were working!

When our efforts were ended and the machines completed, the princes held a council and announced: "Let all prepare themselves for a battle on Thursday; in the meantime, let us pray, fast, and give alms. Hand over your animals and your boys to the artisans and carpenters, that they may bring in beams, poles, stakes, and branches to make mantlets. Two knights should make one mantlet and one scaling ladder. Do not hesitate to work for the Lord, for your labors will soon be ended." This was willingly done by all. Then it was decided what part of the city each leader should attack and where his machines should be located.

Meanwhile, the Saracens in the city, noting the great number of machines that we had constructed, strengthened the weaker parts of the wall, so that it seemed that they could be taken only by the most desperate efforts. Because the Saracens had made so many and such strong fortifications to oppose our machines, the Duke, the Count of Flanders, and the Count of Normandy spent the night before the day set for the attack moving their machines, mantlets, and platforms to that side of the city which is between the church of St. Stephen and the valley of Josaphat. You who read this must not think that this was a light undertaking, for the machines were carried in parts almost a mile to the place where they were to be set up. When morning came and the Saracens saw that all the machinery and tents had been moved during the night, they were amazed. Not only the Saracens were astonished, but our people as well, for they recognized that the hand of the Lord was with us. The change was made because the new point chosen for attack was more level, and thus suitable for moving the machines up to the walls, which cannot be done unless the ground is level; and also because that part of the city seemed to be weaker, having remained unfortified, as it was some distance from our camp. This part of the city is on the north.

Count Raymond and his men worked equally hard on Mount

Zion, but they had much assistance from William Embriaco and the Genoese sailors, who, although they had lost their ships at Joppa, as we have already related, had been able, nevertheless, to save ropes, mallets, spikes, axes, and hatchets, which were very necessary to us. But why delay the story? The appointed day arrived and the attack began. However, I want to say this first, that, according to our estimate and that of many others, there were sixty thousand fighting men within the city, not counting the women and those unable to bear arms, and there were not many of these. At the most we did not have more than twelve thousand able to bear arms, for there were many poor people and many sick. There were twelve or thirteen hundred knights in our army, as I reckon it, not more. I say this that you may realize that nothing, whether great or small, which is undertaken in the name of the Lord can fail, as the following pages show.

Our men began to undermine the towers and walls. From every side stones were hurled from the *tormenti* and the *petrariae*, and so many arrows that they fell like hail. The servants of God bore this patiently, sustained by the premises of their faith, whether they should be killed or should presently prevail over their enemies. The battle showed no indication of victory, but when the machines were drawn nearer to the walls, they hurled not only stones and arrows, but also burning wood and straw. The wood was dipped in pitch, wax, and sulphur; then straw and tow were fastened on by an iron band, and, when lighted, these firebrands were shot from the machines. (They were) all bound together by an iron band, I say, so that wherever they fell, the whole mass held together and continued to burn. Such missiles, burning as they shot upward, could not be resisted by swords or by high walls; it was not even possible for the defenders to find safety down behind the walls. Thus the fight continued from the rising to the setting sun in such splendid fashion that it is difficult to believe anything more glorious was ever done. Then we called on Almighty God, our Leader and Guide, confident in His mercy. Night brought fear to both sides. The Saracens feared that we would take the city during the night or on the next day, for the outer works were broken through and the ditch was filled, so that it was possible to make an entrance through the wall very quickly. On our part, we feared only that the Saracens would set fire to the machines that were moved close to the walls, and thus improve their situation. So on both sides it was a night of watchfulness, labor, and sleepless caution: on one side, most certain hope, on the other doubtful fear. We gladly labored to capture the city for the glory of God, they less willingly strove to resist our efforts for the sake of the laws of Mohammed. It is hard to believe how great were the efforts made on both sides during the night.

When the morning came, our men eagerly rushed to the walls and dragged the machines forward, but the Saracens had constructed so many machines that for each one of ours they now had nine or ten. Thus they greatly interfered with our efforts. This was the ninth day, on which the priest had said that we would capture the city. But why do I delay so long? Our machines were now shaken apart by the blows of many stones, and our men lagged because they were very weary. However, there remained the mercy of the Lord which is never overcome nor conquered, but is always a source of support in times of adversity. One incident must not be omitted. Two women tried to bewitch one of the hurling machines, but a stone struck and crushed them, as well as three slaves, so that their lives were extinguished and the evil incantations averted.

By noon our men were greatly discouraged. They were weary and at the end of their resources. There were still many of the enemy opposing each one of our men; the walls were very high and strong, and the great resources and skill that the enemy exhibited in repairing their defenses seemed too great for us to overcome. But, while we hesitated, irresolute, and the enemy exulted in our discomfiture, the healing mercy of God inspired us and turned our sorrow into joy, for the Lord did not forsake us. While a council was being held to decide whether or not our machines should be withdrawn, for some were burned and the rest badly shaken to pieces, a knight on the Mount of Olives began to wave his shield to those who were with the Count and others, signalling them to advance. Who this knight was we have been unable to find out. At this signal our men began to take heart, and some began to batter down the wall, while others began to ascend by means of scaling ladders and ropes. Our archers shot burning firebrands, and in this way checked the attack that the Saracens were making upon the wooden towers of the Duke and the two Counts. These firebrands, moreover, were wrapped in cotton. This shower of fire drove the defenders from the walls. Then the Count quickly released the long drawbridge which had protected the side of the wooden tower next to the wall, and it swung down from the top, being fastened to the middle of the tower, making a bridge over which the men began to enter Jerusalem bravely and fearlessly. Among those who entered first were Tancred and the Duke of Lorraine, and the amount of blood that they shed on that day is incredible. All ascended after them, and the Saracens now began to suffer.

Strange to relate, however, at this very time when the city was practically captured by the Franks, the Saracens were still fighting on the other side, where the Count was attacking the wall as though the city should never be captured. But now that our men had possession of the walls and towers, wonderful sights were to be seen. Some of our men (and this was more merciful) cut off the heads of their enemies; others shot them with arrows, so that they fell from the towers; others tortured them longer by casting them into the flames. Piles of heads, hands, and feet were to be seen in the streets of the city. It was necessary to pick one's way over the bodies of men and horses. But these were small matters compared to what happened at the Temple of Solomon, a place where religious services are ordinarily chanted. What happened there? If I tell the truth, it will exceed your powers of belief. So let it suffice to say this much, at least, that in the Temple and porch of Solomon, men rode in blood up to their knees and bridle reins. Indeed, it was a just and splendid judgment of God that this place should be filled with the blood of the unbelievers, since it had suffered so long from their blasphemies. The city was filled with corpses and blood. Some of the enemy took refuge in the Tower of David, and, petitioning Count Raymond for protection, surrendered the Tower into his hands.

Now that the city was taken, it was well worth all our previous labors and hardships to see the devotion of the pilgrims at the Holy Sepulchre. How they rejoiced and exulted and sang a new song to the Lord! For their hearts offered prayers of praise to God, victorious and triumphant, which cannot be told in words. A new day, new joy, new and perpetual gladness, the consummation of our labor and devotion, drew forth from all new words and new songs. This day, I say, will be famous in all future ages, for it turned our labors and sorrows into joy and exultation; this day, I say, marks the justification of all Christianity, the humiliation of paganism, and the renewal of our faith. "This is the day which the Lord hath made, let us rejoice and be glad in it," for on this day the Lord revevealed Himself to His people and blessed them.

On this day, the Ides of July, Lord Adhemar, Bishop of Puy, was seen in the city by many people. Many also testified that he was the first to scale the wall, and that he summoned the knights and people to follow him. On this day, moreover, the apostles were cast forth from Jerusalem and scattered over the whole world.[14] On this same day, the children of the apostles regained the city and fatherland for God and the fathers. This day, the Ides of July, shall be celebrated to the praise and glory of the name of God, who, answering the prayers of His Church, gave in trust and benediction to His children the city and fatherland which He had promised to the fathers. On this day we chanted the Office of the Resurrection, since on that day He, who by His virtue arose from the dead, revived us through His grace. So much is to be said of this.

4. *Arrangements for holding Jerusalem.* (July 22—August 7, 1099.)

(*Gesta.*) Then our leaders in council decided that each one should offer alms with prayers, that the Lord might choose for Himself whom He wanted to reign over the others and rule the city. They also ordered all the Saracen dead to be cast outside because of the great stench, since the whole city was filled with their corpses; and so the living Saracens dragged the dead before the exits of the gates and aranged them in heaps, as if they were houses. No one ever saw or heard of such slaughter of pagan people, for funeral pyres were formed from them like pyramids, and no one knows their number except God alone. But Raymond caused the Emir and the others who were with him to be conducted to Ascalon, whole and unhurt. However, on the eighth day after the city was captured, they chose Godfrey as head of the city to fight the pagans and guard the Christians. On the day of St. Peter ad Vincula they likewise chose as Patriarch a certain very wise and honorable man, Arnulf by name. This city was captured by God's Christians on the fifteenth day of July, the sixth day of the week.

(*Raymond*). Accordingly, after six or seven days the princes solemnly began to consider the matter of choosing a ruler, who, assuming charge of all matters, should collect the tributes of the region, to whom the peasants of the land could turn, and who would see to it that the land was not further devastated. While this was taking place, some of the clergy assembled and said to the princes, "We approve your election, but if you proceed rightly and properly, you will first choose a spiritual vicar, as eternal matters come before temporal; after this, a ruler to preside over secular matters. Otherwise, we shall hold invalid whatever you do." The princes were exceedingly angered when they heard this and proceeded the more quickly with the election. The clergy had been weakened by the departure of Lord Adhemar, Pontiff of Puy, who, in his life had held our army together with holy deeds and words, like a second Moses. After him, however, William, Bishop of Orange, a man of good repute, wished to minister to our strength, but he rested in peace at Marra within a short time. Accordingly, therefore, the good men having been taken off, the clergy conducted themselves humbly, all except the Bishop of Albara and some others. However, the Bishop of Martirano,[15] advancing by other than the right road, since he had obtained the church of Bethlehem by fraud, was captured by the Saracens on the third or fourth day and never again appeared among us. The princes, disregarding admonition and opposition, urged the Count of St. Gilles to accept the kingdom. But he said that he abhorred the name of king in that city, though he would consent to have others accept it. For this reason they together chose the Duke and placed him in charge of the Sepulchre of the Lord.

After this, however, the Duke required the Tower of David from the Count. But the latter refused, saying that he wished to stay in that region until Easter, and meanwhile he wanted to keep himself and his men in honorable state. But the Duke said that he would give up other places rather than the Tower. And so the disputes were multiplied. The Counts of Flanders and Normandy favored the Duke. Almost all from the land of Count Raymond did likewise in the belief that if the Tower were surrendered he would thereupon return home. Not alone did the Provençals oppose their lord, the Count, in this matter, but they also made up many vile statements about him so that he would not be chosen King. And so the Count, without the help of companions or friends, handed over the Tower to the Bishop of Albara for the sake of avoiding judgment. But the latter, without waiting for judgment, handed it over to the Duke, and when he was called traitor for having done this, he said that he had been compelled (to do so) and had suffered violence. I found this out, in truth, that very many arms were brought into the house of the Patriarch where the Bishop was staying near the Holy Sepulchre. But he spoke, also, of violence done himself and often secretly charged the friends of the Count with this affair.

So when the Tower had been surrendered, the Count blazed forth into great anger against his people, saying that he could not remain disgraced in that country. Accordingly, we set out from Jerusalem to Jericho, took palms and went to the Jordan.[16] There, as Peter Bartholomew had commanded, a raft was constructed from twigs, and with the Count on it we pulled it across the river; since, forsooth, we had no ship, this plan seemed better to us. When after this the multitude had been called together, we commanded that they pray God for the life of the Count and the other princes. Therefore we proceeded to dress only in a shirt and new breeches, as we had been commanded about baptism; but why the man of God so commanded, we still do not know. When these matters had been accomplished, we returned to Jerusalem.

At this time, Arnulf, chaplain of the Count of Normandy, was chosen Patriarch by some, the good (clergy) opposing it not only because he was not a subdeacon, but especially because he was of priestly birth and was accused of incontinence on our expedition, so much so that they shamelessly composed vulgar songs about him. But, led on by such ambition, and disregarding the decrees of the canons and the infamy of his birth and conscience, he stirred up the people against the good (clergy) and had himself raised upon the patriarchal seat with hymns and chants and the great applause of the people. The divine vengeance exacted from the Bishop of Martirano, who had been the instigator and executor of this affair, not only did not terrify Arnulf, but, furthermore, did not prevent him from depriving of their benefices the clergy who had altars in the church of the Holy Sepulchre, or those in whose custody indulgence funds had been established.[17]

And thus Arnulf, increasing his power, began to inquire from the inhabitants of the city where the Cross was which pilgrims had been accustomed to adore before Jerusalem was taken. Although they denied (this knowledge), and by oath and other signs were willing to show that they did not know, they were at length compelled (to yield) and said this: "It is manifest that God has chosen you, has delivered you from all tribulation, and has given you this and many other cities, not by the strength of your valor, but by blinding the impious in His wrath. Your Lord and Guide has opened to you the most strongly fortified cities and has won fearful battles for you. Therefore, why should we stubbornly conceal from you His good gifts, since we see that God is with you?" After this, they led them to a certain hall in the church, and, unearthing the Cross, they gave it up. Thereupon, all our men rejoiced, and we returned praise and thanks to Almighty God, who not only gave us the city in which He had suffered, but likewise the symbols of His Passion and victory, that we might the more closely embrace Him with the arms of faith, the more certain the signs of our salvation that we beheld.

(*Manasses.*) Manasses, by grace of God Archbishop of Rheims, to Lambert, his brother, Bishop of Arras; greeting in Jesus Christ.

Be it known to you, dearest brother, that a true and joyful rumor has recently come to our ears, which we believe to have come down not from human knowledge, but from the Divine Majesty—to wit: Jerusalem stands on high with joy and gladness which it has so gloriously received from God in our times. Jerusalem, the city of our redemption and glory, delights with inconceivable joy, because through the effort and incomparable might of the sons of God it has been liberated from most cruel pagan servitude. And let us also be joyful, whose Christian faith in such times as these has been placed in a mirror of eternal clarity.

We, therefore, admonished, summoned, and compelled, not only through the letters of Lord Pope Paschal, but, also, through the most humble prayers of Duke Godfrey, whom the army of Christ by divine direction elevated as King, as well as through the mellifluous entreaties of Lord Arnulf, whom they have unanimously chosen as Patriarch of the see of Jerusalem—we command with equal affection that you have every one of your parish churches, without fail, pray with fasts and almsgiving that the King of Kings and the Lord of Lords crown the King of the Christians with victory against the enemy, and the Patriarch with religion and wisdom against the sects and deceptions of heretics. We command, likewise, and admonish, through your obedience, that you constrain by threat all who vowed to go on the expedition and took the sign of the cross upon themselves to set out for Jerusalem, if they are vigorous of body and have the means to accomplish the journey. As for the others, however, do not cease skilfully and most devoutly to admonish them not to neglect aiding the people of God, so that not only the first, but likewise the last, may receive the shilling which is promised to those laboring in the vineyard.[18] Farewell.

Pray for the Bishop of Puy, for the Bishop of Orange, for Anselm of Ribemont, and for all the others who lie at rest, crowned with so glorious a martyrdom.

5. *Battle of Ascalon.* (August 7—August 15, 1099.)

(*Gesta.*) Meanwhile, a messenger came to Tancred and Count Eustace, bidding them make themselves ready to go to take the city of Neapolis. They went forth, taking along many knights and foot-soldiers and came to the city, but its inhabitants surrendered there. A short while after this, the Duke sent word to them to come quickly to battle, because the Emir of Babylon was ready at the city of Ascalon. Then they entered the mountainous region in haste, seeking fight with the Saracens, and came to Caesarea. And then, when they had come near the sea to the city of Ramlah, they found there many Arabs who were the forerunners of the battle. Our men pursued these and captured several of them, who told all the news of the battle, where and how many the enemy were, and where they were planning to fight the Christians.

When Tancred heard this, he straightway sent a messenger to Jerusalem to Duke Godfrey, the Patriarch, and all the princes, saying: "Know that battle is being prepared for us at Ascalon. Go there quickly with all the forces that you can obtain." Then the Duke ordered that all be warned to go to Ascalon faithfully prepared against our enemy. He himself, with the Patriarch and Robert, Count of Flanders, went out of the city on the third day of the week, and the Bishop of Martirano with them. But the Count of St. Gilles and Robert the Norman said that they would not go forth unless they knew that battle was certain. Accordingly, they ordered their knights to go and see whether there was really a battle, and to return quickly, because they were ready to go straightway. They went and saw the battle and returned quickly with the news that they had seen it with their own eyes. Forthwith the Duke sent word to Jerusalem by the Bishop of Martirano, who had been taken along, for the knights who were there to prepare themselves and come to battle. On the fourth day of the week those princes went out and rode to battle. The Bishop of Martirano went back, bearing messages for the Patriarch and the Duke, and the Saracens, coming upon him, carried him off captive with them. But Peter the Hermit remained at Jerusalem, ordering and commanding both Greek and Latin clergy faithfully to hold a procession to God, and to offer prayers and alms that God might give victory to His people. Thus the clerics and the priests, dressed in sacred vestments, conducted a procession to the Temple of the Lord, chanting masses and prayers that He might defend His people.

At length the Patriarch, bishops, and the other leaders were assembled at the river which is in the region of Ascalon. There they took plunder of many cattle, camels, sheep, and goods of all kinds. However, almost three hundred Arabs came up and our men rushed upon them and took two of them, pursuing the rest up to their army. When evening came, the Patriarch had it heralded through the whole host that at earliest morning all should be ready for battle, forbidding any man to pay attention to any spoils until the battle was finished, but saying that when this was done they might return with joy of good fortune to take all that was predestined to them by the Lord.

At early dawn on the sixth day of the week, they entered a very beautiful valley near the sea-coast, where they arranged their lines. The Duke drew up his line, the Count of Normandy his, the Count of St. Gilles his, the Count of Flanders his, Tancred and Gaston[19] theirs. They also arranged foot-soldiers and bowmen to precede the knights; and so they ordered everything and began to fight immediately in the name of the Lord Jesus Christ. On the left side was Duke Godfrey with his line, and the Count of St. Gilles rode near the sea on the right side. The Count of Normandy, the Count of Flanders, Tancred, and all the rest rode in the middle. Then our men began to move about a little, but the enemy stood ready for battle. Each one had his water-bag hanging from his neck, out of which they could drink as they pursued us, but by the grace of God they were not accorded this (privilege). Moreover, the Count of Normandy, perceiving that the standard of the Emir had a kind of golden apple on the top of a spear which was worked with silver, rushed violently upon him and wounded him even to death. On another side, the Count of Flanders very fiercely rushed upon the enemy. Tancred, thereupon, made a charge through the middle of their tents, and when the pagans saw this, they straightway took to flight. The multitude of the pagans was innumerable, and no one knows their number except God alone. The battle was huge, but accompanying us was the Divine might, so great, so strong, that we overcame them immediately. Moreover, our enemy stood blinded and stupefied, and, though looking at the knights of Christ with open eyes, they saw nothing; thus terrified at the valor of God, they dared not rise up against the Christians. In the excess of their fear they climbed trees, in which they thought to hide themselves, but our men brought them to earth by shooting and killing them with lances and spears. Others threw themselves on the ground, not daring to stand up against us. Our men cut them to pieces, just as one cuts animals to pieces for the market. The Count of St. Gilles killed them without number, but some flung themselves into the sea, and others fled hither and hither.

Thereupon the Emir, coming in front of the city, grieving and sorrowfully weeping, said: "O Spirits of the Gods! Who ever saw or heard such things? Such might, such valor, such military skill, never exceeded by any people, is now conquered by a band of Christians so little that they could be enclosed in the hollow of a hand. Alas! Grief and sadness are mine! What more shall I say? I am conquered by a race, beggarly, unarmed, and very poor, a race that has nothing except a beggar's scrip and cloak. They now pursue the Egyptian people who commonly gave them alms when in olden times they begged through our whole land. Hither, according to agreement, I have brought together two hundred thousand knights, and, behold, I see them fleeing with loose bridles along the road to Babylon, and they dare not turn back against the Frankish people! I swear by Mohammed and by the names of all the gods that, since I am driven out by this foreign people, I will no longer retain knights for any gathering. I brought all kinds of weapons and instruments and machines to besiege them in Jerusalem, and they have come before me to battle by two days. Alas! What would be mine, if I had led their people as my own! Woe is me! What more shall I say? I will be forever disgraced in the land of Babylon!" Our men, moreover, took his standard, which the Count of Normandy bought for twenty marks of silver, and gave it to the Patriarch, to the honor of God and the Holy Sepulchre; and some one bought the sword for sixty *besants*. And so, God willing, our enemy were conquered.

All the ships of the pagan lands were there, but when the men on them saw the Emir fleeing with his army, they immediately hoisted sail and rode out to deep water. Our men returned to their tents and took a great amount of spoil, gold, silver, a heap of all kinds of goods, horses and mules, asses and camels, innumerable sheep and cattle and instruments; for all the mountains and hills and all the level places were covered with the multitude of the enemy's animals. Finding piles of arms, also, they carried off what they wished and burned the rest. Our men returned with joy to Jerusalem, bringing along goods of every description; to wit, camels and asses laden with biscuit, butter, grain, cheese, bread, oil, and all the goods they needed. This battle was fought on the day before the Ides of August, our Lord Jesus Christ granting this, who hath honor and glory now and ever, forever and ever. Let every spirit say Amen!

(*Raymond.*) And when, as we said above, it had been arranged that the Duke of Lorraine should keep the city, and when the Count, embittered with grief and wrong because he had easily lost the Tower of David (that is, the capital of the whole kingdom of Judaea), was arranging for this reason to turn with most of our people, it was announced to us that the King of Babylon had come to Ascalon with a countless multitude of pagans. And as it was told us, he had come to take Jerusalem by storm, to kill all the Franks above twenty years, to take the rest, together with the women, captive, to give the males to women of his own race, and the women to his youths, so that the lords of Babylon might then have warlike families of the race of the Franks. But not content with this, he said he would do the same with Antioch and Bohemund; he said, likewise, that he would place upon his head the diadems of Damascus and the rest of the cities. He said that the Turks and the Franks, victors over the Turks, were nothing in comparison with the multitude of his foot-soldiers and knights. But not even content with this, he turned in blasphemy against God, saying. "I will destroy the place of the Lord's nativity, and the place where the Lord very often rested, the place of the Passion, and Golgotha, where they say flowed the blood of the Lord hanging upon the Cross, the place of the Lord's burial, and all the other holy places in the city, or nearby, which are venerated by Christian people. I will tear them up by their roots from the earth and break them; and, after this, I will cast the dust into the sea, so that there will no longer be any memorial of the Lord for the people of the Franks to seek."

Moreover, when this and many other things about the multitude of the people who accompanied that tyrant were announced to us, and that all these had been assembled at Ascalon, a day and a half distant from Jerusalem, all our princes and clergy gathered together. Walking with bare feet before the Sepulchre of the Lord, with many prayers and tears they sought mercy from God that He would now deliver His people, whom He had thus far made victorious over all, and that He who had just purified the place of His sanctification for His own name's sake would not suffer it again to be contaminated. After this, we went, likewise on bare feet, to the Temple of the Lord, and, calling upon God's mercy in psalms and hymns, and on the treasures of the saints, we there poured forth from soul and body before God (the plea) that the outpouring of His blessing might likewise be recorded, saying: "If thy people sin against thee, and, turning again, shall do penance and shall come and pray in this place, hear thou them from heaven, O Lord, and deliver them from the hands of their enemies." After this, when they had received the benediction from the bishops, the princes decided upon the plan of the battle and the guard of the city.

Thereupon, the Duke and his knights set forth to find out for certain if the news about the Emir was as rumor reported it. When they had reached the plains of Ramlah, he sent back word to the Counts at Jerusalem by the Bishop of Martirano.[20] Thus assured of battle, they sent word among all the strong who had remained in Jerusalem. Thereupon, after supplicating God and taking up our arms and the Lance of the Lord, we set out from Jerusalem and came to the plains on that day. On the next day, moreover, with our army joined in squadrons we advanced, stationing garrisons on every side. But at evening when we had come near the river, which is on the way of those who go from Jerusalem to Ascalon, Arabs were grazing their flocks of sheep, innumerable herds of cattle, and camels without number. When our men saw this multitude of men and animals, thinking that there would be a battle, they seized their arms and sent about two hundred knights to reconnoiter; but the other armed men, as we said, were advancing in nine squadrons. There were three on the rear, three in front, and three in the middle, so arranged that from whatever side battle came, it would be met in those three ranks, the middle squadron remaining as a support of all. When the Arab herdsmen, however, saw the knights who had been sent ahead, they deserted their animals. And yet, if God were regarding them as He regarded us, they should have entered upon a fight with all of us. There were about three thousand herdsmen in arms, but to our army we hesitatingly ascribe more than twelve hundred knights, while we dare not put the number of footmen beyond nine thousand. And so when the herdsmen had fled, we took as much plunder as we saw on that day. Some of the herdsmen were killed and a few captured. After this, however, we remained in the same place because it was evening. And then we forced the captives to confess the intentions of the enemy, their condition and number. They confessed, therefore, that it was the will of these people to besiege Jerusalem, take the Franks by storm, kill and capture them, and they added that the Emir was in camp, five leagues away, ready to set forth against us on the next day. Of their number, however, scarcely anyone was certain, since they were being multiplied daily. When questioned about themselves and their companions, they said they were herders of animals which were to be distributed for a price among the forces of Babylonians.

Accordingly, our men, eager and assured of battle, sent back to their companions the causes of trouble and controversy. After this, they confessed their sins and negligence and were so cheered in spirit that it seemed scarcely credible to them that the enemy were prepared for battle. For such security grew up in the hearts of each man that they believed their enemy more timid than hinds, and more harmless than sheep. But we had this security because we believed that God was with us, as in the other matter, and that because of the blasphemy made against Him He would deal (with them) on His own account, even if our cause were valueless. Therefore we regarded Him as our Defender, and ourselves as aids to Him in His (struggle). Then it was proclaimed through the army that all should be ready for battle in the morning, and that each one should attach himself to the princes of his people, and that no one should touch plunder, and that any who touched it before the battle was finished would be excommunicated. We spent that night poorly enough, for we had no tents; a few had bread, no one wine, and very few grain and salt, but meat was as abundant as sand. We ate meat, and for bread we had the soft flesh of sheep.

And now the morning of the following day was dawning, and the watchful host was aroused to the fight by the sound of trumpets and horns. So at daybreak we set forth, drawn up as we have already described, with guards on every side, and directed the army of God against the camp of Mohammed. But the enemy lingered within their camp, thinking that at their approach we would not even stay inside our walls. For when they heard of the death and flight of the herdsmen, they said, "The Franks have come for plunder and have gone back with it." They were being daily informed, forsooth, by those who fled from Jerusalem of our small numbers and of the weakness of our people and horses. Besides, relying on their number and strength, they believed that they could drown us and our camp in their spit alone. Likewise, their stargazers and soothsayers, as it was reported, said that they ought neither to move their camp nor fight against us until the seventh day of the week; that if they wished to do any of these things earlier, matters would turn out adversely. We advanced, drawn up in squadrons, as we have said. God multiplied His army so that we did not seem inferior in numbers to the enemy. For the animals which we had left joined themselves to us and, forming, herds, though no one drove them, they accompanied us, so that they stood when we halted, ran when we ran, and advanced with our advance. The amount of precious spoil was inestimable. Moreover, who can count all the arms or tents? When our enemy saw their multitude cut to pieces and our men securely and eagerly fighting in their tents for victory and spoil, they turned and said to themselves, "Flight is our only protection, and why delay? If these men, worn out from their march, almost half dead from hunger and thirst, have today prostrated all our multitude at one charge, what will they do when rested, refreshed, and victorious against us, half destroyed, lessened in number, and terrified?" Accordingly, the enemy returned with disturbed mind to Ascalon, which was about a mile from our camp—but not all of them.

It then pleased Raymond to send a certain Bohemund, a Turk by birth, to the Emir under pretense of entering upon a friendship, blaming him because he had been unwilling to surrender Jerusalem freely and because he had borne arms against us. Bohemund was at the same time to find out whether the Emir was meditating flight or battle, and how he conducted himself in defeat. This Bohemund, moreover, was a Turk by birth, learned in many tongues, very ingenious and crafty and most loyal to us. He was called Bohemund because the great Bohemund had received him from the baptismal font, for he had come to us with his wife and arms.

The book of Raymond of St. Gilles is ended happily.

6. *Bohemund and Baldwin fulfil their vow.* (November, 1099—January, 1100.)

(*Fulcher.*) . . . . . . Lord Bohemund, a wise and energetic man, was then ruling in Antioch, while Baldwin, a brother of the aforesaid Godfrey, ruled Edessa and the neighboring lands across the Euphrates river. When these two heard that Jerusalem had been taken by those who had set out as their companions, they were made most joyful and humbly gave thanks to God. But if those who preceded them had done well and successfully, it is not to be doubted that these two, with their forces, were to partake of the glory, even though they followed later. For it was necessary that the land and states taken with such difficulty from the Turks should be carefully guarded. These, if left unguarded, might be recovered in a renewed attack by the Turks, who were now driven back to Persia. In this case, great harm would befall all the Franks going to Jerusalem, as well as returning. Perhaps Divine Providence, knowing that Bohemund and Baldwin would be more useful to the army in what remained to be done than in what was already done, had delayed them.

Oh, how many times, in the meantime, this same Baldwin was wearied in making war against the Turks in the land of Mesopotamia! To tell how many of their heads he cut off there would be impossible. Often it happened that he with his few men fought a great multitude of them and, with the help of God, rejoiced in triumph. And when Bohemund, through legates, had advised Baldwin that they and their men should both complete the unfinished journey to Jerusalem, Baldwin, arranging satisfactorily all his affairs, prepared to go. Then, hearing that the Turks had invaded one section of his country, he suspended the execution of his project, and without taking time to assemble his little army, he went against the enemy with a few men. On a certain day when the Turks, unconcerned in their tents, were thinking that Baldwin had already commenced his journey, all at once they saw the white flag which he carried; and, struck with fear, they took to flight. After following them a little way with his few men, Baldwin returned to complete what he had just planned.

Setting out and passing to the left of Antioch, he came to Laodicaea, where he bought provisions for the journey and reloaded the pack animals and set out. It was the month of November.

After we had passed by Gibellum, we overtook Bohemund camped in his tents before the city Valenium. There was with him a certain Archbishop of Pisa, Daimbert by name,[21] who, with some Tuscans and Italians, had come by ship to the port of Laodicaea, and who was there waiting to go with us. The Bishop of Apulia was there, too. With Lord Baldwin there was a third bishop. We estimated the number of those thus assembled in friendship to be twenty-five thousand of both sexes, foot-soldiers as well as knights.

When we had reached the interior states of the Saracens, we were unable to obtain from the wicked inhabitants of the region any bread or food of any kind. There was no one who would give or sell it to us, and, as our provisions were being more and more used up, it happened that many were cruelly tortured by hunger. Horses, too, and mules suffered doubly for lack of food. They traveled, but they ate not. However, in those cultivated fields through which we passed on our march, there were certain ripe plants, very much like reeds, which the people called *cannamelles*. The name is composed of the words *canna* and *mel*, whence, I think, it is also called wood-honey,[22] which is skilfully made from it. Almost famished, we chewed these all day long for the flavor of the honey, which, however, helped but little. Thus for the love of God we endured this and many other ills, such as hunger, cold, and heavy rains. Many, lacking bread, ate horses, mules, and camels. Besides the excessive cold, we were tormented very often by showers of rain; and the heat of the sun was not sufficient to enable us to dry our wet clothes thoroughly before another rain would harass us for four or five days. Then I saw many who had no tents die from exposure to the cold rain. I, Fulcher of Chartres, who was with them, saw many persons of both sexes and a great many beasts die from the very cold rain one day. It would be long to tell and tedious to listen to all the details of their suffering; for no trouble or sorrow escaped the people of God. Often many Franks were killed by the Saracens who lurked along the way in narrow paths, or wherever our men went in search of food. You might have seen mounted knights of noble birth become simple foot-soldiers, after having lost their horses in one way or another. As the baggage animals failed, you might have seen sheep and goats, stolen from the Saracens, heavily laden with baggage, which by its weight skinned their backs. Twice on the way, and no oftener, we had bread and grain, bought at exorbitant prices from the people of Tripoli and Caesarea. From this it is manifest that one can scarcely get any great good without great labor. It was indeed a great blessing when we finally arrived at Jerusalem.

When we reached there, our long fatigue was forgotten. When we viewed the much longed for Holy of Holies, we were filled with joy indescribable. Oh, how often we recalled to mind that prophecy of David which says, "We shall worship in the place where His feet have stood!"[23] We beheld that prophecy truly fulfilled in us, although it likewise pertains to many others. Thither, indeed, did we go up, "the tribes, the tribes of the Lord, to confess His name"[24] in His holy place. On the day of our entrance into Jerusalem, the retreating sun, having fulfilled its winter descent, resumed its ascending course.

After we had visited the Lord's Sepulchre and His Glorious Temple and many other sacred places, on the fourth day we went to Bethlehem, in order that, as we were about to celebrate the anniversary of the nativity of our Lord, we might that very night be watchers in the stable where the Holy Mother laid Jesus, and there assist in the devotions. All that night we filled with appropriate devotions; and in the third hour, after three masses had been celebrated, we returned to Jerusalem. Oh, what a stench there then was around the wall of the city, inside and outside, from the dead bodies of the Saracens, massacred by our colleagues on the capture of the city, wherever they had hunted them down!

But after we and our beasts had been refreshed for some time with a much needed rest, and after the Duke and other leaders had chosen Daimbert, mentioned above, as Patriarch in the church of the Holy Sepulchre, we got new supplies of provisions, and, loading our mules, we went down again to the river Jordan. Some of the army, the last to arrive, chose to remain in Jerusalem; others who had come first preferred to go with us; but Duke Godfrey continued energetically to rule the territory of Jerusalem.

On the third day, before the Ides of August, those sickly days, Urban, Pontiff of Rome, passed away.

On the first day of January 1100 A.D. we all took palm branches, cut in Jericho, to carry them off, as was customary. On the second day we commenced our return journey. Our leaders wished to cross through the city of Tiberias on the sea of Galilee. This sea, formed from a union of fresh waters, is eighteen miles long and five wide. We went from there to Caesarea-Philippi, which in the Syrian tongue is called Paneas, and which is situated at the foot of Mount Lebanon. There two springs gush forth which give rise to the river Jordan. This Jordan, flowing through the Sea of Galilee, then runs into the Dead Sea. The Lake of Gennesaret,[25] according to Josephus, is forty stades wide and one hundred long. The river, then, flowing in one channel, spreads out into a sea which is called

Dead because nothing living flourishes in it. This sea, which is called Lake Asphaltites, is believed to be bottomless and to have buried in its depths the cities of Sodom and Gomorrah. Following St. Jerome, whom I read in his exposition upon the prophet Amos, I conjectured quite carefully with regard to these springs that Dan was located in that part of Judea where Paneas now is; for the tribe of Dan built there a city which they called by the name of their father, Dan. For this reason, I think the one spring was called Dan, and the other Jor which was adjacent to it. Then we came to a very strong city which they called Balbec, built by Solomon, and surrounded by high walls, and called by him Thadamar.[26] This is situated a two days march from upper Syria, about six days journey from great Babylon, and about one day's march from the Euphrates. The Greeks called this place Palmyra. Here springs and wells abound; but water was never found in the lower land.

Then about four hundred soldiers of the Turks of Damascus came out to meet us. Because they thought we were unarmed and greatly exhausted from our labors, they supposed that we were also discouraged. If Lord Baldwin had not on that day cautiously and carefully guarded the rear, perhaps they would have killed many of us. For our bows and arrows were spoiled in a rainstorm, since in that region they were fastened together with glue. Bohemund was leading the first division of our army. So, with the help of God, the pagans got no advantage of us. Then we camped before that town. On the very next day approaching nearer to the sea, we passed over the the cities of Tortosa and Laodicaea. There at Laodicaea we found Count Raymond, whom we had left there. Because food was scarce, we could buy no supplies on which we could live. Therefore we hastened, without stopping, until we arrived at Edessa. . . .

7. *Official summary of the Crusade.* (June 19, 1097—August 12, 1099.)

(*Daimbert.*) To the lord Pope of the Roman Church, to all the bishops, and all who cherish the Christian faith; I, Archbishop of Pisa, and the other bishops, Duke Godfrey, now, by grace of God, Defender of the Holy Sepulchre, Raymond, Count of St. Gilles, and all the army of God which is in the land of Israel; greeting and prayer.

Multiply your prayers and supplications with joy and exultation in the sight of the Lord, since God has enlarged His compassion by fulfilling in us what He promised in olden times. For, after the capture of Nicaea when the whole army departed thence, there were more than 300,000 soldiers. And though this multitude was so great that it could have occupied all Romania, drunk up all the rivers, and consumed all the vegetation in one day, yet the Lord conducted them in such plenty that a ram was bought for one *denarius,* an ox for less than twelve. Furthermore, even though the princes and kings of the Saracens rose up against us, nevertheless, God willing, they were easily conquered and crushed. And so, because some were puffed up at the happy outcome of these events, God opposed to us Antioch, a city impregnable to human might, and detained us there for nine months, and so humbled us in the siege outside the city until every swelling of our arrogance relapsed into humility.

Accordingly, when we had been brought so low that scarcely one hundred sound horses were found in the whole army, God opened up to us the supply of His blessing and compassion, led us into the city, and made subject to our sway the Turks and all their possessions. Since we took this as if it were acquired by our own strength, and did not worthily glorify God, who had conferred it, we were besieged by such a multitude of Saracens that no one dared to go out of the city, great as it was. In addition, famine grew so powerful in the city that some could scarcely restrain themselves from eating human flesh. It is a long story to recount all the misery which was present in the city. However, the Lord looked again upon His people whom He had so long chastised, and consoled them kindly. Accordingly, first, as if to make reparation for our suffering, He gave us His Lance, a gift not seen since the time of the apostles. Then, He so animated the hearts of the men that those whom sickness or starvation had deprived of strength to walk about were now infused with power to take up arms and fight courageously. Then, when the enemy had been triumphantly overcome, the army left Antioch because of famine, disgust, and especially because of the quarrels among the princes.

Setting out into Syria, we took by storm the Saracen cities, Barra and Marra, and acquired all the fortresses of the region. While we were delaying here and there, there was so great a famine in the army that the already fetid bodies of Saracens were eaten by Christian people. At length, when upon Divine admonition we were advancing into the interior of Hispania, we had with us the most generous, compassionate, and most victorious hand of the Omnipotent Father. For the citizens and chatelains of the region through which we were advancing sent ambassadors with many gifts, who were ready to serve us and to surrender their walled places. But because our army was not large, and all were in haste to go to Jerusalem, we accepted their pledges and made them tributary, since, forsooth, one of the many cities which are on that sea-coast had more men than were in our army. And when they heard at Antioch, at Laodicaea, and at Edessa that the hand of the Lord was with us, more of the army who had remained there overtook us at Tyre.

Accordingly, with God thus our Fellow-voyager and Helper, we came even to Jerusalem. And while the army was laboring in the siege of that city with great difficulty, especially on account of the scarcity of water, a council was held, and the bishops and princes announced that a procession was to be made around the city with bare feet. (This was done) that He who had entered it in humility for our sake might, through our humility, open it to us to do justice on His enemies for His sake. Accordingly, the Lord, pleased at this humility, granted the city with His enemies to us on the eighth day after our humiliation, on this day, to wit, when the primitive Church was expelled from Jerusalem, the day when the festival of the Dispersion of the Apostles is celebrated by many of the faithful. And, if you desire to know what was done about the enemy whom we found there, know that in the portico of Solomon and in his Temple, our men rode in the blood of the Saracens up to the knees of the horses.

Then, when it had been arranged who should hold the city, and the others wanted to return home for love of their fatherland, or affection for their parents, it was announced that the King of Babylon had come to Ascalon, with a countless multitude of pagans, to lead the Franks who were at Jerusalem into captivity, and to take Antioch by storm. So he himself had said; the Lord, however, had decided otherwise concerning us. Accordingly, when we had found out in truth that the army of Babylon was at Ascalon, we hastened to meet them, leaving our baggage and our sick at Jerusalem with a garrison. When our army was face to face with that of the enemy, upon bended knees we invoked God as our aid, who in our other times of need had confirmed the law of Christians, (praying Him) in the present battle to break the strength of the Saracens and the devil, and to extend the kingdom of Christ and the Church everywhere from sea to sea. Nor was there delay. God was present with those who cried out to Him, and He administered such strength of courage that any one who saw us rush upon the enemy might have likened us to a sluggish stag thirsting for a fountain of running water. It was, indeed, accomplished in marvelous manner, for in our army there could not have been more than 5000 knights and 15,000 foot-soldiers; in that of the enemy 100,000 knights and 400,000 foot-soldiers. Then marvelous did the Lord appear among His servants, since, before we came into (actual) conflict, He turned this multitude to flight as a result of our charge alone, and snatched away all their arms, so that if they should wish thereafter to fight against us, they would not have arms to rely upon. As to the quantity of spoil, however, which was captured, no question should be asked where the treasures of the King of Babylon were concerned. In that place we killed more than one hundred thousand Moors by the sword. The fear of these people, moreover, was so great that about two thousand of them were suffocated in the gate of the city. Of those, furthermore, who perished in the sea, there is no count. Thickets of thorns, likewise, held many of them. The world was surely fighting in our behalf, and had not the spoils of the camp detained many of our men, there would be few of that great multitude of the enemy able to bring back tidings of the battle. And though it may be tedious, nevertheless this should not be omitted: on the day before the battle was to occur the army captured many thousands of camels, oxen, and sheep. And when the people let them go, at the command of the princes, wonderful to relate, the camels formed many and multiple squadrons, the oxen and sheep likewise. Moreover, these animals accompanied us so closely that they halted when we halted, marched when we marched, and charged when we charged. Clouds, too, protected us from the heat of the sun and cooled us.

And so, when the victory had been celebrated, the army returned to Jerusalem. Leaving Duke Godfrey there, Raymond, Count of St. Gilles, Robert, Count of Normandy, and Robert, Count of Flanders[27] returned to Laodicaea, where they found the fleet of the Pisans and Bohemund. And when the Pisan Archbishop had brought Bohemund and our lords into concord, Count Raymond arranged to return to Jerusalem for the sake of God and our brothers.

Accordingly, in addition to such wonderful devotion of bravery on the part of our brothers, such glorious and coveted retribution on the part of the Omnipotent, such greatly desired remission of all our sins through the Grace of God, and exaltation of the Catholic church of Christ and all the Latin people, we urge that He may cause you also to sit at the right hand of God, who liveth and reigneth God forever and ever. Amen.

We ask and beseech you through the Lord Jesus who was ever with us, shared our labors, and snatched us from tribulations, that you be mindful of your brethren, who are returning to you, by benefitting them, and cancelling their debts, that God may benefit you and absolve you from all your sins, that God may grant you a share in all the blessings which we or they have deserved from God. Amen.

Moreover, Jerusalem was captured by the Christians in the year 1099, on the Ides of July, the sixth day of the week, in the Seventh Indiction, the third year of their setting forth. Their first battle was at the bridge over the river Orontes, in which many Turks were killed on the ninth day before the Kalends of March. The second battle was fought at Nicaea on the third day before the Nones of March, in which the pagans were beaten by the Christians. Their third battle was on the fourth day before the Kalends of July, at Antioch, the Lance of the Lord, recently found, preceding them. The fourth occurred on the Kalends of July. Moreover, the Turks were likewise beaten in Romania. Their fifth battle occurred on the Ides of July, when, after the thirty ninth day of the siege, Jerusalem was captured. Their sixth battle was fought on the fourth day before the Kalends of August, at Ascalon, against the king of Babylon, in which 100,000 knights, and 40,000 foot-soldiers were defeated and destroyed by a small army of Christians. Thanks be to God! The letter endeth.

The Pope's response to the news of the capture of Jerusalem.

(*Paschal*) Paschal, bishop, servant of the servants of God, to all archbishops, bishops, and abbots throughout Gaul; greeting and apostolic blessing.

We owe boundless gratitude to the compassion of Almighty God, since in our time He has deigned to wrest the Church in Asia from the hands of the Turks and to open to Christian soldiers the very city of the Lord's suffering and burial. However, we ought to follow Divine grace with what means He has given us, and effectively aid our brethren who have remained in those districts which were once the lands of the people of Palestine or Canaan. Urge, therefore, all the soldiers of your region to strive for remission and forgiveness of their sins by hastening to our Mother Church of the East; especially compel those who have assumed the sign of the cross in pledge of this journey to hasten thither, unless they are prevented by the hindrance of poverty.[28] Moreover, we decree that those be held in disgrace who left the siege of Antioch through weak or questionable faith; let them remain in excommunication, unless they affirm with certain pledges that they will return. We furthermore command that all their possessions be restored to those brethren who are returning after the victory of the Lord, just as you recall was ordained in a synodal decree by Urban, our predecessor of blessed memory. Do thus in all matters, being so zealous in your duty that by common zeal our Mother Church of the East may be restored to her due state, the Lord granting it.

EPILOGUE

(The accounts of the Crusades of 1101, of the expeditions of the Genoese, of the Pisans, of the Venetians and of the Norwegians, all of them in response to Urban's call at Clermont might well be included as part of the First Crusade but space does not permit. The brief statements of Fulcher about the general condition of the Christians in the Holy Land in 1100 and twenty years later are added in conclusion.)

1. *Conditions in the Holy Land during the first years of the Latin Kingdom.*

(*Fulcher*). . . . In the beginning of his reign Baldwin was the possessor of very few cities and people; yet, through that same winter he protected his kingdom well against enemies on all sides. And because they found out that he was a very courageous fighter, although he had few men, they did not dare to attack him. If he had had more soldiers, he would have met the enemy gladly. The land route was still completely obstructed to our pilgrims—Franks, Angles, Italians, and Venetians—who with from one to four ships came timidly by sea to Joppa, the Lord leading them as they sailed through the midst of hostile pirates and past the cities of the Saracens. At first Joppa was our only port. When we saw that they had come from our western lands, immediately and joyfully we advanced to meet them as if they were saints. Each of us inquired anxiously from them concerning his own home and his loved ones. The newcomers told us all that they knew. When we heard good news, we rejoiced; when they told of misfortune, we were saddened. They came on to Jerusalem; they visited the Holy of Holies, for which purpose they had come. Then some remained here in the Holy Land; but others returned to their native country. For this reason Jerusalem was depopulated and there were not enough people to defend the city from the Saracens, if only they dared to attack us. . . .

2. *Twenty years later.*

(*Fulcher*). . . . Consider, I pray, and reflect how in our time God has transferred the West into the East. For we who were Occidentals now have been made Orientals. He who was a Roman or a Frank is now a Galilaean, or an inhabitant of Palestine. One who was a citizen of Rheims or of Chartres now has been made a citizen of Tyre or of Antioch. We have already forgotten the places of our birth; already they have become unknown to many of us, or, at least, are unmentioned. Some already possess here homes and servants which they have received through inheritance. Some have taken wives not merely of their own people, but Syrians, or Armenians, or even Saracens who have received the grace of baptism. Some have with them father-in-law, or daughter-in-law, or son-in-law, or step-son, or step-father. There are here, too, grandchildren and great-grandchildren.[29] One cultivates vines, another the fields. The one and the other use mutually the speech and the idioms of the different languages.[30] Different languages, now made common, become known to both races, and faith unites those whose forefathers were strangers. As it is written, "The lion and the ox shall eat straw together." Those who were strangers are now natives; and he who was a sojourner now has become a resident. Our parents and relatives from day to day come to join us, abandoning, even though reluctantly, all that they possess. For those who were poor there, here God makes rich. Those who had few coins, here possess countless besants; and those who had not had a villa, here, by the gift of God, already possess a city. Therefore, why should one who has found the East so favorable return to the West? God does not wish those to suffer want who, carrying their crosses, have vowed to follow Him, nay even unto the end. You see, therefore, that this is a great miracle, and one which must greatly astonish the whole world. Who has ever heard anything like it? Therefore, God wishes to enrich us all and to draw us to Himself as His most dear friends. And because He wishes it, we also freely desire the same; and what is pleasnig to Him we do with a loving and submissive heart, that with Him we may reign happily throughout eternity.

NOTES TO INTRODUCTION

[1] Bishop Stubbs, quoted by George L. Burr in the *American Historical Review* for April, 1901, page 439.

[2] Gibbon: *Decline and Fall of the Roman Empire*, Chapters LVIII-LXI.

[3] The following fourteen letters have been translated from the Latin texts edited by Hagenmeyer in his *Epistulae et Chartae . . . Primi Belli Sacri:*

II. Urban II to all the faithful assembling in Flanders. Written about the end of December, 1095. Pages 42-43.

IV. Stephen of Blois to his wife, Adele. Written from Nicaea, June 24, 1097. Pages 100-101; 107-109.

VI. Simeon, Patriarch of Jerusalem, and Adhemar, Bishop of Puy, to the faithful of the northern regions. Written from Antioch, October, 1097. Page 132.

VIII. Anselm of Ribemont to Manasses, Archbishop of Rheims. Written from Antioch about the end of November, 1097. Pages 106-107; 129.

IX. The Patriarch of Jerusalem to all the bishops of the West. Written from camp at Antioch, January, 1098. Pages 142-144.

X. Stephen of Blois to his wife, Adele. Written from Antioch, March 29, 1098. Pages 131-132, 155-157.

XI. Alexius to Oderisius, Abbot of Monte Casino. Written from Constantinople, June, 1098. See Chapter III, n. 26. Pages 110-111.

XII. Bohemund, son of Robert Guiscard, Raymond, Count of St. Gilles, Duke Godfrey, and Hugh the Great, to all the faithful in Christ. Written from Antioch, either October, 1097(?) or April-July, 1098. Pages 130-131.

XV. Anselm of Ribemont to Manasses, Archbishop of Rheims, July, 1098. Pages 157-160; 189-191.

XVI. Bohemund, Raymond, Count of St. Gilles, Godfrey, Duke of Lorraine, Robert, Count of Normandy, Robert, Count of Flanders, and Eustace, Count of Boulogne to Pope Urban II. Written from Antioch, September 11, 1098. Pages 160-161; 192-195.

XVII. The Clergy and people of Lucca to all the faithful. Written from Lucca, October, 1098. Pages 161-162; 191-192.

XVIII. Daimbert, Archbishop of Pisa, Duke Godfrey, Raymond of St. Gilles, and the whole army in the land of Israel to the Pope and all the faithful in Christ. Written from Laodicea, September, 1099. Pages 275-279.

XIX. Pascal II to all the archbishops, bishops and abbots of Gaul. Written about the end of December 1099. Page 279.

XX. Manasses, Archbishop of Rheims to Lambert, Bishop of Arras. Written from Rheims, November or December, 1099. Pages 264-265.

[4] The following are the accounts contained in this book:

1. *Anonymi Gesta Francorum et aliorum Hierosolymitanorum.* Translated in full from Hagemeyer's edition. To read in the order of the

NOTES

original, see pages 28, 57, 71, 57, 80, 62, 93, 98, 101, 113, 118, 120, 123, 125, 132, 136, 144, 151, 163, 169, 174, 182, 195, 204, 214, 223, 242, 249, 256, 262, 265.

2. *Historia Francorum qui ceperunt Jerusalem,* by Raymond of Aguilers. Translated in full from the text in the *Recueil des Historiens des Croisades, Historiens Occidentaux,* III. To read in the order of the original see pages 8, 64, 97, 103, 116, 124, 126, 134, 139, 147, 153, 168, 173, 176, 182, 173, 185, 197, 207, 217, 224, 243, 250, 257, 262, 268.

3. *Historia Hierosolymitana,* by Fulcher of Chartres. Translated in part from Hagenmeyer's edition. Preface: I, chapters 1-14, 33-34; II, chapter 6 *passim;* III, chapter 37 *passim.* To read in the order of the original see pages 24, 26, 28, 40, 24, 44, 45, 56, 61, 67, 99, 104, 105, 116, 118, 119, 121, 272.

4. *The Alexiad,* by Anna Comnena. Translated in part from the edition by Reifferscheid. Vol. II, Book X; chapters 5-6 *passim;* 7; 9 *passim;* 10; 11 *passim;* Book XI; chapters 2-3 *passim;* pages 70, 76, 86, 94, 99, 109.

5. *Historia de Hierosolimitano Itinere,* by Peter Tudebode. Only the variations from the *Gesta* are indicated and are to be found in the notes. The edition used was that of the *Rec. Occid.* III. See also Molinier: *Sources de l'histoire de France,* nos. 2115-2116.

6. *Hierosolymita,* by Ekkehard, Abbot of Aura. Translated in part from Hagenmeyer's edition, chapters VIII-XIII. See pages 41, 46, 53.

7. *Gesta Tancredi,* by Raoul de Caen. Translated in part from the text in *Rec. Occid.* III; chapters 99-103, 108-109. See page 237.

8. *Liber Christianae expeditionis pro ereptione, emundatione, restitutione Sanctae Hierosolymitanae,* by Albert of Aix. Translated in part from the text in the *Rec. Occid.* IV. Included in this translation are I, chapters 2, 6-8, 15-24, 26-30, *passim;* II, chapters 1-17 *passim.* It has been thought necessary to translate only the gist of the matter contained in most of the chapters, as Albert was not, strictly speaking, an eye witness. Pages 48, 54, 57, 73, 80.

9. *Hierosolymitana Expeditio,* by Robert the Monk. The report of Urban's speech at Clermont, as contained in *Rec. Occid.* Vol. III, Book I, chapters 1-2, has alone been translated. Page 30.

10. *Historia Hierosolymitana* by Balderic, Archbishop of Dol. Urban's speech at Clermont; contained in *Rec. Occid.* IV, Book I, chapters 4-5, has alone been translated. Page 33.

11. *Gesta Dei per Francos,* by Guibert, Abbot of Nogent. Here the speech of Urban and the description of Peter the Hermit, contained in *Rec. Occid.* IV, Book II, chapters 4-6, have alone been translated. Pages 36-47.

[5] "He who first wrote this should be believed, since he was on the expedition and saw it with the eyes of his body—to wit, Peter Tudebode of Civray." See Tud. XIV: 6.

[6] For a more detailed discussion of this point, see Kugler: *Analekten zur*

Kritik Albert's von Aachen, and the summary of the discussion in Molinier: *Les sources de l'histoire de France,* no. 2126.

[7] For a comprehensive treatment of mediaeval chronology, consult Grotefend: *Taschenbuch der Zeitrechnung,* or Giry: *Manuel de Diplomatique.*

[8] Delbrück: *Geschichte der Kriegskunst,* III, pp. 228-29.

NOTES TO PROLOGUE AND CHAPTER I

[1] The Maccabees were followers of Judas Maccabeus, whose exploits are described in the Book of Maccabees. The name recurs frequently in the accounts of the First Crusade. The deeds of the Maccabees, recalled by Urban in his speech at Clermont, served as a heroic model for emulation by the Crusaders. It is interesting to note the opinions of the different chroniclers as to the success of the Crusaders in this aim.

[2] This is an interesting example of geographical terminology. These names were not used to designate those particular regions in the mediaeval period, but were all drawn from Fulcher's store of ancient and chiefly Biblical knowledge. His use of the terms must be regarded as a rhetorical device.

[3] Psalms 33:12.

[4] For a thorough analysis of the various accounts of Urban's speech at Clermont see article by D. C. Munro in the *American Historical Review* for January, 1906.

[5] Though Henry had been crowned King of Germany in 1054, he did not receive the imperial crown until 1084, after he had driven Gregory VII from Rome and installed the antipope, Clement III. Under the circumstances, no loyal adherent of Gregory's could recognize Henry as rightful Emperor. Furthermore, Conrad of Franconia was disputing the imperial claims at this time.

[6] Urban II, formerly Odo, Otho, or Odoard of Largny, or Lagny, in the neighborhood of Rheims, was of noble birth. He entered the service of the Church and had risen to the rank of archdeacon in its secular hierarchy when he decided to attach himself to the monastery at Cluny. Here his learning and zeal for reform won him recognition and he was made prior. In 1078 Gregory made him Cardinal-Bishop of Ostia. Gregory esteemed him very highly and in 1084 sent him as envoy to Henry IV, who imprisoned him for a short time on account of his loyalty to the Pope. Just before Gregory's death, his name was mentioned as one of four men whom Gregory regarded as qualified to carry on his policies. The Abbot of Monte Cassino, who took the title Victor III, was chosen first, but upon his early death in 1087, Odo was elected, and in 1088 he was consecrated Pope Urban II. He carried on the fight with Henry IV throughout the eleven years of his pontificate. Usually in exile from Rome, he found the struggle at first very discouraging. The Normans of southern Italy remained true to him, however, and so also did Matilda of Tuscany. Gradually he gained other support, and after the Crusaders started on the journey he was enabled,

with their help, to regain Rome. The last two years of his life were spent in relative quiet, and he died peacefully at Rome July 29, 1099.

[7] Wibert, who was descended from a very influential family in northern Italy, had risen to the highest ecclesiastical dignity in Italy, the archbishopric of Ravenna. In the quarrel between Gregory and Henry he sided with the latter. In 1084, with Henry's help he was installed in Rome as antipope, taking the title Clement III. Shortly afterward, he crowned Henry as Emperor and continued to dispute the papal title until his death in 1100.

[8] Matilda, Countess of Tuscany, had sheltered Gregory VII at Canossa in the winter of 1076-7, and she remained a staunch friend of the Reform Church Party until the time of her death in 1115.

[9] Matt. 5:13.
[10] Matt. 15:14.
[11] Luke 16:19-31.
[12] The Truce of God, which forbade any violation of peace between vespers on Wednesday and sunrise on Monday. The allusion to the former enactment may refer to a similar decree passed by a Church council in southern France in 1041.

[13] Luke 16:24.
[14] Matt. 10:22.
[15] Matt. 10:32.
[16] Matt. 5:12.
[17] Matt. 10:37.
[18] Matt. 19:29.
[19] Ex. 3:8.
[20] Matt. 18:20.
[21] Matt. 10:38.
[22] See the account by Caffaro, *Liberatio Orientis,* XIV.
[23] Psalms 79:12.
[24] Judges 19:10; Gen. 15:21.
[25] Judges 45:3.
[26] Gen. 36:12; Gen. 14:7.
[27] Adhemar (d. August 1, 1098), the Nestor of this expedition, had become Bishop of Puy before 1087. He had won fame not only as a man of great moral worth, but also as a vigorous prelate. On several occasions he had been called upon to supplement his moral precepts by physical force, which he effectively did. His knowledge of fighting men and his great tact made him a worthy choice for the exacting office of papal representative.

[28] Jno. 4:22.
[29] Matt. 27:52.
[30] Isaiah 14:19.
[31] Isaiah 2:3.
[32] Eccl. 1:7.
[33] II Thess. chap. 2.
[34] Luke 21:24.
[35] Jno. 7:6.
[36] Isaiah 43:5.

[37] This recurrence of old Neustria and Austrasia, or West and East Frankland, after so many centuries is an interesting example of the persistence of the Frankish and Carolingian traditions on both sides of the Rhine.

[38] The epidemic which started at the church of St. Gertrude of Nivelle was known as "St. Anthony's fire" and worked widespread devastation at the beginning of the twelfth century.

[39] People of the stem-duchies of Germany. Ekkehard, unlike Fulcher, does not use the term *Alemanni* as a designation for all Germans, but only for those from the region of Swabia.

[40] Alexander II, who occupied the papal throne 1061-1073, and was succeeded by Gregory VII.

[41] Clermont in Auvergne.

[42] August 15.

NOTES TO CHAPTER II

[1] See Graetz: History of the Jews, vol. IV: chap. 10 *et passim*.

[2] Psalms 86:9.

[3] Psalms 18:23.

[4] This legend is apparently one of the older legends of Europe. It was later applied to Frederick II and then to Frederick Barbarossa.

[5] Peter the Hermit, whom later legend made the author of the Crusade, was little known before that time. These statements contain almost all that is known about his earlier career. He was a monk and after the Council of Clermont began to preach the Crusade. There is little foundation for the story of his earlier romantic pilgrimage to Jerusalem. See Hagenmeyer: *Peter der Eremite*.

[6] Coloman, or Koloman, who succeeded his father, Ladislas I, July, 1095.

[7] Hugh, Count of Vermandois, and brother of Philip I of France. Philip was incapacitated for the Crusade, since he was excommunicate at the time. Hugh was one of the older men among the leaders. His forces were small. His prominence was due chiefly to his relationship with the King of France, together with a certain assurance of address, which led the other leaders to entrust him with diplomatic undertakings. Fulcher is at some disadvantage in describing the course of the other bands. His statements about them should be compared carefully with those of the other writers. The statements of Anna and Albert offer a more reasonable explanation of Hugh's predicament.

[8] Bohemund (1058(?)-1111), who appears as the crafty Ulysses of the First Crusade, was the eldest son of Robert Guiscard. He had begun his military training early, serving in many of his father's strenuous campaigns in Italy, Sicily, and Greece. He was with his father in the successful campaign against Durazzo and Corfu, and when his father was called back to Italy by the Pope's plea for help, Bohemund was left in command of the Norman forces in Greece. With these he penetrated the peninsula as far as Larissa, where he was finally repulsed by the Emperor Alexius. Neither Bohemund nor Alexius ever forgot those four years of warfare. Among

the Latin leaders on the First Crusade none understood the problems before them better than Bohemund, for he had had dealings not only with the Greeks, but with the Saracens in Sicily. Because he was born of an early marriage, his mother being a woman of obscure Norman origin, he had inherited only the principality of Otranto, while his younger brother, Roger, son of a Lombard princess, succeeded to his father's title. The Crusade, therefore, offered him an opportunity for improving his fortune.

[9] Godfrey of Bouillon (1065(?)-1100), so called from the feudal principality of that name which he held before he became Duke of lower Lorraine. Through his mother, Ida, he was grandson of Duke Godfrey II and had been designated by the latter as his successor. Henry IV, the Emperor, withheld this duchy from him for some years. The young Godfrey, however, won the Emperor's favor by valiant aid against the Pope and other enemies, and in 1082 he received the duchy. It was said of Godfrey that he was the first to storm the walls of Rome in the Emperor's attack upon the papal city. Nevertheless, after some years, Godfrey was won over to the papal side of the Investiture Struggle and was among the first to take the Crusader's vow.

[10] Raymond of Toulouse (d. 1105), or St. Gilles, had become Count of Toulouse in 1086. He was a religious enthusiast and had probably taken part in the warfare against the Mohammedans in Spain before the First Crusade. Without doubt, he was the first important secular person to volunteer for the Crusade. He made careful disposal of his possessions before going, and on the expedition he was reputed to be the wealthiest of the leaders. For some cause he had lost the use of one eye, a circumstance which may have played a part in his position among the leaders, as it did later in legend.

[11] Robert of Normandy (1054(?)-1135), eldest son of William the Conqueror, had enjoyed a rather turbulent career as Duke of Normandy for some years before 1096. Early recognized as his father's successor in Normandy, he twice revolted against his father and was twice forced into exile. Upon the Conqueror's death, he released many political prisoners, among them being his contentious uncle, Odo, Archbishop of Bayeux. He was engaged in warfare with his brothers, William Rufus and Henry, when the call for the Crusade was announced. Thereupon, he made peace with his brothers, mortgaged his duchy to William Rufus, and started on the Crusade. He had already given proof of those traits which marked him on the expedition—great physical courage, love of pleasure, and lack of ambition.

[12] The *Angles,* or English, are mentioned by other writers, also; e.g., the English fleet which the citizen of Lucca accompanied to Antioch. See p. 161.

[13] See Introduction, p. 6, and Chapter VII, note 28.

[14] Robert of Flanders (d. 1111) became Count of Flanders upon the death of his father in 1093. He was comparatively young and adventurous when he started on the Crusade. His fame rests chiefly upon his exploits as a Crusader.

[15] Baldwin (d. 1118), the younger brother of Godfrey, had been named

for the service of the Church and ecclesiastical preferment, and had, indeed, taken minor orders when the call for the Crusade came. This gave him an opportunity for the more congenial pursuit of armed adventure.

[16] Baldwin, Count of Hainault.

[17] Grez and Ascha were both feudal territories in that portion of lower Lorraine known as modern Belgium.

[18] Albert's idea of this eastern boundary is rather vague. His inclusion of practically all Germany within Gaul may be due to his identification of the Roman province of that name with the empire of Charles the Great, whose memory was and still is cherished on both sides of the Rhine.

[19] *Francavilla*, near Sermis on the Save. It was known by that name as late as the fourteenth century.

[20] Tancred (d. 1112), nephew of Bohemund, was the son of a Lombard prince named Marchisus. He had some military experience in southern Italy and seemed deeply devoted to his uncle. His chief title to fame both in history and legend rests upon his part in the First Crusade and the rule of Antioch, which he held from 1101-1112.

[21] See Hagenmeyer: *Gesta*, p. 154, note 24.

[22] *Roscignolo*, either Rossano in Calabria, or Roscignolo in Salerno, or Roussillon in France.

[23] Not to be confused with Adrianople, which is on the opposite side of the Balkan peninsula. The valley here referred to lay a short distance east of the Adriatic, behind Avlona and Durazzo.

[24] The Turcopoles were a light armed soldiery, possibly of Turkish origin, in the service of the Greek Emperor. Several of the chroniclers describe them as people reared among the Turks, or the offspring of Christian mothers and Turkish fathers.

[25] Curator of the palace, an officer of high rank in the household of the Emperor.

[26] The mercenary army of the Byzantine Empire was drawn from the surrounding tribesmen, including the Turks. The *Tanaces* have not been identified. The name may possibly be a corruption of the term *Patzinaks*.

[27] Possibly modern Wodena, though this is by no means certain.

[28] Romans 11:33.

[29] Isaiah 28:12; Jer. 6:16; Acts 3:20.

[30] The modern Devol.

[31] Either Pella or Cella.

[32] Possibly the Greek Peritheorion.

NOTES TO CHAPTER III

[1] Chalandon: Essai sur le regne d'Alexis Ier Comnène.

[2] Revue Historique, LXXXIII, pp. 160-8.

[3] The meaning of this surname which Anna uses is uncertain. It may be a reference to the monk's hood worn by Peter (*cucullus*). Another conjecture is that the word comes from a Picard term meaning 'short.'

[4] Romania was used rather loosely by different writers to designate: (a)

the whole eastern Roman Empire; (b) Asia Minor; (c) the Sultanate of the Turks in Asia Minor, known as the Sultanate of Rum, or Roum. Here the last is apparently meant.

[5] The inconsistent statements of the different writers make exact identification of *Xerogord* impossible.

[6] September 29.

[7] Matt. 10:28.

[8] See Introduction to Chapter IV, p. 112.

[9] One of the commanders of the Byzantine fleet.

[10] In the original the title of this man is "dux," but to avoid confusion with the Latin title, which conferred a somewhat different distinction, the term is here translated "governor."

[11] An honorary title reserved for members of the imperial family.

[12] Good Friday, April 2, 1081, when, through the treason of German mercenaries within the city, Alexius succeeded in entering Constantinople. His reign is usually dated from this event.

[13] Nicephorus Bryennius, husband of Anna Comnena.

[14] A place just across the Strait from Constantinople, not as yet identified.

[15] See Introduction to Chapter III, p. 69.

[16] A reference to the earlier fighting between the Italian Normans and Alexius—certainly not to the battle at Larissa, when Bohemund was forced to retreat. Anna, in her references to this former hostility between Alexius and Bohemund, is inclined to lay greater stress upon Larissa. The Emperor's war with Robert Guiscard and Bohemund took place from 1082-1084.

[17] The mention of Antioch as a specific part of Bohemund's agreement is not confirmed by the other writers, nor is it mentioned in connection with later disputes about Antioch. The point raises a question as to whether the *Anonymous* wrote this portion of his work before or after Antioch was taken.

[18] The allusion is to William the Conqueror, whose gifts to the knights in his following after the battle of Senlac had evidently become proverbial.

[19] See Introduction, pages 19-22.

[20] See note 19.

[21] A covering of wicker-work used as a shield over the body in approaching a fortified place.

[22] A mound of bones of Crusaders was still pointed out to travellers as late as the fifteenth century. See travels of Bertrandon de la Brocquière in Wright: *Early Travels in Palestine*, p. 337.

[23] See Introduction, p. 14.

[24] Pantaleon, according to legend, was a physician of Nicomedia, who was converted to Christianity and performed wonderful cures. He was martyred in the year 303 under the persecutions of Diocletian. His date in the calendar of saints is July 27.

[25] Georges Palaeologus was a member of one of the most distinguished families in the East and was a trusted friend of Alexius from the beginning of his reign.

[26] This letter undoubtedly was written in the year 1098, but the date, in the month of June, seems almost incredible. In the early days of that month Alexius was on his way to aid the Crusaders. He was met by Stephen of Blois at Philomelium. Placing full faith in Stephen's statement that the Crusaders were probably all destroyed, he had turned back toward Constantinople, laying waste the country as he went, in order to make difficult pursuit by the Turks. He returned to the imperial city toward the end of the month, and the news of Kerbogha's overthrow could scarcely have reached him by that time. Under the circumstances, his assurances to the Abbot about the condition of the Latin Crusaders would be hypocrisy of the basest kind, if written at this time. It is possible that the mention of June as the date of the letter may have reference to the time of arrival at Monte Cassino, the letter having been written a month or so earlier. On the whole, Alexius deserves the benefit of the doubt.

NOTES TO CHAPTER IV

[1] See note 8.

[2] See note 22.

[3] It is uncertain just who these people were. The name occurs only in the accounts of the *Anonymous* and his followers. P. Paris has conjectured that they were people from Fez in northern Africa (Chanson d'Antioche; II, 305).

[4] Not the Publicans of the Scriptures, but rather the Paulicians, a sect of the Manichaeans. They were most numerous in Armenia. Persecution by the Greeks had driven them into alliance with the Saracens. Other adherents of this sect were located in the Balkan peninsula near Philippopolis. The later Albigenses of southern France may have obtained some of their tenets from this sect.

[5] The western writers had great difficulty in reproducing the names of Turkish and Saracen leaders. The title *Emir*, or local governor, apparently seemed to them part of the name. The two leaders here mentioned have not been fully identified. It has been suggested that *Admircaradigum* is a western corruption of Al Emir Korâdjâ, the name of a Turkish prince who died in 1113. *Miriathos* may, in the same way, be a corruption of Emir Atsiz, though it is impossible accurately to identify the persons meant.

[6] Fulcher might have named others to make the list complete, but apparently his object was to enumerate the distinctive varieties of speech to be found in the army. Most of the names are easily recognized today. The Gauls were probably people from central France, the Allobroges from east central France, the Apulians from southern Italy, and the Iberians from northeastern Spain.

[7] There is a difference of opinion among modern scholars as to the location of this valley. Hagenmeyer accepts the identification of *Botrenthrot* with the valley which runs from the north southeastward to Bozanta and then over the Gullek Pass. It is still used as a main road to Tarsus. See Hagenmeyer: *Gesta*, p. 217, note 42.

[8] Probably none of the writers were present on this journey of adventure. The *Anonymous* undoubtedly obtained his account from the gossip of Tancred's men at Antioch, while Fulcher acquired his information from Baldwin on the way to Edessa. Raoul de Caen, whose intimate acquaintance with Tancred several years later renders his account of somewhat more than secondary value, has more to say of this clash between Baldwin and Tancred. The affair at Tarsus, as related by Raoul, is in substantial agreement with the accounts of the *Anonymous* and Fulcher, but he adds that Baldwin followed Tancred to Adana, where the latter was encamped within the city walls. A quarrel arose over the price of supplies, and the two leaders drew up their forces for battle outside the city. Tancred, with fewer troops, refused to advance beyond the support of the hurling machines on the walls, while Baldwin, under the circumstances, was unwilling to risk his superior forces. An equal number of knights from each army advanced to settle the dispute by wager of battle. The outcome was indecisive, an equal number on each side being unhorsed. Finally, better counsel prevailed, and peace was established between the two leaders. Raoul further says that Baldwin was rescued by Tancred when he was surrounded by Turks at Artasia. This seems improbable in view of Fulcher's statement that Baldwin had returned to the army at Marasch and departed thence toward Edessa. See Raoul de Caen: *Gesta Tancredi*, chapters 33-47.

[9] This place is not to be confused with Rugia, from which it was a day's march.

[10] Mt. *Maregart*, according to description, must have been the hill behind Bohemund's camp, although this is not entirely certain.

[11] This title is not exact. Bohemund was Count of Otranto, but from Anselm's rather distant point of view Bohemund's followers came from a region so close to Rome that they might well be called Romans.

[12] These men, most of whom are not mentioned elsewhere, were probably all from the northern part of France, and well known to both Anselm and the readers of his letter.

[13] See Introduction, p. 5.

[14] Possibly a corruption of *protospatharius*, an official of the imperial guard. The name as here written cannot be identified exactly in the Greek of the period.

[15] Assam, or Asam, was a Turkish lord of considerable power who took a prominent part in later wars with the Eastern Empire. The policy of leaving garrisons at various places along the line of march had an important bearing upon the career of the army itself, for, while many of the garrisons were too small to cover the territory assigned to them, their absence did weaken the strength of the main army.

[16] See Chapter I, note 27.

[17] The hill to the south of the city on which Tancred was stationed.

[18] Raymond's use of this term is somewhat uncertain. Spain was so called, of course, but it was clearly not the region here referred to. Ispahan, the name of a town and a large portion of Persia, seems equally out of the

question, for this foraging journey was accomplished in a very few days. The region actually involved was probably the valley of the Orontes, just south and southeast of Antioch. Raymond may have derived *Hispania* from Ispahan, applying the term vaguely to all the land southeast of Antioch. This seems the most probable explanation.

[19] By Goths Raymond probably means the people of Toulouse and even of northern Spain.

[20] The Fatimite Caliphate had been established at Cairo in Egypt since 972 A.D. In recent years they had lost most of their holdings in Syria to the Seljuk Turks, who were attached to the Abassid Caliphate of Bagdad. The Caliph in Egypt at this time was the vigorous Mustali (1094-1101), who was very desirous of regaining Syria from the Seljuks. Hence, his envoys appeared among the Crusaders at Antioch to arrange a satisfactory alliance against the Seljuks, their common foe. The Emir, or Vizier, of the Egyptian Caliph at this time was Al- Afdhal, who is mentioned later.

[21] Probably Tarsus, whose possession Baldwin and Tancred disputed, and which lies near the other two cities mentioned. The actual possession of these places was already in the hands of the Crusaders, so that the only object of this grant would be to forego the rights which the Emperor had reserved in his agreement with the princes.

[22] According to Anna (XI, 4-12 passim), Tetigus, who was in command of the Greek force which had accompanied the Crusaders from Nicaea, was constantly threatened by Bohemund and finally forced to flee. Bohemund is said to have advised his desertion on the ground that the Crusaders were very angry with the Greeks. Anna, of course, regards the whole incident as a part of Bohemund's deliberate scheme to take Antioch and the surrounding country, in violation of his oath to the Emperor.

[23] See note 20. The "King" either refers to the Caliph or his Vizier. Saracen titles were not clearly understood by the Latins.

[24] St. George (martyred, according to legend, at Nicomedia, April 23, 303) was the patron saint of the region about Constantinople. The Strait, the Arm of Saint George, was named in his honor. St. Demetrius (Proconsul at Achaia, martyred October 8, 290) was patron saint of the region of Bulgaria. St. Theodore (probably Theodore Stratolates, who died at Heraclea in Pontus, February 7, 319) was a patron saint of Asia Minor. By Saint Basil is probably meant the great Church Father of the East, Archbishop of Caesarea in the early fourth century, though there are almost thirty saints of this name in the calendar of the Eastern Church. The intervention of these saints, recorded not only in this letter, but also in the accounts of the Latin chroniclers, is an interesting example of religious psychology. The patron saints of the West are little mentioned.

[25] The Turkish ruler of the city, Yâgi Sian by name. See Introduction, p. 14.

[26] *Pirus,* called also *Pyrrhus, Pirrus, Firous, Feirus, Pirus Datianus,* and *Firu* is, for obvious reasons, the object of great difference of opinion. The Mohammedan writers call him an Armenian, a renegade Christian, while the

NOTES

authoritative Latin accounts—*e.g.*, Bohemund's letter, p. 160—speak of him as a Turk.

[27] *Sensadolus,* properly Shams-ad-Daula. The name is also written *Sanxadones.*

[28] Dokak of Damascus, Mo'in ad-Daula Sokman ibn Ortok of Jerusalem, and Roduan of Aleppo. The names *Bolianuth* and *Hamelnuth* are uncertain. See Hagenmeyer: *Epistulae,* p. 284-5.

[29] See note 20.

[30] See note 28.

[31] Kerbogha, called also *Corbaga, Corbagath, Curbanaan,* and *Corbahan,* was Atabek, or Prince, of Mosul. He was a follower of Barkiarok, one of the sons of the Sultan Melikschah, who was disputing the sultanate with his brothers. The expedition of Kerbogha represents the rather feeble effort of the Caliph of Bagdad to unite the quarreling brothers against the Christian invaders.

[32] Robert of Normandy was short and stout in stature and is said to have been thus nicknamed by his father.

NOTES TO CHAPTER V

[1] The name has reference to the unleavened bread used in the communion service. It here probably refers to the Armenians and Maronites who used the unleavened bread.

[2] The *Anonymous* here betrays both his authorship of the letter and his ignorance of the monotheistic character of the Mohammedan faith. In this, however, he was not alone, for several of the Latin writers indicate their belief that the Mohammedans were idolators.

[3] Psalms 68: 30; 79: 6.

[4] Joshua 1: 4.

[5] In connection with the fighting inside the city of Antioch, Tudebode adds: "On that day a certain proved knight, Arvedus Tudebodus by name, was wounded. His companions carried him down below into the city. There he lived until Saturday, when between the ninth and sixth hours he passed away from the world, to live in Christ. A certain priest, Peter, his brother, buried his body before the western door of the church of St. Peter. And he was in great fear of losing his head, as were all the rest in the city. We beg all who read and hear this to give alms and say prayers for his soul and for the souls of all the dead who died on this journey to Jerusalem." See Tud. X; 8.

[6] Anna's account of the meeting at Philomelium and the Emperor's attitude is as follows: "With his forces ready, the Emperor set out to the aid of the Gauls defending Antioch. When he came to Philomelium with his whole army, after killing many barbarians along the way and devastating the cities which had formerly been occupied by them, he met there William Grandmesnil, Stephen, Count of France, and Peter *Aliphae.* These men had escaped by ropes from the walls at Antioch and had set out through Tarsus

to the Emperor, from whom they were sent. They assured the Emperor that the fortunes and hopes of the Gauls were reduced to very narrow straits; nay, they swore that absolute destruction threatened them. The Emperor, much inflamed at this announcement, decided all the more quickly to hasten the aid which he was bringing them, but all dissuaded him from so rash a plan." . . . Anna XI, 6.

[7] Psalms 15:1.

[8] I Peter, 5:5-6.

[9] St. Mercurius, according to legend, was the head of the army of the Emperor Decius in the war with the Persians. His refusal to worship the gods brought down the wrath of the Emperor upon him, and, after a miraculous deliverance at one time, he was finally martyred. For Demetrius see Chapter IV, note 24.

[10] II Kings, 7:1.

[11] Probably Balduc, Emir of Samosata, son of Ibn al Danischmend.

[12] Not the same as Roger of *Betheniville,* who follows.

[13] Mohammed.

[14] June 27.

[15] The Koran.

[16] William of Grandmesnil was Bohemund's brother-in-law.

[17] According to the Gospel, a soldier pierced the side of the Saviour as He hung upon the Cross. The name of this soldier has not been preserved but as early as the sixth century the name *Longinus* occurs as a designation for the man. It seems to have arisen from a careless translation of the Greek word for spear. On this foundation a legend rapidly arose, and *Longinus* became widely known.

NOTES TO CHAPTER VI

[1] Acts 1:11, 2:7.

[2] The Jacobites were of the Monophysite sect, followers of Jacobus Zanzalus, and were fairly numerous in Syria. The Syrians were probably Maronites, who regarded the Abbot of St. Maro in the Lebanon Mountains as their head. The Armenian Christians were also Monophysites. A universal policy toward heretics had not yet been evolved by the Church at Rome. From a political and military point of view, it was highly inexpedient for the Crusaders to adopt a drastic policy toward these heretical Christians in the East. Bohemund's plea was never fully answered, and, in general, the practical policy pursued was one of persuasion rather than force. Bohemund's readiness to adopt extreme measures against them may have been influenced by his desire to retain Antioch, which scheme the Greeks opposed. Softer counsel prevailed in the end, and wisely so.

[3] August 1.

[4] St. Trophim, according to legend, was Bishop of Arles and a disciple of St. Peter.

[5] October 6.

[6] This is an extremely interesting example of how the Crusaders ad-

justed themselves to the changed conditions involved in the Crusade. In this improvised election of Peter as Bishop of Albara there appear all the elements so common in the West—the influence of the Count, the nomination by the clergy, and the approval of the people. The great influence of the secular Count is especially noteworthy in view of the fact that the papal party to which he leaned was at that time engaged in the Investiture Struggle, an effort to free the Church elections from this very influence.

[7] See Chap. III.

[8] Raymond's insistence upon the Emperor's rights is all the more remarkable in view of the fact that he was the only one of the leaders who never took the prescribed oath to Alexius.

[9] This statement must be regarded as an exaggeration of the true condition. "Three hundred and sixty monasteries" might approximate the truth, if by the term "monastery" is meant every building occupied by a monk or monks. As for bishoprics, William, Archbishop of Tyre, counted no more than twenty provinces in the patriarchate of Antioch.

[10] Antiochus, after whom Antioch was named, was the son and successor of Seleucus, the general of Alexander the Great. Seleucus built the city and made it his capital. At this point in his version Tudebode lists the names of the seventy kings over whom Antiochus is said to have ruled, but as they are chiefly fanciful they have not been inserted.

[11] Robert of Flanders, according to Raymond (p. 209), and Robert of Normandy, according to Raoul (chapter 96, *Gesta Tancredi*), had accompanied Count Raymond to Marra.

[12] Tudebode at this point inserts the following: "There, with many others who happily returned their souls to God, for whom they had assembled there, a certain very excellent knight, Arnaldus Tudebodus, was killed." . . . See Tud. XII, 3.

[13] This doubtless has reference to the oath which they took to the Emperor at Constantinople. That the Emperor regarded Antioch as within the terms of the oath is indicated by his later struggles with Bohemund.

[14] Venetians and Greeks had co-operated for centuries. In many respects Venice may be regarded as one of the western trading posts of the Greeks. The presence of the Venetian ships does not signify Venetian participation in the Crusade, but rather the Emperor's contribution to the support of the army. The Venetian expedition of the year 1100 must be looked upon as the first crusading expedition of the Republic.

[15] Ali, Mohammed's son-in-law, whom the Fatimite Caliphs regarded as Mohammed's successor. This constituted one of the essential points of disagreement with the Abassid Caliphs of Bagdad.

[16] See Introduction, p. 17.

[17] See Introduction, p. 15.

[18] Arnulf, who became one of the most powerful clerical leaders in the army, was a native of Flanders. He is said to have been the son of a priest, which, on strict canonical grounds, would have disqualified him for the priesthood. However, large portions of Europe were still unconverted to

the stricter ideals of the Reform Church Party. As a result, he found little to hinder his rapid advancement. Before the Crusade he had gained fame as a teacher, especially in Normandy, where he counted among his pupils Matilda, the daughter of William the Conqueror, and Raoul, famous later as a priest and panegyrist. When the Crusade was preached, Arnulf joined the expedition in the band of Robert of Normandy. His position was that of chaplain to Odo, Archbishop of Bayeux, the fiery brother of the Conqueror. Upon Odo's death early in the march, Arnulf virtually succeeded the Archbishop, becoming chaplain to Robert of Normandy. In this capacity he was soon recognized as one of the ablest churchmen in the whole army. He possessed many qualities aside from his great learning which won him popularity and influence not only among the leaders, but also among the soldiers.

[19] June 24.

[20] It is difficult to determine exactly who are included in these terms. Raoul possibly includes among the Bretons all the Scotch, Irish, or Breton Crusaders; among the Swabians and Alemanni all the Germans. Likewise, by Huns he probably means all the Hungarians, and by Ruthenians all the Slavs. The first two terms were often so used by other chroniclers, while the last two are somewhat inaccurate.

[21] Virgil's *Aeneid*, II, 390.

[22] The silence of the *Anonymous* and the other writers who were doubtless present at the Ordeal is baffling. Possibly they were unwilling to commit themselves on this disputed question of the Lance, whose validity they had practically all accepted at Antioch. Fulcher, who was not present, records the Ordeal and apparently recognizes the outcome as a definite refutation of the Lance. See Fulcher (Hagenmeyer's ed.) I: 18: 5.

[23] The final fate of this Lance is somewhat obscure. Count Raymond kept it and took it along with him to Constantinople. Raoul and Matthew of Edessa, the Armenian writer, say that he presented it to Alexius. Albert says that he lost it in Asia Minor in 1101. In the West the dispute about its validity raged for some time longer. Guibert criticised Fulcher very severely for doubting it.

NOTES TO CHAPTER VII AND EPILOGUE

[1] St. George, according to tradition, was born at Lydda, but had suffered martyrdom at Nicomedia. See Chapter IV, note 24. His remains were brought back to the place of his birth and a church erected there in his honor. The legend which the *Anonymous* here repeats was copied by later writers and widely circulated in the West by later pilgrims.

[2] This was the first Latin bishopric established in the patriarchate of Jerusalem. The Bishop was spoken of afterwards as the Bishop of Ramlah, or Lydda, or St. George. Ramlah and Lydda were but a few miles apart, the church of St. George lying between the two places. All three were in the Bishop's diocese, and one or the other served as his seat, at various times—hence the confusion of names.

[3] See p. 278.

[4] See p. 236. The effect of the death of Peter Bartholomew was to discredit the Lance among most of the Crusaders. The expedition of Hugh of Monteil may be regarded as an effort on the part of the Provençal party to replace the Lance with an equally venerable relic. According to Albert, the opposing party, under Arnulf's leadership, sought to accomplish the same purpose by making a golden image of the Saviour. However, the place which the Lance had held among the Crusaders was not filled until the discovery of the Cross at Jerusalem by Arnulf.

[5] St. Cyprian, not to be confused with the famous Bishop of Carthage, was martyred in Asia Minor during Diocletian's persecutions. Chrysostom was the famous Patriarch of Constantinople, the great preacher, who is numbered among the four great Church fathers of the East. Leontius was probably the Greek theologian of the sixth century, whose surname was Byzantinus. By *Omechios* is probably meant Onesimus, the disciple of St. Paul.

[6] This is the fleet to which Raoul refers in his account. Other English ships are mentioned by the citizen of Lucca in his letter (p. 161). These ships afforded material aid to the Crusaders on the expedition and afterwards helped to carry them back to the West.

[7] Either the author, or the copies of his book are in error, for the eighth day before the Ides of June was Monday, the sixth. Tudebode says that it was the third day of the week and the seventh day of incoming June, which is consistent. See Tudebode, Rec. Occid. III, p. 102. The error of the *Anonymous* may be purely typographical.

[8] A village in the department of Garde.

[9] Psalms 107:33.

[10] Generic term for coins.

[11] Dan. 9:24-27.

[12] Adhemar had died August 1 of the previous year and is mentioned as having appeared in a vision at the trial of the Lance (p. 198).

[13] Eustace, Count of Boulogne, was the elder brother of Godfrey. He succeeded to the title and possessions of his father.

[14] July 15.

[15] Arnulf, Bishop of Martirano, who is described by Raoul as a man of little learning, seems, nevertheless, to have had considerable influence. He was Tancred's chaplain, and, since Tancred captured Bethlehem, his prospect of obtaining the bishopric was a very good one, especially in view of the support he rendered to his namesake, Arnulf, chaplain of the Count of Normandy. In speaking of the capture and death of the Bishop of Martirano, Raymond is here anticipating the event which happened some days later.

[16] The palms were the sign of the completed pilgrimage. It was customary for pilgrims to bring home palms from the Jordan. See p. 274.

[17] Allowance must be made for Raymond's intense hatred of the man who, more than any other individual, was responsible for discrediting the Lance.

The Provençal "good clergy" would scarcely support Arnulf as candidate for the patriarchal office.

[18] Matt. 20: 1-16.

[19] Probably Gaston of *Beert*, who has been mentioned before on several occasions. See page 257. It is uncertain whether he was from northern or southern France.

[20] Arnulf of Martirano, whose death Raymond has already described.

[21] Daimbert, or Dagobert, Archbishop of Pisa, who here enters the history of the Crusade, had become prominent in the affairs of the Western Church. He had been ordained by the anti-pope, Wibert of Ravenna, but shortly thereafter was won over to the side of Urban. He became Bishop of Pisa, and when Corsica was acquired from the Saracens, Urban added Corsica to the diocese of Pisa and elevated the episcopal see to an archbishopric. Daimbert thus became the first Archbishop of Pisa. He was entrusted by Urban with several commissions to various provinces, and in 1098 he took the leadership in organizing a naval expédition to go on the Crusade. Needless to say, Urban approved of this and may have sent Daimbert as his vicar to succeed Adhemar, who had died at Antioch. At any rate, on his arrival in the East Daimbert found himself the leading churchman there, and the only one who by intimate acquaintance was qualified to represent the Pope. Bohemund, whose hold upon Antioch was jeopardized by the claims of Alexius, was anxious for the approval of the Pope as a lever to turn the energy of the Crusaders against Alexius. His immediate friendship for Daimbert, the friend of the Pope, plays an important part in later events.

[22] Sugar-cane. The crusaders introduced it widely in the West.

[23] Psalms 132: 7.

[24] Psalms 122: 4.

[25] Lake of Gennesaret, or Sea of Galilee.

[26] A glance at the map will show that Fulcher's identification of Balbec with Thadamar is impossible. He undoubtedly saw Balbec and had read about Thadamar, which was once a flourishing trading centre, but it is doubtful whether more than the magnificent ruins of the latter place were then in evidence. Fulcher probably never saw even the site of Palmyra, or Thadamar, but applied his learning to embellish his description of Balbec. Thadamar was scarcely on the road from Jerusalem to Laodicaea.

[27] Both Roberts returned home with their armies. Robert of Normandy tarried sometime at Salerno to be healed of a troublesome wound which he had received on the Crusade. When he reached Normandy, he found his brother, William Rufus, dead, and his younger brother, Henry, on the English throne. A quarrel finally broke out between himself and Henry, and in the war which followed Robert was captured and forced to spend his last days as a prisoner. He died in 1126. Robert of Flanders probably bore his letter to the Pope at Rome and then hastened home. During the next eleven years he figured prominently in feudal warfare, though not always to his credit. His chief claim to fame lies in his exploits as a Crusader. He died in 1111.

[28] This insistent plea, that the able-bodied who had taken the vow, and had failed to carry it out, or had faltered on the way should fulfil their vows, has appeared in practically all the letters written by the Crusaders since the capture of Antioch. The papal command to the same effect must have been, therefore, a real consolation to the many who had carried out their vow at such great cost. It seems only an act of bare justice to set down the fate of the two most prominent offenders, Stephen of Blois and Hugh the Great, whose conduct involved not merely the ignominy of negligence but more especially that of desertion in the face of the enemy. The following passage from Ordericus Vitalis (X, 19) as translated by Thomas Forester (Bohn Antiquarian Library) reveals the embarrassing directness of the pressure upon Stephen.

"Being frequently reproved by a variety of persons for this conduct, Stephen was compelled both by fear and shame to undertake a fresh crusade. Among others, his wife, Adele, often urged him to it, reminding him of it even amidst the endearments of conjugal caresses. 'Far be it from me, my lord,' she said, 'to submit any longer to the jibes you receive from all quarters. Pluck up the courage for which you were renowned in your youth, and take arms in a noble cause for the salvation of thousands, so that Christians may have good reason to exult in all parts of the world, to the terror of the pagans and the public humiliation of their detestable religion.'

"This was the sort of language that clever and spirited woman often addressed to her husband. He certainly had already sufficiently experienced the perils and difficulties of the enterprise to make him shrink from undergoing such toils again. At length, however, he took courage, and, putting himself on the march at the head of many thousand French, persevered against most formidable obstacles, until he reached the tomb of our Lord."

Stephen survived but a very short time. He had visited Jerusalem and was at Joppa, waiting for a ship to take him home, when news was brought that hostile bands were in the vicinity. Baldwin, the king, called for volunteers to drive them off and Stephen was among those who responded. The battle was very disastrous for the Christians. To quote Fulcher's words, "Alas, how many valiant knights and how many brave soldiers we lost in this catastrophe . . .! For Stephen of Blois, a prudent and noble man, and another Stephen, Count of Burgundy, were killed."

There is a lack of agreement among the writers as to the fate of Hugh the Great. That he was among the victims of this expedition is accepted by Fulcher, who fixes his death at Tarsus late in 1101, and by William of Tyre (X, 13), who states that his body was buried in the church of St. Paul at that place.

[29] The offspring of these mixed marriages were called *Pullani* and figure prominently in the literature of the twelfth and thirteenth centuries.

[30] This led to the formation of a mongrel speech known generally as the *Lingua Franca,* which was long used in commercial intercourse throughout the East.